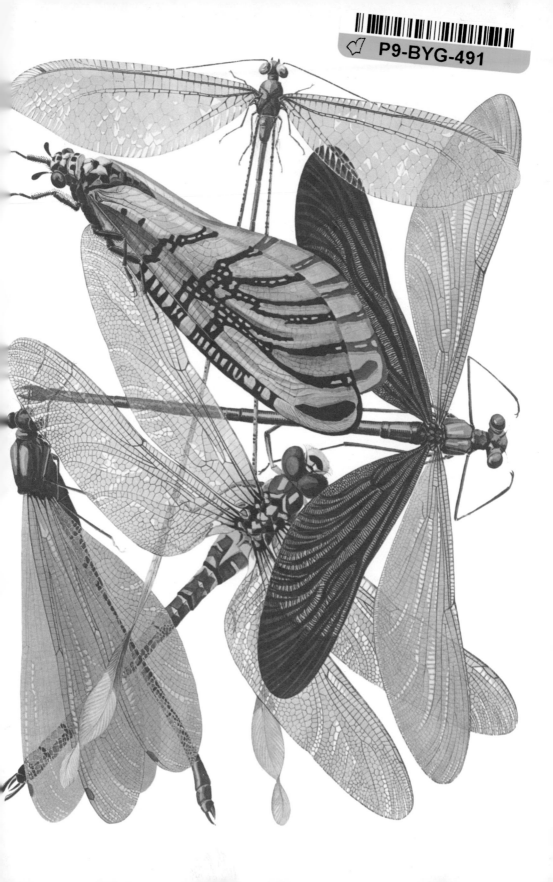

Also by Hugh Raffles

In Amazonia: A Natural History

Insectopedia

Insect pedia

Hugh Raffles

Pantheon Books, New York

All rights reserved. Published in the United States by Pantheon Books,
a division of Random House, Inc., New York, and in Canada by
Random House of Canada Limited, Toronto.

Pantheon Books and colophon are registered trademarks
of Random House, Inc.

Portions of this book originally appeared in different form in the following:
"My Nightmares" in *Anthropology Now*; "Generosity (the Happy Times)" as
"Cricket Fighting" in *Granta* and in *The Best American Essays 2008*, edited by
Adam Gopnik (New York: Houghton Mifflin, 2008); "Chernobyl" as "A
Conjoined Fate" in *Orion*; and "Jews" as "Jews, Lice, and History" in *Public
Culture*.

Grateful acknowledgment is made to the following for permission to reprint
previously published material: The Hokuseido Press: "Oku no hosomichi" by
Bashō Matsuo from *Haiku* by R. H. Blyth. Reprinted by permission of The
Hokuseido Press. • W. W. Norton & Company, Inc.: Excerpt from "Seen from
Above" from *Miracle Fair* by Wislawa Szymborska, translated by Joanna
Trzeciak, copyright © 2001 by Joanna Trzeciak. Reprinted by permission of
W. W. Norton & Company, Inc.

Library of Congress Cataloging-in-Publication Data
Raffles, Hugh, [date]
Insectopedia / Hugh Raffles.
p. cm.
Includes bibliographical references and index.
ISBN 978-0-375-42386-4
1. Insects.   2. Human-animal relationships.   I. Title.
QL463.R34 2010   595.7—dc22   2009024302

www.pantheonbooks.com

Printed in the United States of America
First Edition
9 8 7 6 5 4 3 2 1

For my mother and father,
for my sisters,
for the insects, for their friends,
and, of course,

For Sharon

The minuscule, a narrow gate, opens up an entire world.

GASTON BACHELARD

CONTENTS

In the Beginning . . .   3

Air   5

Beauty   13

Chernobyl   15

Death   41

Evolution   46

Fever/Dream   71

Generosity (the Happy Times)   74

Heads and How to Use Them   116

The Ineffable   123

Jews   141

Kafka   162

Language   171

My Nightmares   201

Nepal   205

On January 8, 2008, Abdou Mahamane
   Was Driving through Niamey . . .   207

Il Parco delle Cascine on Ascension Sunday   241

The Quality of Queerness Is Not Strange Enough   257

The Deepest of Reveries   264

Sex   267

Temptation   291

x   Contents

The Unseen   298

Vision   301

The Sound of Global Warming   318

Ex Libris, Exempla   331

Yearnings   343

Zen and the Art of Zzz's   383

Notes   387

Selected Bibliography   427

Acknowledgments   439

Index   441

Insectopedia

In the Beginning . . .

In the beginning, a long, long time ago, a time before any people were here, a time close to the primordial gas and ooze, a time not too long after the time (we are, after all, talking geological time) when those heroic protozoa created the planet's first encyclopedia by turning themselves into mitochondria and chloroplasts within other cells, which in turn formed alliances that grew into yet other beings, which joined up with yet others to make invisible cities, worlds within worlds . . . Sometime after that time but still long before our time, there were the insects.

For as long as we've been here, they've been here too. Wherever we've traveled, they've been there too. And still, we don't know them very well, not even the ones we're closest to, the ones that eat our food and share our beds. Who are they, these beings so different from us and from each other? What do they do? What worlds do they make? What do we make of them? How do we live with them? How could we live with them differently?

Imagine an insect. What comes to mind? A housefly? A dragonfly? A bumblebee? A parasitic wasp? A gnat? A mosquito? A bombardier beetle? A rhinoceros beetle? A morpho butterfly? A death's-head moth? A praying mantis? A stick insect? A caterpillar? Such varied beings, so different from each other and from us. So prosaic and so exotic, so tiny and so huge, so social and so solitary, so expressive and so inscrutable, so generative and so opaque, so seductive yet so unsettling. Pollinators, pests, disease vectors, decomposers, laboratory animals, prime objects of scientific attention, experimentation, and intervention. The stuff of dreams and nightmares. The stuff of economy and culture. Not just deeply present in the world but deeply there, creating it, too.

There are too many insects, uncountable numbers, more all the time. And they are so busy, so indifferent, and so powerful. They'll almost never do what we tell them to do. They'll rarely be what we want them to be. They won't keep still. In every respect, they are really very complicated creatures.

Air

1.

On August 10, 1926, a Stinson Detroiter SM-1 six-seater monoplane took off from the rudimentary airstrip at Tallulah, Louisiana. The Detroiter was the first airplane built with an electric starter motor, wheel brakes, and a heated cabin, but it was not a good climber, so the pilot leveled off quickly, circled the airstrip and surrounding landscape, held open the specially fitted sticky trap beneath the plane's wing for the designated ten minutes, and soon returned to land. As he touched down, P. A. Glick and his colleagues at the Division of Cotton Insect Investigations of the U.S. Bureau of Entomology and Plant Quarantine ran out to meet him.

It was a historic flight: the first attempt to collect insects by airplane. Glick and his associates, as well as researchers at the Department of

Agriculture and at regional organizations such as the New York State Museum, were trying to discover the migration secrets of gypsy moths, cotton bollworm moths, and other insects that were munching their way through the nation's natural resources. They wanted to predict infestations, to know what might happen next. How could they contain these insect enemies if they didn't know where, when, and how they traveled?

2.

Before Tallulah, high-altitude entomology had barely got off the ground. Researchers sent up balloons and kites fitted with hanging nets, climbed up pylons, and pestered lighthouse keepers and mountaineers. But armed now with the new airplane technology, Glick went down to Tlahualilo in Durango, Mexico. There, 3,000 feet above the valley plain, his pilots trapped the pink bollworm moth, a feared invader of the U.S. cotton crop. Face-to-face with the unanticipated scale of his task, Glick wrote tersely that "the pink bollworm moths are carried in the upper air currents for considerable distances."[1]

There were only a few flies and wasps in that first trap at Tallulah. But over the next five years, the researchers flew more than 1,300 sorties from the Louisiana airstrip and captured tens of thousands more insects at altitudes ranging from 20 to 15,000 feet. They generated a long series of charts and tables, cataloguing individual insects of 700 named species according to the height at which they were collected, time of day, wind speed and direction, temperature, barometric pressure, humidity, dew point, and many other physical variables. They already knew something about long-distance dispersal. They had heard about the butterflies, gnats, water striders, leaf bugs, booklice, and katydids sighted hundreds of miles out on the open ocean; about the aphids that Captain William Parry had encountered on ice floes during his polar expedition of 1828; and about those other aphids that, in 1925, made the 800-mile journey across the frigid, windswept Barents Sea between the Kola Peninsula, in Russia, and Spitsbergen, off Norway, in just twenty-four hours. Still, they were taken aback by the enormous quantities of animals they were discovering in the air above Louisiana and unashamedly astonished by the heights at which they found them.[2] All of a sudden, it seemed, the heavens had opened.

Unmoored, they turned to the ocean, began talking about the "aero-plankton" drifting in the vastness of the open skies. They told each other about tiny insects, some of them wingless, all with large surface-area-to-weight ratios, plucked from their earthly tethers by a sharp gust of wind, picked up on air currents and thrust high into the convection streams without volition or capacity for resistance, some terrible accident, carried great distances across oceans and continents, then dropped with the same fateful arbitrariness in a downdraft on some distant mountain-top or valley plain. They estimated that at any given time on any given day throughout the year, the air column rising from 50 to 14,000 feet above one square mile of Louisiana countryside contained an average of 25 million insects and perhaps as many as 36 million.[3] They found lady-bugs at 6,000 feet during the daytime, striped cucumber beetles at 3,000 feet during the night. They collected three scorpion flies at 5,000 feet, thirty-one fruit flies between 200 and 3,000, a fungus gnat at 7,000 and another at 10,000. They trapped an anthrax-transmitting horsefly at 200 feet and another at 1,000. They caught wingless worker ants as high as 4,000 feet and sixteen species of parasitic ichneumon wasps at altitudes up to 5,000 feet. At 15,000 feet, "probably the highest elevation at which any specimen has ever been taken above the surface of the earth," they trapped a ballooning spider, a feat that reminded Glick of spiders thought to have circumnavigated the globe on the trade winds and led him to write that "the young of most spiders are more or less addicted to this mode of transportation," an image of excited little animals packing their luggage that opened a small rupture in the consensus around the passivity of all this airborne movement and led to Glick's subsequent observation that ballooning spiders not only climb up to an exposed site (a twig or a flower, for instance), stand on tiptoe, raise their abdomen, test the atmosphere, throw out silk filaments, and launch themselves into the blue, all free legs spread-eagled, but that they also use their bod-ies and their silk to control their descent and the location of their land-ing.[4] Thirty-six million little animals flying unseen above one square mile of countryside? The heavens opened. The air column was "a vault of insect-laden air" from which fell "a continuous rain."[5]

3.

From the mid-1920s through the 1930s, high-altitude researchers in France, England, and the United States were making the same discoveries and coming to the same conclusions. Broadly speaking, they decided, there were two kinds of insect travel.[6] The tiny insects of the aerial plankton occupied the air above 3,000 feet, where they moved involuntarily, unable to resist the fast-moving higher-level currents. Stronger-flying, larger insects kept relatively close to the ground, below the 3,000-feet boundary, harnessing the calmer, low-altitude winds and migrating according to their own routes and schedules. These lower-level migrations could be spectacular. Some, such as those of the monarch butterflies and the Old Testament locusts, were already familiar. Others could take an entomologist by surprise. All were somehow mysterious. In 1900, James William Tutt witnessed millions of noctuid Silver Y moths flying with other insects in a steady east-west line alongside migrating birds. A few years later, William Beebe from the New York Zoological Society—the same William Beebe who pioneered deep-sea exploration in his steel bathysphere—found himself caught in a dense mass of purplish-brown butterflies on the Portachuelo Pass in northern Venezuela. Despite his confusion, Beebe managed to calculate that at least 186,000 insects had swept by him in the first ninety minutes. An hour later, with the torrent now "going full strength," he composed himself enough to pull out his high-power binoculars:

> I began about twenty-five feet overhead and then refocussed slowly upward until the limit of vision of the small insects was reached. This, judged by horizontal tests of objects of similar size would be about a half mile zenithwards, and at every fractional turn of the screw, more and more smaller-appearing butterflies fluttered into clarity.
>
> Throughout the entire extent of verticality there was no lessening of denseness of flying insects. . . . For many days this particular phase of migration continued, millions upon millions coming from some unknown source, travelling due south to an equally mysterious destination.

Beebe also reported a different phenomenon: a steady stream of insects of many species—cockchafers, chrysomelid beetles, vespid wasps, bees, moths, butterflies, and "hosts upon hosts of minute winged insect life"—passing together through the migration flyway in a massive motley emigration that apparently took place every year.[7] All that minute insect life was too small to be counted. But aphids, an indistinct haze, will swarm at densities up to 250 times greater than that of butterflies. In fact, these tiny ones—the aphids, the thrips, the microlepidoptera, the smallest beetles, the smallest parasitic wasps, all barely visible to the human eye—form the overwhelming majority of species and individuals of the class Insecta, testimony to the fact that evolution shrank the insects over the millennia even as it exploded their numbers and differences.

The giant dragonflies of the late Paleozoic, with their thirty-inch wingspans, are no more. As insects miniaturized, they developed their near-endless variety of aerodynamic body shapes and their specialized muscles for super-high-frequency wingbeats. Of the million or so species currently described, the average adult body length is at most a mere two tenths of an inch, and the median length is significantly less. Nonetheless, it is the larger, more visible insects, those four tenths of an inch or more in length (that is, at least twenty times larger than the average), that command the attention of researchers. If we subtract the huge volume of genomic studies of the fruit fly *Drosophila melanogaster*, the literature on tiny insects is scant.[8] It seems clear that the relative abundance of miniature insects that Glick recorded in the air column is less a result of their being so easily carried aloft than a result of the fact that they so outnumber their larger relatives.

Glick himself reported strong-flying dragonflies at 7,000 feet over Tallulah, large insects flying well above the 3,000-foot boundary and flying so comfortably that they shifted direction to avoid his plane. Other researchers, including Beebe, recorded minute weak-flying insects—the supposedly involuntary dispersers—close to the ground, well below the proposed threshold. Researchers of insect flight now talk about the boundary layer in more fluid terms, as a variable region near the earth's surface in which wind speed is less than the speed at which a particular insect is capable of flying, a zone that varies with the strength of the wind and the capacity of the insect. Within the boundary layer, the insect is able to orient itself actively. Above the boundary layer, its direction of flight is strongly influenced by the prevailing winds, and the animal adapts to, rather than overcomes, atmospheric conditions.[9] Given that only about 40 percent of known insects fly at airspeeds greater than three feet per second and that such timid winds—so gentle that a human can barely sense them—are generally found only close to the ground, most insects exercise full control over their directionality only at an altitude of three to six feet.[10]

Yet beyond the boundary layer, thousands of feet into the troposphere, it's likely that only a small proportion of these animals—those without wings (such as spiders and mites), those that become too cold, and those suffering from exhaustion—are passively carried. From the tiniest to the largest, migrating insects are out there actively flying, flapping their wings, maintaining or varying their altitude and direction despite the strength of the winds around them. Sometimes they hover, sometimes they glide, sometimes they free-fall, sometimes they soar. They do what they can to evade birds in the daytime and bats at night. Rarely do they drift along like pollen in a breeze. Or plankton in the ocean.

No, aerial plankton is not a good name for these animals. They don't live in this medium; they occupy it temporarily. And their residency is full of calculation and action. Their exodus is triggered by the impulse to find new habitats and to encounter new hosts. Sometimes their flights are short, repeated dispersals; sometimes they are vast migrations from which the traveler may or may not return. In either case, there is little passivity. Takeoff is oriented to wind and light. If the animal is strong enough, flight is often against or across the wind. Butterflies and locusts streaming in formation may suddenly interrupt a low-level journey with a dramatic collective rise to catch a current at thousands of feet. Even tiny insects appear to seek out thermal drafts. In the upper reaches of the air column, the minute ones take paths strongly determined by the wind, but inside the airstream they hold steady, beating their wings, adjusting their direction and altitude. And then they alight, often prompted by scent or reflecting light, using their bodies to bring themselves to earth.

Forty years ago, Cecil Johnson, the author of a classic text on insect migration and dispersal, pointed out that many, perhaps most, individual insects die on these voyages, but "this is the price such species pay for finding their habitats." Johnson conjured an image of a planet under surveillance, "the surface of the Earth is thus scanned very effectively as millions of individuals, flying on air currents, continuously encounter suitable and unsuitable situations." When the situation does not suit, they soon take off again in search of a better location for feeding or breeding (or some other activity obscure to us), following "a direction determined either by the wind or themselves."[11] It is a fact of planetary life, a great "diffusion system" that transports immense populations of animals "day after day, year after year, century after century."[12] What happens to the notion of an invasive species in the face of this continuous and irrepressible traffic of short- and long-range travel, dispersal, and migration? What is left of a notion that everything has its own place, that everything belongs somewhere and nowhere else, that boundaries are inviolable, that with vigilance and chemicals this hyperabundance of willful and random life can be brought under control? Perhaps this was what Glick glimpsed 3,000 feet above Durango, face-to-face with the pink bollworm moth, its flapping wings gleaming in the high-altitude sunshine.

4.

Stop. If you're inside, go to a window. Throw it open and turn your face to the sky. All that empty space, the deep vastness of the air, the heavens wide above you. The sky is full of insects, and all of them are going somewhere. Every day, above and around us, the collective voyage of billions of beings.

That's the letter *A*: the first thing not to forget. There are other worlds around us. Too often, we pass through them unknowing, seeing but blind, hearing but deaf, touching but not feeling, contained by the limits of our senses, the banality of our imaginations, our Ptolemaic certitudes.

Beauty

"What's going on? What is it?" I called out to Seu Benedito as we put-putted along the Rio Guariba in the afternoon sunshine. "What's happening?"

A hundred yards away on the far bank, under the heavy trees, which just yesterday had sheltered a broken wooden house, the poorest on the river, was a shimmering jewel, a glittering vision of fluttering yellow, canary yellow, corn silk yellow, golden yellow. Flecks of gold were spinning from it like cinders high into the dark forest. Sparkling sunbursts were spiraling out from it over the river. "What is it?"

"Oh," Seu Benedito laughed, "the *borboletas de verão,* the butterflies of summer. They're back. You've never seen them?"

That day they were everywhere. An explosion exploding the world, dressing it in strange new color, tripping it out with unexpected beauty. As we chugged along the river, we saw that each house we passed had surrendered to the transformation. Thousands of yellow butterflies had settled on roofs and walls, occupied wooden porches, finally turned Amazonia into El Dorado, encrusted this quiet village in layers of gold.

When we reached home, there were golden-yellow summer butterflies dancing around our house too. High in the eaves, all around the porch, low in the muddy yard where the pigs rooted under the floorboards. They floated and soared, and I took a picture to hold on to that day and the few that followed before the insects left.

This is the kitchen at the back of Seu Benedito's house, near the mouth of the Amazon in the Brazilian state of Amapá. I lived here for fifteen months in 1995 and 1996, and this is what it looked like in the late-afternoon sun on the day the butterflies arrived. Sometimes now it

seems like a dream, someone else's story, so I take out this picture and think back to that day. See the sleepy hunting dog in the foreground? See the *açaí* palms, with their heavy bunches of black fruit? See the two giant tires that little Helton and Rosiane filled every morning with water from the creek, just out of view to the right? See the fenced-off vegetable patch? The thick wire clothesline? See the *borboletas de verão* caught in time and space like mini UFOs, just visiting, just stopping by, entering our lives, transforming everything just for a moment, showing us a glimmer of a different world, then passing on?

Chernobyl

1.

I look at this photo of Cornelia Hesse-Honegger in her apartment in Zürich and try to imagine what she sees through her microscope. Beneath the lens is a tiny golden-green insect, one of the leaf bugs of the suborder Heteroptera that she has been painting for more than thirty years.[1] The binocular microscope magnifies to eighty times. The centimeter scale in the left eyepiece allows her to map every detail of the insect's body with precision.

Cornelia collected this animal close to the Gundremmingen nuclear power plant in southern Germany. Like most of the insects she paints, it is deformed. In this case, its abdomen is irregularly shaped, a little crin-

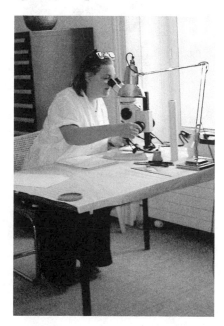

kled on its right side. To me, even under the microscope the deformity is all but imperceptible. But just think, she says, how such an anomaly must feel if you are only two tenths of an inch long!

What does Cornelia see when she focuses so intently on this creature? She tells me that when she's outside, collecting in fields, at roadsides, and on the edges of forests, she "loses herself in the animal." At these moments, she says, she feels "very connected, extremely connected"; she feels a deep bond, as if, perhaps, she herself had once been such a creature—a leaf bug—"and had a body remembering."

But her painting practice, as she explains it, is almost the opposite of this. When she sits down with her microscope, she no longer experiences the insect as a coevolved being but as form and color, shape and texture, quantity and volume, plane and aspect. Her work becomes as mechanical as possible. ("I want to be like a laser that goes from one square centimeter to the next. I see it, I show it; I see it, I show it," she tells me.) At times, as in the painting below, she introduces a principle of formal randomness, selecting specimens from her collection by chance and abstracting a single structure, which she repeatedly positions at designated points on the graph paper, creating an image with no preconceived final arrangement, an image whose aesthetic origins lie squarely in the tradition of concrete art, in which she was raised.

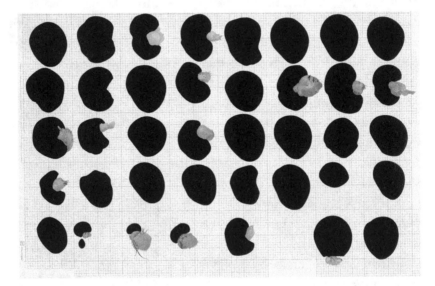

The painting shows a series of eyes from fruit flies, *Drosophila melanogaster*, that had been irradiated by geneticists at the University of Zürich's Institute of Zoology. Although she has chosen not to show the animals' heads, Cornelia uses them as her points of reference, centering each one on corresponding squares of graph paper so that they are situated precisely in relation to the absent bodies to which they belong. But radiation has left the eyes irregularly positioned on the flies' heads, and as a result, despite the orderliness of the arrangement, the horizontal and vertical lines in the paintings are uneven. Cornelia's systematic randomness produces regularity but not uniformity, a graphic expression of

an insight central to her understanding of nature, aesthetics, and science: the world, her paintings say, is governed simultaneously by stabil-
ity and randomness, by principles of both order and chance. The flies'
eyes are bizarre. Their size and shape vary dramatically. Several are
sprouting wing parts, aberrations that allow researchers to investigate
cell behavior—"like someone who studies a train by systematically letting it derail," as Cornelia puts it.[2] One fly, represented by empty space,
has an eye missing entirely. Because she detests naturalism in painting
(naturalism, she tells me, encourages the viewer to focus on the "reality"
of the image, on the skill of the artist, on the artist's "vision") and
because she wants us to pay attention to form, she painted the eyes black
rather than a realistic red.

Cornelia painted that picture in 1987. But she first drew mutated
Drosophila twenty years earlier, as a scientific illustrator at the Institute
of Zoology.[3] In a standard mutagenic protocol, those flies had been fed
food laced with ethyl methanesulfonate. The resulting mutations fascinated her so much that she began painting the damaged insects in her
own time, experimenting with angle and color, even casting some large
heads as plastic sculpture, struggling to make sense of the disturbing
world she was being pulled into. At the institute, her job was to draw the
varied appearance of the so-called Quasimodo mutants. The animals
were crippled and pitifully monstrous, "chaotically" deformed. In preparation for the illustrators, the inner organs of each fly's head were dissolved with a chemical agent that left the disturbed face as a mask. "The
mutants were not to leave me," she wrote. And, indeed, from that point
on her activities are shadowed by the victims, actual and potential, of
induced mutation.[4]

The image opposite is among the last that Cornelia painted before
making a collecting trip in July 1987 to Österfärnebo, in Sweden, the site
she identified as the place in western Europe most heavily polluted by
fallout from the disaster at Chernobyl. That journey signaled the beginning of a new phase in her life, one marked by controversy and not
always welcome attention. In their unsettling combination of blank
abstraction and bleak outrage, the disembodied eyes are a premonition,
an anticipation.

When the reactor exploded at Chernobyl, Cornelia was ready. "Chernobyl was just the answer to the question, What is going on here?" she

told me recently. She was already a witness. She had seen the diminish-ing numbers of leaf bugs in her garden. She had seen the monstrous fruit flies. The laboratory and the world were one. What now stood between them? She already recognized the emerging aesthetic. There was no nature immune to its effect. "We cling to images that do not cor-respond to changing reality," she wrote.[5] Chernobyl was merely the nightmare exposed to the light of day, the invisible made evident.

2.

In 1976, Cornelia Hesse-Honegger was living quietly in the countryside outside Zürich with two young children, a self-absorbed, neglectful hus-band, and a passion for leaf bugs. It wasn't simply the beauty of the insects that attracted her. There was something about their character. ("They have a kind of being aware of certain situations that I find extremely amazing," she says.) Their idiosyncrasies turned collecting into an obsession ("a kind of addiction"; "to find a leaf bug is fantas-tic . . . it's heaven on earth!"). She rapidly grew familiar with the ones that lived nearby and started to recognize individual differences ("the individual differences are in fact astonishing") as well as the more acknowledged distinctions among families and species. Summer vaca-tions were spent at her husband's family's house in the southern canton of Ticino, rising early while the mist still clung to the landscape, roam-ing the wetlands, collecting her insects, becoming closer and closer to the local plant and animal life.

Collecting created one kind of intimacy. Discovering the habits of the insects and uncovering their hiding places ("I know exactly where they will be") cultivated her sensitivity to their senses ("They're lazy people!" she told me, laughing), her feeling that they know when she is near, that they feel when her eyes *touch* them. Through collecting she came to understand their ecology and their character. How could she not? And through the intense attention of painting, she developed another type of intimacy, becoming expert in their morphology and their variety.

Painting, she insists—reaching back to the sixteenth-century Swiss naturalist Conrad Gesner; to her inspiration, the painter-explorer Maria Sibylla Merian; to the autodidact fossil hunter Mary Anning—is research, not merely documentation.[6] It is a way of achieving multidimensional knowledge of the subject, a way to *see* it in its biological, phenomenological, and political fullness. Not simply a way to express what we see, painting is a discipline through which we learn to see—to see, that is, in the broad sense of gaining insight. Through painting, she is able to map anomaly, to recognize patterns and relationships across her archive of collecting sites, to realize that she has encountered this deformity somewhere before: Österfärnebo, Chernobyl, Sellafield, Gundremmingen, La Hague. "It's a discovery of a new world," she says. "The more I look, the more I dive into this world, the more I can connect." If only life would allow her to spend six months painting just one leaf bug. If only . . . "I would like to go deep, deep, deep, deep . . ."

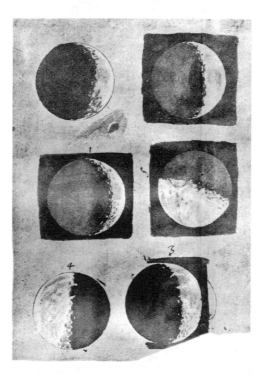

It is late in the evening. We have finished dinner and are admiring Galileo's famous ink washes of the moon, a series of paintings she loves (*"This* is art!"). Galileo made these images in 1610, sketching what he saw through his recently constructed telescope, a novelty that brought an entirely new world into focus. The sense of discovery in these pictures is claustrophobic. They have an urgency about them, as if he drew in disbelief ("what causes even greater wonder . . ." he marveled), racing to capture the unimagined textures before they rotated into shadow, perhaps never to be seen again.[7] Cornelia tells me how Galileo's colleagues examined these drawings of what he'd seen in the night sky but were unable to recognize the objects he showed them. This was not the moon they knew. How could they trust the view through an instrument they did not understand? They were "seeing-blind," Cornelia says. So set in their thinking, so at home in their world, they looked but they didn't see, looked but made no sense of what they saw.

After she left her husband and her country garden, after she moved back to Zürich with her children, after Chernobyl, Cornelia published the first of two cover stories in the Sunday magazine of the leading Swiss newspaper *Tages-Anzeiger*. Under the headline "When Flies and Bugs Don't Look the Way They Should," she presented paintings of leaf bugs, fruit flies, and ivy leaves she had collected around Österfärnebo and Ticino.[8]

Her account of the trip to Sweden is engrossing. Part detective story, part conversion narrative, part conspiracy, it begins with her struggle to track down information about the radioactive cloud that spread west across Europe from Chernobyl in the days after the explosion. She finds maps ("miserably inexact") and identifies the most contaminated places to which she can gain access ("In the evenings, when the children were in bed, I pored over maps and brooded over data at the kitchen table"). Her calculations reveal that the greatest fallout in western Europe was in eastern Sweden ("and that, I decided, was where I wanted to go").

When she arrives, people tell her—as they will years later at Three Mile Island—about the strange feelings, the inexplicable foreboding they experienced the night the rain cloud broke and radioactive particles poured down on their town. A local veterinary surgeon shows her clover growing red leaves and yellow flowers instead of the green leaves and pink flowers of earlier years. She finds odd-looking plants everywhere. She collects insects, and the next day, July 30, 1987, she examines them under her microscope. She already knew that leaf bugs were exceptional biological indicators. She had observed in her garden how the precision of their anatomy made irregularities highly evident, how normal variation was generally restricted to their markings, how one bug could live its entire life on a single plant, and how its descendants might remain there too. She realized that by ingesting fluids directly from leaves and shoots, leaf bugs made themselves vulnerable to contaminants taken up by the plant. But in seventeen years of painting them, she had never seen anything like this. "I felt sick. One bug had a particularly shortened left leg, while others had feelers like shapeless sausages, and something black grew out of the eye of another." She sees everything as if for the first time.

Although I was theoretically convinced that radioactivity affects nature, I still could not imagine what it would actually look like. Now these poor creatures were lying there under my microscope. I was shocked. It was as if someone had drawn back the curtain. Every day I discovered more damaged plants and bugs. Sometimes I could hardly remember what the normal plant shapes looked like. I was confused and afraid I might be losing my mind.

I realized that I had to free myself from all my prior assumptions and be completely open to what was in front of me, even at the risk of being considered mad. The horror of what I had found tortured me in my sleep and gave me nightmares. I began to collect and paint feverishly.[9]

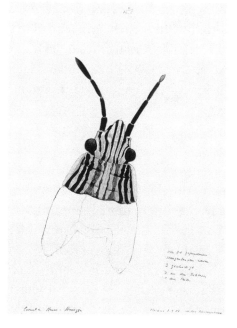

She had planned it as a temporary detour.

[Chernobyl] happened and I thought I'd do this quickly. A year, two, maybe three—and then I'd go back to my mutated fly eyes or something. This was actually the kind of work that I liked. I didn't like to leave this work. I only did because I thought it was necessary. All those paintings [in the magazines] are on cheap paper, the cheapest paper, just from my sketching pad. It wasn't serious artwork. I was convinced that after I painted the first ones, the scientists would say, "Yes, that's really interesting. Let's run to those places and collect."

She traveled back to Ticino, to the area near her ex-husband's family's home and to the insects she knew so well. Although fallout from Chernobyl had been less concentrated here than in Sweden, the climate was milder. As the contamination rained down, insects in Ticino were already feeding on vegetation that had not yet sprouted further north. She collected bugs and leaves, and she found three pairs of *Drosophila*, which she brought back to Zürich and bred in the kitchen of her apartment. "I sat in front of the microscope night after night trying to keep up with the rapid propagation," she wrote. It was a full-time job, but she was "possessed by the need to see and discover," and I don't think she really thought about the difficulties. She prepared special food, cleaned out the jars, accustomed herself to the stench, and tended to the exploding population. The prize, her terrible reward, was quickly apparent. "I was horrified by what I saw," she wrote.[10] And again and again, in counterpoint to the refusals of the scientists, this horror is the root of compulsion.

3.

In outline, it's quite simple. The international nuclear regulatory agencies—principally the International Commission on Radiological Protection (ICRP) and the U.N. Scientific Committee on the Effects of Atomic Radiation—calculate the dangers of radioactivity to human health using a threshold. Although many scientists admit that the mechanisms of radiation damage to cells are poorly understood, that the composition of emissions from nuclear installations vary substantially, and that different bodies (not to mention different organs and different cells at different points in their development) respond to contamination in quite distinct ways, the threshold establishes a universal tolerance level below which emissions are considered safe. In the tense days following the disaster at Chernobyl, it was the logic of a fixed threshold that allowed government experts to reassure their nervous publics that the dangers were negligible.

The ICRP derives its threshold from a linear curve extrapolated from rates of genetic (reproductive) irregularities, cancer, and leukemia among the survivors of large-scale nuclear events. Since those calculations began, the prime data set has been drawn from survivors of the 1945 bombings of Hiroshima and Nagasaki. The initial radiation dosage at those sites was extremely large and distributed in a short period. The resulting curve emphasizes the effects of exposure to artificial radioactivity at high values. Low-level radiation, such as that emitted over long time periods by normally operating nuclear power plants, appears relatively, if not entirely, insignificant, its effects falling within the range of the "natural" background radiation emitted from elements present in the earth's crust. The assumption is that large doses produce large effects; small doses, small effects.

A number of scientists unaffiliated with the nuclear industry and frequently in alliance with citizens' groups from areas close to nuclear plants describe an alternative curve. Following work carried out in the 1970s by the Canadian physicist Abram Petkau, they argue that the effects of radiation are best captured not by the official linear curve, in which a double quantity produces a double effect, but by a "supralinear" curve, which registers far higher effects at low doses. In the supralinear curve, there is no safe minimum dose above zero.[11]

These researchers often begin with epidemiology, carrying out their own population surveys downwind or downstream of nuclear installations, looking for statistically significant correlations between localized clusters of disease and sites of low-level radiation emissions. Working from the assumption of a causal relationship between emissions and sickness—an assumption reinforced not only by the epidemic proportions of some of these clusters but also by the secrecy of the industry—their focus is on the identification of the mechanisms by which low dosage disrupts biological function.

For example, Chris Busby, a British physical chemist and anti-nuclear campaigner, emphasizes two critical but overlooked variables: cell development and the random behavior of artificial radioactivity.[12] Under normal conditions, Busby argues, a cell (any cell) is hit by radiation approximately once a year. If the cell is in its normal quiescent mode, it is fairly robust. However, during times of active replication—a repair mode that can be triggered by various forms of stress—the same cell is highly susceptible to radiation. At those moments, it exhibits considerable genomic instability, and two radioactive "hits" produce a far greater effect than just one.

Moreover, Busby says, the ingestion of radioactive materials through food and water has effects quite distinct from those of external exposure. Certain types of internal radiation associated with, for instance, drinking contaminated milk can produce multiple hits on an individual cell within hours. If a cell receives a second hit of artificial radiation while it is in active replication mode, he claims, it is up to 100 times more likely to mutate.

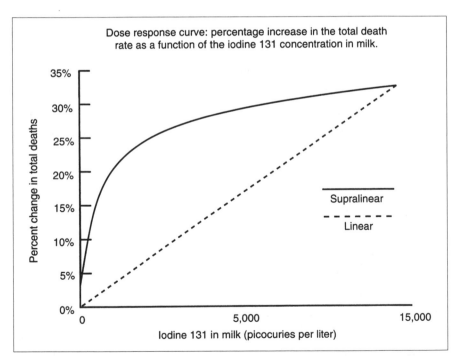

Dose response curve: percentage increase in the total death rate as a function of the iodine 131 concentration in milk.

In Busby's second-event theory, the level of vulnerability of a cell to radiation is a function of its state of development at a given moment. And this vulnerability is further exacerbated by the random, discontinuous waves characteristic of artificial radiation. Cornelia explained the randomness of artificial radiation to me using the analogy of bullets: it doesn't matter how many are fired, whom they're fired by, or even when and where they're fired; you need only be hit by one at the wrong time and in the wrong place to suffer its effect. The ICRP linear curve assumes a constant distribution of particles and a predictable effect. If, as many argue, those are invalid assumptions, the levels of environmental susceptibility to the effects of radioactive contamination are likely to be dramatically elevated—indeed, they are likely sufficient to explain the epidemiological evidence of elevated mortality in human, animal, and plant populations in sites subject to more or less routine radioactive emissions.

Low-level-radiation campaigners would no doubt have predicted the experts' response to Cornelia's articles in the *Tages-Anzeiger Magazin*. Reiterating the official position that the fallout from Chernobyl was too small to induce mutations, scientists stated simply that the explanation must lie elsewhere. Cornelia's methodology, they argued, did not adequately control for alternative causal factors, such as pesticides and parasites. She offered no comparative baseline, no reference habitat free of contaminants in which a normal rate of variation for the species could be measured. In fact, they pointed out (ignoring the limited character of her claims), she offered no numbers at all, either for dosage or for incidence of deformities.[13] The scientists dismissed her evidence, rebuffed her appeals to their expertise, and retreated without explanation from the occasional unguarded expressions of interest. It was a scenario she would witness repeatedly: "I showed my bugs and flies to all the professors with whom I had previously worked. I even brought the director of the Zoological Institute, a professor of genetics, a little tube of deformed living flies. He didn't bother to look at it, and said an investigation would cost too much time and money. He said that since it had already been confirmed that small doses of radiation would not cause any morphological damage, the expense was in no way justifiable."[14]

From the outside, of course, it seems almost too obvious: her amateur status, her gender, the sensitivity of the issue, the closed character of the industry. Always the same questions: What qualified her to attribute causality to the deformities she found? What qualified her to distinguish mutations induced by radiation from the naturally occurring variation expected in any given population? What qualified her to develop her own methodology? What qualified her to feed the hysteria of a public made paranoid by Chernobyl? What qualified her to contradict those who were qualified? How could she live with the rash of abortions her reports had provoked among women in Ticino?

But beyond the scientific community—and, it is important to say, among the few scientists already sympathetic to the anti-nuclear movement—the response was far from entirely hostile. She made radio appearances and received large quantities of encouraging mail. After the first article, the opposition German Social Democratic Party called for an investigation into the local effects of Chernobyl. After the second, the Swiss government, forced to respond to public pressure, agreed to sponsor a doctoral dissertation on the health of heteropterans across the federal territory.

Nonetheless, the antagonism of the scientists unsettled her, and perhaps we should remember just how controversial nuclear power was in Europe following Chernobyl. The Swiss anti-nuclear movement was vocal and politically effective, and Cornelia's bombshells exploded in the media just as activists were canvassing for the 150,000 signatures required to enforce a third referendum on the restriction of the industry. The first two votes (in 1979 and 1984) had been narrowly defeated, but this one, held in September 1990, would result in a ten-year moratorium on the construction of new reactors. It was impossible to intervene in this issue and remain innocent. Yet Cornelia appears to have thought of herself still as within the fold of science, if not openly acknowledged as a lay expert then at the least as a fellow traveler contributing through her skills as an artist. Perhaps she was a little too independent for the supporting role expected of the scientific illustrator, but wasn't she nonetheless a collegial participant in a common project of investigation and understanding?

She finds a cicada with a grotesque stump growing from one knee and takes it to a former professor. "Years before," she wrote, "I had collected insects with him for the fauna courses at the university. I had learned from him how to set up a professional collection of insects. It was his schooling that had made me the meticulous scientific illustrator I had become." The professor admits he has never seen this kind of deformity before but dismisses its significance and scolds her like a child for the articles in the *Tages-Anzeiger*. Don't think you are a scientist just because you have drawn pictures for me and my colleagues, he tells her.[15]

The closed ranks shocked her. The reactions bore the marks of an expulsion. It was a decisive moment, and again it seems that—to use her word—she was "possessed," taken over by a visceral conviction of vision, of seeing something invisible to others, seeing the minatory sicknesses of these invisible insects. Remembering those turbulent months, she wrote, "I knew a task had found me."[16]

I don't want to write a hero story. But let me tell you what she did. In Sweden, she was amazed to discover that no one was investigating the effects of Chernobyl on animals and plants. Returning to Switzerland, she reviewed the criticism of her first article. If, as the scientists insisted, low doses of radionuclides were not producing these disturbances, there should be none around the famously clean Swiss nuclear plants. Unsure of what to expect, she traveled to the cantons of Aargau and Solothurn and hiked around their five nuclear installations. The deformed bugs she found at every turn were the subject of her second article in *Tages-Anzeiger Magazin*, a focus of even more controversy than the first. "I believe," she wrote in her conclusion, "we must pursue [the causes of these disturbances] with the best and most sophisticated methods at our disposal, and with a level of funding I cannot afford. With my illustrations I can only point out changes. I make them visible. With this work I allow myself to point to a crisis in the investigation of the effects of artificial low-level radiation, and further to call for scientific clarification at a broader level. I cannot go further with the means at my disposal. But more detailed investigations are both possible and necessary."[17]

4.

The garden bug on page 28 is from Küssaberg, in Germany, close to the Leibstadt nuclear power plant in Aargau. The entire neck plate is distorted; the bulging blister on its left includes an unusual black growth. Cornelia's painting is delicate but meticulous. In color—many shades of gold—and at full size (this one is seventeen by twelve inches; some are far larger), it is strikingly beautiful.

The composition, unsparing, is typical. On featureless white backgrounds, she emphasizes the insects' architectural properties, their structure and monumentality as well as their decorative surface. The poses are formal and explicitly contrived. She repositions legs and wings to expose deformity; often, for the same reason, she leaves out limbs or body segments or just sketches them in outline.

Leaving behind scientific illustration, which, she explains, relies on nineteenth-century techniques of "light and shadow," she adopted the color perspective pioneered by Cézanne and the cubists, creating spatial effects through relations between colors (employing contrasts of inten-

sity, temperature, and value) and—like Goethe, Rudolph Steiner, and Josef Albers—attending to the subjective and relational nature of color perception. Light and shadow, she says, is "historical": it captures one particular moment, freezing light and, with it, time; color perspective, on the contrary, is timeless, outside time. Then she shows me how, as she paints, she shifts the position of the insect under her microscope so that the finished image is a composite of several angles, again calling up the cubists and their multifaceted renderings of simultaneity.

These watercolors are realistic but not naturalistic. With rare exceptions, her animals lack all animation. Their physicality foregrounded, they have the aura of specimens. Each painting is a portrait, and each insect is a subject, a specific individual. She tells me, "I like that the insect can be itself. That's why I choose to paint the individual as it is. I could, for instance, paint one that has five different defects that I find in an area. I don't do this. I want to show the individual." On display, the insect hangs, massive, stunning in its detail, supplemented by a label that identifies the date and site of its collection, as well as its irregularities, and that grounds the atemporal image in time, place, and politics. Sharing much of the visual grammar of the biological sciences, the paintings seem mutely dispassionate, resolutely documentary. But so thoroughly in the world, they shimmer with emotion.

Cornelia once told me that the first time she saw a deformed leaf bug, so tiny, so damaged, so irrelevant, she lost her mental balance, her perspective, her sense of scale and proportion. For a moment, she was unsure if she was looking at herself or the animal. She paused in her narrative. "Who cares about leaf bugs?" she said. "They're just nothing." She was recalling her earlier life, as the teenage daughter of famous artists, describing how she hung back in the shadows, unobserved, as her parents entertained Mark Rothko, Sam Francis, Karlheinz Stockhausen, and other luminaries in New York, Paris, and Zürich ("No one would even see me or recognize me. . . . I would never interfere"). And she was recalling how in twenty years her husband never visited her studio, and how, when her son was born, the doctor came into her room and made a drawing for her to break the news that her child had a club foot, and how, when she saw that first deformed leaf bug in Sweden, it had a crippled foot too. And she was telling me how, when she saw that first crippled insect, in the shock of all those experiences colliding so suddenly with such unanticipated force, she had to fight physically to stop herself from throwing up.

And just a few moments later, in the failing afternoon sunlight in her Zürich apartment, she said, "In the end, the picture is everything. Nobody sees the insect itself." And it was my turn to pause, because I didn't quite know what she meant. It sounded like a lament, a disappointment that her images are too instantly domesticated, reduced to the iconic, that they too easily make the leap from invisibility to enormity, too effectively stand in for human fears, too readily bring self-concern to the fore, so that the individual insect—the one she found ("It's heaven on earth!"), captured ("They can move very quickly"), killed with chloroform ("I always tell myself this is the last summer"), pinned, labeled, added to the thousands already in her collection, and finally came to know so intimately through microscope and brushes—seems again and again to be overlooked, to become lost.

But then I remembered Cornelia saying that if she were freed of the compulsion to paint deformities, if she were free to paint whatever she chose, her work would follow the path laid out in the painting of the mutant eyes she completed before her life was interrupted by the journey to Österfärnebo. And I realized that her lament was not only for the loss of the individual insect. In that painting, she offers the insect not as being or subject but as its antithesis: the insect as aesthetic logic, as coalescence of form, color, and angle. This is work that draws explicitly on her history in concrete art, an international movement centered in postwar Zürich, in which—because of the prominence in the group of her father, Gottfried Honegger—she received her initial aesthetic training. (Cornelia's mother, Warja Lavater, was widely known as an innovative graphic artist and maker of artists' books.)

Concrete paintings tend toward geometric patterns, high-contrast color blocks, glassy planes, and the refusal of figurative or even metaphorical reference. Kazimir Malevich's programmatic *White on White* (1918), a white square painted on a white ground, is perhaps the movement's founding document. Casting themselves as aesthetic radicals breaking with the conservatism of representational art, Max Bill, Richard Paul Lohse, and the other founders of concrete art looked to Soviet constructivism, to the geometry of Mondrian and De Stijl, and to the formalism of Bauhaus. In his 1936 manifesto, *Konkrete Gestaltung* (*Concrete Formation*), Bill wrote, "We call those works of art concrete that came into being on the basis of their own innate means and laws—without borrowing from natural phenomena, without transforming those phenomena, in other words: not by abstraction."[18]

Abstract art, searching for a visual language based in symbols and metaphor, is still "object painting," is still tied to the object it mimics, is still asking what that thing is, how it can be made sense of, how it can be communicated. For concrete artists, the work should speak of nothing but itself. It should reference nothing outside itself. It should leave the viewer complete interpretive freedom. Its signs and its referents should be one and the same: form, color, quantity, plane, angle, line, texture.

From the 1940s, the group was centered in Zürich, a wartime refuge for critical intellectuals. Its influence, though, was felt throughout Europe (notably in the op art of Bridget Riley and Victor Vasarely), in the United States (in color-field painting and minimalism), and in Latin America (especially among Brazilian concrete and neoconcrete artists, such as Lygia Clark, Hélio Oiticica, and Cildo Meireles). The movement was varied, but it found an early unity in the search for an art that would be the visual and tactile expression of pure logic ("the mathematical way of thinking in the art of our times," as Bill put it).[19] As the concretization of the intellect and the removal of interpretation, it was a direct riposte to Surrealism's appeal to the unconscious. Yet subjectivity proved to be a stubborn presence. Concrete paintings and sculptures were also the product of the artists' arbitrary choices. Probability, chance, and randomness promised a solution, and the search for effective ways to integrate them into the artistic process became an important preoccupation.

It took me a long time to understand the importance of these aesthetics for Cornelia. On the one hand, it seemed clear that her sensuous attention to the insect contravened their most basic premise: the adherence to Malevich's "nonobjectivist" determination to shatter the connection between art and material objects. Yet I knew from our conversations that in the moment of painting, Cornelia sees form and color, not the independent object. Nor is there anything accidental in the formality of her portraits or the repetition of the poses. All is geometric, the insects located on a grid that she systematically completes. Her method is both highly precise and, in the sense that the outcome is contingent on what is present under the microscope, substantially random. It is not unusual that after finishing a painting, she discovers that the insect is deformed in ways she hadn't noticed before. Her painting practice, she insists, creates a rigorous break, removing her environmentalist politics and her sympathies for the animal from the image, so that the paintings themselves are freed of her presence. "My task," she told me, echoing Max Bill, "is just to show [the insect] and to paint it, not to judge it." Viewers, she says, must search for meaning in the picture unburdened by her message.

But, I wondered, with the strength of her commitment to anti-nuclear politics and to the insects themselves and with the descriptive labels accompanying the images and all the controversy that has surrounded her work, how could either she or the viewer avoid judgment? "I do think it's possible," she replied. "When I sit there and draw, I want nothing else than to be as precise as possible. It is not simply politics: I have a deep interest in structure in nature." But what kind of non-object art can be based so strongly in objects? Can her pictures be both "deeply in the world," as she puts it, and speak of nothing beyond themselves? Isn't there a contradiction between these twin impulses of her painting: to recognize the individual insect and simultaneously to efface it into an aesthetic logic of form? Yes, she says without hesitation, her work is really neither concrete nor naturalistic. And according to many, it is also neither science nor art. Perhaps, she laughs, that's why she so rarely manages to sell any of it!

Much later that evening, with both of us fading fast and our conversation faltering, she returns again to this question. We are talking about her involvement in campaigning, how an exhibition of her paintings organized by the World Wildlife Fund toured sites slated for nuclear-waste disposal, when she abruptly shifts the topic. "It's the artistic question," she says suddenly. "How to show structure . . . It's a question of how can I show the structure of what I find." It is not simply politics. But how to assert this when the politics overshadows everything and the painting is far more complex than it appears?

And then, in frustration and from more than a little exhaustion, her voice dropping to little more than a whisper: "Everything is always so focused on those watercolors . . ."

5.

In the years since the *Tages-Anzeiger* articles, Cornelia has devoted herself to investigating the health of insects near nuclear power plants in Europe and North America. She has collected at Sellafield, in northwest England (the location of the 1957 Windscale disaster); around the Cap de la Hague reprocessing plant in Normandy; at Hanford, Washington (site of the plutonium factory for the Manhattan Project); on the perimeters of the Nevada Test Range; at Three Mile Island, Pennsylvania; in Aargau during every summer from 1993 to 1996 (the map below is based on data from 2,600 Aargau insects); and as an invited participant on a 1990

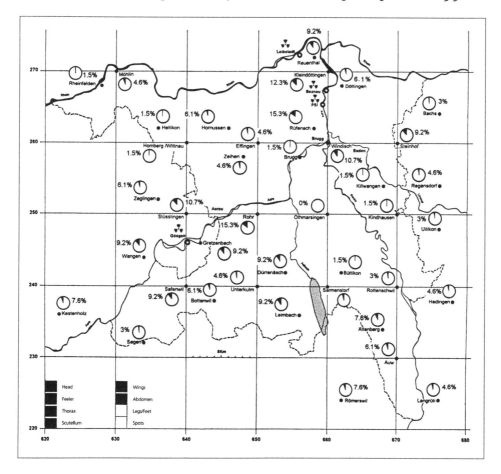

tour of the zone surrounding Chernobyl. She lectures, speaks at conferences, organizes exhibits of her paintings in collaboration with environmental groups, and is working on a large-scale project with the group
Strom ohne Atom (Electricity without Nuclear Power) to document the
distribution of eleven types of morphological deformities (missing and
misshapen feeler segments, wings of different lengths, irregular chitin,
misshapen scutella, deformed legs, and so on) among sets of fifty insects
she is collecting at each of twenty-eight locations in Germany.

She has succeeded in forming some important relationships with scientists. At Cap de la Hague, for example, Jean-François Viel, a professor
of biostatistics and epidemiology at the University of Besançon who has
identified a leukemia cluster among local residents, collaborated on the
statistical analysis of her collection. But in general she is more cynical
now about enlisting experts and instead responds to critics directly
through her research design: her data collection is more systematic, her
documentation more rigorous, and her paintings are no longer the rapid
sketches of those first frenetic field trips. In interviews and publications,
she has begun to explicitly address methodological questions, arguing
that there can be no reference habitat on a planet thoroughly polluted by
fallout from aboveground testing and emissions from nuclear power
plants and being careful to point out that she is documenting induced
deformities to somatic cells rather than heritable mutations. ("I cannot
say they are mutations because I cannot prove it, and if I cannot prove it,
I don't think I can say it," she tells me.) In this way, she emphasizes her
own expertise, strengthening her intervention in those nonscientific are-
nas where her talents are valued, publicizing her findings through environmental organizations, mass media, and cultural institutions.

These tactics free Cornelia to act as an environmentalist, to participate
in a world in which the politics of scientific proof are inverted by the precautionary principle, which asserts that a well-founded fear of potential
danger is a sufficient basis on which to oppose the deployment of a policy,
practice, or technology. They free her from the shadow of science, from
having to assert herself against a set of methodological and analytic stan-
dards that are always impossible to achieve because they are always initially institutional—that is, recognized only among those with the requisite
credentials (a doctorate, an affiliation, a professional network, a funding

history, a publishing record). The irony, of course, is that no one understands her scientific inadequacies better than Cornelia herself. And no one—as the tone of those early articles and her petitioning of professors showed—was more willing to accept the conventional subordinate role of the amateur as the handmaiden of the scientific expert. It strikes me that the relentlessness of her work has grown in direct proportion to her understanding of its importance. And that her understanding of her work's importance has increased as it has become clear how isolated is her quest for recognition of the effects of low-level radiation on insects and plants. Where would she be now if she hadn't faced such hostility and rejection? "It's something I don't understand," she told me in Zürich, "because if I had only found one leaf bug with its face shifted that would be enough to ask what was going on." And yet somehow, despite all this, there are signs of change. Perhaps the current interest in nuclear power as a "green" fuel has given new urgency to her message, perhaps it is the fruit of her relentlessness, but she has recently had an unexpected success, publishing a prominent (and beautifully illustrated) article—which, as we would expect, pulls no punches—in the specialist peer-reviewed journal *Chemistry and Biodiversity.*

But it is not as if acceptance in the art world has been any easier. In a sympathetic essay, the painter and critic Peter Suchin writes that "for one audience Hesse-Honegger's practice is invalidated by its 'artistic' manner, for another it is simply not artistic enough." In this arena, her work is too assertively realist and too tied to illustration, which, Suchin continues, "many would claim . . . is not 'art' but mere technique, a formulaic manner of record-making, largely devoid of the innovative, critical, and transformative qualities frequently associated with artistic production."[20]

Cornelia's unwillingness to respect epistemological boundaries seems to make art critics as uncomfortable as it does scientists. Her paintings insist that it is the boundary itself, rather than its breaching, that is the problem, that science and the visual arts belong together, that their separation is, as Galileo's vibrant lunar washes make clear, an artifact of the historical slicing of knowledge into ever more specialized and ever less ambitious disciplines. She claims scientific ancestors in Gesner, Merian, and Galileo, all of whom understood that active seeing through painting and drawing is the basis of scientific inquiry, that the empirical method begins with the artist's development of a mode of attention grounded in the close observation of nature.

But vision, perception, and attention are just a part of the story. After the publication of her second *Tages-Anzeiger* article, Cornelia traveled to Sellafield. Because contamination from the reactor there was known to be severe, she expected to find a larger number of damaged insects and deformities more serious than those she found near Aargau. But the difference between the sites was insignificant. Soon after, when she visited Chernobyl, she was appalled by the bleak conditions in which the local population lived, and she was surprised—and awkwardly disappointed—to discover that even there insect life was no more disturbed than in Switzerland. A period of introspection followed, a moment, it seems, of a more profound breaking with the science in which she had been trained at the Institute of Zoology:

> My intention had been to find a scale that would show that there was less damage in places with low radioactivity than in places with high or extremely high levels. I had read about radioactivity, and also about the Petkau Effect, but I didn't know what to make of the different opinions. Nor could I fall back on scientific inquiries because there were none. Now I was moving into new territory. Sitting gloomily in my rooms in England, I had to admit that my work was still based on the beliefs of scientists in Zürich and on a linear, or proportionate, increase of the effects of radiation. I was the one wearing blinders. I'd been looking for evidence that would confirm my own assumptions.[21]

The solution lay in a return to the principles of concrete art, to its affinity for science as a shared site of rationality, and in particular to its understanding of randomness. Random thinking was something Cornelia had already integrated into her painting practice and her aesthetics. It was a key component of her struggle to allow the insect to be itself rather than merely a vehicle for her artistic expression. Staring gloomily down the lens of her microscope in those rooms in northwest England, she sees the evidence of her observation again and again contradicting the preconceptions she is imposing on the irradiated landscape. She sees contingency at every turn: "Reality is different. Each nuclear power plant emits its own nuclear cocktail. Every landscape with its own characteristic meteorological and topographical conditions reacts differently.

In Switzerland, where weather conditions with inversions prevents, or at least mitigates, the dispersal of waste material and radioactivity in the atmosphere, the situation is entirely different from an area where a strong wind is constantly sweeping over the countryside."[22]

Such symmetry! And what grim satisfaction when it all comes together: the contingency of landscapes and bodies, the concrete aesthetics of chance, and the random behavior of artificial radionuclides. Something like randomness, a combination of contingency and chance, is now an analytic as well as an aesthetic:

> If one wants to systematically explore the relationship between one thing and another, one should not expect to find a neat equation of cause and effect. One has to abandon the idea that truth will visibly impose itself. Things need space in order to express themselves. Each individual peculiarity in a population (or combination of peculiarities) could prove itself to be a possibly relevant characteristic.
>
> This is certainly not a revolutionary discovery. Every statistical investigation is based on the random distribution of characteristics. But in my opinion, this is important not only in science and statistics, but also in art. In art I consider it increasingly important to experiment with chance, because the strength of artistic representation lies in perceiving every single thing as a unique event.[23]

With her growing alienation from mainstream science and her increasing proximity to anti-nuclear activism come not only a willingness to critique nuclear science as a corrupt enterprise but also a renewed sense of science's epistemological limitations. Some of this comes from her sensitivity to the vulnerability of the nonhuman universe of bugs, flies, and leaves. Some comes from personal disenchantment. And some seems to derive from lectures she attended two decades ago by the Austrian physicist and philosopher Paul Feyerabend, famous for arguing against proscriptive method and for the equivalence of multiple ways of knowing.[24] I think I hear echoes of Feyerabend's iconoclastic "epistemological anarchism" when she tells me how scientists conceive too much in linearities, and I think I hear them again when she tells me how they visualize in discrete, unconnected objects, quarantining the issues they study and relieving themselves of the problem of politics, as if both systematic and random connections did not exist, as if the problem of the atom were not deeply tied to the problems of clean water, clean air, dying forests, and poisoned food, as if this were not a problem of ways of living as much as ways of knowing.

6.

I found an upstairs window seat on the double-decker train. Zürich gleamed in the morning sunshine, all strong colors, deep shadows, and crisp air. The lake glistened. The clouds cleared. I saw the mountains for the first time. The train rattled out to the airport.

One of the last things Cornelia told me was "I think I cannot show myself as a whole." She brought out a work I hadn't seen before and set it down in front of us, a large picture of brightly colored paper cuts, silhouettes of outsize insect body parts arranged in series on a white background. The insects stripped bare. One type of essence. Color, form, quantity.

It was the other pictures, the portraits, that she described as "brutal paintings." But as the city flattened into suburbs and objects beyond the window blurred into indistinctness, I began to think that these more concrete images were the truly violent ones. After all, it is in these paintings, the paintings that show less of the insect and more of herself, that Cornelia renounces her intimacy with the individual leaf bugs and finds a way to discard all her attachments.

But the portraits—the brutal portraits—dissatisfy her. By too effectively standing in for human fears and too readily bringing viewers' self-concern to the fore, they elicit the wrong response. People see only the iconic figure of the insect, she said, never the individual insect itself. They see a biological indicator pathetic in its beauty, a warning sign, a prophecy of a day already dawned. They see neither the individual insect nor her painting, the non-object painting that refers to nothing except itself.

Yet somehow the portraits also achieve a doubling, a breaching of the lines between human and animal. These intensely direct paintings embedded so strongly in fears of invisible poison and malevolent corporate power enforce identification across the most radical of gaps by insisting on the most fundamental of commonalities—physical vulnerability, mortality—and by evoking a sense of humility in the face of complex beauty. Her portraits and the controversy she generates around them force people to transcend species difference by recognizing a conjoined fate, a common witnessing, a shared victimhood. It is quite unsettling: the eye of the painter and the viewer suspended between the clinical and the empathetic, a loss of stable distinction between subjects and objects, between humans and insects, between intimacy and distance.

Cornelia makes meticulous spiral-bound books of her field trips, just a few copies of each. Over the years they have become more elaborate and now include her photographs of the sites she visits, as well as color photocopies of her paintings, maps, statistical appendices, and lists of the collected insects, with records of any deformities. All these are inserted around her journal, a day-by-day account of the trip that includes descriptions of her encounters with people, plants, and insects. The books are beautiful objects, and the journal is relaxed and personal, full of anecdotes, reflections, and asides. She recalls how in Moscow, Idaho, two teenage girls in town for a football game entered her room, examined her microscope and collecting equipment, one of them asking if she were a witch, taking her hands, and sensing an intense vibration, a vibration that Cornelia sensed also. "She asked me what she had to do to become a person like me. I told her that she has to always listen to her heart and never worship a human being. If she wanted to find solace, she had to turn to an animal or a tree for help."

Nearby, in Connell, Washington, close to the Hanford reactor, she became friendly with the woman who cleaned her hotel room. The woman and members of her family—including her pets—have become sick with illnesses that the woman attributed to unacknowledged radioactive releases from the plant. But "her husband, neighbors, and even her 22-year-old son say she is nuts. She was happy to find in me a person who listened for once and agreed. I will never forget Donna. For me she represents all the people suffering not only from radioactivity but also from [the] brutality of the experts who claim that health problems are purely a form of imagination or bad nourishment. What these people sense is denied, so how can they trust their own senses when the experts tell them they are crazy?"[25]

In Omonville-la-Petite, in Normandy, she tries to dissuade a man who has been recruited to work in the COGEMA nuclear plant at Cap de la Hague:

He should think of his wife and children, and that he could get sick and that then COGEMA wouldn't pay him anything. I told him that in Switzerland foreigners are hired for dangerous work and that one lets them go after paying them well for three months. No one knew later how they fared, and no one cared. The same had been done to the cleanup workers in Chernobyl, the so-called liquidators. . . . I think that the young African heard me and I hope that he had the courage to look out for himself. But when an unemployed father gets such a well-paying job what should he do?[26]

The journals catalog her collecting. She finds seventeen ambush bugs on the borders of Zion National Park, in Utah. "When I narcotized them, they let out a sweet smell, which hurt my eyes and made me nearly faint. They really tried to defend themselves, but alas I was stronger."[27] Weeks later, on arriving in Connell, she writes: "I was tired of looking for and killing insects."

Here she is at the entrance to the Hanford reactor. She includes this photograph at the end of her journal. Mindful of the hostility she faces, she calls it "a document, necessary to make people trust that I was really there."

She looks happy in the picture, the "scientific artist" laughing with the guard who helped her select the best angle for the shot. She is doing something important, deeply in the world, living with the disappointments, managing the contradictions, feeling part of everything, feeling very connected, showing herself as a whole, very much alive.

Death

Diligence

One summer many years ago, I found work in a restaurant kitchen out-side London. Arriving early one morning during my first week, I was led by the manager to a white door on the far side of a small, open courtyard. He removed the padlock, and we stood there as our eyes slowly adjusted to the gloomy interior. A small storeroom gradually came into view, with piles of supplies: cases of oils and canned vegetables, sacks filled with flour.

The floor was a mottled white, and it was only after a few moments that I realized, with some horror, why we were standing on the threshold as if at the seashore, silent under a lowering sky. No one else will do it, the manager told me. You'll need a broom and those bottles of bleach.

* * *

As with many repulsive tasks, once the shock of entering the field of action has passed, disgust generates an energy of its own. Partly, it's the desire to finish rapidly. Partly, the activity itself blocks out reflection and produces a kind of drunkenness, a giddiness that sees off doubt.

I waded in. Thousands, tens of thousands of maggots, "slippery finger-length maggots,"[1] white maggots, writhing on the floor, shiny and wet. In an hour it was over: the room clean, the floor sluiced, the job still mine.

Doubt

With careless hands a child kills an ant, many ants. Flies are far trickier, though once caught, they have little chance. And if darting birds don't grab them first, butterflies die a natural death; few people—collectors excepted—willfully still such tremulous beauty.

* * *

It has the marks of permanent war. Beetles, good at hiding, keep close to the ground. Wisława Szymborska finds one dead on a dirt road, "three pairs of legs . . . neatly folded across its belly." She stops and stares. "The horror of the site is moderate," she writes. "Sorrow is not contagious." But still doubt remains:

> For our peace of mind, animals do not pass away,
> but die a seemingly shallower death
> losing—we'd like to believe—fewer feelings and less world,
> exiting—or so it seems—a less tragic stage.[2]

An uncommon sensibility. Almost like a child meeting death for the first time, grasping analogy, tentatively building a bridge. Tentatively. The poet is tentative. Her knowledge of the small (and sometimes large) acts of bad faith through which we live our lives is what makes the poem.

Difference

Three years ago, Sharon and I walked through the entrance doors of the Montreal Insectarium, down the curved staircase to the open-plan exhibition hall, and within minutes, were absorbed in the displays. All those insects in one place got us thinking about the megacategory the museum had taken on, about the unreachable diversity contained within that word *insects,* and about how unfortunate it is that the negative connotations of the word sweep up so much. Such are the perils of taxonomy in the public sphere. And what a huge task it leaves a place like this.

* * *

But pretty soon, realizing that everyone else—people of all ages—was just as absorbed, we began thinking how well the curators, designers, educators, and other staff had succeeded in their mission to "encourage . . . visitors to think more positively about insects." We were struck by the combination of exhibits on topics that are more familiar (insect biology) and less familiar (cultural connections between humans and insects). The exhibits were thoughtful and fun; the text was smart and didn't talk down. The examples were diverse and intriguing.

And then, like a thought unthought, like that peculiar biblical image of scales falling from Saul's eyes, like waking from a dream, like that moment when the drugs wear off (or, alternatively, when they kick in), we both realized, at what seemed like the exact same instant, that we were in a mausoleum and that the walls were lined with death, that those gorgeous pinned specimens, precisely arranged according to aesthetic criteria—color, size, shape, geometry—were not just dazzling objects; they were also tiny corpses.

* * *

How strange that we look at insects as beautiful objects, that in death they are beautiful objects whereas in life, scuttling across the wooden floor, lurking in corners and under benches, flying into our hair and under our collars, crawling up our sleeves . . . Imagine the chaos if they came back to life. The impulse, even in this place, would be to lash out and crush them.

But if you watch people going from case to case around the room, you see right away that many of these objects (not necessarily the largest, not necessarily the ones with the longest legs or spindliest antennae) possess intense psychic power. It's clear in the way that everyone—myself included—navigates the displays, in the way that we move along the rows a little tentatively and then pull up short and sometimes back off sharply. And it's a little odd that we act like this, because the animal is not only locked behind Perspex in a display case but is, besides, not at all physically dangerous, if, in fact, it ever was. It is as though, along with their beauty, these animals find their way to some deep part of us and, in response, something taboo-like draws us in. Despite death, they enter our bodies and make us shiver with apprehension. What other animal has this power over us?

* * *

So much about insects is obscure to us, yet our capacity to condition their existence is so vast. Look closely at these walls. Even the most beautiful butterfly, observed Primo Levi, has a "diabolical, mask-like face."[3] Unease has a stubborn source, unfamiliar and unsettling. We simply cannot find ourselves in these creatures. The more we look, the less we know. They are not like us. They do not respond to acts of love or mercy or remorse. It is worse than indifference. It is a deep, dead space without reciprocity, recognition, or redemption.

Defeat

Flies, Saint Augustine wrote, were invented by God to punish man for his arrogance. Was that what the people of Hamburg were supposed to feel in 1943 as they stumbled through the smoldering ruins of their city during the pauses between Allied bombing raids? Flies—"huge and iridescent green, flies such as had never been seen before"—were so thick around the corpses in the air-raid shelters that, across the floors writhing with maggots, the work teams detailed to collect the dead could reach the bodies only by clearing the way with flamethrowers.[4]

And then, here and elsewhere, on the heels of imposed vulnerability come the images of famine and disease, flies sipping from the corners of dull eyes, sucking at the edges of crusted mouths, crusted noses. Child and adult too weak, too pacified, to keep brushing them away. Animals, too, dogs, cows, goats, horses. Flies taking over, moving in, preparing the generations, the eggs, the larvae, the feast. Heralding the transition, only slightly premature.

Evolution

1.

"The maggot is a power in this world," wrote Jean-Henri Fabre, the Insect Poet, in a moment of characteristic awe. He was philosophizing about flies—bluebottles, greenbottles, bumblebee flies, gray flesh flies—and their capacity "to purge the earth of death's impurities and cause deceased animal matter to be once more numbered among the treasures of life."[1] He was pondering the rhythm of the seasons and the cycles of mortality, and he was exploring the grounds of his new house in Sérignan du Comtat, a small village in Provence close to Orange where he was unearthing his own treasures: decaying bird corpses, fetid sewer ducts, ruined wasps' nests—secret refuges of nature's alchemy.

Fabre had called this house, with its large garden, l'Harmas ("the

name given, in this district, to an untilled, pebbly expanse abandoned to the vegetation of the thyme"), and it is now a national museum, recently reopened after six years' renovation.[2]

It is a beautiful house, large and imposing, glowing pink in the summer sunshine, thick walled to keep out the mistral, pale-green shutters. A handsome house that was known locally as *le château*.[3] Fabre was fifty-six when he moved here. Almost immediately he had a two-story addition built onto the main residence: on the first floor, a greenhouse where he and his gardener grew plants for the grounds and for his botanical studies; above, a naturalist's laboratory, in which he spent the greatest part of his time. The property is on the outskirts of Sérignan, and one of Fabre's first acts was to surround its nearly two and a half acres with a stone wall six feet high, isolating it still further. Indeed, Anne-Marie Slézec, the director of the museum, told me, in his thirty-six years here, Fabre never once ventured the few hundred yards into the village.

Mme. Slézec had been assigned to l'Harmas from her position as a research mycologist at the Muséum national d'Histoire naturelle, and now, after six years in the provinces, her task complete, she was eagerly anticipating her return to Paris.

There was a good reason to select a mycologist for this posting: among the chief treasures of l'Harmas are 600 luminous aquarelles of local fungi, delicate portraits that Fabre painted in an effort to preserve the colors and substance of objects that, once collected, rapidly lost all relation to their living form. The paintings are justly famous, and they seem in some way to distill Fabre's entire life's work. Powerfully descriptive and immediately accessible, they strive to capture the ecological whole and, in doing so, to convey the beauty and what he saw as the mysterious perfection of nature. They are the product of exceptional observational skills. They utilize a talent that was largely self-taught. And they reveal a profound intimacy with their subject.

But Mme. Slézec's task was to be less mycological than antiquarian. She rapidly turned detective. To reconstruct Fabre's study, she hunted down old photographs, securing the crucial lead from a librarian in Avignon who found a contemporary image, which the director set out to reproduce in every respect. Somehow she turned up the very same framed pictures; the same books; the same clock (which she had restored to working order); the same globe; the same chairs; the same cases of snails, fossils, and seashells; the same set of scales. She reinstated the famous writing desk, just two and a half feet long, a school desk really, insubstantial enough for Fabre to pick up and move as needed. She brought the photograph back to life. Or rather, she brought it into the present and, in the process, re-created the study as a memorial. Only Fabre himself is missing (and he is missing from the image, too), though the sunlight that still floods through the garden window fills the room with the aura of his life, a life lived fully right in this space.

The grounds presented a different challenge. When Fabre arrived, in 1879, he discovered that the nearly two and a half acres of land he now owned had once been a vineyard. Cultivation had involved the removal of most of the "primitive vegetation." "No more thyme, no more lavender, no more clumps of kermes-oak," he lamented.[4] Instead, his new garden was a mass of thistles, couch grass, and other upstarts. He ripped it out and replanted. By the time Mme. Slézec arrived, however, the Muséum national d'Histoire naturelle, which had taken possession on the death of Fabre's last surviving son, in 1967, had turned much of the land into a botanical garden. Scouring Fabre's notebooks, his manuscripts, and his correspondence, studying photographs taken on the grounds, Mme. Slézec searched for clues that would enable her to restore what Fabre had intended to persist after his death. She cleared the shrubs obstructing his much-loved view of Mount Ventoux, the isolated outlier of the French Alps that—following in Petrarch's famous footsteps—Fabre often climbed. She reintroduced bamboo, forsythia, roses, and Lebanon oak, and she protected and managed the surviving Atlas cedars, the Aleppo and Corsican pines, and the graceful lilac walk that leads from the entry gate to the house.

The garden, she determined, had been planned in three sections. In front of the house, Fabre had laid out a formal flower garden surrounding a large ornamental pond. This was where he entertained his not inconsiderable number of visitors: members of the local intellectual elite and, toward the end of his life, dignitaries and admirers from further afield. Beyond the flower beds, he established the *harmas* for which the house was named, an area of native shrubs and trees that were planted, nurtured, then left to grow with minimum management. Finally, beyond the *harmas*, he planted a large area of trees, a *parc arboré*, again allowed to thrive with relatively little intervention. These latter two areas were his "laboratory of living entomology," the habitats for his insect

studies.[5] Viewed from the flower garden, they looked wild and untamed, but as in the Romantic tradition of landscape gardening, this naturalness was an effect of much art and labor.

Fabre lived at l'Harmas until his death in 1915 at age ninety-two, and it was here that he wrote nine of the ten volumes of his *Souvenirs entomologiques,* a massive work with a mass readership on which his fame and reputation rest. It was a labor he conceived as an irrefutable demonstration of the "Intelligence [that] shine[s] behind the mystery of things"[6] and as a monument against "transformism"—that is, the evolution of plants and animals through the adaptive transformation of species descended from common ancestors, a formulation of evolution general enough to include both Darwin and his French forerunner, Jean-Baptiste Lamarck. It was here in the *harmas* and the *parc arboré* that Fabre encountered the animals that fill those volumes and bear the burden of his calling: the wasps, bees, beetles, grasshoppers, crickets, caterpillars, scorpions, and spiders whose behavior he describes in such vivid detail. It was here, in this "Eden of bliss," as he put it (with one eye ever trained on his legacy), that he would "live henceforth alone with the insect."[7]

2.

The garden at l'Harmas and the countryside surrounding it were a naturalist's paradise, and Fabre's interests were voracious, his knowledge encyclopedic. He studied birds, plants, and fungi. He collected fossils, seashells, and snails. But above all, it was the insects that fascinated him.

Fascination, though, is not always twinned with affection. Hundreds of cicadas lived in the two plane trees outside his front door, and each day in summer he heard their calls. "Ah! Creature possessed," he despaired soon after arriving, "the plague of my dwelling, which I hoped would be so peaceful!" He considered hacking down the trees to be rid of them. He had already eliminated the frogs from his pond ("by means perhaps a little too rigorous," he admitted).[8] If he could, said Mme. Slézec, he would have silenced the songbirds too.

The cicadas were a "real torment."[9] But like all of nature, they were also an opportunity. As a child, Fabre had been deeply impressed by La

Fontaine's *Fables*, though less by their moral complexity and social satire than by their ability to make the natural world serve as a vehicle of moral instruction. Nature was everywhere and at every turn offered occasion for inquiry and education. Insects, especially, were around every corner and beneath every footstep. And so were their secrets. Insects struggled, they triumphed, they failed. Their lives were full of drama both epic and homespun; they had personalities, desires, preferences, habits, and fears. Indeed, their lives were much like his own. Unearthing an insect's biography was both an exploration of the unknown and something more: a journey on which everyone was invited and for which Fabre was both the guide and the subject. "Fabre's accounts of insect life," writes the historian Norma Field perceptively, "convey both the drama he found in it and the drama he experienced in exploring it. . . . The narrative of insect life becomes the narrative of Fabre's life."[10] Field sees in this convergence a persuasive narrative structure that gives Fabre's writing its exceptional force. And perhaps it's not only his readers who are being persuaded. All this narrative blurring signals an ontological blurring between the man and his insects, an effect of deep affinities. What does it take, we might wonder, to become a true insect poet?

Everyone could participate in Fabre's narrative. Scientific inquiry demanded specialized skills, patience, and ingenuity. But its dissemination would be accessible and democratic. Each insect was a mysterious neighbor whose true identity was revealed only through the patience and ingenuity of its biographer. By the time he is done, each insect has given up its secrets, surrendered its life story. And, Fabre insists, this biographical approach is a surer route to knowledge than any science that takes as its object the dead animal pinned to a card and viewed under a microscope. Morphological similarities might be meaningful to the elite theorists in their metropolitan studies, but what counted out here in the world was behavior: who did what to whom, how, and why.

The great institutions of natural history, botany, and zoology were increasingly preoccupied with questions of classification. For Fabre, such activities and (what he saw as) their newly distanced ways of engaging with nature—as object, specimen, icon—were, quite simply, "burying us."[11] Insects were all around, yet we scarcely knew them. If, like La Fontaine, we observed their behavior with patience and dedication, they could provide an unrivaled source of moral and scientific education. Even the cicadas. Even the maggots. And even—perhaps especially—those ruthless hymenopteran hunters, the solitary wasps.

3.

Work on the high wall surrounding l'Harmas started soon after Fabre and his family arrived in 1879, but construction was frustratingly slow. For the naturalist, however, the delays were serendipitous. The builders left large piles of stone and sand in the garden, and these were soon occupied by bees and wasps. Two wasps, the *Bembix* and the Languedocian sphex, were old friends that Fabre knew well from previous encounters. They made homes in the sand, and he spent much of his days observing and recording their behavior.

Fabre truly loved wasps. Along with beetles, they occupy more of the *Souvenirs* than any other group. (He wrote little on ants and butterflies.) He loved that they were still so unknown. He loved their determination—so close to his own—to overcome the largest obstacles. He loved their precision. Above all, he loved that they allowed him to disclose the astonishing complexities of their behavior and then, like a magician, reveal that this behavior, no matter how much it looked like problem solving and ingenuity was—contra Darwin—entirely devoid of intelligence. He loved the wasps because, as exemplars to him of both the "wisdom" and the "ignorance" of instinct, they were his accomplices in the campaign against transformism.

He seeks them out. Knowing their habits, he finds a likely spot—a sand dune, a steep roadside bank, a small clearing in the undergrowth, a south-facing garden wall, a kitchen fireplace—and he waits. He watches each species prepare its nest in its own style. Here is the *Bembix rostrata* digging like a puppy ("The sand, shot backwards under the abdomen, passes through the arch of the hind-legs, gushes like a fluid in a continuous stream, describes its parabola and falls to the ground some seven or eight inches away").[12] Here is a small group of *Cerceris tuberculata*, "industrious miners" who "patiently remove with their mandibles a few bits of gravel from the bottom of the pit and push the heavy mass outside."[13] Here are some yellow-winged sphex (*Sphex flavipennis*), "a troop of merry companions encouraging one another in their work; . . . the sand flies, falling in a fine dust on their quivering wings; and the too bulky gravel, removed bit by bit, rolls far away from the workyard. If a piece seems too heavy to be moved, the insect gets up steam with a shrill note which reminds one of the woodman's 'Hoo!' ")[14] And here are the *Eumenes* wasps, whose nest is so "gracefully curved" and so carefully decorated with snail shells and pebbles that it is "both a fortress and a museum."[15]

Their nests complete, the wasps fly off. Fabre waits, his patience inexhaustible. Finally, they return, laden with food for the larva that will hatch in their nests. A *Cerceris* lands with a metallic *Buprestis* beetle. A hairy *Ammophila* (a sphex) arrives with an outsize lepidopteran larva. Here is a *Chalybion* (another sphex) clasping a spider between her legs. Here comes a yellow-winged sphex dragging a cricket far larger than itself.

Facedown on the ground, lens in hand, as close as his quarry allows, Fabre permits no detail to escape him, hour after hour, an eager giant spying on a Lilliputian world. Sometimes, anxious for discovery, he goes further, dislodging the nest and prizing it open with his knife. Maybe there's a lone victim, paralyzed and positioned on its back, a single egg placed on its abdomen just beyond reach of its feebly flickering legs; maybe there are several victims in a cell, stacked on top of one another or arranged front to back, the freshest farthest from the egg.

"Observation sets the problem," he writes; "experiment solves it."[16] Sometimes he tests the animal in situ. He might wait for the moment when the wasp, descending to check the nest, leaves its captive momentarily unguarded. Swiftly, Fabre purloins the immobilized victim and, breath bated, observes the wasp's agitation on surfacing. Or he allows the wasp to position her prey in the nest and then enters stealthily, removes the victim, and watches to see if she will nonetheless deposit her egg and seal the entrance as usual (or as he would have it, as predetermined).

Sometimes he carries the nest carefully back to the house. Often, he captures the insect, brings it to his laboratory, and creates controlled and convenient conditions in which to observe its behavior and devise more complex experiments of longer duration. Perhaps, searching for answers in anatomy as well as psychology, he chloroforms and dissects it.

His first dissection was a revelation. It catalyzed his decision to abandon a career teaching mathematics and to make a living from his true passion, natural history. It was 1848. The Second Republic had just been established, and France was in uproar. Fabre was in Corsica, twenty-five years old, teaching physics in the college at Ajaccio and as entranced by the luxuriant landscape ("the infinite, glittering sea at my feet, the dreadful masses of granite overhead")[17] as any Humboldt setting foot in the New World.

He had leaped at the posting, eager to escape Carpentras ("that accursed little hole").[18] Just a few months previously, he had resigned his job as a schoolmaster there, revealing the sense of outrage that would never fully desert him, his hurt at the exclusions that refused to end no matter his achievements. It was the memory of his ejection from school when his parents—Provençal peasants who tried (and failed) to make a living keeping cafés in a series of towns—could not keep up the monthly fees. It was his frustration as a young man laboring on railroad-construction sites, repeatedly passed over for academic postings and denied the opportunity to show his capacities ("The injustice was too unheard-of," he wrote to his brother, Frédéric, in September 1848, ". . . to give . . . [me] two licentiate's diplomas, and to make . . . [me] conjugate verbs for a pack of brats!").[19] It was his disappointment at the commercial failure of his decade's work on a process to extract madder, the red dye used for military uniforms, an enterprise designed to provide him with the income he would need to take up academic employment (which, at the time, was unpaid and intended only for men of means). It was his distress when the clerical backlash against Napoleon III's educational reforms led to his dismissal from teaching (he had been giving free science classes that were open to girls), throwing his family into poverty and upon the charity of a close friend, the English liberal theorist John Stuart Mill (who had moved to Provence to live and die near the grave of his wife, the early feminist Harriet Taylor).[20] It was bitterness that all this misfortune was compounded by the failure of those with power over him to appreciate that his successes (his baccalaureates in letters and mathematics, his degrees in the mathematical and physical sciences, his doctorate in the natural sciences, his more than 200 publications: textbooks as well as volumes of popular science written at a time when the genre scarcely existed; as well as his major scientific discoveries: the first demonstrations of taxis in animals and the proof of hypermetamorphosis in beetles) were won against odds unimaginable by the Parisian scientific elite. It was more bitterness that when recognition finally came, at the end of his long life, the university, the scientists, even the entomologists, rarely paid homage; it was the literary lions—Victor Hugo (who dubbed him the Homer of insects); Edmond Rostand, the author of *Cyrano de Bergerac* (who, not to be outdone, anointed him the insects' Virgil); the playwright Romain Rolland (for whom Fabre was *"un des Français que j'admire le plus"*); and the Provençal poet Frédéric Mistral—who campaigned for Fabre's nomination for the 1911 Nobel Prize—not for a scientific prize, please note, but for the prize for literature.[21] It was his helpless anger at the sudden loss of his eldest son at sixteen and the subsequent deaths of two young daughters and two wives, tragedies that were to cast a pall over his life but tragedies, it must be admitted, from which he himself created a badge of lifelong suffering that became an against-all-odds story of the homespun genius, the poverty-stricken hermitlike poet of science at work in his garden,

alone with his insects, simplicity, sacrifice, naïveté in the strict sense, the story that would thrill the Parisian cultural set in his last days and draw them down to the unfamiliar environs of Sérignan.

It was a raw anger that fueled a vigorous populism. Addressing an imagined audience of elite scientists, the men who had responded to his antagonism to evolutionary theory by removing his textbooks from classrooms and once more plunging him into grim poverty, he articulates a passion so consuming that it temporarily absolves the cicadas: "You rip up the animal and I study it alive; you turn it into an object of horror and pity, whereas I cause it to be loved; you labor in a torture chamber and dissecting room, I make my observations under the blue sky to the song of the Cicadas, you subject cell and protoplasm to chemical tests, I study instinct in its loftiest manifestations; you pry into death, I pry into life."[22] He meant, of course, that he studied the living animal, the animal in its true form, as God intended it to be known, a being of spirit, mystery, and definite purpose, a being accessible through experience not theory, through intimacy not abstraction.

But he was, as we already know, not averse to prying into death, and indeed, according to his friend and biographer, the doctor-politician Georges Victor Legros, it was with that first dissection, in Ajaccio, that his story began. In Corsica, he had befriended Alfred Moquin-Tandon, a professor of botany at Toulouse, a man of letters twenty years his senior who wrote poetry in vernacular Provençal and talked of the importance of an accomplished style, even in the writing of biology. Over dinner, Moquin-Tandon, improvising instruments from his sewing basket, dissected a snail. "From that time forward," wrote Legros, Fabre "began to collect not only dead, inert, or desiccated forms, mere material for study, with the aim of satisfying his curiosity; he began to dissect with ardor, a thing he had never done before. He housed his tiny guests in his cupboard; and occupied himself, as he was always to do in the future, with the smaller living creatures only." Soon after, Fabre wrote Frédéric from Corsica, "My scalpels are tiny daggers which I make myself out of fine needles; my marble slab is the bottom of a saucer; my prisoners are lodged by the dozen in old match-boxes; *maxime miranda in minimis.*"[23]

Maxime miranda in minimis. Of the many tiny marvels he would encounter over the succeeding decades, the most miraculous were the hunting wasps. Some of what they revealed to him was already known, but some was entirely new. Not even the illustrious René-Antoine Ferchault de Réaumur—the pioneer of entomological observation who described the *Odynerus* wasp at length in his six-volume *Mémoires pour servir à l'histoire des insectes* (1734–42)—knew that instead of laying their egg directly on the "swarming heap" of two dozen captive weevil larvae, the *Odynerus* (and the *Eumenes*) suspend it from a fine thread attached to the domed roof of the nest.[24] After years of trying to engineer the opportunity, Fabre was finally a witness. It was, he confessed, "one of those moments of inward joy which atone for much vexation and weariness." The hatched wasp larva lowers itself to feed ("head downwards, it is digging into the limp belly of one of the caterpillars"), and then—when its meal becomes too agitated—it hoists itself safely out of reach.[25]

4.

Each of his insects confirmed the power of instinct. It might seem, he said, as if these animals know what they're doing. It might appear as if their astonishing behavior is an exterior manifestation of an interior life. But that would be entirely wrong. They act without consciousness and without self-knowledge. They follow instincts they have possessed since the Creation, instincts that are blind, rigid, and innate, that are not learned but are instead possessed fully formed from birth, perfect and infallible, highly specialized to their function and peculiar to each species. These instincts possess "wisdom": they generate flawless behavior that solves the most complex problems of physical existence. Yet under the stress of experimental disruption, they prove themselves completely "ignorant," unresponsive to the simplest changes in familiar conditions.[26]

Over and over he told this story, believing—as many creationists still do—that in instinct he had found evolution's Achilles' heel, proof that species are fixed and immutable and have been so since the beginning. Because—and his argument is quite this simple—how could intermediary stages exist for such extraordinarily complex and precisely calibrated behavior? Think of the hunting wasps, he says; it's a zero-sum game: "The art of preparing the larva's provisions allows of none but masters and suffers no apprentices."[27] If the prey isn't adequately immobilized, he says, it will destroy the egg or the larva; if the prey is so badly wounded that it dies, the egg will hatch but the larva's food source will putrefy and the hatchling will starve. What animal genius enables the delicate calculation by which, time after time, the prey is rendered insensate but with all vital functions intact? As he watches the hairy *Ammophila* paralyze its victim, he faces life's most profound truth, the mystery of mysteries, before which even grown men of science can only weep: "Animals obey their compelling instinct, without realizing what they do. But whence comes that sublime inspiration? Can theories of atavism, of natural selection, of the struggle for life interpret it reasonably? To me and my friend, this was and remained one of the most eloquent revelations of the unutterable logic that rules the world and guides the ignorant by the laws of its inspiration. Stirred to our innermost being by the flash of truth, both of us felt tears of undefinable emotion spring to our eyes."[28]

Any of his insects could bring him here. But it was the wasps, he believed, that presented the most forceful case against the Darwinian view that instincts are inherited adaptive behaviors; that, as Darwin put it in 1871 in *The Descent of Man,* complex instincts are gained "through the natural selection of variations of simpler instinctive actions," and "those insects which possess the most wonderful instincts are certainly the most intelligent." Darwin's instincts were, of course, inherited, and they were far from fixed and far from perfect. They were adaptive, not prescient. As he summarized it, "intelligent actions, after being performed during several generations, become converted into instincts and are inherited."[29]

It was against these heresies that Fabre marshaled the wasps. And it was the wasps that gave him license to state categorically, "I reject the modern theory of instinct." "Modern theory," his disparaging term for evolution, was "an ingenious game in which the arm-chair naturalist, the man who shapes the world according to his whim, is able to take delight, but in which the observer, the man grappling with reality, fails to find a serious explanation of anything whatsoever that he sees."[30]

The hairy *Ammophila* chooses for her prey the larva of the lepidopteran *Agrotis segetum,* a creature up to fifteen times her weight. Fabre's description of the struggle between the tiny wasp and the large "gray worm" is one of his most famous. "Never," he wrote, "did the intuitive science of instinct show me anything more exciting."

He is walking with his friend close to home when they catch sight of the agitated *Ammophila.* The two men "at once lay down on the ground, close to where she was working," so close, in fact, that—in a typically Doctor Dolittle detail—the wasp briefly settles on Fabre's sleeve.[31] They watch as she scours a narrow patch of ground, evidently on the track of her prey. Ill-advisedly, the larva surfaces. "The huntress was on the spot at once, gripping him by the skin of his neck and holding tight in spite of his contortions. Perched on the monster's back, the Wasp bent her abdomen and deliberately, without hurrying, like a surgeon thoroughly acquainted with his patient's anatomy, drove her lancet into the ventral surface of each of the victim's segments, from the first to the last. Not a ring was left without receiving a stab; all, whether with legs or without, were dealt with in order, from front to back."[32]

Note the key observation: the wasp delivers nine stings, each injected at a precise point in a different segment of the caterpillar's body. And note also that the stings are delivered in sequence. Fabre's subsequent dissection seems to prove the wasp's foresight. These are surgical strikes, each taking out one of the caterpillar's motor ganglia. But the best is to come.

The victim's head is still unscathed, the mandibles are at work: they might easily, as the insect is borne along, grip some bit of straw in the ground and successfully resist this forcible removal; the brain, the primary nervous center, might provoke a stubborn contest, which would be very awkward with so heavy a burden. It is well that these hitches be avoided. The caterpillar, therefore, must be reduced to a state of torpor which will deprive him of the least inclination for self-defence. The Ammophila succeeds in this by munching his head. She takes good care not to use her needle: she is no clumsy bungler and knows quite well that to inflict a wound on the cervical ganglia would mean killing the caterpillar then and there, the very thing to be avoided. She merely squeezes the brain between her mandibles, calculating every pinch; and, each time, she stops to ascertain the effect produced, for there is a nice point to be achieved, a certain degree of torpor that must not be exceeded, lest death should intervene. In this way, the requisite lethargy is obtained, a somnolence in which all volition is lost. And now the caterpillar, incapable of resistance, incapable of wishing to resist, is seized by the nape of the neck and dragged to the nest. Comment would mar the eloquence of such facts as these.[33]

In a classic paper first published in 1972, the psychologist Richard Herrnstein (now remembered less fondly as co-author of *The Bell Curve*), located Fabre as a major figure in the "intuitional approach to instinct," a position Herrnstein neatly summarized as "a set of denials held together by a sense of awe."[34]

In this late-nineteenth–early-twentieth-century post-Darwinian moment of intense debate about the nature and origins of human and animal behavior, instinct was a central, much-contested philosophical and empirical concept. The intuitional position—with its idea of instinct as a special and undefined "capacity for adaptation"[35] distinct from intelligence—was only one of several key poles. Herrnstein identified three and contrasted Fabre's account with what he called the "reflexive view," which brought together such diverse figures as Herbert Spencer, the behaviorists Jacques Loeb and (in his early work) John B. Watson, and the psychologist-philosopher William James, who was quite clear on the distinction between his own position and that of a Fabre: "The older writings on instinct are ineffectual wastes of words . . . [that] smothered everything in vague wonder at the clairvoyant and prophetic power of the animals—so superior to anything in man—and at the beneficence of God in endowing them with such a gift. But God's beneficence endows them, first of all, with a nervous system; and, turning our attention to this, makes instinct immediately appear neither more nor less wonderful than all the other facts of life."[36] In this intuitional account, says James, instincts are little more than complex, differentiated reflexes ("compound reflex action" was Spencer's famous phrase).

Herrnstein's third position, which, like the reflexive view, assumed that instincts are subject to selective pressures in ways similar to morphological traits, was termed hormic (as in hormonal) psychology by William McDougall, its main proponent. According to McDougall, instincts are highly malleable and susceptible to environmental influence but organized around a stable core, which is driven by a striving toward a defined outcome (the building of a nest, the imprisoning of prey, and so on) and is the impulse behind almost all human and animal behavior. Instincts, wrote McDougall, are "the mental forces that maintain and shape all the life of individuals and societies."[37]

With the rise of behaviorism in the 1920s, instinct fell out of favor as an explanation of animal behavior and reemerged only in the 1950s with the popularization of the ethologists, especially Konrad Lorenz and Nikolaas Tinbergen, who, though Darwinians, enforced a sharp division between instinct and learning. There is a line here that reaches across the decades from Fabre to these more recent students of animal behavior and is held together by simple behavioral experiments in natural settings, by close observation, and by the familiar combination of science and wonder. It's a line that somehow bypasses Fabre's hostility to evolution and instead picks up his commitment to popular pedagogy—the impulse to accessibility that led Lorenz, Tinbergen, and their colleague Karl von Frisch to cultivate an eager reading public and capture the Nobel Prize that eluded their predecessor.

It is a line of flight. The wasps fly straight through here, veering off in unanticipated directions, touching down at decisive moments. They flee science to foment Fabrean wonder among the modern creationists, for example, and sometimes they appear in more intriguing places, as in the imagination of the influential philosopher Henri Bergson, a great admirer of Fabre's (he attended the celebration at l'Harmas organized by Legros in 1910 that heralded the Provençal hermit's belated journey to the limelight). Bergson listens to the description of the nine-times-stabbing *Ammophila* surgeon and develops his own idiosyncratic metaphysics of evolution, which draws on Georges Cuvier's early-nineteenth-century notion that animals, like sleepwalkers, are equipped with a "somnambulist" consciousness ("a kind of consciousness which is intellectually unaware of its purpose").[38]

Bergson offers an intuitional view of instinct as a "divinatory sympathy" and, like Fabre, opposes instinct to intelligence. But the opposition has a different basis. Where Fabre sees intelligence as the mark of human superiority, to Bergson it is a limited form of understanding, cold and external. Where Fabre sees instinct as mechanical and shallowly automatic, to Bergson it is a profound understanding, a kind of knowledge that takes us to "the very inwardness of life," reaching back through the common evolutionary history of wasp and caterpillar, back before they diverged on the tree of life, back to a deep intuition of each other, so that the *Ammophila* simply knows how to paralyze the caterpillar without ever having learned and so that their dramas "might owe nothing to outward perception, but result from the mere presence together of the Ammophila and the caterpillar, considered no longer as two organisms, but as two activities."[39]

Still, as Bertrand Russell noted as early as 1921, "love of the marvellous may mislead even so careful an observer as Fabre and so eminent a philosopher as Bergson."[40] Fabre got a lot wrong about the hairy *Ammophila*, and it is on plain empirics that his critique of natural selection has been most effectively dismissed. This is not, it seems, a zero-sum game after all. It is true that, in general, the wasp paralyzes its Lepidoptera larvae with multiple stings, one to each segment. But the operation is not so miraculously accurate, nor so consistent, nor does it always follow the same order. Nor does the caterpillar even survive every time. Sometimes the larvae feed off its putrefying body. Sometimes they are killed by its thrashing torso. Moreover, as both reflexive and hormic theorists suggested, the wasp adjusts its behavior in response to changing external stimuli, such as climate, the availability of food, and the condition and behavior of its prey. And it readily alters the sequence and (what, for want of a better term, we might call) the logic of its actions for reasons that may be self-evidently necessary or, on other occasions, quite opaque. Wasps have been observed stinging forty separate larvae and then choosing to drag the forty-first, unparalyzed, to their nest. They have been recorded paralyzing their prey but not following this action with any kind of nest building. They have been seen stinging at random, opportunistically, apparently just trying to get a good shot in. And it has been discovered that their sting is an injection as well as a stab and that it contains poison that produces instant paralysis and the longer-term effect of inhibiting metamorphosis and maintaining the larval body in a supple state, the effect on the victim less percussive than chemical.[41]

There's something uncanny here. And it's not only the wasp. Herrnstein was right to point to the mysticism at the heart of Fabre's account. He understood that the "vague wonder" that readers take from Fabre is the most potent legacy of the intuitional position. Yet it has its paradoxes too. Fabre pleads with us to understand that these animals are acting blindly, automatically, without will or intention. And to get there, he revels in the animals' behavior, believing that the more complex it is and the more rational it appears, the more devastating his unmasking of it as no more than blind instinct, the more crushing his denunciation of the transformists that follows. These wasps are "surgeons" who "calculate" and "ascertain." Their victims "resist." But the effect is unforeseen. Fabre is enthralled. And the wasps claim the stage. He is their host. They speak through him, live through him. His prose leaves us not with a sense of the insects' insufficiencies but with a profound impression of their capacities. A profound impression of the wasps' capacities, that is, and of Fabre's too. Despite his insistence, it is not instinct that is miraculous but the animals themselves.

5.

The celebrity Fabre enjoyed in his final years did not long survive his death. Though there was little possibility of his embrace by the scientific community, literary fashion ensured that his stature as a nature writer would also rapidly fall. Nowadays, he is largely forgotten both in France and in the English-speaking world. Not even the creationists claim him.

Only in Japan is Fabre now a household name. There, he is a stalwart of the elementary school curriculum and is often a child's first introduction to a natural world that soon comes alive in summer insect-collecting assignments. He frequently returns in later life too, as parents introduce their children to the pleasures of natural history and recall the carefree days of their own youthful insect love. ("I write above all things for the young," Fabre, a schoolteacher for a full twenty-six years, once told his critics in the scientific establishment; "I want to make them love the natural history which you make them hate.")[42]

As we might expect, he is a fixture of Japan's numerous insectaria. But he also pops up in less likely places: incarnated in the resourceful boy hero of a current manga (*Insectival Crime Investigator Fabre*) in the top-selling biweekly omnibus *Superior;* as an anime character (in the series *Read or Die,* he is cloned as an evil genius with the power to turn insects loose against civilization); as a free promotional plastic figurine (a *souvenir entomologique*)—along with models of the cicada, the scarab beetle, the hairy *Ammophila,* and other favorites—in any of the thousands of 7-Eleven convenience stores throughout the country; and in luxury advertising, as a marker of male cosmopolitanism, intellectual curiosity, and a certain spiritual yearning.[43]

But it is not just in schools, nature centers, and Japan's vibrantly commodified popular culture that Fabre's presence is felt. While his writings are available in English only in haphazard and elderly translation, a recent tally calculated that Japanese scholars produced forty-seven complete or partial editions of the *Souvenirs* alone between 1923 and 1994.[44] Okumoto Daizaburo, literature professor, insect collector, and founder-director of Tokyo's new Fabre Museum, points out that the early history of these translations is especially interesting.[45] It was, after all, Osugi Sakae, the famous anarchist and author of the memorably subversive aphorism "Beauty is to be found in disarray," who completed the first systematic translation of Fabre into Japanese and whose plan—cut short by his brutal murder in the police repression that followed the great Kanto earthquake of 1923—was to translate the entire *Souvenirs.* In 1918, around the time he first read Fabre, Osugi wrote: "I like a spirit. But I feel a repugnance when it is theorized. Under process of theorizing, it is often transformed into a harmony with social reality, a slavish compromise, and a falsehood."[46]

Though a committed Darwinian (he had already translated the *Origin of Species*), Osugi felt he had found a kindred spirit in Fabre. Captivated by

雲の上のリラグゼーションは、いかがですか。

www.ana.co.jp **ANA**

the energy of Fabre's prose and by the pedagogical possibilities of popular science, Osugi was also drawn strongly to Fabre's hostility to theorizing. The problem of theory, the charismatic writer-activist believed, lay less in its ability to explain than in its desire to order, less in its ambition to make sense of the world than in its appeal to the analytic over the experiential. The ordering impulse was a constraining impulse, one driven by the desire to dominate, to master, both intellectually and practically. The elevation of the rational, he asserted, impoverished the possibilities of apprehension. "To desire collapsing the universe into a single algorithm and to master all of reality with the precepts of reason" was, Fabre had written, a "grandiose enterprise," not a grand one.[47] It didn't seem to matter to Osugi that this suspicion of global explanation arose from Fabre's constant rediscovery of God's hand in nature, a very different basis for wariness than his own.[48]

I don't know whether Okumoto is correct in his argument that Fabre's appeal for Osugi lay in their shared nonconformity, but I like where it leads us. As Okumoto tells it, the revolutionary labor leader took inspiration from the schoolteacher-naturalist's rejection of authoritarian pedagogy, his insistence on teaching girls as well as boys, and above all, his attitude toward categorization. ("A fig for systems!" Fabre exclaims in the *Souvenirs* when discussing taxonomists' refusal to classify spiders as insects.)[49] Fabre's celebration of the sensuality of inquiry, his rejection of authority, and his democratic accessibility fascinated Osugi—as it does Okumoto, who places Fabre alongside the celebrated naturalist and folklorist Kumagusu Minakata (1867–1941), another household name in today's Japan and another figure honored for his nonconformity and independence: "These two idiosyncratic autodidacts never simplified their own thoughts into laws and formulas. Some people criticized their lack of strong, consistent theories, but they kept searching for the diversity of the world and kept seeing everything with a fresh eye. They are, indeed, what Rimbaud calls '*voyants*.' "[50]

"Insect lovers are anarchists," writes Okumoto elsewhere; "they hate following other people's orders and try to create something like 'order' by themselves—or else they don't care about such a thing at all!"[51] Insect lovers, he says, see the world from the place of the insect, from inside the life of the animal, from within its micro world. They pry into life, not death.

There's another insect lover who might help here. Imanishi Kinji, ecologist, mountaineer, anthropologist, founder of Japanese primatology, and best-selling theorist of nature study (*shizengaku*), began his career in the 1930s studying mayfly larvae in the Kamo River, in Kyoto. A theorist of evolution, Imanishi was no theoretical Fabrean. But he was no Darwinian either. Like Osugi's hero, the great anarchist Peter Kropotkin, Imanishi saw cooperation as the motor of evolution, rejecting both inter- and intraspecific competition as the basis of natural selection. Imanishi stressed the connection and harmonious interaction among living things but insisted that the meaningful ecological units are societies, outside of which an individual cannot survive. Individuals come together not for reproduction but because they have needs in common, which they meet through collaboration. With its interest in cooperating groups rather than competing monads, his *shizengaku* is, he maintained, a Japanese view of evolution, distinct from a Darwinian system ideologically rooted in Western individualism.[52] Like Fabre, Imanishi attracted considerable condescension from professional biologists in Europe and North America, who scented an anti-scientific anti-Darwinism at work. But Imanishi's ideas have widespread popularity in Japan.[53] Even though there is little overlap between the architecture of Imanishi's thought and Fabre's natural historical theology, there is an unambiguous affinity. "There are people in the world," Imanishi wrote in 1941,

> who have spent their whole lives dressed in white smocks, and have never once been out of the laboratory. There are probably even famous scholars who have never once seen animals and plants as they exist in nature. I will not stand for the lumping together of people who have views of nature like that, and people like me, who have shaped their views of nature by spending their lives in the midst of nature; this feeling, perhaps an undercurrent, is somewhere behind my work. Even if there are no natural sciences, nature will still exist. No matter how great the natural sciences make themselves look, they can know only a part of nature. Having subdivided nature and become a specialist in some field, one is a mere specialist of constituent nature (*bubun shizen*). In the schools they do not teach us that, in addition to constituent nature, there is also total nature (*zentai shizen*). It was the mountains and exploration which taught me of the existence of total nature.[54]

The "anti-science" rejection of mechanistic theory, the intuitive connection of observer and observed, the immersive affinity of person and world, this enfolding of a life and its work. Remember Fabre: the simplicity, the patience, the life eked out far from metropolitan glamour, the attempt to grasp the living whole, the disdain for authoritarianism, the ethical independence, the moral life, the scholarly life, the pedagogical life. These are lessons that appeal just as strongly to old and young, to radical and conservative.

And what's more, for Imanishi as for Okumoto, Fabre's pursuit of the godly in insects is recognizable in another way. It has a sensibility that is easily assimilated to a set of ideas often invoked by Japanese nature lovers (and foreign commentators on Japanese attitudes toward nature) seeking to explain what nationalists, Romantics, New Agers, and others frequently consider a unique Japanese affinity to nature and, in particular, to insects: that animist, Shintoist—and subsequently Japanese Buddhist—notion that divinity (*kami*) "take[s] abode in natural features that give people a feeling of awe or spirituality," that "nature is divine," that nature *itself* is divine.[55] (Not, I should emphasize, as Fabre would have it, that nature is an expression of the Divine.)

And there's something else. Osugi and Okumoto reveal the inadequacies of literal-meaning-centered reading. They remind us that to understand Fabre and his appeal, we have to listen for other languages in his work, not simply to what the linguistic philosopher J. L. Austin would call his "constative" meanings—his unconvincing theory of instinct, his poorly reasoned rebuttal of transformism—but to his poetics, the poetics of his storytelling and of the writing that unexpectedly pulls you through the hand lens and into the wasps' nest, the poetics of his haunted life and of his consummate self-mythologizing, the poetics of grand affinity with the natural world, the poetics of his insects, of the impossible, uncertain intimacy between you, me, and those others that are simultaneously most commonplace and most alien.[56]

6.

In one of his famous monthly essays in the magazine *Natural History,* the evolutionary biologist and historian of science Stephen Jay Gould noted that the parasitic wasps—both the endoparasites, which consume their living prey from the inside out, and those ectoparasites described by Fabre, who eat from the outside in—confronted Western theologians of the eighteenth and nineteenth century with their most terrifying problem, the problem of evil. If God is benevolent and the Creation an expression of his goodness and wisdom, "why," they agonized, "are we surrounded with pain, suffering, and apparently senseless cruelty in the animal world?"[57] It was easy to understand that predation was intrinsic to survival in nature, but why would a compassionate God allow the horrors inflicted by the wasp on its victims, the "slow death by parasitic ingestion," a death made more nightmarish in that it was suffered by living, evidently conscious beings in a manner that, as Gould put it, recalled "the ancient English penalty for treason—drawing and quartering, with its explicit object of extracting as much torment as possible by keeping the victim alive and sentient."

"As the king's executioner drew out and burned his client's entrails," Gould wrote, "so does the [wasp] larvae eat fat bodies and digestive organs first, keeping the [victim] alive by preserving intact the essential heart and central nervous system."[58]

It is hardly original to point out that nature has long been an irresistible mirror to the human condition, its laws seen as expressions of God's laws, its every gesture embodying a moral lesson, its "societies" taken as atavistic versions of our own. Faced with the frightening inscrutability of the parasitic wasp, two roads were possible to these observers. One involved the painful acknowledgment of nature's evil followed by the necessary next step of a determination to transcend animality and fulfill the promise of humanity through goodness. The second, more common nowadays than in earlier centuries and more aligned with the contingency of modern evolutionary theory, rested on the moral disenchantment of nature, on the claim that there are in fact no lessons to be found in the behavior of nonhuman beings or phenomena, that nature, in Gould's word, is "nonmoral," that, as he put it, "Caterpillars are not suffering to teach us something; they have simply been outmaneuvered" (and that, although currently improbable, they and their fellow victims may one day even turn the tables on the wasps).

But parasitic wasps don't lend themselves to disenchantment. Somehow, in their presence, observation is filled with drama. "We cannot," Gould pointed out, "render this corner of natural history as anything but story, combining the themes of grim horror and fascination and usually ending not so much with pity for the caterpillar as with admiration for the [wasp]."[59]

Poor parasitized Fabre! A fine host indeed. If he had only seen it this clearly perhaps he would not have told us quite so much about the *Sphex*, the *Bembix*, and the rest. He might have thought twice before dwelling so long on the details of their hunting strategies and, in particular, on the precision of their surgical skills. But the point, of course, is that he couldn't help himself. From the moment he wept before the *Ammophila*, the die was cast. And that surrender was both his undoing and his triumph. When it came to it, he let the animals tell their tales. In this, at least, his instincts were exactly right.

Fever/Dream

1.

That too-hot, too-shadeless morning, pushing the outboard motor to its very limit, first one river, then the next, those never-ending Amazon rivers—never realized anywhere could be so far, worrying about the gas tank, worrying about fallen trees in the water, worrying about the time, heading for the medical post with poor, sad Lene, her hair hacked short in an act of rebellion that only confirmed her madness; Marco, her husband, stone-faced, watching over her, her body now sprawled under the bench seats in the hull of the bouncing dinghy, motionless, lifeless but not quite dead, lifeless on the outside, but everything happening within, malaria coursing through her veins, bloating her liver, fevering her poor, troubled brain.

2.

Everyone got sick. It made no difference that the area around the house had been cleared of forest, as the public health leaflets insisted. Nor did it matter that each house had its neat, handwritten number on the doorpost to confirm that it had been sprayed with DDT. Everyone got sick, some worse than others, the weakest—the children and the elderly—as always, worst of all. When it was my turn, I just lay in my hammock, burning with icy shivers, my body racked from top to toe, eyes dull, mind listless, utterly dependent on the kindness of people who knew there was nothing to do but wait it out. Every day as night fell, it returned. And then, afterward, in the morning, a feeling of weakness that was pleasantly ascetic, as if I had been purged and cleansed, had survived a trial. But within, the knowledge that my body was stitched fatefully to the rhythm of the day in a new and previously unanticipated pattern.

And my sickness was as nothing compared with that of others. Dora, young and strong, my best friend here, came that close to death. She, like Lene, had *falciparum*, the most dreaded, she told me. I'd been away when she took ill, and that absence gave her the chance later to narrate with the full melodrama that the crisis deserved. It was the *três cruzes*, three crosses, she said, though, like me, she had never quite figured out why it was called that. *Um cruz, dois cruzes, três cruzes.* Some people said it referred to the intensity of the infection. But the printed slip they had given both of us at the clinic in town had three Latin names (although there are really four *Plasmodium* protozoa that inhabit human hosts) and a space for a tidy little cross beside each. Mine had just one cross, and the box next to *P. falciparum* was unmarked. Lene and Dora both had three crosses, so one cross had to be inside the box for *P. falciparum*, the parasite that swims all the way to your brain.

3.

It makes little difference if you clear the vegetation around your house the way the leaflets tell you. It can even make it worse. This is the Amazon floodplain, for heaven's sake; the houses are on the banks of the river, and when the tide falls, it leaves pools of standing water everywhere. For a few weeks each year, the mosquitoes are so thick in the air at dawn and dusk that everyone burns wood inside the house, hoping that the thick smoke will force the devils to leave. With streaming eyes, slapping ourselves repeatedly on thighs, arms, sides, even the face, hitting each other when we see one land, jumping around like Keystone Kops, we try to eat the evening meal but more often than not simply give up. It's impossible to sit down or even stay still, and if the needle-sharp bites weren't so painful, we'd probably find it comical. Within minutes we retreat to the safety of mosquito nets or cover ourselves with cotton blankets, frustrated, sore, hungry.

In the city there are various contraptions for seeing off mosquitoes. But here, without electricity, there is only smoke. With no effective recourse, the insects exhaust us. I never talked to anyone about this, but those insects made me feel like an interloper. Not—as when I first arrived—an awkward intruder in the lives of the people who became my hosts (making me their parasite). Now, when we ran from the clouds of mosquitoes and the billowing smoke, together in our pain and annoyance, it was clear that we all were intruding on this landscape and its forms of life.

4.

Although *P. malariae* can make a home in a range of primates, *falciparum* and the others live in humans only. Between the female *Anopheles* mosquito and its parasitic protozoa, these are life cycles of awe-inspiring elegance, devastation, and persistence. In September 1658, Oliver Cromwell died from malaria he contracted in Ireland. Now Europeans know it only as a disease of the tropics, of poverty, distance, and underdevelopment, a disease without profit. According to the World Health Organization, malaria kills 1.5 million people each year. Thankfully, Lene was not one of them. At least, not then. At the health post, they gave her an injection and some tablets, and we took her back home, more slowly, less anxious.

So many problems, so overwhelming, where even to begin? No nearby health post, no sanitation, insufficient food in summer, the insupportable inequalities of health, life expectancy, and well-being. And then the shame, so much shame, so much uselessness, the overwhelming boredom that drove this woman beyond restlessness and consigned her family to the margins of this margin. The day I went to say my final good-bye, Lene stayed inside the two-room wooden house with her daughters—the four preteen girls who cared for her. I sat outside with Marco on a tree trunk overlooking the creek and his field of maize. He drew on his cigarette and listened patiently as I lied for the last time, telling him about my journey and promising I'd come back to see them all again soon.

Generosity (the Happy Times)

1.

On the way to the cricket fight, Mr. Wu slipped us a piece of paper. It looked like a shopping list. "More numbers," said Michael. He read:

Three reversals
Eight fears
Five fatal flaws
Seven taboos
Five untruths

It was Mr. Wu's answer to a question I'd asked him earlier that day in the smoke-filled, gold-papered private banquet room upstairs at the Luxurious Garden in Minhang, an industrial district in southwest Shanghai. But it wasn't the answer we'd expected. Ask him anything you want, said Michael, and I thought we were all relaxed enough, too. Boss Xun and Mr. Tung, the charming gambler from Nanjing, were telling funny stories; tight-lipped Boss Yang was red-faced and expansive; we were toasting health and uncommon friendship. But when I told Mr. Wu that I didn't yet understand the Three Reversals, he looked straight through me without a smile.

Michael had taken time out from college in Shanghai to work as my translator. But he'd quickly become my full-fledged collaborator. Together, we were trying to find out as much as we could about cricket fighting and what everyone said was its revival. We spent our days running around the city, finding ourselves in places new to both of us, meeting traders, trainers, gamblers, event sponsors, entomologists, and all kinds of experts. By the time we sat down to eat in the Luxurious Garden, we already knew two of the Reversals and suspected the third, and my question was supposed to be an uncontroversial conversation starter. But Mr. Wu was having none of it. Like so many people we met in Shanghai, he wanted us to understand how deep was the world of Chinese cricket fighting—and how shallow were our questions.

2.

As everyone knows, the speed of urban growth and transformation in Shanghai is stunning. In less than one generation, the fields that gave the crickets a home have all but gone. Now, dense ranks of giant apartment buildings, elongated boxes with baroque and neoclassical flourishes, stretch pink and gray in every direction, past the ends of the newly built metro lines, past even the ends of the suburban bus routes. The spectacular neon waterfront of Pudong, the symbol of Shanghai's drive to seize the future, is barely twenty years old but already under revision. I marvel at the brash bravery of the Pearl Oriental Tower, the kinetic mul-

ticolored rocket ship that dominates the dazzling skyline, and think how impossible it would be to build something so bold yet so whimsical in New York. Michael and his college-age friends laugh. "We're a bit tired of it, actually," Michael says.

But they also know nostalgia. Only a few years ago, in what seems like another world, they helped fathers and uncles collect and raise crickets in their neighborhoods, among close circles of friends, in and out of one another's homes and alleyways, sharing a daily life that the high-rise apartments have already mostly banished. Downtown, remnants of that life are visible in pockets not yet rebuilt or thematized. Sometimes, though, residents are merely waiting, surrounded by their neighbors' rubble, holding out against forced relocation to distant suburbs as the government clears more housing, now for the spectacle of Expo 2010.

Eleven miles from the city center and a crowded fifteen-minute bus ride from the huge metro terminus at Xinzhuang, the township of Qibao is a different kind of neighborhood. An official heritage attraction, a stroll through a past disavowed for its feudalism during the Cultural Revolution but now embraced for its folkloric national culture, Qibao is newly elegant, with canals and bridges, narrow pedestrianized streets lined with reconstructed Ming- and Qing-dynasty buildings, storefronts selling all kinds of snack foods, teas, and craft goods to Shanghainese and other visitors, and a set of specimen buildings skillfully renovated as sites of living culture: a temple with Han-, Tang-, and Ming-dynasty architectural features, a weaving workshop, an ancient teahouse, a famous wine distillery, and—in a house built specifically for the sport by the great Qing emperor Qianlong—Shanghai's only museum dedicated to fighting crickets.

All these crickets were collected here in Qibao, says Master Fang, the museum's director, standing behind a table laden with hundreds of gray clay pots, each containing one fighting male and, in some cases, its female sex partner. Qibao's crickets were famous throughout East Asia, he tells us, a product of the township's rich soil. But since the fields here were built on in 2000, crickets have been harder to find. Master Fang's two white-uniformed assistants fill the insects' miniature water bowls with pipettes, and we humans all drink pleasantly astringent tea made from his recipe of seven medicinal herbs.

Master Fang has considerable presence, the brim of his white canvas hat rakishly angled, his jade pendant and rings, his intense gaze, his animated storytelling, his throaty laugh. Michael and I are drawn to him immediately and hang on his words. "Master Fang is a cricket *master*," confides his assistant Ms. Zhao. "He has forty years' experience. There is no one more able to instruct you about crickets."

Everyone at the museum is caught up in preparations for the Qibao Golden Autumn Cricket Festival. The three-week event includes a series of exhibition matches and a championship, with all fights broadcast on closed-circuit TV. The goal is to promote cricket fighting as a popular activity distinct from the gambling with which it is now so firmly associated, to remind people of its deep historical and cultural presence, and to extend its appeal beyond the demographic in which it now seems caught: men in their forties and above.

Twenty years ago, everyone tells me, before the construction of the new Shanghai gobbled up the landscape, in a time when city neighborhoods were patchworks of fields and houses, people lived more intimately with animal life. Many found companionship in cicadas—"singing brothers"—or other musical insects that they kept in bamboo cages and slim pocket boxes, and young people, not just the middle-aged, played crickets, learning how to recognize the Three Races and Seventy-Two Personalities, how to judge a likely champion, how to train the fighters to their fullest potential, how to use the pencil-thin brushes made of yard grass or mouse whisker to stimulate the insects' jaws and provoke them to combat. They learned the rudiments of the Three Rudiments, around which every cricket manual is structured: judging, training, and fighting.

The irony is that despite the erosion of the popular base needed to guarantee its persistence, cricket fighting is experiencing a revival in China. Even as it loses out to computer games and Japanese manga with the young, it is thriving among older generations. Yet it's an insecure return that few aficionados are celebrating. For even as the cricket markets flourish, the cultural events blossom, and the gambling houses proliferate, much of the talk is marked by the same anticipatory nostalgia, a sense that this, too, along with so much else about daily life that only a few years ago was taken for granted, is already as good as gone, swept away—not for the first time in recent memory—into the dustbin of history.

Master Fang pulls an unusual cricket pot from the shelf behind him and runs his finger over the text etched on its surface. In a strong voice, he begins to recite, drawing out the tones in the dramatic cadences of classical oratory. These are the Five Virtues, he announces, five human qualities found in the best fighting crickets, five virtues that crickets and humans share:

> The First Virtue: When it is time to sing, he will sing. This is trustworthiness [xin].
> The Second Virtue: On meeting an enemy, he will not hesitate to fight. This is courage [yong].
> The Third Virtue: Even seriously wounded, he will not surrender. This is loyalty [zhong].
> The Fourth Virtue: When defeated, he will not sing. He knows shame.
> The Fifth Virtue: When he becomes cold, he will return to his home. He is wise and recognizes the facts of the situation.

On their tiny backs, crickets carry the weight of the past. Zhong is not ordinary loyalty; it is the loyalty one feels for the emperor, the willingness to lay down one's life, to not shirk one's ultimate duty. *Yong* is not ordinary courage; it is, once again, the readiness to sacrifice one's life and to do so eagerly. These are not simply ancient virtues; they are points on a moral compass, codes of honor. As anyone will tell you, these crickets are warriors; the champions among them are generals.

The passage on Master Fang's pot is from the unquestioned urtext of the cricket community, the thirteenth-century *Book of Crickets* by Jia Sidao.[1] No mere cricket lover, Jia is remembered still as imperial China's cricket minister, the sensual chief minister in the dying days of the Southern Song dynasty, so absorbed in the pleasures of his crickets that he allowed his neglected state to tumble into rack, ruin, and domination by the invading Mongols. The story is told by his official biographer:

> When the siege of the city of Xiangyang was imminent, Jia Sidao sat on the hill of Ko as usual, busying himself with the construction of houses and pagodas. And, as usual, he continued to welcome the most beautiful courtesans, streetwalkers, and Buddhist nuns as his prostitutes and to indulge in his routine merry-making. . . . Only the old gambling gangsters, looking for play, approached him; no one else dared peek into his residence. . . . He was squatting on the ground with his entourage of concubines engaged in a cricket fight.[2]

The historian Hsiung Ping-chen points out that whatever this incident might say about Jia's sense of responsibility and his personal rectitude, it also casts him as a man whose failings were at least irredeemably human and whose passion for crickets had a democratic stubbornness. From this point on, Jia "was enthroned as the deity in China's game world," she writes. "For centuries, his name liberally adorned all covers of books on crickets, call them collections, histories, dictionaries, encyclopedias or whichever title you wish, concerning catching, keeping, breeding, fighting, and, of course, gambling."[3]

There is much ambivalence surrounding these crickets, even in this one story. It's so many things: a sorry tale in which crickets are just another expression of feudal decadence—the counterpoint to socialist modernity and the ready analog for contemporary injustices; a cautionary tale in which the moral effects of compulsive cricket fighting on individual and society are only too plain; a seductive tale in which the problem of desire—with its ever-present threat of addiction or other disorder—is part of the crickets' magic, in the spell they cast over the most important man in the empire, a spell at once enthralling and enslaving. And more prosaically, it's a cultural tale in the blandest sense, extending through the centuries, demonstrating the historical reach of crickets as socially important beings, as historical agents of the first degree.

As if all that weren't enough for one figure (who, of course, had another public career as a politician of considerable importance), there is the *Book of Crickets,* the very foundation of cricket knowledge, the mostly unnamed source to which everyone—Master Fang, Mr. Wu, Boss Xu—is referring when he tells me that this cricket culture is very deep knowledge, that it comes to us directly from the ancient books. And we can put this in another language to say simply that Jia Sidao's *Book of Crickets* is not only the earliest extant manual for cricket lovers, it is also perhaps the world's first book of entomology.[4]

There are written records of people fighting crickets in China as early as the Tang dynasty (618–907). But it's only with Jia's *Book of Crickets,* with its detailing of intimate insect knowledge, that we can be sure that cricket raising and fighting had become a widespread and elaborate pastime. In fact, it was in the 300 or so years between Jia's Southern Song dynasty and the mid-Ming dynasty that an organized market developed around these animals.[5] This market reached its height during the Qing dynasty (1644–1911), linking town and country in commerce and culture and stimulating an extraordinarily beautiful material culture of implements and containers.[6] It eclipsed the crickets' older role as singing companions, producing an extensive network of gambling houses with specialized workers and complex rules, an equally energetic but largely ineffectual series of state attempts at prohibition, and—as if it were the expression of Jia's extravagant desire—sweeping up people of all ages in an activity that was accessible to all social groups and for several centuries was truly popular, as can be seen quite clearly in paintings and poetry and in classic stories like Pu Songling's "The Cricket," a tale of bureaucratic oppression and mysterious transformations, a tale of depth, subtlety, and social criticism familiar to everyone I met in Shanghai, a tale that I was able to find in a used-book stall as a finely drawn comic from the early 1980s, a storytelling form once as popular in China as it still is in Japan and Mexico.[7]

But let's not lose sight of Jia Sidao just yet. His book is too important and too interesting. It ranges across philosophy, literature, medicine, and lore, as well as the knowledge that falls under today's more restricted nineteenth-century model of natural history. In its scope it is reminiscent of other great early-modern insect compendia such as book VII of Ulisse Aldrovandi's *De animalibus* (1602) and Thomas Moffett's *Insectorum sive minimorum animalium theatrum* (1634), the first European books dedicated entirely to insects (which, we might note, were not published until more than 300 years after the *Book of Crickets*).

Jia's ambitions were different from those of the European naturalists, and he writes not with their unrestrained desire to assemble and, in their own ways, possess the natural universe but with the more modest impulse to serve the community of gamblers, of which he was a part. Like Aldrovandi's and Moffett's volumes, the *Book of Crickets* is a work of compilation and systematization. But, whereas the impending post-Enlightenment disciplining of European natural philosophy doomed Aldrovandi's and Moffett's often-fanciful encyclopedias to long-term obscurity, Jia's approach is so rigorously empirical and so calibrated to the demands of his fellow insect lovers that—notwithstanding the critical orientation to classical erudition that permeates today's cricket community and the corresponding periodic complaints about Jia's unscientific lapses—his detailed diagnostic key to the morphological characteristics of successful warriors is still the basis of cricket knowledge. When Master Fang and other experts tried to instruct me in the distinctions that allow them to judge a cricket's fighting potential simply by observing the insect in its pot, they used the taxonomy that appeared first in Jia's *Book of Crickets* and was modified and supplemented—but not overthrown—across the centuries.

The system is fearsomely complex. It begins with body color. Jia identifies and ranks four body colors: first yellow, then red, black, and finally white. The authoritative Xishuai.com cricket-lovers' website adds purple and green—for which cricket people always use the ancient term *qing*—to this list but does not rank them. By contrast, most cricket experts I talked to in Shanghai describe only three colors: yellow, *qing*, and purple. Yellow crickets are reputed to be the most aggressive of the three but not necessarily the best fighters because *qing* insects, though quieter, are more strategic and—according to the annual illustrated list of cricket champions—include a greater number of generals.

Color is the first criterion by which crickets are divided and it confers an initial identity that, as we can see, is held to correspond to differences in behavior and character. Below these gross distinctions, however, is a further set of divisions into individual "personalities," whose total number is often put at seventy-two.[8] To entomologists like my friend Professor Jin Xingbao, these personalities relate only to individual—and therefore taxonomically insignificant—variations among crickets that belong to a very limited number of formal species. In the Linnaean terms that she prefers to use, most of the fighting crickets kept in Shanghai are either *Velarifictorus micado*, a black or dark-brown species that grows to seven tenths of an inch and is highly territorial and aggressive in the wild, or, in smaller numbers, the equally bellicose *V. aspersus*.[9]

Because it identifies breeding populations and evolutionary relationships, Professor Jin's type of classification is essential if, for example, the goal is conservation. However, I suspect she would agree that it's not much use to cricket trainers seeking ways of identifying potential champions. Their classification system is based on an agglomeration of numerous physical variables, complex clusters of characters.[10] Length, shape, and color of the insect's legs, abdomen, and wings are all system-atically parsed, as is the shape of the head—current manuals might include seven or more possibilities—and differences in number, shape, color, and width of the "fight lines" that run front to back across the crown. Experts also consider the energy of the antennae; the shape and color of the animal's "eyebrows" (which should be "opposite" in color to the antennae); the shape, color, translucence, and strength of the jaws; the shape and size of the neck plate; the shape and resting angle of the forewings; the sharpness of the tail tips; the hair on the abdomen; the width of the thorax and face; the thickness of the feet; and the animal's overall posture. The insect's "skin" must be "dry" (that is, it must reflect light from inside itself, not from its surface); it must also be delicate, like a baby's. The cricket's walk must be swift and easy; it should not have a rolling gait. In general, strength is more important than size. The qual-ity of the jaws is decisive.

Innumerable manuals are dedicated to the identification of especially desirable crickets. Books are filled with color photos of such admirable personalities as Purple Head Golden Wing, Cooked Shrimp, Bronze Head and Iron Back, Ying Yang Wing, and Strong Man That Nobody Can Harm. But as Professor Jin points out, these are ideal types, individ-ual crickets that display prized combinations of traits and are unlikely to recur in precisely this form.

Though from a natural science perspective, this method may appear to be characterized above all by imprecision and taxonomic confusion, it is closer to zoological classification than it might at first appear. The cricket-lovers' system is a practical one directed at the identification of signs of fighting prowess and the circulation of these signs within the cricket community in a spirit of democratic scholarship. It is also, in its own way, a moral system, a manual of a perhaps archaic masculinity (though it would be foolish to assume that because these characteristics are valued in crickets, they are therefore admired in men). The mastery of such knowledge can require decades of dedicated application, both book study and hands-on learning. It is comprehensive and also intuitive. It is largely inaccessible to a novice. Scientific classification, though substantially more recent and directed to different goals, shares many of these features, and it, too, is based on type specimens—the first individuals of a given category to be collected and described, the specimen against which all subsequent individuals will be measured. Moreover, in both systems, so long as individual variation falls within given parameters, it is disregarded.

Taxonomy doesn't simply require judgment; it is itself a set of judgments. And it is the key to the early-autumn task of acquiring the best possible insects. As Michael and I were told repeatedly, judging a cricket's quality requires deep knowledge. Nonetheless, judging is only one of three rudiments of cricket knowledge, and for Master Fang it is of less significance than the work of training, which fills the two-week midautumn period between *bai lu*, when collecting ends, and *qiu fen*, which marks the official start of the fighting season.

Master Fang tells me that the trainer's task is to build on preexisting natural virtues to develop the animal's fighting spirit (*dou xing*). This indispensable quality is revealed only at the moment the insect enters the arena. Though a cricket might look like a champion in all respects, though the judgment of its physical qualities may be correct, it can still turn out to lack spirit in competition. This, Master Fang insists, is less a matter of the individual cricket's character than a function of its care. It is the task of the trainer to build up the cricket's strength with foods appropriate to its stage of growth and individual needs, to respond to its sicknesses, develop its physical skills, cultivate its virtues, overcome its natural aversion to light, and habituate it to new, alien surroundings. Fundamentally, says Master Fang, a trainer must create the conditions in which the insect can be happy. A cricket knows when it is loved, and it knows when it is well cared for, and it responds in kind with loyalty, courage, obedience, and the signs of quiet contentment. In practical terms, this is a quid pro quo because a happy cricket is amenable to training, and as its health, skill, and confidence increase under the trainer's care, so too does its fighting spirit.

And as he was explaining all this to me, describing the sexual regimen he provides, outlining the many symptoms of ill health that one must be alert to, displaying the purified water, the home-cooked foods, the various pots, explaining that everything relies on communication and that the yard grass is the "bridge" between him and the insect (that, in other words, they understand each other in a language beyond language), Master Fang removed the lid from one of his pots and, in emphatic response to my increasingly unimaginative line of questioning, took his yard grass straw and barked orders at the cricket as if at a soldier: "This way! That way! This way! That way!" And the insect—to Michael's and my real astonishment—responded unhesitatingly, turning left, right, left, right, a routine of exercises that, Master Fang eventually explained, increases the fighter's flexibility, makes him limber and elastic, and shows that man and insect understand each other through the language of command as well as beyond it.

Training is a matter of nutrition, hygiene, medicine, physical therapy, and psychology. Each of these is addressed by Jia Sidao in the *Book of Crickets,* and like the principles of judging a warrior, each has been passed down through the generations of cricket lovers and amended, supplemented, and revised during its travels. Nutrition, hygiene, and medicine now rely both on principles of Chinese medicine—on the requirement to correct imbalances of the five elements with therapeutic baths and appropriate foods—and on the principles of scientific physiology, that is, on the need to find not only cooling and heating foods but also substances rich in, for example, calcium, targeted at the insect's exoskeleton.

And that's what Master Fang told me the last time we met. A wild cricket is always superior to one raised from eggs in captivity, he said. And when I asked him why, he answered that the wild animal imbibes specific qualities from the soils of its birth. I at once thought I was hearing him identify a quality in wildness that I also like to hold on to, an ineffable, holistic quality that escapes molecular logic. Hearing this response reminded me of Igarapé Guariba, that village in the Amazon invaded by yellow summer butterflies, and how when Seu Benedito felt ill and prepared remedies for himself, he would leave the mixture outside, near the river, for several days in a capped soda bottle to absorb the nighttime air. That impressed me greatly because to me the bottle was sealed and nothing could enter, but to Seu Benedito those days under the changing sky were a vital ingredient, as essential to the mixture as any of the roots and leaves. But when I asked Master Fang what exactly it was that the cricket absorbed from his environment—Did it get strong by fighting against a difficult climate or inhospitable soil? Were there perhaps atmospheric spirits that fortified its own fighting spirit?—his response was entirely without mystery: the best crickets come not from the harshest soils but from the most nourishing; their characteristic physical powers are a result of their early nutrition; you should look at the soil before you collect; you should know the quality of the earth from which the animal comes; you should administer baths and supplements accordingly.

And as sometimes happened when the topic became more specialized, Michael and I found ourselves in an area in which the experts disagreed. Xiao Fu, an antiques dealer, recently returned from his annual cricket collecting trip to Shandong, explained that the northern crickets are strong precisely because of the harshness of the dry environment against which they have to battle. Mr. Zhang, who generously spent a day taking us to cricket markets in Shanghai, impressing us with his considerable bargaining skills and sharing his substantial knowledge of cricket culture, also preferred wild crickets to home raised but explained that the wild insects absorb their spirit and "soul" from the elements in which they are raised, from the earth, air, wind, and water.

Some months later, when I read Jia Sidao's *Book of Crickets*, I discovered that the terms in which Jia described the ecological relationship between land and insect were difficult to specify, that he left room for all these views, but that, like most of the people we talked to about this, he, too, insisted on the importance of the initial environment to the insect's fighting quality. His discussion of this point won approval from his modern editor, who, though quick to criticize unscientific lapses in the 800-year-old text, interjected only that there was in fact more ecological variation in the crickets' range than Jia had known of and then, no doubt wisely, declined to arbitrate.

3.

Crickets leap into Shanghai in early August and stay until November. Michael often referred to these three months as the "happy times," and it took me a while to realize he wasn't translating this term literally from our conversations with cricket people but extracting it from the pleasure he heard in their accounts. It was an evocative translation, far better than my very English "cricket season." Even if it ignored the anxieties of what for many was the highlight and sometimes the very purpose of the year, "happy times" captured those irrefutable delights of cricket culture: the play and the camaraderie, the expertise in a world of arcane knowledge, the intimate connection with another species, the willing abandonment to obsession, the security of an erudition that reached back many centuries, and of course, the circulation of money and its possibilities.

The happy times are tethered to the rhythms of the lunisolar calendar, which are themselves tied to the lives of insects. *Li qiu*, the nominal start of autumn, in early August, is also the time when the crickets in eastern China undergo their seventh and final molt. They are now mature and sexually active, and males are able to sing and—as their color darkens and they gain strength over the following days—ready to fight.

It is now that the happy times officially begin. I haven't seen it myself, but it's easy to visualize from the stories: whole villages out in the moonlit fields; young, old, men, women, flashlight bound to the head, listening for the crickets' song, searching around tombstones, poking the earth and brickwork with sticks, throwing water, pinning the insects like startled rabbits in the beams of light, gathering them in small nets, trapping them in sections of bamboo, taking care not to damage their antennae, carrying them home, ordering them by their diagnostic qualities. In a few days of night- or daytime collecting, a family can amass thousands of crickets, ready to be sold directly to visiting buyers or to be carried to local or regional markets.

Li qiu rings alarm bells throughout China's eastern cities. In Shanghai, as well as in Hangzhou, Nanjing, Tianjin, and Beijing, it is the signal for tens of thousands of cricket lovers to head for the railway stations. They pack the trains to Shandong Province, which, during the twenty years in which crickets have become scarce in Shanghai, has established itself as the regional collecting center, the source of the finest warriors, known for their aggression, resilience, and intelligence.

Who knows how many answer the crickets' call and make the ten-hour journey from Shanghai to Shandong? Mr. Huang, feathering a client's hair in his storefront salon, tells us it can be near impossible to find a rail ticket during this period. Xiao Fu, seated in the doorway of his antiques stall, showing us his collection of rare cricket pots—presenting me with a pair from Tianjin (thick walled and pocket-size to warm the cricket close to your body)—estimates that he is 1 of up to 100,000 Shanghainese who go. Others reckon that 500,000 people arrive from eastern China during this four-week period and that upward of 300 million yuan flows into the local economy from the Shanghainese alone.[11]

Who travels to Shandong? Always the same answer: if, like Mr. Huang and Xiao Fu, you habitually bet more than 100 yuan on a fight, you make the journey; if, like Mr. Wu, you bet less, you wait for the cricket markets in Shanghai to fill with insects from the provinces and make your selections there. Xiao Fu tells us that he is like most cricket lovers, just a small-to-middling gambler. But the 3,000 to 5,000 yuan he spends each year in Shandong seems sizable next to the 12,000 yuan he brings in from antiques. Still, there are millionaire cricket lovers taking the train these days who are willing to slap down 10,000 yuan to scoop up a single general. So this year Xiao Fu did what more and more visitors do: he rented a car with his friends and toured the villages dotted throughout the countryside on the roads of Ninyang County, and he avoided the crowds in the main market at Sidian.

Often, I'm told, when buyers like Xiao Fu arrive in outlying villages, the first thing they do is pay five yuan for a table, a stool, some tea leaves, a thermos, and a cup. Then, within moments of settling down, they are besieged by villagers pushing cricket pots under their noses, crying, "Look at mine! Look at mine!" Some of the sellers have pricey, good-looking crickets, but others are children and elderly people with only the cheapest insects to sell.[12] The more successful sellers establish and maintain connections to buyers, perhaps have them come to the village to trade with them, perhaps even have them lodge in their home. The visitors might be gamblers like Xiao Fu, or they may be Shanghainese traders looking to purchase in bulk. Or they might be wealthier farmers or small businesspeople from local towns and villages who have found ways to cross the far-higher entry barriers to sell on the markets in Sidian or Shanghai or both. Or perhaps they are Shandongnese who do business by selling insects to others—Shanghainese or Shandongnese—who sell them on the urban markets. While it's clear that for the village collectors who every year turn to crickets for direly needed cash income, this is a moment of real, though perhaps desperate, opportunity, it's also clear that those who prosper the most in this economy are those who have the most to begin with and that the cricket trade, a vital supplement to the rural economy in Shandong, as well as in Anhui, Hebei, Zhejiang, and other eastern provinces, is also an engine of social differentiation serving to deepen what are already widening chasms of inequality.

Yet it's an insecure and destructive engine. Through the 1980s and '90s, as the cricket markets in Shandong took off, the county of Ninjing was the most popular destination for buyers. But after more than a decade of intensive collecting, the quality of the crickets began to decline noticeably, and Ninjing's preeminence was usurped by its neighbor Ninyang, which now markets itself as "China's Sacred Fighting-Cricket Location." In recent years, however, the overexploitation of crickets in Ninyang has forced local collectors (as well as visitors like Xiao Fu) to expand their range, so that they now comb the countryside and villages within a radius of more than sixty miles from their temporary bases. The pressure of unregulated collecting on the crickets is "like a massacre," writes one contemporary commentator.[13] Night hunting, which used to occupy villagers from nine in the evening until four in the morning, now takes them away from their homes until noon.

Just one month after *li qiu*, as warm August nights ease into cold September mornings and white dew appears on country fields, *bai lu* marks the end of the collecting season. Sensing the chill in the air, the crickets call a halt, heading back into the soil, digging down with their powerful jaws, weakening their most precious fighting asset, and ruining their value as commodities. Carefully packing up their haul, the last Shanghainese retrace their journey home, though this time they share the trains with Shandongnese traders off to stake their claim in the city's cricket markets.

At Wanshang, the largest flower, bird, beast, and insect market in Shanghai, these traders, mostly women, sit in rows in the center of the main hall with their crickets laid out neatly before them in small pots with lids cut from tin cans. Around the market's edges, permanent stalls are occupied by Shanghainese dealers, also newly returned, their clay pots arrayed on tables, the insects' origin chalked up on a blackboard behind them.

The same pattern is repeated at cricket markets throughout the city. At Anguo Road, in the grim shadow of Ti Lan Qiao, Shanghai's largest jail, and again in what Michael called new Anguo Road—rapidly opened in a disused lot following a police raid—Shanghainese sellers sit at tables while traders from the provinces, squatting on stools, lay out their pots on the ground in their own distinct areas. This visible geography mirrors pervasive tensions in Shanghai and throughout contemporary China between urban residents and what is officially known as the "floating population," a vast number of people to whom the government denies urban residency status (with its associated permit and social benefits) but who anyway fill the lowest-paying and most dangerous jobs in the construction, service, and sweatshop sectors.[14]

Even though the provincial traders at these markets don't plan to stay in Shanghai and even though they are likely to be relatively prosperous in rural terms (some are farmers; some are year-round traders of various products; one man I talked to dealt in cell phones), once in the city they are simply migrants, subject to harassment, discrimination, and expulsion. Nonetheless, for those who've made it here, these are potentially happy times too. No matter that unemployment is up, gambling is down (after a series of police crackdowns), and business accordingly slowed, most expect to do well. By minimizing their expenditures—traveling with relatives, going home infrequently, carrying as much stock as possible when they return, and sleeping in cheap "basement hotels" close to the market—provincial traders can make considerably more in these three months than they will in the entire rest of the year. At least that's what traders—including an impressively organized woman from Anhui who said that last year she took home a full 40,000 yuan—told me again and again.

Shanghainese traders don't sell female crickets. Females don't fight or sing and are valued only for the sexual services they provide to males. It's the provincial traders who deal in these, selling them in bulk, stuffed into bamboo sections in lots of three or ten, depending on their size (bigger is better) and coloring (a white abdomen is best). Females are cheap, and at a first glance that takes in these traders' apparently subordinate situation in the market, it seems they sell only cheap animals, female and male.

The signs in front of the Shandongnese traders say ten yuan for each male, sometimes two for fifteen. The buyers file past their pots, browsing the rows with an air of detachment, occasionally lifting the lids to peer inside, taking the grass brush, stimulating the insect's jaws, perhaps shining a flashlight to gauge the color and translucence of its body, trying to judge not only its physical qualities but also that less tangible and even more critical fighting spirit. Despite their studied indifference, they're often drawn in, quickly finding themselves bargaining for an insect priced anywhere between 30 and—if the buyer is a genuine big boss—as much as 2,000 yuan. Only children, novices like me, the elderly, the truly petty gamblers who play crickets for fun, and bargain hunters who believe their eye is sharper than the seller's will buy the cheap crickets, it seems.

But how do you judge an insect's fighting spirit without seeing it fight? Groups of men crowd around the Shanghainese stalls. Michael and I aren't tall or short enough to see between shoulders or legs. Eventually, someone moves aside to share the view: two crickets locking jaws inside their tabletop arena. The stallholders tend to the animals like trainers at a real fight. But they're seated in chairs, pots piled around them, and as the match progresses, they deliver relentless patter, inciting interest like auctioneers, talking up the winner and attempting to raise its price.

This is a risky sales strategy. No one buys a loser, so the defeated are quickly tossed into a plastic bucket. And if, as often happens, the winner isn't sold either, he has to fight again and may be beaten or injured. The seller relies on his ability to inflate the winner's price enough to compensate for the collateral losses. But the woman from Shanghai who eagerly waves us over as she spoons tiny portions of rice into dollhouse-size trays, tells us that the Shanghainese insist on watching the crickets fight before they put their money down, that they like to shift the risk to the seller. It is starting to look as if the divisions between metropolitan and provincial are expressed not only in the spatial arrangements (which make the market look like an allegorical tableau of society at large) but also in the distinctive selling practices of the different groups, so that buyers stroll in and out of two distinct worlds as they browse, two worlds with explicit boundaries marked by distinct codes, aesthetics, and experiences, two racialized worlds perhaps.

"Shandongnese don't dare fight their crickets," the woman continues in a tone that seems congruent with the discriminations that surround us. She is lively and straightforward, generous too, inviting us to share her lunch and giving me a souvenir cricket pot, disappointed that I won't take the insect as well, enjoying initiating us and not about to be silenced by her irascible husband no matter how many times he looks up from his warriors to sound off in our direction. She's expounding on her neighbors, the Shandongnese traders. "They sell their crickets as brand-new to fighting," she says, and then—so casually it almost slips past, and it is only thanks to Michael's quickness and to the violence of her husband's reaction that I realize it—she is telling us that crickets circulate throughout the market, unconstrained by social and political division. She explains that they pass not only from trader to buyer but also, without prejudice, from trader to trader, from Shanghainese to Shandongnese and from Shandongnese to Shanghainese. And as they travel through these crowded spaces, they gain and even recover value; they're born again: losers become ingenues, cheap crickets become contenders; they change their character, their history, and their identity. Caveat emptor.

But how fascinating and even inspiring that the politics of racial difference diagrammed so concretely in this highly spatialized marketplace and conforming so fully (too fully, in a game of double bluff, it turns out) to social expectation is not only an expression of a dismal social logic but also a technology of commerce that creates lively crosscutting dependencies and solidarities. And this thought led me again to the animals who make all this possible, confined to their pots, traveling like slaves really, like chattels, making their way between stalls and pitches, completing circuits, breaching boundaries, and forging new connections, gathering new histories and new lives, unable to prevent themselves from minimizing their captors' exposure to loss, unable to avoid collaborating in their own demise.

In the city, the happy times have no center; they are everywhere, wherever there are crickets. On working-class street corners, groups of men cram themselves around an arena, watching the battles unfold. In the newspapers, it's high culture and low life, elite sponsorship and police raids. The happy times bring the gambling houses to life and make possible cultural events and neighborhood tournaments. They light up the stores that sell cricket paraphernalia, the elaborate implements that every fighting cricket and every cricket trainer needs: tiny food and water dishes (maybe in sets with coordinated designs of Buddhist deities), wooden transfer cases, "marriage boxes" with room for one male and one female, various grades of grass and whisker, nudging brushes made of duck down, tiny long-handled metal trowels and other cleaning implements, large wooden carrying cases, pipettes, scales (both weighted and electronic), technical manuals, specialized foods and medicines, and of course, pots in an enormous variety, some old (and often fake), some new, most of clay but some of porcelain, some large, some small, some with inscriptions, mottoes, or stories, some to commemorate special cricket events, some with intricate images, some simply plain.

The happy times are here again. While they last, the money flows, the people travel, and the insects circulate. It's a period of possibility, an opening in which many projects unfold and many lives are changed. It's an intense period but a short one. It's the length of a cricket's adult life.

4.

Would we see cricket gambling before I left Shanghai? We'd watched crickets fight in Master Fang's museum, and we'd seen traders "test" them at Wanshang and other markets. But it was all starting to feel like *Hamlet* without the Prince. Hadn't gambling and crickets been associated since the earliest records? Hadn't Jia Sidao written for his gambling friends? Didn't *cai ji*, the term for crickets in Shanghainese, mean "collect fortune"? Wasn't it gambling that made the markets possible and kept cricket fighting alive when so much else considered "traditional culture" was disappearing? Wasn't it gambling that made these transactions crackle and our conversations pop?

Master Fang, by no means a moralist, did not agree. He said: Gambling debases cricket fighting. And: Cricket fighting is a spiritual activity, a discipline of man and animal. And: Most gamblers know nothing about crickets and have little interest in them; they might as well be betting on mahjong or soccer.

It wasn't only experience that made Master Fang's words authoritative. He spoke with a persuasive combination of purism (his master's rigor) and enthusiasm (his unaffected pleasure in the crickets themselves and the dramas they create). Nonetheless, there seemed something artificial about gambling's absence. Despite its active exclusion, it always found its way into the tabletop talk. It was as if—for the trainers and audience, if not for the animals—these nongambling fights were merely rehearsals.

But perhaps it was simply timing that made it seem this way. Two weeks later, when the tournament in Qibao reached its final stages, there would be scores, if not hundreds, of people watching the fights in the courtyard of the museum on closed-circuit TV, and as I write this, I remember a Saturday spent in cricket markets with Mr. Zhang, who described how his uncle fought crickets for honor, not money, in the early years of the twentieth century, how in those days the trainers of champions were proud to win red ties, and how, he continued, telescoping the century, cricket fighting began to involve big money only with Deng's reforms and the spread of disposable incomes. Even in Qibao, though, it was hard to enforce purity and hard to imagine that there was no betting taking place in the wings. The discussion at the museum was all about gambling (winners, losers, champions, bets), with Master Fang as caught up in the gossip as everyone else. Even he admitted that gambling made fights more exciting, that it gave them a raw, compulsive edge.

Still, it didn't look as if Michael and I would find out for ourselves. It was a too-illegal, too-closed world, and our connections just weren't good enough. Mr. Huang, the hairstylist, didn't want to take us. I had just arrived in Shanghai and was wilting under the twin debilities of jet lag and brutal humidity. Michael and I hadn't yet figured out our translation rhythm, and we made a distinctly unsparky team. The conversation in Mr. Huang's salon was awkward, and although he was informative and more than courteous, he was wary of taking our relationship further. "It wouldn't be convenient," he said decisively.

Xiao Fu, our second contact, was more enthusiastic. His brother, Lao Fu, was an old classmate of Michael's father, and the four of us quickly hit it off. Xiao Fu was knowledgeable about crickets and generous with his expertise. He brought a selection of his insects and an array of implements to our meeting at his stall and patiently explained many aspects of his passion. Like Mr. Huang, Xiao Fu faced hardships in his life, but he was lucky that in Lao Fu he had a brother who was also a rock, contributing his own expert knowledge of Chinese antiquities to the business and fulfilling a promise to their mother to keep his younger sibling safe and strong. It wasn't Xiao Fu's decision not to take us to a fight. The other members of his circle vetoed the proposal and left him with the awkward task of letting us down gently.

In the end it was Mr. Wu, fulfilling an obligation to a friend of his who was also a friend of a friend of mine in California, who made the arrangements. He met us on a dark street corner opposite the model ball bearing factory in the Minhang Heavy Industrial Zone, folded himself into our minuscule Chery QQ taxi, led us to a warren of rundown apartments blocks, through an open front door, and into a side room just big enough for a TV, a fish tank, and a gold plastic love seat.

Mr. Wu was close with the father of Boss Xun, the sponsor of a cricket casino here. Boss Xun not only provided the premises but also handled the local police, guaranteed a referee to arbitrate the fighting and the cash, and made available a secure and well-organized public house. For all this, he and his partner, Boss Yang, took 5 percent of the winnings. Mr. Wu was a cricket lover of the first order and, we would find out, a gifted judge of cricket form, but he was only a small gambler and not a participant in this underworld. It was this discomfort, he later explained apologetically, that accounted for any erratic behavior.

Boss Xun, though, was relaxed and welcoming. Track pants, T-shirt, plastic flip-flops, and a gold chain, gray hair close-cropped, nails carefully manicured, extra-long and tapered on thumbs and pinkies. "Please feel at home," he said. "Ask me anything you like." But Mr. Wu was chain-smoking and on edge. I remembered the instructions he'd given us in the cab: no smoking during the fight, no alcohol, no eating, no cologne, no scent of any kind, no talking, no noise of any kind. "We will be like the air," Michael had assured him.

But it was hard to be unobtrusive. With what I discovered was characteristic graciousness, Boss Xun insisted on seating us at the head of the long, narrow table next to the referee, the best possible view of the crickets and directly opposite the only door. The casino was basic—a whitewashed room stripped bare—and its simplicity was a measure of its transparency. As the men of Boss Xun's circle entered, they could take in the scene at a glance, the entire room and all its occupants.

A few days earlier, Michael and I had watched a TV exposé of a cricket-gambling den, complete with hidden cameras and pixelated interviewees, and we expected a darkened cellar full of shadowy dealings. But Boss Yang and Boss Xun's casino was lit by an antiseptic fluorescent strip that threw its glare into every corner, and their table was covered with a white cloth on which sterile implements (yard-grass and mouse-whisker brushes, down balls, transfer cases, two pairs of white cotton gloves—all handled only by their staff) were arrayed with surgical precision on either side of the clear plastic arena.

But transparency and security (windows stuffed with thick cushions to keep noises in and noses out) were perhaps just the enabling conditions. This was serious, but it was entertainment too, men's entertainment. Boss Xun worked the room with his self-contained charisma, and the referee was engaging and quick-witted. He treated the men in the now-crowded casino with respect, called the bets with finesse, moved everything along swiftly, and managed friction with boisterous humor, all despite the large amounts of money flying across the table.

"Who will call first?" the referee began, addressing the trainers on either side of him. Their motions were slow and deliberate, densely concentrated. They had pulled on the white gloves, lifted the lids from the pots to examine their animals, and aroused them with the yard grass, and now they were delicately transferring them to the arena. One man was a little clumsier, faltering as he eased his fighter out of the transfer case, sweating slightly, his hand trembling slightly, knowing that much of the betting happens before the animals are even visible, that many people wager on the trainers more than on the insects. As the crickets emerged under the lights, everyone leaned in, strained for the closest view, hungry for that moment when the animals' spirit, power, and discipline would come into the open.

For several minutes, the bets mounted on one animal, then on the next, stopping only when the second pile of cash in front of the referee had grown to equal the first. The packed and steamy room turned raucous. Men with fistfuls of 100-yuan notes clamored to have their bets

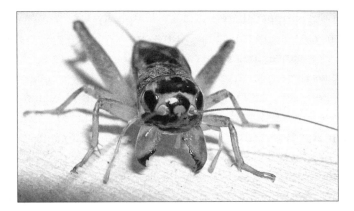

acknowledged by the referee or, once the house bets had closed, called odds to entice others with whom they might deal laterally. The referee's voice boomed above the rest, building up the crickets and the stakes. Some men loudly offered commentary on the animals and the wagers. Others simply watched. (And observing these men, Michael—without animus of his own but in an effort to convey to me the resonances that haunt the gambler's world—recalled one of the scathing essays on political passivity and complicity that the great Lu Xun wrote during the turmoil of the 1930s. Michael couldn't reproduce the exact wording, and I haven't managed to find the text, but the gist was clear and, as he remembered it, sour too: We Chinese like to say we love peace, but in reality we like fighting. We like to watch other things fight, and we like to fight among ourselves. . . . Let them fight; we do not get involved, we just watch.)

And then, at the instant the referee directed the trainers to prepare their crickets, silence snapped into place; the room seemed to hold its breath. The two trainers began again to stroke their animals gently with the yard grass (back legs, abdomen, jaws). The crickets remained motionless. If you were close enough, you could see the beating of their hearts.

Eventually, the insects sang, indicating their readiness. The referee called, "Open the floodgate!" and lifted the panel that divided the arena. Around the table, postures stiffened, the silence intensified. And at once, it was obvious to Michael and me that these animals were far more combative than any we'd seen before, more—we had to say—warrior-like. They looked conditioned, ready. A sudden assault, a dart, a lunge at an opponent's jaw or leg, and the room emitted a sharp, involuntary gasp. All the energy in this tightly packed space concentrated on this tiny drama. A singularity. And at that moment, I realized I was right there, and I looked at Michael squeezed in beside me and saw that he was too, everything focused on the insects.

Yes, this is typical of a gambling house in the industrial zone, Mr. Wu tells us later as we pour out of the building, flooding the empty streets of the housing projects, everyone lighting cigarettes, muffled talking, car doors slamming. Downtown, the sponsors rent hotel suites and hand-pick their high-rolling punters, he says, and at those places the minimum bet is 10,000 yuan and the total stakes can far exceed 1 million. Tonight in Minhang, though, the referee opened the bidding with modest encouragements: "Bet what you like, we're all friends here, even one hundred is fine tonight." Still, at one point during the evening, as the stakes climbed over 30,000 yuan, Mr. Tung, the gambler from Nanjing, showed his hand for the first time and with no change of expression—almost, it seemed, absentmindedly—tossed a bankroll of 6,000 yuan into the middle of the table and then watched impassively as the referee delegated an observer to count and recount the cash until the gate was lifted in the arena and the crickets rapidly and aggressively locked jaws, wrestling, flipping each other over, again and again, incredibly lithe, a blur of bodies, circling each other, hurling themselves at each other. And then—as if abruptly losing interest—disengaging, walking away to opposite corners and refusing their trainers' attempts to incite them back into the fray. Even the referee's effort to stimulate them by eliciting

singing from the two crickets kept for this purpose in pots beside the arena had no effect. It was a draw, a rare outcome, which provoked a contemptuous clucking from Mr. Wu, who stage-whispered to us that really good crickets fight to exhaustion, that although athletic and well matched, these animals were poorly trained.

Afterward, with the fighting over, it was as if a spell had broken. It was only then that I wondered about the violence of this spectacle, about the sovereignty that forces other beings to perform such unwonted acts, about cruelty, and yes, about my failure to wonder. Well, you might say, the ethical suspension (if that's what it was) is unsurprising; the affinities are not so visceral. These are insects, after all—no red blood, no yielding soft tissue, no untoward vocalizations, no expressive faces—not dogs, not songbirds, not even roosters, certainly not boxers wrestling the stark brutalities of race and class.

And yet that concentrated "being there" that Michael and I experienced during the fight was grounded in sympathy for these animals, and it felt like a more profound sympathy than that more familiar feeling of pity-sympathy for animals in distress. Perhaps it was a case of being swept away in the intensity that gripped the room, perhaps it was a case of the magic of money and risk. Even so, the wave that carried us was a wave of identifications shaped by the cultural literacy we were learning from Master Fang, Mr. Wu, and the rest. There was no question about that.

It had been such a short time—less than two weeks in the country of the crickets—yet already I was having trouble separating these animals from their social selves (their virtues, their personalities, their circulations), and already, to me at least, these fights were their fights, their dramas. But I want to be clear about this: the power of this association between the elaborate culture of the cricket-lovers' world and the crickets themselves, the ability of this alliance to produce an effect that those of us not accustomed to thinking of ourselves as ontologically entangled with insects might experience as a suspension of the order of natural things (such that these animals were neither objects nor victims nor even a simple projection of human aspiration), is possible only because of the insects themselves, which are not merely the opportunity for culture but its co-authors. (And here is a moment when, yet again, language—at least, the English language—is not adequate to its task, because even to write about the "association" between the crickets and their cultural selves is absurd. What is a cricket in these circumstances without its existence in culture? What is this culture without the existence of the crickets?)

If the crickets appear to tire, if they hang back, losing interest in confrontation, or if one turns away, dejected, the referee will lower the gate to separate the fighters, reset the sixty-second timer, and invite the trainers to minister to their prospects. Like corner men at a boxing match, they work away to restore their charges' fighting spirit, using different brushstrokes now, testing their technique. But often, like a boxer after a heavy pummeling, the cricket will simply slump, through loss of spirit or other injury, while his opponent will puff up and sing, and the referee will call an end to the fight. Then, all at once, the hubbub in the casino restarts with a rush, and cash again begins to fly—large notes to the winners, 5 percent in small bills coming back to the referee.

And the crickets? The winner is returned carefully to his pot, ready for the journey home or back into the public house to prepare for another fight. The loser, no matter how valiant, no matter how many of the Five Virtues he displayed, no matter that he is likely to be physically unscathed, has finished his career. The referee collects him in a net and drops him into a large plastic bucket behind the table, to be released "into nature" everyone tells me, to which Michael adds that it's okay, I shouldn't worry, he'll be all right: the curse on anyone who harms a defeated cricket guarantees it.

5.

As the happy times approach their November climax, the phalanx of pots creeps further along the table and the contests stretch deeper into the night. But that evening of our first visit to Boss Xun's casino was in late September, and there were just a handful of fights. After they were over, Boss Xun asked if we wanted to see the public house.

The public house is designed to counter some of the more underhand tactics said to be popular among cricket trainers. Of these, the most sensational is doping, especially with ecstasy, the head-shaking drug of Shanghai's teen dance clubs.[15] As anyone who's taken ecstasy can imagine, a high cricket is likely to be a winning cricket. However, it might not be the rush of energy and confidence or the elevated sense of personal charm, attractiveness, and well-being that assures victory. In this type of doping, the real target is the opposition. Crickets are acutely sensitive to stimulants (hence the no-smoking, no-scent rule). They rapidly detect when their adversary is chemically enhanced, and they respond instantly (and no doubt sensibly) by turning tail, forfeiting the contest.

We left the casino and drove through downtown streets lined with new trees gleaming synthetically under fluorescent light, past sleeping factories and darkened office buildings, along wide, empty boulevards, past bright restaurants, dazzling neon karaoke palaces, late-night stalls selling vegetables, DVDs, and hot food, past the round-the-clock construction I'd so quickly grown to expect, along partly paved side streets, beside what could have been a canal, drawing up at another faded apartment building, ducking in through another anonymous door.

I enjoyed the feeling of anticipation as the car slipped through the quiet streets. My mind drifted to the discussion earlier that day in the golden banquet room at the Luxurious Garden between Boss Yang and Mr. Tung, the gambler from Nanjing, about what makes a successful casino. Mr. Tung had traveled from Nanjing to escape his circle—it was too small and too professional, he said; the crickets were too strong and the competition too fierce. Here in Minhang, he told Boss Yang with no sign of awkwardness, his chances of winning were greater, greater too than if he would go to downtown Shanghai.

Perhaps unsurprisingly, Mr. Tung's perfect casino would be a place of comfort as well as security, a place with an appealing atmosphere. He conjured an image of expansive largesse, a scene peopled by relaxed and prosperous gamblers, frank and open, not the kind of men who would argue over small change. He seemed to be casting himself as Chow Yun-Fat in Wong Jing's classic *God of Gamblers* or as Tony Leung in Hou Hsiao-hsien's *Flowers of Shanghai*—or maybe that was my gambling fantasy, not his. He said: The crucial thing is connection; you should be cultivating the successful gamblers, encouraging them to bring more and more of their associates.

Boss Yang and Boss Xun's casino attracted gamblers from Hong Kong, Zhejiang, and elsewhere, as well as from Nanjing. However, the two men were not focused on pampering their clients. There were reasons to keep the atmosphere congenial—an argument could lead to a killing and make the police feel that they had to put on a show—but, Boss Yang countered, the surest route to a successful business was through a reputation for fairness. The most important quality of a casino was the trust between the sponsor and his clients. Owners, trainers, and gamblers (often the same people) should feel safe and should be confident that their animals were safe too.

The public house was an impressive place, part maximum-security zone, part clinic. Every cricket slated for Boss Xun's casino spent at least five days undergoing prophylactic detox here. There are thousands of such houses throughout Shanghai, he tells us, and he's run one for many years, though of course in a variety of locations. It's no game. The risk is large, increased tonight by the novelty of bringing me here. Several sponsors had been arrested and some executed in the anti-gambling drive that swept Shanghai the year before, and as we talk, Boss Xun's right leg stutters rhythmically.

The public house is a four-room apartment stripped and retooled. Three rooms have multiply padlocked steel gates; the fourth is a social space equipped with couch, chairs, TV, and PlayStation, its whitewashed walls decorated with color close-ups of crickets, glamour shots. Nobody drinks or smokes. Two of the gated rooms are caged storage areas lined with shelves, on which I make out stacks of cricket pots. The third has been unlocked, and like the casino, it is brightly lit. Boss Xun leads us inside, and I see a long table and a row of men—owners and trainers here to care for their insects—each tending to a pot. Two assistants, men I recognize from the casino, are stationed across the table. One of them fetches the labeled pots from a cabinet behind him while the other closely observes the visitors. But what makes the scene genuinely startling and momentarily disorienting, even surreal, is that the men lined up at the table, silently intent on their crickets, are dressed identically in white surgical gowns and matching white masks.

Biosecurity is everything. Trainers in the public house give animals only the food and water provided on the premises, and in the casino use only those implements provided by the sponsor. It is well known that trainers dip their yard grass in solutions of ginseng and other substances, which, like smelling salts in a boxing corner, can revive even the most battered fighter. It's well known that they try to contaminate the food and water of their competitors' animals, that they try to engulf them in poisonous gas. It's well known that they'll insert tiny knives into their own yard grass and put poison on their fingertips in the hope of getting close enough to touch the opposition.

Nonetheless, the public house isn't foolproof. One chink in the armor is the moment the insects first enter, when they're fed and then weighed on an electronic scale. The weight is recorded on the side of the pot, along with the date and the owner's name, and it then becomes the basis on which to assign the insects to fighting pairs. Great care is taken to match crickets as precisely as possible, to make the fights as even as possible, an effort that is institutionalized in the system of raising equal stakes on both animals at the start of a fight. Weights are recorded in *zhen*, a Shanghainese cricket-specific measure now used nationally. One *zhen* is around a fifth of a gram, and there must be no more than two tenths of a *zhen* difference between paired fighters. Recognizing an opportunity, trainers have become adept at manipulating their insects' weight. In the past, they would subject the animals to an extended sauna to extract liquid just before the weigh-in. Nowadays, it's more common to use dehydration drugs, which are impossible to detect and, by all accounts, produce few ill effects. Once fed, weighed, and admitted, the animal has at least five days under the care of the public-house staff and his visiting trainer to recover his strength, and if all goes to plan, he'll ultimately fight below his weight—imagine Mike Tyson versus Sugar Ray Leonard!

It wasn't long before we were back in Boss Xun's casino, once more in seats of honor and once more in the grip of the crickets. Again I was impressed by the professionalism of it all. From the secured metal trunk carried in by the public-house assistants to the quickness of the referee and Boss Xun's own congenial working of the crowd, this was a smoothly run operation. We caught the last train back to the city, and I again recalled the lunchtime discussion between Boss Yang and Mr. Tung. Boss Yang had stuck tenaciously to his view that nothing was more important than the casino's reputation for fairness, and now I understood why. After all, only the sponsor and his staff had unsupervised access to the animals. With little difficulty, they could influence the contest in various hard-to-detect ways: by hiring a partisan referee, by matching the fighters unevenly, by neglecting to care for particular individuals adequately or by lavishing extra care on favorites (including their own—Boss Xun liked to fight his crickets here too). I remembered Boss Yang's vigorous defense of his staff in response to Mr. Wu's request to bypass the public house, and I saw that of course there must be no exceptions. Without full confidence in the sponsor's probity and in his ability to create an environment safe from violence, corruption, and the police, there could be no circle, no event, no gambling, no profit, no entertainment, no culture.

6.

Dr. Li Shijun of Shanghai Jiao Tong University invited us to his home. A few journalists, some cricket experts, and a university colleague or two would also be there. We must be sure to show up as planned.

I was keen to meet Dr. Li. I'd seen him interviewed on a TV program included on a DVD I'd picked up on Anguo Road. The reporter was enthusiastic about the professor's campaign to promote cricket fighting as a high-culture activity free of gambling. "Gambling," she said in the final voice-over, "has ruined the reputation of cricket fighting. Cricket fighting is like Beijing opera; it is the quintessence of our country. Many foreigners regard it as the most typically Oriental element of our culture. We should lead it to a healthy road." Just a few days before I arrived in Shanghai, Dr. Li had again featured prominently in the media, this time in a newspaper article about a gambling-free tournament he had staged downtown. The newspaper journalist identified Dr. Li as the "cricket professor." The TV reporter had called him the "venerable cricket master."

Dr. Li's apartment was tucked away in a corner of a low-rise housing complex close to the university campus. He was a charming host, warm and welcoming, a youthful sixty-four-year-old, his lively features crowned with what I can only describe as a mane of silver hair. Several people were already there when we arrived, and he swiftly corralled us all in his office, all the while pointing out the prizes from his lifelong passion: the cricket-themed paintings, poems, and calligraphy created by him and his friends that enlivened the walls and bookcases, the large collection of southern cricket pots, which are the focus of one of his four published books on cricket-related matters.[16]

The professor ushered us into a large sitting room, in which he had laid out a variety of pots and implements. Selecting two pots, he carried them over to a low coffee table positioned in front of a couch. He transferred the crickets to an arena on the table and invited me to sit beside him. He put a yard grass straw in my hand and, as people often did, encouraged me to stimulate the insects' jaws. I was clumsy with the brush and always felt as if I were tormenting the insect, which more often than not simply stood still and suffered my attentions. But I obliged and was jiggling my wrist as best I could when I looked up to find that all the other people present, with the exception of Dr. Li, who continued to stare intently at the crickets as if he and I were alone in the room, had somehow, from somewhere, produced digital cameras and were lined up in formation, snapping away at close range like paparazzi at a premiere. Michael too! And now Dr. Li turned creative director, instructing me how to position the grass, how to hold my head, what to look at, how to sit . . .

Maybe I'm unusually dense about this kind of thing, perhaps insufficiently entrepreneurial. It was only later, on the crowded bus back to the metro with Michael and Li Jun, a smart young reporter whom Dr. Li had invited to join us for lunch, chattering away about my research and my impressions of Shanghai, that it dawned on me what was going on. Even Michael, who, it seems, had merely wanted to capture the moment, was startled by my naïveté.

A few days later, under the headline "Anthropologist Studying Human-Insect Relations, U.S. Professor Wants to Publish a Book on Crickets," Li Jun's article appeared in the mass-circulation *Shanghai Evening Post*. The photo caption, adapting a well-known saying, read "United by their love of crickets, these two strangers immediately became friends."[17]

Li Jun subtly traced Dr. Li's erudition. She noted his eager recourse to

the yellowing books on his shelves, his willingness to take me on as his acolyte as well as his friend. ("Questions flew out of his mouth like bullets," she wrote of my reaction to the crickets.) She identified Dr. Li as one of Shanghai's modern literati, a person of refinement cultivating a set of scholarly arts, among which the contemplation, appreciation, and manipulation of what I would call nature—and which includes the judging, training, and fighting of crickets—have long figured prominently.[18] In offering me guidance, she wrote, Dr. Li was *chuandao jie huo*, a Confucian term for the teacher's task of passing on the knowledge of the ancient sages and resolving its interpretive difficulties. She let her readers know that his pro-cricket, anti-gambling campaign was a matter of culture, that it reached out from the whirlpool of the present to a higher ground that was both an available safe haven of the past and an anchor for the future. And she was right to do so, because without pointing to those capacities and desires, the rest didn't make sense.

Dr. Li grew up in Shanghai, and like other men of his generation whom I met, his early fascination with crickets had been sparked and nurtured by an older brother. He describes passing the large (now long-gone) cricket market at Cheng Huang Miao every day on his way to school in the late 1940s; he remembers using his pocket money to buy crickets; he fondly recalls the circle of insect friends (*chong you*) that grew around him, boys his own age and, from time to time, the adults who would stop to play with them.

At twenty, he graduated from the Shanghai Film Academy and was assigned to the Shanghai Science and Education Film Studio, where he developed his skills as a cameraman and animator. In the mid-1980s, he was appointed professor of photography and animation arts at Jiao Tong University.

We didn't talk about this, and he doesn't discuss it in his writing, but the history of Shanghai during this period is well known: the falling out of favor of the cosmopolitan city that had given birth to the Chinese Communist Party; the never-implemented plan to dismantle the metropolis and disperse a population rendered suspect by the city's decadent colonial past; the forced closure of hundreds of its factories, schools, and hospitals and the relocation of 2 million of its residents during the Great Leap Forward and the Cultural Revolution; the city's precipitous decline and stagnation until its belated incorporation into Deng's reform strategy with the Pudong policy of 1992; its spectacular return to eclipse Hong Kong, looking out across the East China Sea not only toward the West but toward Japan, Korea, and Southeast Asia.[19]

And all the while, Li Shijun cultivated his passion for crickets. He married, raised a family, carried out his responsibilities, advanced his career, expanded his cricket-loving circle, and refused to gamble. He told the story of how he would wander his Shanghai neighborhood seeking a cricket partner, someone willing to pit his insect against his own, but to do so without staking money. Time after time he was rebuffed. He offered to fight simply "for exercise," just for practice, but no one would place his animal at risk without potential reward. He returned home dejected, embittered by the "poor condition of the world around him." It was then that his wife, seeing his distress, made herself his special *chong you*, and there, alone in their apartment, together they fought crickets.[20]

This was the early 1980s, as the restless wake of the Cultural Revolution gave way to the new turbulence of reform. Cricket fighting was already experiencing the stirrings of a revival that would bring teams of enthusiasts from Jiao Tong and Fudan universities for intervarsity competitions at Dr. Li's apartment, where his wife and daughter would prepare lavish banquets (as they did for Michael and me) and nurture a sort of cricket salon under the professor's patronage and sponsorship, a salon of real friends, he wrote, not the kind of friends one makes through gambling, who fall out over money and become strangers forever. Unlike those gamblers who travel together, collect together, fight together, but keep their own knowledge secret from one another, these cricket lovers share their experience. They are a circle of constant friends united by their love for crickets, a circle of men among whom he is the acknowledged big brother.

I can't shake Dr. Li's image of himself and his wife in their Shanghai apartment, refugees from the deterioration they sensed all around them yet on the cusp of a florescence in the activity they love, which is fueled not by a return to the elite traditions of cricket culture he values so highly but by a relaxing of moral codes and a rising tide of both surplus income and financial desperation, a rich matrix for the regeneration of gambling, the source of so much of Dr. Li's anxiety. And this is all deeply ironic for the professor, as well as disturbing and perhaps disorienting, because for Li Shijun the care and combat of crickets is a matter of *yi qing yue xing*, which corresponds to something like the cultivation of moral character, the elevation of one's self and, by extension, of society as a whole.

Both in person and in his writings, the professor is direct. At the end of his book *Fifty Taboos of Cricket Collecting* (don't buy a cricket whose jaws are shaped like the character /\, don't buy a cricket with rounded wings, don't buy a cricket with just one antenna, don't buy a cricket that is half-male, half-female, and so on), he remarks that it is no mystery that society looks down on cricket fighting. Whereas at the university he teaches in a suit and tie, at the insect market, surrounded by "low-level people," he is compelled—for fear of appearing ridiculous—to wear slippers, T-shirt, and shorts like everyone else. The lack of cultivation— evident in the smoking, cursing, and spitting all around him—is not simply a personal matter: "If you want others to treat you with respect you must first act decently," he insists.[21]

Nor is it merely a question of deportment. The circle he is creating is both a refuge and an example. There is, he says, a crisis of civility in Chinese society, and cricket fighting, with its long history as a cultivated art, is a discipline, a spiritual road, the ideal vehicle for the cultivation and elevation of the self. With its traditions, knowledge, and scholarly demands, cricket fighting is a rare practice, more akin to tai chi than mahjong. But it is a practice debased by gambling. How nightmarish that an activity so elevated has become the vehicle of such degeneration.

Campaigns against gambling have been a feature of the People's Republic since the liberation. But despite periodically aggressive policing and especially since the post-Mao reforms, the party has had little success in controlling its expansion. Unlike the attempt to outlaw mahjong, which failed during the 1980s, the assault on crickets has been indirect, paralleling policy during the Ming and Qing dynasties, when imperial prohibitions ran up against the emerging professional network of urban cricket houses and legislation targeted gambling rather than crickets.[22]

Even during the Cultural Revolution, cricket fighting wasn't formally banned. However, as Master Fang and others recalled, one way or another it was driven to the margins. Except for small children, no one could find time for crickets; even when lives remained relatively intact, adults were too busy attending meetings. But there was no ambiguity about gambling. It was violently disavowed as a feudal evil, a vice with particularly tenacious roots in Chinese society. And it was through its association with gambling and elite corruption that cricket fighting suffered—through its affinity with a complex of indulgences marked as male (sex, drugs, drink, easy money; luxuriance, hedonism, or whatever gesture might be possible in its direction). In other words, crickets suffered through their association with social evils that—like the cricket fighting on which they were both parasitic and enabling—were distinguished by their cultural and historical depth, by what was understood to be their profound Chineseness.

Despite the uncompromising public line, party people I talked with were pragmatic about the anti-gambling campaigns. Journalists and scholars, they responded to the issue as engaged intellectuals, debating whether gambling was a product of poverty and would thus wither away as income increased (an argument shadowed by anxieties about escalating inequalities) and whether its recent resurgence was due to the explosive combination of higher disposable income and chronic underemployment resulting from the shuttering of state enterprises. Cricket fighting had a peculiar status in this debate. Thoroughly contaminated by gambling, it was also the source of a new and highly valued commodity: traditional culture. With the flush of money and a giddy sense of a physical world disappearing before their eyes, a new nostalgia seemed to be gripping the burgeoning urban middle class. New value was being conferred on vernacular architecture, classical painting, antique ceramics, scholars' rocks, teahouses, and other material histories. One sign was the vigorous trade in counterfeit imperial antiques for the domestic market. If there was ever a moment to promote those elevating elements of cricket fighting to which Dr. Li had devoted so much of his life, this was it.

We were surrounded by abundance. The delicious sixteen-course lunch prepared by Dr. Li's wife and daughter sat mostly uneaten. Dr. Li told us about his scheme to promote development in Henan Province by helping local farmers enter the Shanghai cricket market in competition with traders from Shandong, Anhui, and elsewhere. He was spending significant sums of his own money on this project and investing a great deal of his considerable energy, even traveling to the countryside to donate equipment and teach villagers how to distinguish among different insect species. The village he was working with was on the same latitude as Ninyang, and he had every reason to expect its crickets to be as strong as Shandong's. The pilot project had produced promising results. It was now only a question of convincing the buying public.

I wondered how the market in crickets could survive without gambling cash. I thought of all those men at Boss Xun's casino, the intense gazes, the sudden silence, the blur of crickets under the lights, the explosive laughter. I thought how, despite all its evident dangers, it is gambling—with its illicit pleasures, its secure masculinity, its justification of obsession, its profound cultural rooting, its incentive to commodification, and its underwriting of an entire informal economy—that has kept cricket fighting alive, and it is Boss Xun and his associates who, like it or not, are the guardians of this world and its dynamic traditions.

Gambling isn't just economic, I said. There's a culture of gambling, and a sociality, and a living history, too, of gambling on anything, not only on crickets—though crickets are especially fantastic for this! Gambling is as much "traditional culture" as cricket raising. Even Jia Sidao was a gambler! To which Dr. Li replied evenly that the government's target was not gambling itself but the social problems it generated. Anyway, he could never gamble no matter how exciting it might be. How could he take his friends' money? Such behavior was inappropriate for a scholar. And look, he said, the problem is not small gambling, a few coins here and there to spice up a game. The problem is when people wager their house, their possessions, gamble away their lives. Of course, we could never eradicate something so deep in society. But over time, by example, an alternative could grow. And he sketched a vision of a future Shanghai in which a cricket fight was much like a cross between a sports tournament and a pet show—much like the world of Japanese stag and rhinoceros beetles, in fact—a world in which restrained but enthusiastic people, young and old, studied and collected, formed clubs and shared knowledge. He was already promoting such events, he said, and they were attracting his students from Jiao Tong University.

And much later, long after lunch was over, after I had learned so much and enjoyed such kind hospitality, after most of the other guests had left, after we had talked for several hours about his project in Henan (crickets can help those people escape their poverty, he had said), about his idea of reforming cricket classification (it's too complicated even for the experts, he had said with much amusement), and about his belief that far from dying out (as all my other insect friends thought it was), cricket culture was in fact thriving among the young, after the long journey home across this ever-growing city, and after Li Jun had quizzed me up and down on the bus to the metro station, only then, back in my downtown hotel room, with its view across the sparkling cityscape, did Michael and I reconstruct the day's conversations and—remember that by now we both felt ourselves to be so deep in the world of Shanghai cricket fighting and were both somehow so invested in its realness—he said, and I had to agree, that although he had great respect for Professor Li, this idea of reforming cricket culture through example would lead to two types of cricket fighting: one would be elite, aboveground, and organized around well-funded official championships; the other would be underground and illegal, it would involve gambling, it would continue to be treated with fear and disdain, and it would have better crickets, better matches, and more excitement. And, Michael said, he thought that Dr. Li and his friends understood this, that they were far from naïve. And, he continued in that wise and generous way of his, that was okay. They just want their world, he said, and that's not necessarily such a bad thing.

7.

Centuries before anyone thought of placing crickets in pots and provoking them to fight with yard grass, their evocative singing and their presence in the home cast an annual blow against loneliness and gave them a special place in Chinese life. In this poem from *Shijing* (*The Book of Songs*), an anthology compiled around 3,000 years ago, it is the cricket that seeks out human company and finds its way into the intimate heart of the household:

> It is in the wild in the seventh month,
> Under the eaves in the eighth month,
> In the house in the ninth month,
> and under my bed in the tenth month.[23]

There is a deep, deep history of cricket friends—people who become friends through crickets and crickets who themselves become friends with people. It wasn't only Xiao Fu who told me how his crickets were his friends and how he tries to make them happy, how he can tell when they are happy and how they can tell that he cares, how, as Jia Sidao suggests, he chews sesame seeds before feeding them to his insects just as mothers sometimes chew their babies' food before feeding it to them. But crickets are friends, not babies. And that is something cricket lovers (unlike some pet lovers) are unlikely to forget. Because, as well as the Five Virtues, they have the Three Reversals.

You remember that the Five Virtues show the similarities between crickets and people? They are five classical qualities (loyalty, courage, trustworthiness, and so on), exemplary virtues that can be found in ancient heroes and toward which ordinary people (like you and I) can aspire. The Five Virtues reveal a deep ontological connection between people and crickets, a shared being in the world that forms the basis for the attachments and identifications that, along with gambling, have kept cricket fighting alive for so many centuries. The Three Reversals recognize the complementary reality: they acknowledge the definitive difference between crickets and people.

The First Reversal: A defeated cricket will not protest the outcome of a fight; he will simply leave the arena without bluster or complaint.

The Second Reversal: A cricket requires sex before a fight and performs better for the stimulation it provides; rather than having an enervating effect on athletic performance (as, according to this reversal, it does in men), pregame sex among crickets promotes physical prowess, mental focus, and a fighting spirit.

The Third Reversal: Crickets have sex with the female on the male's back, a position functionally impossible for people (without complicated equipment). Moreover, as the entomologist L. W. Simmons points out in what we might think of as a decisive commentary on the Third Reversal, "Since the female must actively mount a courting male there is little if any opportunity for forced matings by males."[24]

Like the Virtues, the Reversals are both empirical and symbolic, derived from close observation and pointed at things bigger than themselves. Psychological, physiological, and anatomical—they are systematic, comprehensive, and economical. When taken together, the Virtues and the Reversals offer a way of forming relationships with other beings that accepts that they are both like and unlike ourselves, not in some generalized abstract way, but in quite particular respects that provide grounds for connections and empathies as well as points of utter disconnection. I don't think it matters whether you're committed to crickets through gambling or you're committed to ending gambling in the name of a higher culture. I think the Virtues, the Reversals, the Flaws, the Taboos, and all the other entryways into the world of cricket fighting take you to a place governed by the laws of us/not us, where similarity/ difference simply persists as a fact of existence and does not require res- olution. I think this is just as it should be, even if there is little else that can be relied on to persist right now in Shanghai.

The last time I saw Boss Xun, he invited me to travel with him to Shandong next year. We would spend two weeks there collecting crick- ets, he said. He knew everyone and had excellent relations with the local authorities. His offer tugged at me strongly. It would be good to experi- ence the happy times once more. It would be good to be around cricket friends, human and insect, again. It would be good to live, just for a while, in that space of acceptance where things are simultaneously one thing and another. Michael was enthusiastic too. Perhaps, he said, we could spend the entire season with the crickets. That, we agreed, would really be something to come back for.

Heads and How to Use Them

1.

I missed the crickets. I missed their friends. I opened *The New York Times* and missed them even more.

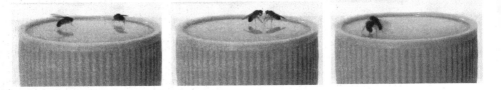

Flies, fruit flies, *Drosophila melanogaster,* the experimental animal par excellence, arguably more important even than rats or mice in the history of modern science. These haunting video stills were shot in 2006 in a neuroscience lab in southern California. The flies are fighting, and the U.S. government—channeling its money through the National Science Foundation—is betting on the winners.[1] The arena is a telegenic blue.

Herman A. Dierick and Ralph J. Greenspan, lead researchers at the Neurosciences Institute in San Diego, are breeding fruit flies for aggression. Flies, they tell Nicholas Wade of the *Times,* are militantly territorial in the wild but lose their edge in captivity. Professors Dierick and Greenspan fill pots with fly food and encourage individual males to defend them. They call this the "arena assay." They rank the flies on an "aggression profile" based on four criteria: the frequency of fighting, the rapidity with which the animals engage, the amount of time a pair spends in combat, and the fervor of the battle ("the number of high-intensity elements such as holding or tossing").

Dierick, Greenspan, and their colleagues separate the most belligerent fighters to use as breeding stock. After twenty-one generations, they report aggression-profile differences of more than thirtyfold compared with their control population of standard laboratory flies. "Because aggression levels are likely to be strongly influenced by the brain," they decapitate generation 21. They grind the heads. They want to know if genes expressed in the fighters' brains can be correlated with the newly aggressive behavior. "Dr. Greenspan said an understanding of how genes set up circuits to govern behavior would be of broad significance in understanding what makes either flies or people tick," writes Wade.[2]

2.

Fruit flies are well suited to the experimental life. Perhaps too well. They breed fast (in ten days, a female can complete her reproductive cycle and produce 400 or even 1,000 offspring). They have a relatively simple genetic structure (only four to seven chromosomes). And like every other organism, they mutate.

In 1910, the Columbia University geneticist Thomas Hunt Morgan stumbled on the capacity of *Drosophila* to produce startlingly visible mutations—and to produce them in quantity. Almost at once, fruit flies were no longer just minor annoyances that breezed in through the open summer windows in upper Manhattan, nosed around, and stayed or left. They were "fellow laborers," as their biographer Robert Kohler puts it.[3] Morgan's lab soon became their lab (the internationally famous Fly Room), and Morgan and his colleagues soon became their scientists (they called themselves fly people and drosophilists).

Very rapidly, the fruit fly became a fixture of genetics laboratories worldwide. Indeed, writes Kohler, without its capacity to act as "a biological breeder reactor" and produce enormous quantities of mutants, we might still be awaiting the arrival of modern genetics.[4]

In those early years, as Morgan and his fly people incorporated *Drosophila* into their experimental work, they found themselves struggling to keep up with its prodigious ability to produce mutations. They were overwhelmed by, swamped by, mutants. Such a quantity of new data demanded a new experimental method, one characterized by high-

volume efficiency, and mass gene mapping rapidly took shape as the new signature of genetic research. In turn, the constraints of the new method demanded a new fly, a consistent fly that could be compared to other flies with confidence. It required an animal free of the high natural variability of the nonlaboratory population, an animal in which all observed variation would be unmistakably a product of experimental mutation, "The little fly," writes Kohler, was "redesigned and reconstructed into a new kind of laboratory instrument, a living analogue of microscopes, galvanometers, or analytical reagents."[5]

A fly was born. A novel animal, so long as it could be prevented from combining with its nonstandard relatives. The researchers sought parental material in the most desirable mutants, the ones that were robust, keen to mate, fecund, and easily distinguishable from those other *Drosophila* buzzing busily beyond the Fly Room. These were also, Morgan noted, the ones that were "free from such bad habits as getting drowned, or stuck in the food, or refusing to be emptied from the culture bottle, etc., which alienate the affections of the experimenter."[6]

The new fly was cooperative, amenable to experiment, attuned to the production of precise, numerical data. Unlike its increasingly distant cousins outside the lab, who took to the air only at dawn and dusk, it was active all day long and bred around the clock. It was mass-produced to produce experiments in mass. By the best estimates, in creating the genetic map of the standard fly between 1919 and 1923, Morgan and his colleagues "etherized, examined, sorted, and processed" between 13 million and 20 million of them.[7] And in the midst of such attention to numbers, the enormous imprecision of that figure says as much about the animal's status as does the enormous figure itself.

You might argue that by entering the laboratory, the fruit fly guaranteed itself a life of ease and plenty. No more foraging for food or dodging predators, no more vulnerable larvae. Up to that moment, along with dogs, rats, cockroaches, and a few other household familiars, the fly had been an opportunist, a companion animal sharing human history, finding a home alongside and among us, neither fully wild nor truly domesticated (*commensal* might be a good term), eating where we ate, thriving where we thrived, and no doubt surviving where we failed.

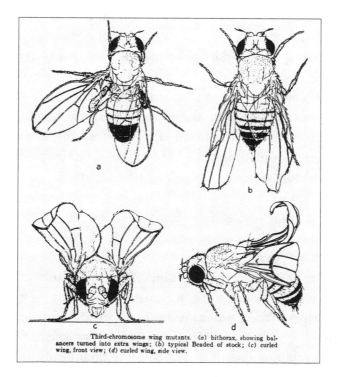

Third-chromosome wing mutants. (*a*) bithorax, showing balancers turned into extra wings; (*b*) typical Beaded of stock; (*c*) curled wing, front view; (*d*) curled wing, side view.

But laboratory life isn't much of a bargain. Countless billions of *Drosophila* have been subjected to induced mutations since Morgan's day. As Cornelia Hesse-Honegger witnessed, they grow too many body parts—or too few—and they grow them in the wrong shapes and in the wrong places (legs from their eyes, legs from their legs—you know how it goes). With a little help, they develop Huntington's, Parkinson's, and Alzheimer's diseases. They experience sleep and memory disorders. They get addicted to ethanol, nicotine, and cocaine. In short, as Cornelia realized, they not only bear the burden of our dreams of health and longevity, but they also assume the task of living out our nightmares.

3.

As the industrial fruit fly became more standardized, as it changed and grew apart from its unfettered cousins, and as—at the same time—it became more and more a product of the Columbia Fly Room, Morgan and the drosophilists came increasingly to admire and respect it, to regard it, as did the geneticist J.B.S. Haldane, as a "noble animal." Considering how much of themselves they'd put into creating it, how much time they were spending in its company, and how closely it was collaborating in their work, it isn't surprising that they personified the fly. But still, this intimate bundling of admiration and slaughter is telling and a little strange too, until one thinks of the ways in which nobility is often twinned with sacrifice and how all of them—flies and fly people—had embarked on a great voyage, the kind of scientific voyage of discovery that often includes suffering and self-sacrifice as integral components of its narrative.[8]

Maybe the limits of this little strangeness can help us understand a bigger strangeness too: how this fly can be so like us that it seems natural to think of it as our biological surrogate and simultaneously can be so entirely unlike us that it seems equally natural to subject it, without remorse or even concern, to unconstrained destruction.[9]

Those images of the fighters are disconcerting. So far from Shanghai, so unexpected, flies not crickets, such a blunt instrument, thrust into a culture of no culture, caught on video, losing their heads. In Shanghai, the lines are clear: there's ambiguity and attachment but no confusion. In San Diego, too, the lines are drawn, and there's also no confusion. But there's no ambiguity either. In San Diego, similarity is quantifiable. Even if the numbers aren't entirely solid yet, the facts still count: humans and fruit flies share many of the same genes; we share metabolic and signaling pathways at the cellular level, and, many neuroscientists are willing to argue, we overlap substantially in behavior and (what the scientists contend are) its molecular mechanisms.[10]

There are few niceties here. Animal experiments are blunt instruments, and the logic of the model organism is to separate body and soul, biology and consciousness, physics and metaphysics. It's easy when similarity and difference are not ranged on the same scale, when the basis for judging one is not the same as that for judging the other, when the criteria of similarity are genetic and the criteria of difference do not even require articulating: they are ancient, Aristotelian, now commonsensical, obvious, tedious to enumerate. Let's say only that these are insects, that their difference—and what it allows—is not in question. Elias Canetti understood this. Insects, he wrote, "are outlaws":

> The destruction of these tiny creatures is the only act of violence which remains unpunished even *within* us. Their blood does not stain our hands, for it does not remind us of our own. We never look into their glazing eyes. . . . They have never—at least not amongst us in the West—had the benefit of our growing, if not very effective, concern for life.[11]

Annemarie Mol, the Dutch philosopher and anthropologist, has studied the social life of atherosclerosis, a disease that narrows the arteries and inhibits circulation, first in the legs and eventually in the heart. Mol is an acute observer. She attends autopsies on atherosclerosis patients, many of whom died under hospital care. She notices that as the pathologists slice through the heavy flesh to enter the circulatory system, they often take a moment to cover the corpse's face with a piece of cloth.[12] Mol considers this gesture and concludes that there are in fact two corpses—one body but two beings. One being, the body being sliced, is the biological body, the scientific body, freed of the metaphysics of humanity and free to be dissected as a piece of meat, anonymous. The second being, the body being sliced, is the social body, a body with history, family, and friends, a body that has loved and suffered and demands modesty, respect, and attention. Mol's point is not to choose which of these bodies is lying on the autopsy table but to show that both bodies are present and that the simple gesture with the cloth—the covering of the face—is also a simple gesture of recognition.

Maybe for now that cloth can also mark the difference between the fighting crickets of Shanghai and the fighting flies of San Diego. Maybe the difference is ontological. In Shanghai, each cricket is many crickets, many beings with many histories and many friends are compressed into its limber frame. Around it, many dreams unfold, many projects rise and fall. If they are warriors, so are we. In San Diego, there is only the scientific fly, "an instrument, a living analogue of microscopes, galvanometers, [and] analytical reagents" whose purpose is clear, whose role is defined, whose death is not at issue, whose life is not at stake.

The Ineffable

1.

The most beautiful images of insects I have ever seen are in *Ignis*, the first volume of Joris Hoefnagel's natural history masterpiece *The Four Elements*, a compendium of the world's animals that this great Flemish miniaturist completed in 1582.[1]

Painted in delicate but still-vibrant gouache on seventy-eight vellum pages only five and five eighth inches high by seven and one quarter inches wide, many of Hoefnagel's insects sit poised, on the point of motion, as if holding their breath, their shadows appearing almost to flicker on the featureless white ground. Others fly within the simple gold border that bounds them like a magic circle. Still others, spiders, dangle from the frame. Sometimes they seem to acknowledge one another, sometimes not. Sometimes they touch, most often not. Sometimes they seem so close, so *present* in the viewer's time and space, that as the pages fell open in the National Gallery of Art in Washington, D.C., where Greg Jecmen, curator of old master prints and drawings, was showing me the precious volume, I caught my breath in involuntary wonder.

It felt odd to be surprised like that. For just a second, I let myself fancy that mine was the same sharp gasp as that of Hoefnagel's sixteenth-century viewer, someone for whom (it is likely) insects were lowly and loathsome, still buried at the foot of an Aristotelian natural order that held them firmly in the thick darkness of excrement and decay, unworthy of contemplation, until—and surely this was Hoefnagel's intent—the page fell back to reveal their astonishing perfection.

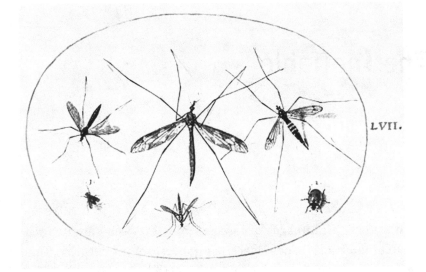

2.

"In minimis tota es." That's how the London physician Thomas Moffett puts it in his *Insectorum sive minimorum animalium theatrum,* an encyclopedic study of insect life and lore conceived and written in the same years as *The Four Elements,* although not published until 1634.[2] Moffett's insects are exemplary in many large ways. They are industrious; they are thrifty; they demonstrate good governance, respect for the elderly, and devotion to their offspring. Their metamorphosis is a resurrection, not merely a transformation. Their wondrousness stimulates piety. Their tiny perfection leads us to cry out, "How wonderful are thy works, O Lord!"[3]

The *Theatrum* was the second great compendium devoted to insects. The first was *De animalibus insectis libri septem,* published in 1602 by the prominent Bolognese naturalist and collector Ulisse Aldrovandi, a volume of such authority and ambition that it opened the door through which insects would eventually find their way into academic natural history.[4] Both texts followed in the wake of *Ignis,* making Hoefnagel's not only "one of the founding monuments of entomology" but also the first book of any type devoted to insects "as a separate kingdom rather than [as] a group appended to other major classes of animals."[5] All three books formed part of a continent-spanning project of early-modern natural history, a project fueled and provisioned by New World exploration and the expansion of maritime and overland trade. Far-reaching networks of correspondence and perilous travel linked scholars, merchants, and patrons—often with overlapping functions—to Prague, Frankfurt, Rome, and other centers of late-Renaissance learning.

It wasn't only self-justification that provoked Moffett's insistence that the greatest was contained even in the meanest. He was also appealing to a widely held Platonistic cosmology, in which the relationship between small and large was conceived as that between microcosm and macrocosm, with each being containing within it a seed of the entire cosmos.[6] How well this notion lent itself to the study of insects! Their miniature world astonished not simply by the scale of its infinitely intricate social, biological, and symbolic life but, above all, by the contrast between the density of activity and meaning compressed into such physical tininess and the vastness of the cosmos to which it so unerringly but so mysteriously corresponded. Where better to locate the structure of the cosmos than in its most compact form? Given that the paradoxical was often a defining trait of the wondrous, Moffett could convincingly argue that the miniature was saturated by the immensity of the Divine to an even greater extent than were nature's more conspicuous phenomena. Such micro/macrocosmic reasoning was so well established in the humanist circles to which these naturalists belonged that it was even the principle on which Hoefnagel's final patron, the Holy Roman Emperor Rudolf II, organized his Prague cabinet of curiosities, the greatest *Kunstkammer* in Europe and the eventual home of *The Four Elements.*[7]

Yet these were complex impulses. While Moffett, Hoefnagel, and Aldrovandi were extending the reach of piety to insects, they were also developing an observational practice that, as the art historian Thomas DaCosta Kaufmann writes, was leading to "the investigation of matter and of the processes of the natural world considered *as ends in themselves.*"[8] And Hoefnagel was also perfecting a complementary painting practice, which would establish him as a crucial figure in the development of the secular still life. Like others in his circle of Netherlandish humanists, Hoefnagel appears to have embraced Neostoicism, political moderation, and confessional indifference, making a self-conscious stand against intolerance at a time of the religious violence that saw his home city of Antwerp sacked by Spanish soldiers, his merchant family dispersed, and he himself consigned to a peripatetic future that would lead to Munich, Frankfurt, Prague, and finally Venice.

Nonetheless, it would be a mistake to imagine Hoefnagel in modern terms as a secular scientific illustrator. His work was governed by an ethic that drew deeply on the religious, albeit one motivated by an ecumenical striving for a peaceful resolution of the post-Reformation divisions in the Christian church.[9] Indeed, Hoefnagel provided most of his paintings in *The Four Elements* with biblical aphorisms lauding divine providence and design. However, this piety is also not easily translated into present-day terms. Firm distinctions among sacred, secular, and what might now count as the domain of the occult were by no means settled.[10] These were critical decades in the formation of modern modes of investigation, yet they were also decades in which esoteric traditions flourished among European intellectuals and in which revelation of the deep systematic ordering of the world was a guiding principle of natural philosophy and the arts it generated. Early-modern scholars deployed occult experiment, numerology, the symbolics of emblems, and a broad range of other forms of magic to close the gap between "the observation of appearance and the intuition of an underlying reality" and thus make nature's secrets visible.[11]

The difference of insects—so small, so alien in appearance, so prodigious in their reproductive capacities—was profound and troubling. It placed them as simultaneously natural, that is, unexceptional and God-given, *and* on the borders of the inexplicable. Perhaps this paradoxical nature helps explain why insects became such popular objects of inquiry at this time, and perhaps it also explains why studies of them in this period reveal so many of the tensions present in natural philosophical practice. Consider, for example, Francis Bacon's deeply Aristotelian account of "vivification"—reproduction—in *Sylva sylvarum* (1627), the collection of natural history observations on which he was working at the time of his death. Bacon, widely—if perhaps too easily—regarded as the founder of empirical philosophy, devotes much of the seventh section of his book to insects, "*Creatures bred of* Putrefaction," because, as he says, echoing Moffett, "the *Nature* of *Things* is commonly better perceived, in small, than in Great."

The "*Contemplation* . . . [of insects] hath many *Excellent Fruits*," writes Bacon:

> First, in *Disclosing* the *Original* of *Vivification*. Secondly, in *Disclosing* the *Original* of *Figuration*. Thirdly, in Disclosing many things in the nature of *Perfect* Creatures, which in them lie more hidden. And, Fourthly, in *Traducing*, by way of *Operation*, some *Observations* on the *Insecta*, to work *Effects* upon *Perfect Creatures*.[12]

He has little interest in insects in themselves. Their value lies in what they reveal about higher creatures. Even in this short passage, his detachment from the object of study is radically at odds with Hoefnagel's intimacy. Yet the tension that insects manifest between difference and sameness in their status as microcosms of nature writ large allows Bacon to generalize as to the character of fundamental physiological processes common to all beings. This willingness to take insects seriously as objects of study while reinforcing their pejorative association with waste and imperfection (in the Aristotelian sense of spontaneous generation) indicates the obstacles faced by Moffett, Hoefnagel, and their insect-loving colleagues. The struggle would continue right through the eighteenth century, dogging the first generations of professional entomologists, Enlightenment savants such as Jan Swammerdam and René-Antoine Ferchault de Réaumur, who, despite their scientific eminence, faced ridicule for the disproportion between the status of their scholarly attention and that of its humble object.[13]

Moffett's strategy in these circumstances was the appeal to wonder through facticity, the heaping of fact upon fact, anecdote upon anecdote, observation upon observation, example upon example, impressing through the weight of evidence, understanding that the empirical was the source of the wondrous rather than, as Bacon might have preferred, its antidote. Again and again, in language of striking everydayness, Moffett expresses his astonishment at the marvels of the insect world. In a characteristic moment (and just before advising the use of a hand lens), he makes what must have seemed an incredible assertion, at least to those unfamiliar with Pliny, and he does so through a vocabulary of homespun analogy that emphasizes that the ubiquity of his subjects is also part of their miraculousness. "Thou shalt finde in the body of Bees," he writes with obvious excitement, "a little bottle which is the receptacle of Honey sucked from flowers, and their legs loaded with Bitumen which sticks fast to make wax."[14]

Like Moffett's, Hoefnagel's insects are at one and the same time familiar and unprecedented. The more time I spend with *Ignis,* the clearer it becomes that he focused all his substantial powers on turning these creatures into beings that are, quite literally, wonderful. Under his hand, beetles, moths, crickets, ants, butterflies, dragonflies, a mosquito, three mosquito hawks, a rather hairy black caterpillar, a ladybug, many bees, numerous spiders (of varying size and appearance), and even some wood lice are transformed into subjects and agents of the late-Renaissance capacity for wonder, a very particular emotional sense, a "cognitive passion" in which feeling and knowing were combined and cultivated.[15] This sixteenth-century wonder was a type of faculty, the possession of which was itself the mark of the cultivated person.

The historians Lorraine Daston and Katharine Park have described wonders—that is, the objects that provoked the response of wonder—as "the aristocracy of natural phenomena." The identification and collection of wondrous objects in cabinets of curiosity were central to the self-definition of the European cultural elite.[16] Within a few decades, objects once wondrous would become vulgar and undesirable, too gaudy and too unreliably emotional to satisfy the rising imperatives of rational discrimination.[17] But in Hoefnagel's day, people sought out wonders in objects of all kinds that tied the transcendent to the earthly, and they found them as readily in nature as in those exceptional human-made imitations (like Hoefnagel's insects) that revealed the bonds between people and the natural world with which they were so deeply entwined. Through the incitement of wonder, wondrous objects led to philosophical reflection and from there to true knowledge, a point that could be underlined by direct citation from Aristotle.[18]

At first, Hoefnagel's images tugged at me with what I took to be their tenderness, so sensitively wrought, so decorative. But once I recovered from my gasp as the page fell open, I began to wonder—in that rather disconnected, secular, modern way—if that response wasn't merely a product of my schooling in the contemporary aesthetics of biodiversity and its associated ethic of conservation and protection. Hoefnagel, I began to recognize, was doing something else. He was demanding that I not only see, look at, and observe the insects but that I do so with entirely new eyes, that I meet difference and dwell in it, that I discover grounds for empathy in the encounter with these beings' biological and social marginality. I began to understand that he wanted me eye to eye with these insects, as close as could be, in direct and transformative confrontation.

3.

As its title makes clear, *The Four Elements* presents the animals of the world in four groups. Each group is in its own volume, each is tied to its particular element, and each element is filled with symbolic meaning. Hoefnagel grounds the quadrupeds and reptiles on earth, submerges the fish and mollusks in water, frees the birds and amphibians to the air, and from the outset—*Ignis* is the first volume—signals his intention to surprise by associating fire, *ignis,* not with the salamander (which was believed to pass through flames unscathed) but with the "*animalia rationalia et insecta,*" a new category all his own that brings insects together with human prodigies, two forms of the marginal and marvelous.

Though with less fidelity than Bacon, Hoefnagel, too, reached back to Aristotle for his zoology. But perhaps this is a misleading way of putting it, given how widespread was the enmeshing of early-modern European natural philosophy in Aristotelian thought.[19] Central elements of Aristotle's biology persisted in Europe with little challenge through the mid-eighteenth century and beyond, long after the dismantling of the structural cosmology with which Aristotelianism is centrally identified. And specifically in terms of emerging entomology, it would be impossible to overestimate the significance of the observations and taxonomies developed by Aristotle in *Historia animalium* (*History of Animals*), *De partibus animalium* (*On Parts of Animals*), and *De generatione animalium* (*On the Generation of Animals*), continued by his student Theophrastus in his work on plant-insect interactions, and collected and extended by

Pliny in book XII of *Naturalis historia* (*Natural History*). With the introduction of the taxonomic class he called the *entoma*—animals with
notches or segments—Aristotle was the first to make systematic attempts
to group and describe the insects.[20] Prior to that, only those insects considered dangerous or useful—principally in medical terms—had figured
as objects of natural historical attention.

Aristotle derived his classificatory characters from observed morphology, adding layers of differentiating features to build up the higher
taxa.[21] Yet unlike Linnaeus, whose attention to distinguishing characteristics was rigorously morphological, Aristotle looked to the soul of the
animal—that is, to its vital functions—rather than to its body, for defining characters. And although he did dichotomize on occasion—into
winged and wingless insects, for example—he sought distinction on the
principle of unique constellations of features rather than in binary oppo-
sitions. Moreover, his taxonomy and the entire ontology from which it
derived were underwritten by the cosmological conviction that nature
was motivated by a teleology embodied in an ascending hierarchy of perfection, at the terrestrial summit of which, predictably enough, was the
human male. As G.E.R. Lloyd succinctly explains, the edifice presup-
posed a close relationship among an animal's humoral qualities, its
mode of reproduction, and its degree of perfection. "Aristotle," Lloyd
writes, "differentiates groups of animals by their faculties of sensation,
their means of locomotion, their methods of reproduction. These capacities are, in his view, closely correlated with certain primary qualities, the
heat, coldness, dryness and wetness of the animal. Thus the viviparous
animals, the ovoviviparous ones, the two main divisions of ovipara
(those that produce perfect, and those that have imperfect, eggs) and the
larvae-producing animals are arranged in a descending order of 'perfection,' where the hotter, and wetter, the animal the more perfect it is."[22]

Cold and dry, the *entoma* form one of the four genera of bloodless animals. Some of them are winged; all have more than four feet; all possess
sight, smell, and taste; some have hearing. Most significantly, as Lloyd
indicates, the *entoma* reproduce by spontaneous generation, the most
imperfect of the four methods that Aristotle identifies. Houseflies, for
example, arise from manure, as do fleas; lice originate in flesh; worms
grow from old snow; moths come from dry and dusty wool; others emerge

from dew, mud, wood, plants, and animal hair. The examples demonstrate Aristotle's close observation—without the benefit of lenses—and the application of a somewhat dogmatic theoretical apparatus. These little animals have sex, as he witnesses, but the offspring are always an inferior, more imperfect organism: the progeny of flies and of butterflies, for example, are tiny worms.[23] And without evolution, there can be no improvement, no upward progress from excrement to ether. In every respect, then, Aristotle's insects (with the exception of the highly regarded bees) are as far from perfection as is possible for animal beings.[24]

Ignis was in rebellion against this Aristotelian order. Where earlier artists had focused on the most emblematic of the insects—the stag beetle, the bee, the grasshopper—or had worked local species into illuminated texts to commemorate pilgrimages, Hoefnagel used *Ignis* to revise their standing as a class.[25] By granting them such prominence and cohesion and by implicitly maintaining equivalence across the group—lavishing as much attention on the pestilential mosquito and the prosaic wood louse as on the industrious bee—Hoefnagel insisted on the value of all the creatures known to him as *insecta*.

To establish his case, he turned to physical principles that owed much to Aristotle. The cosmos that held sway in Renaissance Europe was divided into two realms: above, filled with the perfect and incorruptible ether, which moved in perfect and uniform motion, were the celestial heavens; below, abutting the lunar sphere, lay the terrestrial realm, constant only in its flux, composed of fire, earth, air, and water, the four types of terrestrial matter. Of those four elements, it was fire, the outermost surface of the terrestrial region, that occupied the most elevated natural place. Unimpeded, fiery bodies would always rise naturally toward the celestial realm, and in this sense they were closest to perfection.[26] By attaching his insects to fire, Hoefnagel fused them to the most exceptional element, the element associated with generation and dematerialization, the most protean, the most dynamic, the most unfathomable, and in early-modern Europe, the most wondrous. And crucially, in contrast to the logic of the other volumes of *The Four Elements*, fire is not the medium in which the insects live. Instead, it represents the properties they embody.[27]

4.

Rather than insects, though, the opening folio of *Ignis* depicts a human couple. The strange man with the penetrating gaze, whose wife rests her hand on his shoulder in a protective gesture, is Pedro González, the first of Hoefnagel's *animalia rationalia*.

Encountered on Tenerife and brought back to France, where he received a humanist education at court, González, as Hoefnagel's inscription relates (and there is other historical documentation, too), was a man of letters well known in European society. His dress and demeanor indicate considerable cultivation, but his congenital hirsutism, as well as that of his similarly somber children, depicted in the following folio, places him in a tradition of wildness, a wildness further suggested by the blasted landscape. The landscape accentuates the couple's solitude, and the golden circle within which they, too, are enclosed seems an ironic comment on their civilized careers. Imprisoned as they are by physical accident and perverse celebrity, any doubt as to their aloneness is dispelled by the verse from the book of Job beneath the portrait: "Man born of woman, living briefly, a life replete with many miseries."[28]

But what kind of man? González and his children—as well as the projected, though never painted, giant and dwarf of folio 3—are the *animalia rationalia*, the only humans (along with González's wife) in the entire *Four Elements*. Hovering on the edge of humanity, they are more wondrous still for remaining within its fold, bringing together rationality (which defines the human) and animality (against which the human is defined), unsettling the very idea of natural order. Physically, they are instantly recognizable as members of the races of wild men and monsters that populate the outer shores of the Renaissance imagination, beasts rather than men, the opposites of men through which we come to understand what men really are. Culturally, though, there can be no question that González is human; indeed, as Hoefnagel's inscription makes clear, that he is a humanist. And in this decisive sense, his outsideness poses a profound challenge to the very idea of a humanity defined by its capacity to reason, a challenge that echoes that posed in the same years by Montaigne in his essay "On Cannibals," in which it is the encounter with native Brazilians at the French court that throws into question the superiority of European civility.[29]

The exotic problem of the Gonzalez family was widely recognized at the time. Important portraits were commissioned. Prominent physicians were consulted. Aldrovandi himself examined the family and included images of them in his *Monstrorum historia*.[30] But of all the commentaries, Hoefnagel's goes furthest. If these are victims, their sad situation is an indictment of intolerance, and in being invited to see them in this way, we are also, as the art historian Lee Hendrix suggests, reminded of the intolerance sweeping Europe that made a victim and a refugee of Hoefnagel himself.[31] If these are victims, then, like the victims of religious persecution, they are radically misunderstood. And these victims—and perhaps all the victims—are unmistakably wondrous. Imbued with fire, they rise above their earthly condition to soar naturally toward the celestial sphere. It is a powerful image, and it has stayed with me since that day at the National Gallery of Art in Washington, D.C. The strange man whose penetrating gaze is fixed unflinchingly on the viewer. The sad but self-possessed woman who looks neither at her husband nor at the artist but instead stares with blank resignation into an undefined distance and who is perhaps the most haunting figure of all: the one who chooses to transgress and thereby elects to suffer, the one positioned to mediate between the fully human and the *animalia rationalia*, the one about whom nothing is written, the one whose name and biography don't appear to have been recorded.

Why does Hoefnagel bring the González family together with the *insecta* in this novel order of nature? Or more precisely, why does he use these human prodigies to frame and preface his book of insects? The answer must lie in what these beings share: a wondrousness brutally misconceived as imperfection, a common existence at the margins of nature. If González stands on the borders of humanity, insects stand both at the edge of nature and on the lip of the visible. On the threshold of hidden truths, they point beyond themselves, portals to the deep unknown, taking us—in this age before the microscope—"on an optical voyage into uncharted terrain."[32]

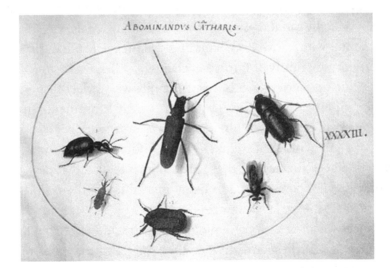

5.

It took me a while to recognize *Ignis* as a form of what Sir James Frazer, the encyclopedist of early anthropology, called homoeopathic magic, that form of sympathetic magic based on the law of similarity, in which like begets like.[33] I already knew that the work of the early-modern natural philosopher was to use the *ars magica* to reach through that gap between the visible and the intuited universe.[34] So why was I so slow to see that *Ignis* and its insects were themselves magical objects?

Perhaps it was that none of Frazer's innumerable examples— refracted as they are through the imperial prism of early-twentieth-century social science[35]—appeared to correspond. Hoefnagel didn't seem much like the "Ojebway Indian" who works his evil with "a little wooden image of his enemy and runs a needle into its head or heart." Nor did he remind me of the "Peruvian Indians [who] molded images of fat mixed with grain to imitate the persons whom they disliked or feared, and then burned the effigy on the road where the intended victim was to pass."[36] Nor were Hoefnagel's so precisely realized insects reminiscent of these fetishes of wood and fat whose morphological likeness to their victims seems in Frazer's account to be casually and abstractly gestural, perhaps even irrelevant.

Although he has his doubts, Frazer allows that when intentionality is clearly evident, the term "mimetic magic" may be permissible. This should have alerted me, or at least would have if I hadn't been thinking of imitation as ruled by tragedy, of mimicry as always haunted by the repetition of its failure to become its object. I could still think of Hoefnagel as some sort of (very-ahead-of-his-time) Surrealist and of his mimetic method as a tactic of disruption calculated to destabilize his viewer and produce the psychic conditions for revelation. But maybe there was more? Frazer's phrase reminded me of how, in his strange essay "On the Mimetic Faculty," Walter Benjamin argues that the aspiration is not in vain. In Benjamin's understanding of mimesis, there is no limit to the identification with the object made possible by the copy. Instead, in the words of anthropologist Michael Taussig, under the right circumstances, the object "passes from being outside to becoming inside. . . . Imitation becomes immanence."[37]

As were the insects it revealed, so was *Ignis* itself a wonder, its revelatory images the fruit of Hoefnagel's astonishing capacity to breathe life into his subjects. Even though, like most painters of the time, he based much of his work on other artists' representations, his was a celebrated ability to move beyond simple copying. In his hands, even Dürer's famous stag beetle was re-inspired and in its new aliveness took the viewer that much closer, tantalizingly closer, to the promise of whatever lay beyond.[38]

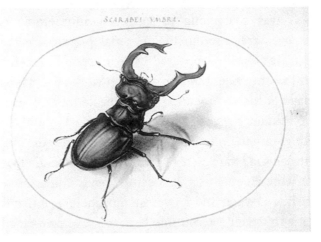

Try not to think of this copying as imitation. Think of it as philosophical art in the service of something greater and more mysterious. It expresses piety, of course—these are God's creatures—but also the associated desire to reach deeper, to cross the gap between representation and the real, between vellum, paint, and insect, between subject and object, between human and divine, between human and animal. Rather than producing a likeness of a being to act upon that being—as in Frazer's examples—Hoefnagel's likenesses aim to bring us to a point of identity with the being depicted. This is imitation striving for immanence and doing so through empathy—an empathy generated through wonder and a wonder created by an array of destabilizing tactics (those tactics that let me imagine Hoefnagel as an early-modern Surrealist).

Central to it all is the work of active viewing which Hoefnagel demands. It is impossible to pass lightly over his insects. Just as Pedro González locks us in his stare, holds our attention, and insists that we acknowledge him as subject (as person, as citizen, as topic, and as victim), so the detailed precision of Hoefnagel's insects draws us into their individuality and elicits the same type of concentrated focus on the being in itself as would a lens, pulling us into the mysterious vitality of animate nature.

The dramatic staging heightens the effect: the background, usually blank, offers both depth and surface (note the delicate shadowing) yet removes the distraction of earthly context, leaving the insects in an independent, featureless space, a space I think of as ontological rather than—as we might expect today—ecological or historical. Abruptly, and this is part of what provokes that sudden gasp, Hoefnagel draws us into the tiny creatures' scale. We become small, as if we have passed through his looking glass. Variations in the animals' size—from the teeniest flies to the most monstrous spiders—are startling, frightening, but also exciting. He emphasizes their movement, their sense of purpose, intimating a motivating intelligence. Such wonders demand humility. They confront us with the limits of our understanding and with the poverty of the normality in which we dwell. This encounter wrought by mimetic magic takes us further and further into a secret realm. Deeper and deeper, closer and closer, up against the limits of communication, up against the ineffable.

6.

High on its hill overlooking Los Angeles, the J. Paul Getty Museum and Research Institute holds another of Hoefnagel's masterpieces: the *Mira calligraphiae monumenta* (*Model Book of Calligraphy*), an illuminated writing book of rare beauty and sly wit. The original manuscript was inscribed by the master calligrapher Georg Bocskay from 1561 to 1562. Some thirty years later, at the request of Rudolf II, Hoefnagel began to illuminate the text, adorning Bocskay's work with fruit and flowers and with perfect little insects of all descriptions that climb over and around the intricate lettering, balance on serifs, slide down descenders, dart through flourishes, and nibble their way along crossbars, poking irreverent fun at Bocskay's ornate virtuosity as they demonstrate Hoefnagel's conviction that the visual image communicates on a plane inaccessible to the written text.[39]

Despite the airy touch of the *Mira calligraphiae*, Hoefnagel's belief in the capacity of the image to access the truly recondite is utterly serious. In this, he reminds me again of Walter Benjamin, who, similarly intent on transforming relations between people and the world in which they move, struggled to find words to paint his "dialectical images"—images that would seize life in all its contradictions and blast a hole through the world of appearances.[40] In the moment of danger in which Benjamin found himself as a Jew and a Marxist (albeit an idiosyncratic one) in pre–Second World War Europe, his faith in words rested in this ability to explode reality with the densely compressed image. A rather flimsy faith, we might think. But we would be wrong. Even if their power resides in their capacity to appropriate the image and even if the ability of the most daring of them to act on the world is frail and tentative, there is, in this idea, no barrier that the magic of words cannot breach.

Although their views on the relationship between word and image differ, I like to think that Hoefnagel and Benjamin would have understood each other's approach to the task of the philosopher. For both, inspired as they are by traditions of piety, the work of criticism is a work of revelation. For both, revelation involves a drastic and transformative disruption of the everyday. For both, the method of revelation is something we might call mimetic shock: a psychic disordering that is accomplished best in moments of supreme artistry.

The centuries have softened the power of Hoefnagel's insects. It is the arresting beauty of the images that strikes the viewer now, rather than the sudden vision of unanticipated difference. It didn't take me long to realize that the gasp that escaped my lips when Greg Jecmen turned the page as we sat together that morning in the National Gallery of Art was a gasp of awe at Hoefnagel's talent rather than a reaction to the fullness of the insects' presence—a quite different kind of interruption from the one I imagine Hoefnagel intended. I was deeply impressed by the perfection of his imitation of life but less astonished by the life itself. And I didn't at first recognize his mimesis as a magic designed to act upon the world. Perhaps, as Benjamin foresaw, familiarity with the reproduction has inured us to the magic of the original.[41]

But what a labor Hoefnagel set himself! Committed not simply to achieving perfection in representation but to capturing a deeper quality, something elusive and invisible that he knows is there and believes can be made apparent through the art of the copy. What kind of agony is this, working in miniature, striving not simply for realism but for a version of the real that is *so* real—more real even than the copy from which he is working—that it takes him beyond what he can see, takes him into the unknown inside, takes him across the species barrier to a place in which difference dissolves, to the immanence at the end of imitation.

Was he successful? Was his mimetic magic strong enough to jump the gap between representation and real, between vellum and paint and wondrous beings, between human and divine, between human and insect? Perhaps it's enough to recognize the possibility, the weight that beauty once contained. Perhaps. But I suspect it wasn't sufficient for Hoefnagel.

Greg turned another page, and we both gazed down at folio 54. Realizing that I hadn't noticed, he pointed to the unusually worn wings of the two lower dragonflies. They were *real*, he told me, *real wings* that Hoefnagel had detached from his real insect models and carefully, with a care we can only imagine, pasted on to his painting. I saw then that they looked different. Rubbed through and disintegrating, they were decayed, far less lifelike now than the delicately robust imitations he had painted on the central insect. There was, I knew, a tradition of attaching found objects to medieval manuscripts—badges, seashells, pressed flowers—as a sign of witnessing. The objects, relics of a kind, were proof of a visit to the pilgrimage site and tactile mnemonics with which to recall the

experience.[42] But this was something else. This was Hoefnagel staring at the failure of his desire, staring at the limits of representation, staring at the ineffable. I heard Moffett's exclamation—"How wonderful are thy works, O Lord!"—but less as celebration than lament. "How wonderful are thy works, O Lord," I heard Hoefnagel's echo, "How inadequate are my own!"

Jews

Antisemitism is exactly the same as delousing. Getting rid of lice is not a question of ideology. It is a matter of cleanliness. In just the same way, antisemitism, for us, has not been a question of ideology, but a matter of cleanliness, which now will soon have been dealt with. We shall soon be deloused. We have only 20,000 lice left, and then the matter is finished within the whole of Germany.

HEINRICH HIMMLER, April 24, 1943

1.

Traveling alone through a ravaged and hostile postwar central Europe, the narrator of Aharon Appelfeld's searing novel *The Iron Tracks* encounters a man on an empty train who unhesitatingly identifies him as a Jew.[1] But how could you tell? Siegelbaum asks, bewildered. It's nothing physical, the man replies matter-of-factly. It's your anxiety. You have the anxiety of the Jew. The anxiety of the guilty and the hunted. The anxiety of the degenerate. He might have added, You have the scuttling neurosis of the cockroach, the parasitic temerity of the louse. However many we killed, there were always some left. Now, wherever we see one, we know there are many more.

2.

"Antisemitism is exactly the same as delousing," said Heinrich Himmler.[2] And although at times he would strain for the apposite euphemism, the SS *Reichsführer* was famous for choosing his words with precision. Antisemitism is not *like* delousing, nor is it merely *a form of* delousing. It is *exactly the same as* delousing. Did he mean that Jews actually are lice? Or only that the same measures should be taken to eradicate both evils?

Himmler is a constant presence at the U.S. Holocaust Memorial Museum in Washington, D.C. Controlled and confident among his famous colleagues—Göring, Goebbels, the führer himself. The calm within the storm. Downstairs, when I visited in the summer of 2002, the museum had hung an exhibition by the painter and propagandist Arthur Szyk, student of medieval illumination, savage caricaturist, and activist for the Revisionists, the ascendant militarist wing of the Zionist movement.[3] Szyk captured the SS commander's clinical impassivity well.

In summer 1943, soon after the U.S. State Department had for the first time officially confirmed conservative reports of 2 million Jews killed by the Nazis, Szyk, exiled in New York and aggressively campaigning for an interventionist rescue policy, produced a drawing of characteristic clarity.[4] Himmler, Göring, Goebbels, and Hitler complain: "We're Running Short of Jews!" On the table, the Gestapo report: "2,000,000 Jews Executed." In the upper-right-hand corner: "To the memory of my darling mother, murdered by the Germans, somewhere in the Ghetto of Poland . . . Arthur Szyk." He was only guessing this last part, but he was right: his mother had already been herded onto the transport from Lodz to Chelmno.

A year later, at the end of 1944, with Majdanek already liberated, Szyk again drew his Nazi gang, this time for the cover of the Revisionist journal *The Answer*. The dead are present in skulls, bones, and tombstones etched with the names of the camps. The Nazi leaders, towering over the ruined landscape, are tattered and facing defeat; Goebbels, at the front, throws up his hands in disbelief and a kind of surrender as Ahasuerus, the Wandering Jew, passes through, grimly grasping the Torah, the emblem of collective survival. Where we see one, many lurk in the shadows. "An eternal people," as the magazine's caption says.

The Answer was the house journal of the Bergsonites, Revisionist militants in the United States who had thrown themselves into the task of publicizing the destruction of the European Jews. Szyk's drawing, used

THE

ANSWER

MAGAZINE

A NON-SECTARIAN APPROACH
TO THE PROBLEMS OF
THE HEBREW PEOPLE IN
EUROPE AND PALESTINE

COVER. Once again Arthur Szyk gives the
world a masterpiece of thought and art.
The powers of evil, gigantic though they
loom above the wandering Jew, cannot stop
him. Though they block his path with skulls
of his own dead, they cannot prevent the
Torah from infusing life into an eternal
people.

On he goes, though infinite the night,
And ghouls of blackness mercilessly stalking.

Dr. Jacob   Paul   Henry F.   Dr. Johan J.   Z. H.   November   15c
KLATZKIN   ELDRIDGE   PRINGLE   SMERTENKO   WACHSMAN   1944

prominently in the group's materials, displays his gift for distilling programmatic politics into complex yet visceral imagery. The Wandering
Jew—that enduring and ambivalent icon of antisemitism, who mocked
Christ on his progress to the cross and was condemned to roam the
earth until the Second Coming—had been reclaimed by Jewish artists,
and Szyk drew from at least two prominent versions. One—a late-
nineteenth-century image by Shmuel Hirszenberg in which a stripped
and panic-stricken Ahasuerus, victimized to the point of derangement,
flees the grisly horrors of the 1881 pogroms—circulated throughout Jewish Europe on postcards and posters. The second, a sculpture, is by
Alfred Nossig.

With its assertive response to suffering, Nossig's statue transforms
Hirszenberg's traumatized vision. It is an image of Jewishness that—in
an awkward irony that will soon become clear—fit well with Szyk's taste
for the heroic.[5]

Der ewige Jude.
Skulptur von Alfred Nossig.

3.

Lice are parasites (as are Jews). They suck our blood (as do Jews). They carry disease (as do Jews). They enter our most intimate parts (as do Jews). They cause us harm without our knowing it (as do Jews). They signify filth (as do Jews). They are everywhere (as are Jews). They are disgusting. There is no reason they should live.

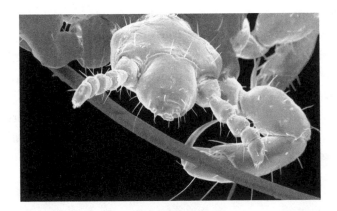

4.

Although the Nazis imposed the borders with unprecedented ferocity, they did not initiate the expulsion of the Jews from the kingdom of humanity. In early-modern France, for example, "since coition with a Jewess is *precisely the same* as if a man should copulate with a dog," Christians who had heterosexual sex with Jews could be prosecuted for the capital crime of sodomy and burned alive with their partners—"such persons in the eye of the law and our holy faith differ[ing] in no wise from beasts" (who were also subject to trial and execution).[6] In a minor key, long-standing German identifications of Jews with dogs (mongrels) and, sometimes, pigs, persisted through the Nazi era.[7]

More destructive—and more insinuating—was the association of the Jew with the shadowy figure of the parasite, a figure that infests the individual body, the population, and of course, the body politic, that does so in both obvious and unexpected ways, and that invites innovative interventions and controls.

Three streams converged in the Jewish parasite—modern anti-semitism, populist anti-capitalism, and the new social sciences (eugenics was one example)—streams that made sense of the world through the concepts and metaphors of biology. The historian Alex Bein tracked the figure of the parasite prior to its modern connection to race.[8] He found it in Greek comedy as a destitute person, a stock character who sparred wittily with host and guests intent on extracting humiliation in return for a meal. Bein then followed its entry into the European vernacular along with the early-modern humanist return to the classical texts. In this later incarnation, its comedic qualities flattened by the centuries, "parasite" reappeared as an expression of contempt for people who fawn on the rich and for people who profit without labor at the expense of those who sweat. It was in this moralistic form that the word was taken up by the eighteenth-century sciences: first botany, then zoology, and finally, fatally, by the sciences of man.

Bein argued that it was the physiocrats, liberal political economists of the mid-eighteenth century, who brought the parasite into European political philosophy. They sliced society neatly into three: the *classe pro-*

ductive of agriculturalists, the propertied class of landowners, and the unproductive *classe stérile,* made up primarily of merchants and manufacturers. It was, Bein argued, the introduction of the "parasitic" *classe stérile* into political discourse that would give antisemitism its populist base in anti-capitalism.

Parasites drain the lifeblood from the body politic. But in order for this commonplace to sustain violence, a decisive metamorphosis has to take place: a people must become vermin in fact as well as in metaphor.[9] "Every living being except Man can be killed but not murdered," writes Donna Haraway.[10] And indeed, somehow, people must be made as killable as animals. Drawing parallels between the genocides in Nazi Germany and Rwanda, the anthropologist Mahmood Mamdani talks about *race branding* ("whereby it [becomes] possible not only to set a group apart as an enemy, but also to exterminate it with an easy conscience").[11] "Ordinary" dehumanization of this type—"the Tutsi 'cockroaches' should know what will happen, they will disappear"[12]—requires two associations: the identification of a targeted group with a particular type of non-human life-form and the association of the being in question with adequately negative traits.

There is no doubt that this happened in the Holocaust. But something more happened, too. Explaining it is at the heart of understanding the fate of the Jews, who, after all, would be killed like insects—like lice, in fact. Literally like lice. Like Himmler's lice. With the same routinized indifference and, in vast numbers, with the same technologies.

5.

Alfred Nossig, the sculptor of that assertive Wandering Jew, was seventy-nine when he was arrested in the Warsaw Ghetto by the ZOB, the Jewish Fighting Organization, the underground group that would lead the iconic uprising. It was February 1943, one of those dead days of terror between the Gestapo's January incursion and the April revolt, and the details are confused. There was a secret trial, a conviction for treason, and a summary execution. After Nossig's death, an incriminating document, a report he had prepared for the Germans on the impact of their routed action, was found in his pocket, or perhaps in the desk drawer of his apartment, or perhaps not at all. No one could say for sure, and by that point it didn't really matter.

Nossig was not only a sculptor. He was also a well-known writer of philosophical and political treatises, a poet, playwright, and literary critic, the author of an opera libretto, a journalist, a diplomat, a polymath trained in law and economics (in Lvov), philosophy (in Zürich), and medicine (in Vienna), and as the historian of Zionism Shmuel Almog puts it, "a conceiver of great schemes."[13] He was a mysterious figure, and a tireless one, always organizing, always arguing, and somehow always on the losing side. For decades, he reveled in the furious center of early Zionism as Jewish intellectuals and activists wrestled bitterly to make sense of their situation in the midst of new ideologies, new possibilities, and unprecedented dangers. Other Jews—though not many—were executed by the ZOB, but none were as prominent as Nossig.[14] The untidy death of the elderly man at this moment of enduring redemption is still a moral, political, and historical problem.

Nossig's vigorous statue of the Wandering Jew was premature in aligning the Torah with resistance and "fell quickly into oblivion."[15] It was Hirszenberg's image of suffering that captured the mood of a Jewish world undone by the vicious pogroms that followed the assassination of Czar Alexander II in 1881, a world soon to experience the explosions of 1903 and thereafter, cataclysms that sent 2.75 million Jews from the Pale of Settlement pouring west across Europe between 1881 and 1914. Still, as we know, the traces of Nossig's vision would reappear in Szyk's rendering of the theme some forty-three years later, a vision that found in suffering a wellspring of defiance.

But defiance can take strange forms. At the time of the pogroms, Nossig was arguing that emancipation and assimilation had directly provoked antisemitism by fomenting insecurity among Christians. Like Hirszenberg, he believed that Jews and Christians were fundamentally incompatible. Among Jews, historical "exile" had led to degeneration. "The average Jewish type," he wrote in 1887, "exhibits strength in the struggle for survival but is morally on a lower level than the non-Jew; he possesses more shrewdness and endurance, but at the same time more ambition, vanity, and a lack of conscience."[16]

Nossig's writings caused a sensation. But not through offense. Instead, his explicit call for the rededication of a Jewish homeland in Palestine as the only solution to the problem of the European Jews thrust him to the forefront of Zionist polemicists—a prominent rival to Theodor Herzl, whose famous manifesto, *Der Judenstaat*, would be published in 1896. Yet it is sentences like the one above, overlooked at the time, that now reveal the latent symptom.

6.

It's all so cinematic. Nossig's arrest, the hurried trial, the secret execution, and—jump-cut—across the Soviet border, the *Einsatzgruppen*, the SS paramilitaries, unleashed, systematically butchering the frozen Ukrainians. The bleached-white landscape, the cabins engulfed in flame, black smoke pluming into an empty sky, red blood soaking out across the crisp snow. It is February when Nossig dies in Warsaw. The uprising begins on April 19, and the fighters are still holding out five days later as Himmler lectures on lice to his SS officers in Kharkov.

This is a difficult history, a story shadowed by the disaster about to fall. There are others, but the late-nineteenth-century words that matter most here are the following: *degeneracy, science, nation,* and *race.* There are Jews, Poles, and Germans. Soon, Europe and its colonies will burn in war upon war. The *Judenfrage,* the Jewish Question, is also the Jewish problem, and new solutions are beginning to appear. Nossig will travel. Before he comes back to die in the filth of the ghetto, he will crisscross the continent, studying; sculpting; writing books and plays; editing journals; organizing museums, exhibits, and research institutes; founding a Jewish publishing house and attempting to establish a Jewish university; addressing meetings and conferences in Paris, Vienna, London, Berlin, and many other cities; building a reputation as a social liberal and committed pacifist; doing anything he can to further the cause of Jewish emigration.

He channels his immense energy into the new cultural and political activism of *Gegenwartsarbeit,* the practical work of transforming the present. By his late thirties, he is one of the best-known Jews of his genera-

tion. But he will end up barely a footnote, his name tied always to that worst of all words: *collaborator.* Could there be a more terrible fate?

Nossig will fall foul first of Herzl and the political Zionists, then of the Zionist Organization itself. But none of that stops him. He negotiates with the Ottomans, the British, the Germans, the Poles. He cultivates around himself the kind of mystery no one likes or trusts, something malign maybe; no one can say for sure. People know he's driven. They're no longer sure by what. It's as if he sensed the disaster about to fall. (But did anyone really sense the disaster about to fall?)

People don't know what to make of him. He has the kind of mystery no one likes or trusts. (Adam Czerniakow, chairman of the Judenrat, the Jewish administrative council in the Warsaw Ghetto, calls him the *tausend Künstler,* the conjurer, the man of a thousand parts.)[17] When he appears in the ghetto, he is taciturn and haughty. ("A word from him was rare indeed.")[18]

Whatever else he may be, Nossig is a modern man of social science. He is a man who grasps the solidity of facts. As if the reality of facts could hold back whatever disaster may befall. He forms the Verein für jüdische Statistik, the Association for Jewish Statistics, and enlists many of the most dynamic Jewish intellectuals of central Europe. They want Jews to know who Jews are and how they live; they want to reveal the corrupting effects of assimilation and the new antisemitism; they want to organize and regenerate.

So they publish surveys of Diaspora life and they produce statistics. It's *Gegenwartsarbeit*. And Nossig (like others who are not Jews) realizes at once that survival will be a question of social hygiene. That the words that matter most are *degeneracy, science, nation,* and *race*.

7.

From Berlin, the center of German Jewish intellectual life, Nossig used his substantial organizational talents to found, in 1902, the Association for Jewish Statistics; to edit, in 1903, its initial publication, *Jüdische Statistik;* and to launch, in the following year, the Büro für Statistik der Juden. The bureau stood at the center of Jewish political and intellectual life in the pre-Nazi period, "the focal point of Jewish social scientific activity in Europe . . . until the mid-1920s."[19]

Jewish social science was a direct response to the Jewish question. The historian John Efron described this succinctly: "The question revolved around accounting for the physical, cultural, and social differences between Jews and Germans. The central issue was why, after their initial emancipation in 1812 in Prussia, their subsequent integration into German society, and their adoption of German culture, the Jews remained a distinct, visible, and easily identifiable group. Why had they failed to shed themselves of their Jewishness—that rarely described, but often observed, essence?"[20]

That this was also a preoccupying question for non-Jewish Germans can be seen in the scale and intensity of the research it provoked. Most famous, perhaps, were the comparative craniometric studies of almost 7 million German and Jewish schoolchildren carried out by Rudolf Virchow in the 1870s, which demonstrated the impracticality of distinguishing phenotypically between Aryans and Jews and, accordingly, of claiming that race and nation were one and the same.[21]

Nossig argued that the loss of cultural distinctiveness through assimilation was destroying the individual Jewish body and the body of the Jewish race. People in exile were subject to diseases of the flesh and the psyche and in need of physical and spiritual regeneration.[22] Because both Jewish social scientists and antisemitic intellectuals were committed to the new logics of physical anthropology, evolutionary theory, and medicine, this was a crisis about which all could agree. Yet there were, obviously, crucial distinctions. In particular, Jewish scholars followed the French naturalist Jean-Baptiste Lamarck in emphasizing the role of the environment in evolution and argued for the social and historical rather than biological and racial determinants of national pathologies.[23] For assimilationists, Lamarck provided a wedge between themselves and antisemitic attempts to roll back the gains of emancipation; for Zionists, he promised that a new land would produce a new Jew.

As did modern antisemitism, eugenics, and what Germans were beginning to call *Rassenhygiene*—race hygiene, rather than social hygiene—captivated thinkers across the political spectrum.[24] It can be difficult now to recognize the idealism tied up in this form of social engineering. And it can be hard also to appreciate the extent to which even the most catastrophic of outcomes was contingent. Darwinism did not have to devolve to a crude sociology of competition; eugenics required commitment to neither nation nor a hierarchy of races, only to the scientific improvement of a given population.[25] But what is so stunning about this moment is how the confluence of these ideologies—and the associated transformation of politics into a form of biological science—proved so irresistible and how it took so many people to such unnerving places.

8.

Degeneracy, science, nation, and race. Nossig stayed within the Zionist Organization for a decade following its first congress in 1897. He threw himself into activism but was more and more at odds with a leadership he considered elitist and anti-democratic. He vied constantly for the diplomatic ear of anyone who might hold a key to the gates of Palestine. He negotiated with British, Polish, and American officials. But his most persistent contacts were with the Ottoman Empire, which at the time controlled the territory of Palestine. His ceaseless travel to clandestine meetings produced anxiety, even among his allies, and a sense of unreliability and danger around his person that would precede him all the way to Warsaw. Even worse perhaps, he failed to disguise his distaste for his Zionist rivals and so created enemies, powerful ones, through displays like the public showdown in Basel in 1903, when he denounced Herzl for his *"jüdische Chuzpeh."*

"All nations got their countries thanks to conquest or labor," he wrote that year in language that could only deepen his isolation; "only the Jews, who buy and sell everything, bought themselves a homeland too."[26]

Nossig's most consuming project at this time was the statistics enterprise. The first task—a task never completed—was to demographically identify the Jewish people; the second was to diagnose their condition. The people were sick: life in the primitive East (or, for later writers, the degenerate West) made this plain.[27] Here again, Jews and antisemites found common ground, even if, for Jews, sickness demanded regeneration and transformation, not extermination.[28]

In 1908, Nossig finally left the Zionist Organization, increasingly uncomfortable with what he thought was its extreme and indistinctively non-Jewish nationalism and its counterproductive and unethical "cult of power" in relation to Palestinian Arabs.[29] Believing also that the organization was neglecting settlement, he established a new broad-based colonization body, the Allgemeine Jüdische Kolonisations Organisation (AJKO), which he hoped would become an institutional rival to the Jewish Agency, the official organization. At that point, many Zionists envisaged a "home for the Jews" within the framework of the Ottoman Empire and were encouraged by the sultanate's developing policy of limited territorial autonomy based on religion and ethnicity.[30]

In the years leading up to the First World War, Nossig maneuvered aggressively to get the Ottomans to recognize the AJKO, not foreseeing the empire's collapse and the British capture of Palestine. Even though German Jews overwhelmingly allied as patriots with the Central Powers in the First World War, Nossig's agitation was sufficiently high profile to mark him as a German agent—a whisper circulated by British and American diplomats in the region, as well as by the Zionist Organization itself, and a rumor that would have an altogether more sinister resonance when it resurfaced twenty years later.

As conditions deteriorated during the 1930s, Nossig threw himself into peace activism, even organizing a peace movement for young Jews. But eventually he felt forced to leave Berlin for Prague, where he devoted himself once more to his sculpture. Europe was becoming increasingly precarious for Jews, but he somehow succeeded in publicly exhibiting in Nazi Berlin a scale model of a monument he planned to erect on Mount Zion in Jerusalem. It was called The Holy Mountain and consisted of more than twenty outsize statues of biblical characters, a symbolic landscape of Judaism, now lost, which I imagine was peopled by figures as vigorous and resolute as his Wandering Jew.

Nossig is in his seventies by this point, and as Almog tells it, is offered asylum in Palestine "as a veteran Zionist."[31] But he doesn't go. The old man who has spent so much of his life working for Jewish emigration refuses to leave without his sculptures. The next we hear he has arrived in Warsaw as a refugee.

9.

To Marek Edelman, a ZOB commander in the Warsaw Ghetto, the execution of "the notorious Gestapo agent, Dr. Alfred Nossig," was a necessary action in "a programme designed to rid the Jewish population of hostile elements."[32] I like to think the contrast between Edelman's military language and his retention of Nossig's title signals unease. But it could just as easily be the voice of bureaucracy.

Remarkably, Edelman survived the uprising. Days after emerging from the sewers of the razed ghetto with a few battered comrades, he took a tram through the bustling streets of Aryan Warsaw and found himself staring at his own image. It was a poster that had appeared immediately following the uprising, and on seeing it, Edelman was instantly "seized by the wish not to have a face."[33]

"Jews—lice—typhus"—the poster that confronted Edelman shows a monstrous louse crawling into a hideously deformed "Jewish" face. It was part of a concentrated campaign that accompanied the liquidation of

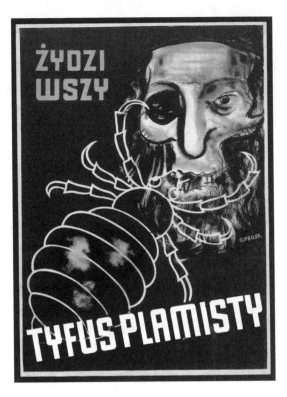

the ghetto.[34] Edelman's panicked reaction testifies to the potency of the image. He drags himself out through the bowels of the ghetto to find that his racialized self, the parasitic louse, has been forced into daylight too. It truly is a shock of recognition.

We already know something of the darkening histories buried in this horror. We, too, recognize the louse and its biology. We remember that there was a moment, not long before, when Jews like Edelman and Nossig could imagine themselves as children of emancipation, as heirs to European science and letters. We know they saw that the old judeophobia had become a new antisemitism. We know that many reacted to this new antisemitism by abandoning their dreams of assimilation and grasping at the Zionist nation.

We didn't know—though it's surely no surprise—that in 1895 (the year after Nossig published his *Social Hygiene of the Jews*) the German physician Alfred Ploetz responded to the general fear of social and racial degeneration in the wake of industrialization by publishing *Die Tüchtigkeit unsrer Rasse und der Schutz der Schwachen* (*The Fitness of Our*

Race and the Protection of the Weak), the founding statement of German *Rassenhygiene*, in which he warned that "traditional medical care helps the individual but endangers the race."[35] We also didn't know that in 1904 and 1905—just after Nossig and his colleagues had launched the Association for Jewish Statistics and prepared its publications—Ploetz, also in Berlin, established the journal and institutional apparatus of the new racial-hygiene movement. It's time to return to the problem we started with. How could the *Reichsführer* say those things? Do you remember? "Antisemitism is exactly the same as delousing. Getting rid of lice is not a question of ideology. It is . . . a matter of cleanliness, which now will soon have been dealt with. We shall soon be deloused."

Perhaps Himmler was indulging in an intimate irony with his men. As is well known, prisoners at Auschwitz were treated to an elaborate charade. Those selected for death were directed to "delousing facilities" equipped with false-headed showers. They were moved through changing rooms, allocated soap and towels. They were told they would be rewarded for disinfection with hot soup. Despite the fears of disease, the hunger for cleanliness, and the routine character of such hygienic procedures for migrants, there is evidence of considerable confusion and recalcitrance. The prisoners massed uncertainly in the shower room. Overhead, unseen, the disinfectors waited in their gas masks for the warmth of the naked bodies to bring the ambient temperature to the optimal 78 degrees Fahrenheit. They then poured crystals from the cans of Zyklon B—a hydrogen cyanide insecticide developed for delousing buildings and clothes—through the ceiling hatches. Finally, the bodies, contorted by the pain caused by the warning agent (a life-saving additive in other circumstances), were removed to the crematoria.[36]

In this grotesque pantomime, the victims—and we must remember they were not only Jews—move from objects of care to objects of annihilation. To diseased humans, delousing promises remediation, a return to community, a return to life; to lice, it offers only extermination. Too late, the prisoners discover they are merely lice.

The politics of life as the politics of death. Life stripped bare of its humanness. (Even if this work of turning humans into lice also makes lice human.) Such things were possible not because of the inferiority of the Jews—a fact never securely established: how could they be so power-

ful and so subhuman all at once?—but because of their unsettling alterity.[37] This is the moment when sovereign power is vested in the medical
professionals. Not the Jewish physicians like Nossig (and Edelman), of
course, but others who had debated the science of national survival in
ways that were at once similar and different.[38]

Himmler's language contains metaphor, euphemism, and at some
level, I suspect, a statement of belief. The word the Nürnberg lawyers
translate as "getting rid of"—"getting rid of lice is not a question of
ideology"—is *entfernen,* to remove or make distant, one more euphemis-
tic ambiguity in the self-consciously legalistic series that has Himmler
elsewhere evade naming the killing, talking instead of "mortality rates,"
"special treatment," "emigration," and "known tasks."[39]

Yet this alone cannot explain the literalization of Himmler's speech
that takes place in the gas chambers. As well as metaphor, euphemism,
and belief, there is the most material of histories underlying his parasitic
insects. It is a history that finally dissolves the distinction between those
things that enter from outside (the individual body, the body politic, the
foreign body) and those that are always present within (the parasitic ani-

mal inside). It is the final collapse of distinction between human and insect; the collapse that allows for extermination.

10.

For Germans, the association of Jews with disease was a long one, encased in the memory of the Black Death as a *Judenfieber,* a Jewish sickness, penetrating from out there, beyond the eastern borders.[40] Of the modern black deaths, it was the lice-borne typhus, with its sudden and catastrophic mortality rate, that was the most feared, and even though by 1900 it was "virtually dormant," its menace was palpable—and also locatable: in Jews, Roma, Slavs, and other "degenerate" social groups associated with "the East."[41]

The national fear of disease only intensified with the rise of the bacteriological sciences. Even though Robert Koch, the pioneer of German bacteriology and winner of a Nobel Prize in 1905 for his work on cholera and tuberculosis, refused to link pathogens with race (instead emphasizing transmission), his research was fully compatible with the new ideologies of racial hygiene, and introduced a logic of extermination that would resonate ever more strongly during succeeding decades.

Koch's most significant legacy in this respect lay in the formalization of a set of authoritarian protocols, including compulsory testing, quarantine, and household disinfection, that he developed and put into practice in colonial Africa. In 1903 in German East Africa, for example, he established a "concentration camp" for the isolation of sleeping sickness. Though the authoritarian management of populations was only one lesson that could be drawn from his work, it was an influential one.[42] Claus Schilling, an assistant of Koch's who would go on to direct a department for tropical medicine at his mentor's Koch Institute, was eventually executed for his malaria experiments at Dachau.[43]

Advances in the scientific control of all kinds of pests—bacteria, parasites, and insects—were by no means restricted to Germany. Medical science stimulated both rivalry and a degree of cooperative research among the imperial powers as shared concerns became evident. Hygiene was the rubric that invited investigation into the intertwined vectors of human, animal, and plant disease as researchers worked to safeguard the health of colonial settlers and their livestock and crops.

At the same time, concern about contamination in Europe and the United States led to restrictive border policies and punitive inspection procedures targeted at particular social groups, with quarantine laws enacted in the United States specifically to prevent the entry of Jews fleeing the Russian pogroms.[44] Disease both necessitated and facilitated the isolation of particular groups as sites of medical intervention and social control. The apparent predisposition of Jews and certain others to infection was self-evidently a mark of cultural primitivism.[45] We might therefore imagine that hygienic interventions expressed a kind of missionary modernity. But it seems instead that regimes of cleansing were dispensed and experienced as punitive, not redemptive. The implication was that disease, at least for these parasitic populations, was an inherent trait rather than a curable condition.

This is the period in which we see the development of those technologies of disease control that achieve a kind of fulfillment at Auschwitz: collective showers, bacteriological soaps, chemical gas, cremation . . . These technologies were already compulsory features of a network of border-control stations that fortified the German frontiers with Russia and Poland and encouraged migrants from the east to regard German territory as implacably foreign ground. Following a severe cholera outbreak in Hamburg in 1892, which was widely attributed to Russian Jews, Germany closed its eastern borders, relenting only to establish a hygienic transport corridor to the ports of embarkation for Ellis Island. For a while, the major shipping lines took over the financing and expansion of the border-control posts.[46]

The outbreak of war in 1914 soon produced mass epidemics among refugees, troops, and enemy captives. In a lightning typhus outbreak in Serbia, more than 150,000 civilian refugees and prisoners died in six months.[47] Hygiene became an urgent political priority, and sanitary regimens became correspondingly more severe. It was Russian soldiers— rather than the atrocious conditions—who were blamed for the appalling mortality rates in the POW camps. "Eastern peoples" were characterized not as victims of disease but as its carriers. State efforts were directed toward protecting the civilian population from contamination (Russian prisoners were to be tended only by Russian doctors).

The critical scientific breakthrough just prior to the war—the identification of lice as the typhus vector—led to an industrialization of delousing and its expansion to civilians. The historian Paul Weindling describes what this meant:

> The routine demanded total nudity, and special attention to the hair, skin folds, and the "Schamgegend" where the lice might lurk in pubic hair or between the bottom cheeks. If any person resisted the shaving of all their hair (and it was noted that women often protested), then a louse-killing substance like petroleum or eucalyptus oil was to be used on those parts of the body defended from more radical hygienic intervention. . . . Clothing, bed linen, and mattress covers had to be placed in ovens or steam chambers. For disinfestation of rooms either steam or canisters of sulphuric acid or sulphur dioxide were used. Items of low value were burned.[48]

Weindling describes the mass application of such procedures by German disinfectors throughout German-occupied Poland, Romania, and Lithuania in response to typhus outbreaks during the war. He documents an increasingly strident association of disease with Jews and others regarded as racial degenerates. Jewish-owned stores in Poland were closed until the owners had undergone delousing. Lodz, a city with a large Jewish population, was ringed by thirty-five detention centers for persons considered infested.[49]

But military defeat in 1918 radically changed the calculus. Rather than expanding into purified colonial living space, medical authorities now found themselves confined to a dramatically reduced national territory. They also found themselves confronting an unmanageable crisis of refugees—mostly ethnic Germans and *Ostjuden*—as well as sick and wounded military personnel returning from the front. In the years following the Treaty of Versailles, highly restrictive immigration controls and draconian inspection practices were imposed in an effort to protect the newly vulnerable *Volk* against contamination from the east.[50]

Nonetheless, and despite the terrible events of the Russian Civil War—25 million typhus cases and up to 3 million deaths from typhus between 1917 and 1923[51]—it was becoming clear that the real danger was no longer external. As early as 1920, police in Berlin and other cities were invoking "hygienic control" as they rounded up *Ostjuden* and transported them to disease-infested camps along the national borders.

Not only the discourses of hygiene (themselves an amalgam of eugenics, social Darwinism, political geography, and pest biology) but also specific technologies, identifiable personnel, and particular institutions dedicated to the eradication of disease shifted rapidly and quite seamlessly to the eradication of people. The elimination of typhus would enable a simultaneous purification of race and polity—one and the same by the mid-1930s—and increasingly the disease's human victims became functionally and perhaps ontologically indistinguishable from its insect vectors.

From 1918, this trajectory accelerated as a conservative political and medical consensus formed around the understanding that contagion was directly tied to degeneration, that a body politic whose health had been shattered by the humiliation of Versailles was now dangerously contaminated, that disease had reached the racial heartland, and that exorcising the phantasm of infection was the only solution. The interwar period is striking for the radical conflation of political philosophy and medicine, such that ghettos, for example, become places of confinement that protect the excluded German population from disease, and simultaneously—and inevitably, given the conditions inside them—diseased sites that generate a pathological anxiety around fears of contamination from escapees. The rest is too well known to bear further repetition.

11.

An elderly Alfred Nossig appears repeatedly in the diary of Adam Czerniakow. The entries are cryptic and irritated, perhaps even condescending. Nossig runs to Czerniakow with prattle from the ghetto streets; he is short of money; he bombards the Germans with letters; on one occasion, they throw him out of their offices.[52] It all raises the suspicion that the old man is senile.[53] Czerniakow describes him as "pleading" and "babbling." He talks about Nossig's "antics." At one point he "admonishes" him.[54]

It is clear that even though Czerniakow may not find Nossig directly threatening, he does not trust him. For a start, Nossig is too familiar with the Nazis. It is the Germans who introduce him to the Jewish administration, to whom he is already known, and it is the Germans who insist on a position for him. Appropriately enough, he is appointed the council's emigration officer. But what kind of farcical task is that? Ghettos were soon to be liquidated all across the Reich, and Nossig is negotiating resettlement with the SS as if this is 1914, as if we are all still Germans! Nonetheless, the work seems to energize him, and for a while he appears to convince himself (if no one else) that there is real hope of relocating the Warsaw Jews to the French colony of Madagascar.

When the ghetto is sealed in November 1940, the Nazis appoint Nossig director of its Department of Art and Culture. It seems another absurd position. But opening the committee's first meeting, the elderly Nossig speaks with characteristic force about the role of art in Jewish Warsaw, by now a place of acute desperation, advancing starvation, and disease. "Art means cleanliness," he is reported to have said, momentarily bringing together those deeply tortured histories of social hygiene. "We have to introduce culture into the streets," he insists. The ghetto must be made clean "so that we are not ashamed in front of our German visitors."[55]

Kafka

Now I am ready to tell how bodies are changed
Into different bodies.

TED HUGHES, *Tales from Ovid*

1.

We know this story. A solitary *Ammophila hirsuta* captures and paralyzes a larva of the turnip moth, *Agrotis segetum*. She drags it to her nest, lays an egg on its soft belly just beyond reach of its feebly waving legs, and exits, barricading the entrance to the burrow behind her. The egg hatches, and the emerging wasp larva at once starts to feed. It grows fat and strong. The caterpillar, unable to move with force but still discerning shape and shadow, sensing atmospheric and chemical changes, and experiencing pain, is slowly consumed, first the nonessential tissue, later the vital organs.

2.

This morning, I read that less than 1 percent of caterpillar eggs survive to adulthood. Such is the ferocity of the predators they face: the birds, reptiles, and mammals (large and small); the parasitoid wasps and flies, the ants, spiders, earwigs, and beetles; the viruses, bacteria, and fungi. Not to mention the gardeners. This state of affairs accounts for the caterpillars' spectacular battery of defenses: toxic flesh, chemical sprays, aggressive sounds, spiny bristles, garish coloring, biting mouths, silky escape ropes, unpleasant fluids regurgitated, repellant odors diffused, the precision mimicry of eyespots, horns, faces, and camouflage, the barbed hair, the stinging hair, the intimidating postures, the alliances with ants.[1]

Still, less than 1 percent survive to adulthood, to that moment when "with a reckless smile," as Roberto Bolaño put it, they emerge anew.[2]

3.

Less than 1 percent survive to adulthood? It must be difficult to establish this fact with confidence when there is no reasonable estimate of numbers to begin with and when each caterpillar instar—each larval stage, of which there are often five or six before pupation—can look quite different.

In short, consider the difficulty of establishing this statistic with confidence when caterpillars, as the ecologist Daniel Janzen recently pointed out, "are the last unknown group of big things on the terrestrial world."[3]

4.

One claim, two problems: the problem of quantifying survival and the problem of conceptualizing adulthood. If the first problem is insurmountable, the second is harder.

The textbooks explain that a caterpillar is a Lepidoptera larva, the stage in the life cycle of a butterfly or moth between the hatching of the egg and the formation of the pupa. It is the stage that leads to metamorphosis and the adult form, the stage during which some animals increase their mass a thousandfold and repeatedly molt as they travel through their various instars.

Jules Michelet, the historian and naturalist, considered the ways in which this extended journey of the insect from one state to another might parallel the passage of other animals "from the embryonic existence to the independent life." Unlike mammals, he wrote in L'insecte in 1857, for pupating insects "the destination is not merely different, but contrary, with a violent contrast." This "is not a simple change of condition," and these are not "the gentle manoeuvres" by which the rest of us achieve maturity. These beings that are one and the same could not be more different: clay-footed yet ethereal, earthbound yet aloft in the skies, scurrying to the shadows yet drawn to the light, a grinder of leaves yet a sipper of nectar, unencumbered by genitalia yet dedicated to sex. "*The legs will not again be the legs. . . . The head will not be the head*," wrote Michelet. This transformation, he saw, "is a thing to confound and almost to terrify the imagination."[4]

Michelet no doubt knew that the word *larva* had entered the Romance languages accompanied by older, darker associations. In a time of meaningful correspondences between natural phenomena and everyday life, an age when people discerned potent signs in stones and storms, the word *larva* conjured disembodied spirits, ghosts, specters, and hobgoblins, and it seized on its insect in a fit of recognition. The duality of the word expressed the occult ambiguity of the creature. It was Linnaeus who insisted on the restrictive modern meaning of the term and, with that shift of logic and sentiment, began the textbook entry that still stands between us and the uncanny reality of the thing.

Here is the larva and there is the adult. For Michelet, author of a celebrated seven-volume *Histoire de la Révolution française*, the event that lies between these states of being was a "revolution," an "astonishing tour de force."[5] It was perhaps possible for Linnaeus to disenchant the word but quite another matter to pacify the thing itself.

5.

As stubborn as its goblin nature was the idea—still with us—of the larva as a mask behind which lies the animal's truth. One being enters the chrysalis. Another comes out. "All is thrown aside with the mask," said Michelet. "All is, and ought to be, changed."[6]

Michelet was fifty-nine when he published *L'insecte*. He would live for another seventeen years, but he was nonetheless already preoccupied with death. His massive works of history were works of resurrection, of bringing back to life. And, indeed, the dead were always around him.

When he was seventeen, his mother died. Six years later, it was his clos-est friend. When he was forty-one, his first wife died. Seven years after that, it was his father, with whom he shared a house. At fifty-two he lost a baby son, the only child of his new marriage; five years after that, his thirty-one-year-old daughter.[7]

And his health was poor, riven by a series of psychosomatic com-plaints brought on by his agonized response to the upheavals that shook France from 1848: the February revolution that created the Second Republic and the subsequent imperial reaction under Napoleon III. A believer in the unity of nations, he was horrified by the assertion of class on all sides. But the restoration of the emperor led—as it did for Fabre—to a dramatic reversal of Michelet's fortunes; in his case to his sacking from a prestigious position at the Collège de France and his untimely departure from Paris.[8]

Death was all around Michelet. "I have drunk too much from the black blood of the dead," he had written in 1853. Yet he is still drawn relentlessly to resurrection.[9] And that surely is why he is drawn also so relentlessly to the larvae.

He is unconvinced by the primacy of the butterfly, the assumption that this most seductive of animals is the fulfillment of the caterpillar in the same way that the adult human is understood to be the fulfillment (for better or worse) of the child. Some of that assumption anticipates Darwinian teleology: the emphasis on reproduction as the purpose of existence confirms that the sexually mature form is the only one that counts. Some of that assumption is more generally evolutionary: the logic of immaturity and development, the progression through ever greater, more advanced stages to ever more advanced, more perfect states that would become so deeply lodged in post-nineteenth-century politics, culture, and personal life—even though our experience of poli-tics, culture, and personal life tells us emphatically that there really is no guarantee of directional progress.

But perhaps, suggests Michelet, the lesson of metamorphosis is not teleology but impermanence and its immortalities. "Throughout my life," he writes, ". . . each day I died and was born again; I have under-gone many painful strugglings and laborious transformations. . . . Many and many times I have passed from the larva into the chrysalis, and into a more complete condition; the which, after awhile, incomplete under other conditions, has put me in the way of accomplishing a new circle of metamorphosis." He is a moment in the midst of many connected lives. Occasionally he catches himself making a gesture, an intonation, and feels his father alive inside him. "Are we two? Were we one? Oh! it was my chrysalis."[10]

6.

More than a century and a half earlier, as 1699 rolled over into 1700, financially independent but hardly wealthy, twenty years of marriage and five more of ascetic withdrawal into the mystical Labadist community in West Friesland firmly behind her, twenty-something daughter and Amerindian slaves in tow, the fifty-two-year-old Maria Sibylla Merian, already a noted painter of European insects, rode a donkey through the tropical forests of the Dutch colony of Suriname, "the only European woman who journeyed exclusively in pursuit of her science in the seventeenth and eighteenth centuries."[11]

Merian traveled with slaves, but as colonial travelers go, she was relatively benign, never speaking ill of the natives, bemoaning their vicious treatment at the hands of the Dutch settlers, and acknowledging with unusual candor (though in general terms rather than by name) the locals' substantial contributions to her collection.

Raised in a family of artists and publishers—her maternal grandfather was Théodore de Bry, whose iconic engravings made the New World real for readers of the first European travel narratives—Merian developed an early fascination for nature study that never left her. She began at thirteen with silkworms (another family connection: her mother's second husband's brother was in the silk trade) but was soon preoccupied by caterpillars in general and, above all, by their transformations.

The beauty of butterflies and moths, she wrote later, "led me to collect all the caterpillars I could find in order to study their metamorphoses."[12] It was an eccentricity in a girl, but as with the famous and similarly youthful heroine of the twelfth-century Japanese story "The Lady Who

Loved Worms" (who did not pluck her eyebrows, did not blacken her teeth, who was, indeed, not very ladylike at all), the peculiarity was one of sensitivity and insight that perhaps indicated a philosophical refinement.[13] It proved to be a tolerable eccentricity—despite the dark associations that crawling creatures often carried.

Surrounded by books and artists, Merian had access to a large library of natural history illustration. She collected her own insects and bred their larvae through their transformations, drawing and painting from life. She honed her conventional drafting skills, copying from the leading emblem books, including *Archetypa studiaque patris Georgii Hoefnagelii* (1592), a popular collection of insect engravings executed by Jacob Hoefnagel in the style of his father, Joris.[14] But Merian's times were different, and so was her vision: if the Hoefnagels' incandescent insect universe was dedicated to the revelation of the microcosmic, she occupied a world refreshed by the introduction of the microscope, in which the new preoccupation was with observation and the classifications it made possible. Where Hoefnagel had arranged his insects in a symbolic order, Merian placed hers in a different relation, one that was drawn from her own life studies and revealed a fascination with the profusions of time, place, and connection.

Intensely colored, intensely subjective, dedicated on the opening page to both "lovers of art" and "lovers of insects," Merian's animals are oversize, the plants are shrunk, the proportions distorted; the animals in Merian's *Metamorphosis insectorum Surinamensium*, the masterpiece she published in Amsterdam in 1705, "appear palpably close, yet imaginary and distant at the same time," as if we, too, are running a lens over their surfaces.[15] Yet as never before, the drama of metamorphosis is given unity. On the same page, she paints the larva, the chrysalis, the butterfly, and the plant on which the caterpillar feeds. (Sometimes she includes the eggs, proof that she had assimilated Francesco Redi's 1668 demonstration that maggots developed from eggs and not via Aristotelian spontaneous generation.) It is a dynamic, interactive world. Its principles are transformation, holism, and the overthrow of that earlier taxonomy of Aristotle, Aldrovandi, and Moffett, which segregated the insects into those that crawl and those that fly and, without knowing what it had done, sundered the butterflies and moths from their larvae.

7.

Michelet greatly admired Merian's paintings. He embraced his fellow traveler in the land of the insects and felt a secure bond across the centuries. Her paintings, he thought, not only expressed the feminine qualities that he expected to find—"the softness, breadth, and fulness of the plants, their lustrous and velvety freshness"—but remarkably also had "a noble vigour, a masculine gravity, a courageous simplicity."[16]

He examined the hand-colored copperplates that fill the *Metamorphosis*. All is change, all is impermanence, all is connection. The vitality of life itself erupts against the artificial tidiness of scientific categories.

Nonetheless, the questions that gnawed at him are not solved here. What is the germ that carries through from one form to another, from one being to another? What is it that persists? What kind of creature is this? Is it one or is it many?

In Japan many centuries earlier, the Lady Who Loved Worms spent her days collecting caterpillars from her garden, ordering them, examining them, admiring them, exclaiming over them. She was contemptuous of butterflies, worthless things compared with the larvae from which they came and which could furnish her with, for example, silk. She liked the little crawly things. She was drawn to things that lacked pretense. She admired the fundamental phenomena—that is, the ever-changing reality behind the "reality" in which we foolishly live. It was, she said, "the essence of things" that interested her; it was the *honji*, a Buddhist term that the unknown author of the famous twelfth-century story uses to mean something like "original form," "original state," "primary manifestation."[17] "The way people lose themselves in admiration of blossoms and butterflies is positively silly and incomprehensible," said the young lady. "It is the person who is sincere and inquires into the essence of things who has an interesting mind."[18]

But Merian, riding her colonial donkey through the forests of Suriname, sailing to Amsterdam in a flurry of self-publishing entrepreneurship, found herself somewhere else entirely, completely disconnected from such thoughts. Her energies were observational, her analytics were visual. She must have abandoned ontological rumination when she quit West Friesland and tired in the most profound way of self-denial. Her principle is beauty, its creation, its appreciation, the surrender to its ineffability. "One day," she writes in one of her unaffected commentaries on the Suriname engravings, "I went far out into the wilderness and found, among other things, a tree the natives call a medlar. . . . There I found this yellow caterpillar. . . . I took this caterpillar home with me, and it soon turned into a light-wood-colored pupa. Fourteen days later, near the end of January 1700, a beautiful butterfly emerged. It has the look of polished silver, covered with the most appealing ultramarine, green, and purple; it is indescribably beautiful. Its beauty cannot be rendered with a brush."[19]

And Michelet, straining too—though in a different way—to grasp both the poetics and the mechanics of transformation, found himself meshed in a metaphysical limbo. History plays strange games with historians. Have you ever visited the Puces de Paris Saint-Ouen, the famous flea market in central Paris? To get there, exit the metro at Porte de Clignancourt and look for the junction of avenue Michelet and rue Jean-Henri Fabre.

Wherever life takes you, there is always something that refuses to follow. However you travel, there is always something that tags along uninvited. "Everyone who walks this earth feels a tickling at his heel," Kafka's famous ape, Red Peter, tells the assembled academy. Kidnapped from his jungle, carried in chains across the ocean, forced to choose between the zoo and the vaudeville, transformed into something new, something part man, part greater than a man, no longer able to reach back to the old ape truth.[20] "Whatever you do," wrote Max Brod, Kafka's friend and literary executor, "it is always wrong." How symptomatic is it that, amid all the literature dedicated to butterflies and moths, until recently there was no authoritative field guide to the caterpillars of any region? Conceptually and taxonomically, their existence is somehow doubtful. Despite all their defenses, less than 1 percent survive to adulthood.

Language

When I wish to attract some bees for training experiments I usually place upon a small table several sheets of paper which have been smeared with honey. Then I am often obliged to wait for many hours, sometimes for several days, until finally a bee discovers the feeding place. But as soon as one bee has found the honey many more will appear within a short time—perhaps as many as several hundred. They have all come from the same hive as the first forager; evidently this bee must have announced its discovery at home.

KARL VON FRISCH

1.

Karl von Frisch won a Nobel Prize in 1973 for his discovery of "the language of bees." It was the year of ethology, and along with von Frisch, the prize in Physiology or Medicine was also awarded to Konrad Lorenz and his Dutch colleague Nikolaas Tinbergen. There was nothing recondite here, no obscure fiddling at the margins of theory. The 1973 prize was awarded for populist research that illuminated the mysteries of animal existence and promised profound and far-reaching truths about the human condition.

Honeybees, said von Frisch, though so tiny and so different, possessed language, the capacity long definitive of humanity. Through a series of elegant experiments carried out over nearly half a century, he showed that they communicated symbolically, that, in a manner more complex than that of any other animals apart from humans, they drew on experience and memory to convey information to each other and to their fellows.

More than ninety years after his first reports, these discoveries are still exciting. And they are made more so by von Frisch's way of telling. By inclination and early training a naturalist, he offered nature not in today's technical language of genomics but in his own deeply personal language of bees, a remarkably affective language that imbued his subjects with purpose and intentionality, that made them appealing and familiar.

Von Frisch offered a science of "what animals do, and how and why they do it" that was as comfortable with ontological difference and abiding mystery as it was with the more familiar scientific impulse toward revelation.[1] Unashamed in his confessions of affinity, he made readers believe—just as he did himself—that they could understand bees, psychologically and emotionally. He turned his public into animal analysts. And in doing so, he gave new impetus—though, perhaps, despite himself—to the Darwinian notion that not only the morphological but also the behavioral, moral, and emotional basis of human existence could be found in the lives of nonhuman animals.[2] Von Frisch spoke for honeybees. And he made them speak. He didn't just give them language; he translated it. Is there anything that is more irresistible?

Nonetheless, these affinities were deeply fraught in a discipline barely born yet already haunted by the specter of fallibility. Ethology's ghost was Clever Hans, the celebrity horse whose cleverness unfortunately lay not in mathematics but in an uncanny sensitivity to the nonverbal cues of his unwitting trainer. Clever Hans's much-publicized debunking by the psychologist Oskar Pfungst in 1907 pushed questions of animal cognition to the very margins of scientific legitimacy and made it clear that ethology was at mortal risk from the allure of its subjects.[3]

It was a foundational temptation to which the resolutely antipsychological behaviorists would not succumb. But it was the seduction to which von Frisch, caught between affect and object, preoccupied, as he himself wrote, by the interplay between "psychological performance and the physiology of the senses," would forever be in thrall.[4]

Because von Frisch loved his bees. Loved them with a gentle passion. Tended and nurtured their generations. Warmed them in his cupped

hands when the brisk air stiffened their wing muscles. Held them as his "personal friends."[5] They were his bees in the way that anthropologists of the past may have fancied the remote tribes among which they lived to be their tribes. That same heady mix of science, sentiment, and proprietorial pride, the same willingness to assume responsibility for another's fate.

So even as he took such care over the tiny creatures' welfare, von Frisch would lovingly (with another love), painstakingly (with a professional patience), and delicately (with such safe hands) snip their antennae, clip their wings, slice their torsos, shave their eye bristles, glue weights to their thoraxes, and carefully paint shellac over their unblinking eyes, modifying their bodies, mutilating their senses, manipulating their behavior according to the experiment's requirement, reconciling his will to suture the yawning gap that separated human from insect with his unspoken assertion of a natural sovereign power.

2.

In April 1933, the Nazi-dominated Reichstag passed the Law for the Restoration of the Professional Civil Service. Jews, spouses of Jews, and political unreliables could now be legally dismissed from the universities.[6]

By then, von Frisch was director of the new Rockefeller-funded Institute of Zoology at the University of Munich and a leading figure in German science. Years before, in the landscaped and columned courtyard of the institute, he had, as he recalled in his memoir, fallen "irresistibly under the spell of the honey-bee."[7]

His enchantment by those he would come to call his little "comrades" had in fact begun even earlier. In 1914, with a magician's flair, he publicly demonstrated what now seems the rather unsurprising truth that honeybees—whose livelihood, after all, depends on their identification of flowering plants—are able to discriminate by color (despite being red-blind). Using the standard behavioral method of food rewards, he trained a group of bees to identify blue plates. He then showed them small squares of colored paper and watched delightedly as they congregated "as if by command" for his skeptical audience.[8]

But it was in the garden in Munich that the bees first danced for him: "I attracted a few bees to a dish of sugar water, marked them with red paint and then stopped feeding for a while. As soon as all was quiet, I filled the dish up again and watched a scout which had drunk from it after her return to the hive. I could scarcely believe my eyes. She performed a round dance on the honeycomb which greatly excited the marked foragers around her and caused them to fly back to the feeding place."

Although beekeepers and naturalists had known for centuries that honeybees communicated the location of a food source among themselves, no one knew how. Did they lead one another to the nectar? Did they diffuse scent trails? "I believe," von Frisch wrote more than forty years later, that this "was the most far-reaching observation of my life."[9]

Under the civil service law, von Frisch and his academic colleagues—as well as all other civil servants in the Reich—were required to produce documentary proof of their Aryan ancestry. Already suspect for his willingness to sponsor Jewish graduate students even when their theses were far from his own specialties, von Frisch found himself in an even more dangerous dilemma.[10] His mother's mother, now deceased, the daughter of a banker and the wife of a philosophy professor, was a Jew from Prague. At first the university protected its star zoologist, arranging for his safe classification as "one-eighth Jewish." But imagine the virulent mixture of ideology and ambition that began to ferment, fed by a rigid institutional hierarchy and the lack of opportunity for advancement among scholars locked out of academic privilege despite their years of training. In October 1941, the campaign against von Frisch succeeded in forcing his reclassification as "second-grade *Mischling*"—one-quarter Jewish—and securing the order for his removal from his post.

As we know, von Frisch survived the Nazis. Inevitably, though, it was far from straightforward. Influential colleagues mobilized on his behalf, arranging a platform in *Das Reich*, a new weekly in which Goebbels contributed the editorials. Von Frisch wrote about the national-economic contribution of the Zoological Institute and how its work was vital to the resilience of the home front.[11] Eventually, though, if in somewhat tortuous fashion, it was the bees that saved him. For two years, an outbreak of the parasite *Nosema apis* had ravaged German hives. Both the national honey crop and agricultural pollination were threatened. Through the intervention of a highly placed ally, von Frisch was appointed as a special investigator, and a panicked Ministry of Food was induced to defer his dismissal from academia "until after the war."[12]

The indifference of the honeybees to politics did not prevent their recruitment to the National Socialist war effort. The ministry soon expanded the *Nosema* remit to include a search for ways of persuading bees to rationalize pollination by visiting only economically desirable plants. Years before, von Frisch had experimented with scent guidance—training bees to respond to a particular odor before freeing them to visit the associated flower—but he had been unable to generate commercial interest. This time, galvanized by looming calamity, national enthusiasm, and news of a large-scale Soviet research project along similar lines, the Organization of Reich Beekeepers rushed to sponsor his work.

Exhausted by the intensifying air war on Munich, von Frisch and his lifelong co-worker, Ruth Beutler, evacuated to the village of Brunnwinkl on the shore of Lake Wolfgang, southwest of Salzburg. This was where von Frisch had spent his childhood summers, and attached to the family house was the natural history museum he had founded as an eager seventeen-year-old. It was here, pursuing adolescent obsessions, that young Karl had enrolled relatives and family friends in scouring the nearby woods and shoreline for local fauna. It was here, at the old mill on the edge of Lake Wolfgang, under the quiet hand of his uncle, the prominent Viennese physiologist Sigmund Exner, that he developed the classical skills in observation and manipulation that would characterize his experimental research.

And it was also here, here among the animals, that von Frisch found his "reverence before the Unknown," less a formal religious conviction than a commitment to a pantheistic relativism. "All honest convictions deserve respect," he insisted, "except the presumptuous assertion that there is nothing higher in the world than the mind of man."[13] And it was here, as he tells it in straightforward yet often lyrical prose, that his liberal Catholic family—doctrinally liberal in an era when Austrian biologists were routinely dismissed for espousing evolution—created a bourgeois haven, a home for science and the arts, for the gentle satisfactions of polite culture far from the upheavals of early-twentieth-century Mitteleuropa: his spirited mother and his caring if reserved father, his three older brothers, all preparing merely for the uneventful unfolding of long and distinguished academic careers.

And it was here, in the cocoon of family memory, as the Allied bombs rained firestorms on Munich and Dresden and as the air thickened over Auschwitz, that von Frisch and Beutler took advantage of their Reich permits to revisit the work on bee communication that he had laid aside some two decades earlier.

In those long-ago studies in the courtyard of the Institute of Zoology, von Frisch had identified two "dances"—he named them the round

dance and the waggle dance—and concluded that bees used the former to indicate a source of nectar and the latter to indicate a source of pollen. Beutler had continued this work in the intervening years but had begun to doubt the hypothesis. Resuming their experiments together in 1944, they discovered that when they positioned the feeding dishes more than 100 yards from the hive, it didn't matter what substance the bees were carrying: on their return, they all performed waggle dances. Rather than a descriptor of material, the variation they observed in the dances must be the bees' way of communicating the far more complicated information of location. This ability to accurately describe distance and direction "seemed," von Frisch wrote, "altogether too fantastic to be true."[14]

It was the complexity of the bees' behavior that was so arresting. Making connections between the intricate sociality of honeybees—which live in self-reproducing "colonies" of thousands of individuals—and the development of sophisticated forms of communication is commonplace now. But early-twentieth-century animal studies were dominated by the conviction of biologists and psychologists that animal behavior was fully explicable in terms of a range of simple stimulus responses, such as reflexes and tropisms. And von Frisch's bees were doing something that leading behaviorists such as John B. Watson and Jacques Loeb considered impossible: they were communicating symbolically, representing information through a form—a predictable pattern of physical movements—that was tied to its object "by social convention, tacit agreement, or explicit code."[15] What was more, this representing could take place several hours after the flight it described. It relied on registering the details of that flight, recalling its content, and, of course, translating and performing the significant information. Moreover, it also required an audience able to interact effectively in its interpretation. To Donald Griffin, the tireless advocate of animal consciousness and the sponsor of von Frisch's 1949 lecture tour of the United States, this was "the most significant example of versatile communication known in any animal other than our own species."[16] Von Frisch went further. It was, he believed, an accomplishment "without parallel elsewhere in the entire animal kingdom."[17]

Contemporary bee researchers have refined von Frisch and Beutler's wartime revisions of the dance theory. There is, most now believe, no difference between the types of information contained in the two main

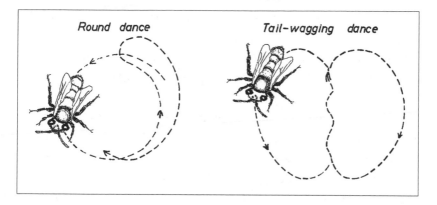

Round dance   Tail-wagging dance

dances.[18] Both use waggling to communicate distance and direction, and in both it is the enthusiasm of the performance that conveys the quality of food. Similarly, in both, the type of flower is revealed by the scent clinging to the insect's body.

In Munich, von Frisch had placed feeding stations directly alongside the hive to facilitate communication between his assistants observing the dances and those stationed at the feeders. However, in the round dances that the bees perform to indicate nearby food, the waggles are abbreviated, occurring just as the dancer turns to begin her new circle. Von Frisch and his team failed to observe those subtle cues, and it is likely that the bee audience doesn't take much notice of them either, relying instead on sense of smell to locate such proximate feeding places. But when food is further away—the transition occurs at a point between 50 and 100 yards for the Carniolan bee, the bee favored by von Frisch— bees returning to the hive interpose an additional sequence of steps, a straight run that contains a "vigorous wagging" of the abdomen, a side-to-side movement they may repeat thirteen to fifteen times per second.[19] It is this distinctive stretch that contains the critical information. Gyrating in darkness amid the crush of bodies on what von Frisch called the hive's "dance floor," the returning forager is closely shadowed by three or four followers, who receive the dance information with their antennae, utilizing scent (to identify the type of flower), taste (to gauge the quality of its product), touch, and an acoustic sensitivity that allows them to pick up the near-air movements produced by the dancer's wings.[20]

The dancer uses the sun as her reference point. Illuminated by daylight on the horizontal platform at the hive entrance, her movements are indexical, pointing directly ahead, "just as we point to a distant goal with raised arm and outstretched finger."[21] Dancing in the open, she orients herself by angling her body so that the sun is at the same angle relative to her body as it was during her recent flight to the food source.[22]

But the vast majority of dances take place inside the hive, in total darkness, on the surface of a vertical comb. Those conditions present the bee with a significant set of problems, which she resolves by reconfiguring the indexical association between the dance and the food source. This interior dance involves a temporal and spatial displacement as the bee converts the angle of the sun, which has permitted her to mime her flight during the outdoor dances, into gravitational terms. To succeed, the bee must note optically the angle between the direction of the sun and the food source on her outbound flight, remember that information, accurately transpose it to an angle that relates to gravity, and in doing so, include a calculation that corrects for the movement of the sun in the time that has passed between her outbound flight and the dance.[23]

If food is located in the direction of the sun, the bee runs upward along the comb; if the feeding place is away from the sun, she runs down. If the material is located at, say, eighty degrees to the left of the sun—as in feeding table II in the diagram on page 181—she points her waggle run eighty degrees to the left of vertical (II'), and so on.[24] Even if the sun is obscured by clouds, she can locate its position by recognizing patterns of polarized light invisible to humans.[25]

Von Frisch tracked bees foraging some seven miles from their hive and discovered that they convey distance through some combination of number and rate of waggles, velocity of forward movement, and length and duration of the straight section.[26] However, distance is a "subjective" quality, which bees measure in terms of the amount of effort they expend on their outward flight. Von Frisch demonstrated this by appending weights of different kinds to various parts of the animals' bodies, exposing them to head winds, and forcing them to walk. In each case, they reported a greater distance than they did without the handicap.[27]

Von Frisch liked to work with "calm and peaceful" bees.[28] They were cooperative, and he was responsive, designing experiments and apparatus around their needs and desires. The bees were affected by wind and temperature. They revealed astonishingly subtle senses of smell and touch. They responded actively to changing light conditions. They grew

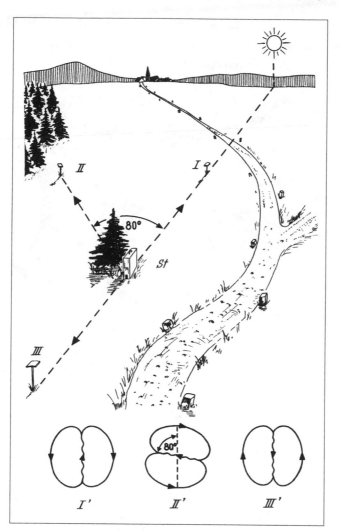

to recognize individual field-workers. Alert to their sensitivities, he could never be certain that their observed behavior was not symptomatic of the artificiality of experimental conditions and so allowed them to force him into exhaustive (and exhausting) replications of his tests as he struggled to find ways to repeat controlled experiments in natural conditions. When his discoveries were too astonishing, he wondered whether his attention had created "a sort of scientific bee."[29]

He began by building an observation hive. This was a standard bee-keeping hive fitted with glass windows, through which the bees could be watched relatively undisturbed. But he soon realized that bright sunlight and the visibility of patches of sky distorted the dances, so instead he developed his own range of hives with removable panels that allowed him to manipulate external conditions.

He designed feeding stations and special food dispensers. And he invented an automatic counting apparatus disguised as a flower to record bee visits when it was impractical or unnecessary to use volunteers.

He devised a coding scheme—an ingenious one—that allowed visual identification of hundreds of individuals. And he used a fine brush to number each bee with spots of colored lacquer while they fed from his sugar water.

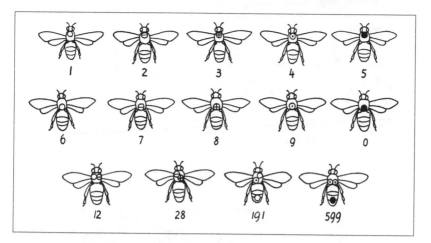

But his true gift was in the design of simple and effective experiments of exceptional elegance. (He initially translated the dance language, for example, by systematically removing to progressively greater distances from the hive the food source that his bees had been trained to seek and then closely observing the dances performed by the returning foragers.) And what underlay this—in addition to patience, self-criticism, and a creatively methodical practice—was his natural historical eye for bee ecology, temperament, and habit, and a deep affinity with bee ontology, the being of a bee.

It was all this that enabled him to recognize the individuality of the members of the hive, their characteristic predilections and tempera-

ments, their shifting moods, and their subtle variations of activity. It was, without doubt, a profoundly anthropomorphic commitment. His bees are "shrewd," "eager," and "phlegmatic"; at one point they even exhibit "class consciousness."[30] But it would be a mistake to think that anthropomorphism, which we could think of here as the impulse to understand other beings by reference to human interiority, is a sufficient framework through which to make sense of his work. For von Frisch, the honeybees were personal friends, but they were also profoundly mysterious in their difference. And it is this gap and its crossings that permit both reverence and subjection, both the relentless search for some kind of redemptive communion and the willingness to brutalize along the way.

Perhaps it is just the moment in which all this is taking place (the terrifying, dehumanizing political-historical moment that is also the thrilling moment in which all these discoveries are entirely new). Or perhaps it is the revived ethological determination to find the human in the animal. But it is clear that both in von Frisch's estimation and in the unfolding of his study, the bees were his collaborators as much as his subjects. He tests them—and makes no effort to hide his disappointment on the rare occasions when they fail to demonstrate their acuity. But they also test him: challenging him to devise experiments sufficiently sensitive to approximate their enigmatic way of being.

Von Frisch plunged into the Brunnwinkl research as into the lustrous depths of another world. "I tried to bury myself in it completely," he recalled, "taking as little notice as I could help of the events around me." Life outside Brunnwinkl was beyond control. In Munich, the Institute of Zoology lay in rubble, his house, too, "a gaping hole." The hostilities of professional life confounded him. He persuaded his wife to burn her diary.[31] Who could be trusted? Who was reading? Who might be listening? But the bees . . . The bees spoke, but they were indifferent to politics. Theirs was a language unsullied by the corrupting jargon of the Third Reich. The bees had a purity. The bees had an intelligible rationality. The bees offered refuge.

We don't know how Ruth Beutler felt, but Martin Lindauer, eventually von Frisch's most distinguished student, describes returning severely wounded to Munich from the Russian front, expressing the desire to study science, and being sent by his doctor to attend a lecture on cell division by Karl von Frisch. Lindauer recalls the event as an epiphany that opened the prospect of a normal, meaningful life for a confused twenty-one-year-old who had refused to join the Hitler Youth and had been sent instead to dig the foundations of Dachau, who had volunteered for the German army after an earlier lecture—this by SS officers recruiting at his high school—and who found in von Frisch a stern mentor with a "zeal for science . . . [who] tolerated no fraud . . . [who was] an extremely exacting person."[32]

Perhaps it's no surprise that, like his teacher, Lindauer experienced a profound attachment to the bees. As the national authoritarian order descended into chaos and conditions for professional science crumbled all around, von Frisch created an island of calm on Lake Wolfgang, finding in his honeybees a regularity, an ordered way of being in which, as in all well-run institutions, none need fear the unpredictable, none need feel unmoored. It was again the Germany of the amateur museum beside the Austrian lake, the Germany before the 1918 revolution, before the Weimar inflation, before the irruption of the Nazis. "After experiencing the senseless regime of the Hitler time, which was malicious, dishonest, and wrong from all perspectives," Lindauer told an interviewer half a century later, "I drew strength from having work based on absolute correctness, honesty, and objectivity. Out of this material and spiritual collapse, this hopelessness, I was able, with Karl von Frisch as a teacher, to build a new way of life. I found a new home with the bees. It was really a new home, the bee colony."[33]

3.

It is not hard to understand. The honeybee colony has tens of thousands of members whose everyday life is a wonder of self-regulated complexity, a productive order continuously brought into being through the intricate fluidity of its social relations, exchange practices, and division of labor. The very first thing von Frisch tells us in his 1953 work *The Dancing Bees* is that honeybees are obligate social beings, that the level of task integration and cooperative interdependence is such that a bee alone cannot survive outside the hive: "There is no smaller unit [than the colony]. . . . One single bee, kept all by itself, would soon perish."[34]

Like ants, termites, and the other social insects, honeybees live in what entomologists call caste societies, an analogy zoologists use to indicate the presence of morphologically distinct occupational groups: the egg-laying queen, the multitude of nonreproductive female workers, and the few hundred fat male drones with big eyes whose sole purpose—so far as we know—is to have sex with the queen on her single mating flight and who ultimately, as winter approaches and food resources dwindle, will be dragged from the hive by the workers, expelled to starve or, if resistant, stung to their death. "From that time onwards until the following spring," wrote von Frisch, evoking the feminist utopias of writers such as Charlotte Perkins Gilman, "the females of the colony, left to themselves, keep an undisturbed peace."[35]

Not surprisingly, it was the workers that attracted the researchers' attention. Von Frisch and Beutler catalogued their dances, and they made far-reaching discoveries concerning their orientation abilities. Lindauer extended their findings to swarming, nest location, and the extraordinary process of nest selection, which I describe below. All three carried out detailed studies of workers' division of labor and time allocation, although Lindauer pushed this furthest, by tracking the entire life history of a bee he called 107.

Below is Lindauer's first schematic of worker labor allocation. It shows what Thomas Seeley has called a "division of labor based on temporary specializations" and comes from Lindauer's classic 1961 account, *Communication among Social Bees,* a collection of lectures he gave at universities in the United States.[36] The column of figures indicates age in days. The whimsical bee people on the left are carrying out the activity associated with a particular point in a bee's life (cell cleaning, caring for

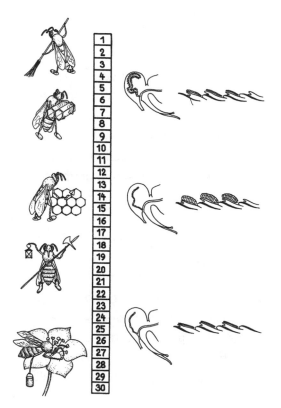

the brood, building and repairing the hive, guarding the nest, foraging for nectar, pollen, and water). The sketches on the right show the corresponding development of glands in the animal's head (the nurse, or feeding, gland) and abdomen (the wax glands). Despite this tight linkage of activity, physiology, and life cycle, Lindauer was fully aware that under critical circumstances—for example, a sudden food shortage—these relationships could be radically interrupted. In such a situation, the glands might stop developing and the bee begin foraging before its appointed day. A bee's physiology and behavior were flexible, adaptive, and responsive to changing conditions.

But that isn't all. When Lindauer tracked 107, he realized that she was not only spending more of her time multitasking than attending to the one expected assignment, but she was also doing an awful lot of wandering around ("patrolling," indicated in Lindauer's diagram on page 189 by the bowler hat and walking stick) and a considerable amount of what appeared to be nothing (40 percent of her time, in fact, "resting" on the chaise longue). Lindauer found explanations for these observations. Patrolling, he reasoned, was a form of site monitoring that allowed the bee to identify immediate needs and allocate her time accordingly. "Loafing," he claimed somewhat less convincingly, maintained the "reserve troops," who could swing into action as occasion demanded.[37]

Both of these unexpected activities suggested the importance of horizontal, peer-to-peer communication in a society organized without leaders or centralized decision making. The honeybees' ability to maintain the hive's internal environment—despite changes in external ambient conditions and the availability of critical resources—relies on contact between returning foragers and those already inside. The alacrity with which foragers are relieved of their loads, for instance, shows the degree of collective need for the substance in question. And not only is the recognizably sign-based language identified by von Frisch involved. Something more fundamental to social life is also going on. The bees are in constant physical contact, palpating each other's head and antennae, sensing each other's odor, passing compressed pollen to each other, sharing and exchanging the sugary contents of each other's stomach, receiving each other's near-field vibrations. Together, constantly, in the deep communal darkness, exchanging substances, sucking and regurgi-

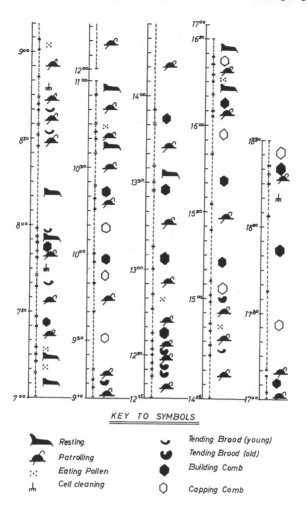

KEY TO SYMBOLS

▬	Resting	⌣	Tending Brood (young)
▲	Patrolling	⌣	Tending Brood (old)
∴	Eating Pollen	●	Building Comb
⊥	Cell cleaning	○	Capping Comb

tating, touching, feeling, smelling, tasting, sensing. Together, touching, in the warm darkness, sucking, feeling, touching, smelling, tasting, touching. Another country. Another language of bees.

And this language is somehow tied to that other language that is all around us here: the language of colonies, of castes and races, of sisters and half sisters, of queens and workers, the language of dance. The language of language, for heaven's sake! This language didn't disappear with von Frisch and Lindauer either. Today's bee scientists speak it too, even if they often bury it in a mechanical discourse of bioenergetics, a dissonance apparent in the distance between the anthropomorphic terminology and the machine-like organism it describes.

The new bee is an evolutionary bee for whom (as for all social insects) society is the individual and whose relationship to the hive is equal to that between the cell and the body. Out of these metaphors comes a compelling narrative of bee evolution in which selective pressures operate at the level of intercolony competition for food, foraging area, and other resources, a narrative supported by the absence of observable tension within the hive.[38]

But von Frisch suggests a supplement. It is not only—as all beekeepers know—the hives that exhibit different personalities (some tidy, some messy, some peaceable, some aggressive). In von Frisch's story, the interplay between individual and collectivity leaves room for individual variability and for the role of varying bee capacities and talents in furthering collective success. In his version, the hive is the expression of a culture of cooperation among its thousands of distinct individuals.

4.

Ernst Bergdolt, lecturer in botany at the Institute of Zoology in Munich, joined the Nazi Party in 1922, when he was just twenty years old. A presciently premature fascist, in 1937 Bergdolt became an editor of the *Zeitschrift für die gesamte Naturwissenschaft* (*Journal for the Entire Natural Sciences*), the most significant attempt to wrestle the biological sciences into conformity with Nazi ideology.[39] It was Bergdolt, the leading light of the German National Socialist Lecturers' League, who led the campaign to remove von Frisch from the Institute of Zoology. This is from a letter he wrote to the Ministry of Education, calling for the director's dismissal:

> Professor v. Frisch has an unusual ability to make propagandistic use of the results of his research, the sort of ability we know from Jewish scientists. In contrast, he lacks entirely the ability to survey his work from a broader point of view, let alone to find connections to the natural establishment of a volkish polity, something that seems so self-evident and would be so easy given his areas of expertise, bees.[40]

Bergdolt had already tried and failed to arrange von Frisch's prosecution for cruelty to animals.[41] His opening shot here is little more than a conventional invocation of "Jewish science." But the second charge was more unusual. While the logic of the hive offered von Frisch and Lindauer refuge from what they experienced as the disorienting chaos of the Nazi Reich, for Bergdolt that same systematicity embodied the utopian promise of Nazism itself. The bees readily provided a mirror of the human. But they did so through lives that—despite the transparency of language—were sufficiently opaque to allow such apparently conflicting fantasies. Even if, in this instance, the fantasies were structured in the same feverish milieu.

This is only partly a matter of different ideas of order. For the Nazis, of course, order required and enforced a savage and exemplary hierarchy. In the hive, however, hierarchy was profoundly ambiguous. Not only were the gender relations of the bee world drastically at odds with the ideals of National Socialism, but the nominal leader—the queen—was a figure of doubtful autonomy, subject in almost all respects to the workers who serviced her. Yet such inconvenient details of bee order were as nothing in light of the allegorical possibilities of formal orderliness: the disciplined subjection to the well-being of the greater good, the self-sacrificial altruism of the nonreproducing workers, the dissolution of the individual in the anonymity of collective purpose, the efficient disposal of lives not worth living, the dedication to a civilizational temporality. And perhaps what also drew Bergdolt to the hive was the brute visuality of that bounded world, self-sufficient and regimented despite its teeming energy, so evocative of totalitarian aesthetics.

Unlike his Nobel co-laureate Konrad Lorenz, who was not only an active member of the Nazi Party but also a key figure in its Office for Race Policy, von Frisch—as Bergdolt realized—had little interest in the larger analogy.[42] Where Lorenz explicitly established racial-hygiene correspondences between the degeneration of domesticated animals and the decline of the civilized human races, von Frisch most often restricted his own editorializing to remarks on the majesty of the bees' senses. In this period, instinct for Lorenz had a particular meaning, in which "instinctive action"—common to humans and other animals—is directed to the preservation of the species and the category "species" is homologous to the *Volk*. Evolution, he maintained, is imbued with moral purpose, selection operates at the level of the community, the subordination of the individual is a social good, and further, the elimination of individuals of "inferior value" is a social necessity. These ideas were also promoted by Alfred Ploetz and the Nordic strand of German *Rassenhygiene* that underwrote Nazi race policy. And Lorenz drew them even more directly from Ernst Haeckel's 1874 idiosyncratic *Anthropogenie oder Entwickelungsgeschichte des Menschen* (*The Evolution of Man*), in which social insects in their hive are a model for the relationship between citizen and state.[43] Lorenz's eagerness to buttress such notions with the authority of science was appropriately rewarded.[44]

It's no wonder that Bergdolt was dissatisfied with von Frisch's bees. Instinct, which could so easily be cast as the motor of racial progress, was decidedly muted in their hive. Only rarely does genetics escape mediation by consciousness.[45] In contrast to Lorenz's persistent diminution of animal capacity—what appears to be intentional action is revealed again and again as merely, if complexly, mechanical—von Frisch's work, focused principally at the level of individual behavior, is motivated by a spirit of valorization, in which the dominant registers are affinity and wonder. (Could we call it a humanism generous enough to include the nonhuman?)

Von Frisch's status as a founder of ethology rests on his revelatory account of the sensory world of the animal. It was an account that called into question simplified stimulus-response models of animal behavior and reoriented debates on animal cognition toward sensory complexity.[46] In contrast to his behaviorist antecedents, von Frisch directed attention to the mind of the animal, not merely to its external expression. His honeybees—"the most perfect insects with sheer incredible instincts"—are conscious, purposeful, able to learn, and capable of making decisions.[47] His language of language is far from accidental. There is, he leaves little doubt, a species of subjectivity in this species. It's a simple claim with complex implications. Perhaps the best way to follow them is through the famous research that von Frisch's student Martin Lindauer carried out on honeybee nest selection.[48]

When the population has grown and the hive is crowded, when nectar is abundant, stores are full, and the foragers are unable to pass off their loads, the bees prepare to swarm. The queen stops laying eggs, and workers tending the larvae begin feeding royal jelly to those they have selected to take her place. The foragers, for their part, stop collecting foodstuff and start searching abroad for cavities, inspecting holes in trees, buildings, and any other likely spots. Within days, the old queen exits the hive, escorted by about half the workers, perhaps 30,000 bees, leaving "house, honeycomb, and food supplies behind for her successors," as Lindauer wrote. They settle, all one living cluster, often on the branch of a nearby tree.[49]

The foraging workers fly missions from this temporary home, still scouring a huge area but looking now for potential nests that meet a set of precise criteria: appropriate size, small and well-positioned entrance, protection from wind, sufficient distance from the original colony, dry, dark, free of ants. And as they locate possible sites, they return to the cluster and—just as they do for food sources—they signal their discovery by dancing, though now they perform on the massed bodies of their assembled fellows.

Lindauer observed this behavior and realized that the returning foragers were dancing but no longer exchanging nectar or pollen. He identified and marked them, interpreted their dances, mapped the coordinates they were pointing to, and on reaching the designated locations found that, instead of collecting from flowers, the bees were "busily inspect[ing] holes in the ground, hollows of trees, or a crack in an old wall."[50] These foragers, he realized, were now "house hunters." This is his description of what happens as they return to the cluster:

If one follows for some time the dances of the scouting bees in the cluster and records their announcements of location, one comes to a very surprising conclusion: not just one nesting place is reported, but rather announcements are given of different directions and distances, and this means that several possible dwellings are announced at the same time. For example: on 27 June 1952 I noticed a dance in a cluster, which reported a nesting place 300 meters to the south. A few minutes later, a second dance could be observed which announced another nesting site 1400 meters to the east. In the next 2 hours, five more announcements came in, from the northeast, north, and northwest, with varied reports of distance. . . . On the next day 14 new reports of locations of nesting sites were added, so that now there were 21 different possibilities to choose from. The scout bees showed at the first glance that they had inspected various quarters: some were powdered over with dried dirt, because they had burrowed in a hole in the ground; others came from a cave in a ruin and were covered with red brick dust; once these seekers of quarters were soiled with soot, having discovered a suitable nesting place in a narrow chimney that was not in use during the summer.[51]

So how are these options weighed? With just one queen—a queen who may be old and weak and have difficulty flying—the swarm must hold together. To avoid disaster, it must reach not only decision but consensus. Yet this does not always happen. If a suitable site cannot be found, the bees may simply nest in the open, consigning themselves to certain death, victims of predators or the first frost. If, on the other hand, two cavities generate more or less equal interest, the swarm may split, each group following a different faction but only one containing a queen. Ultimately, the other will have no alternative but to end its secession and rejoin the swarm, often while both are still in flight to their new home.[52]

At this moment of danger, the survival of the colony depends entirely on the scouts. Nest selection, Lindauer discovered, as well as location, is up to them. They are both dancers and followers. Yet how these scouts "elect themselves" from the other foragers and persuade the rest of the swarm to follow them is still not known.[53]

Just as for nectar and pollen, the intensity of the dance corresponds to the appeal of the resource. A lively dance, a dance that indicates a nest of superior quality, can last for hours, its length and energy making it evident to a large number of scouts. The overall dancing in the swarm continues for days—up to two weeks even—and as it progresses, the number of cavities performed declines. Finally, if all is well, an overwhelming majority of the dancers will be proposing the same location, and any remaining "dissenters" are then disregarded.[54] A general excitement seizes the colony. With the queen at its center, the swarm takes wing for its new home.

But there is more. In the first place, as the debate unfolds, the scouts revisit and redescribe their cavities. And their opinions are likely to change. On return trips, they might find their site less appealing—it leaks in the rain, ants have moved in, a change in wind direction has made it vulnerable. If so, the enthusiasm of their dancing declines, and quite possibly they shift their support to a competing option.

Observing marked house hunters, Lindauer realized that those bees that dance with relatively little energy for one site are likely to eventually transfer their allegiance to another, more popular location. Flexible and open to persuasion, scouts invest decision making with appropriate seriousness. Rather than taking their fellow dancers at their word, they visit a number of sites in person, making inspections for themselves. Nor do they restrict themselves to the most popular options. Scouts attend a variety of dances and visit a range of proposed cavities. Only then, armed with comparative evidence and eyewitness authority, do they make a final decision on how to cast their lot.[55]

To James Gould and Carol Gould, this interaction illustrates "the basically democratic nature of certain colony activities."[56] For Donald Griffin, "These exchanges of dance communication resemble conversational exchanges."[57] They have the back-and-forth quality of a committee meeting, he suggests. And I, too, am impressed by the effectiveness and suitability of the process through which this life-or-death decision emerges, as well as by the mental subtlety it reveals. It is not easy to dismiss the insistence on determination and confirmation, the allowance for change, the hesitations and doubts, the willingness to reevaluate, the calculus of commitment and compromise, the comparative method.

But what kind of language is this? And what types of conversations does it make possible? We know the scientists will gladly speak on the honeybees' behalf. But can these tiny insects truly speak for themselves?

5.

Despite his eighty-seven years, von Frisch traveled to Oslo in the winter of 1973 to receive the Nobel Prize. In his lecture he recalled his life's work—his science, his bees, his colleagues—but he said nothing about his language of language. It was only his title that offered a clue: "Decoding the Language of the Bee."[58]

This was characteristic reticence. Along with his wonder at the bees' capacities was a reluctance to move from documentation—from the tooled-up natural history in which his new bees could be simply displayed for admiration—to a more reflectively theoretical mode in which those capacities could be assessed, evaluated, perhaps found wanting. In fact, it was through this reserve that the bees' linguistic lives became self-evident in his work. And it was through this silence that his analogy gained its effective concreteness—even if, more often than not, he took particular care to cover that special word *language* within the uncertain shelter of quotation marks.

So he is cautious. The bees have "language" but never speech. They do not talk (though he listens and understands). And when he describes Lindauer's research in Asia and Africa on the evolutionary lineage of bee communication as a "comparative philology" of *Apis* "dialects," he is pursuing the established plot. The terminology is descriptive, the comparisons will not reach beyond the honeybees, and the Latinate pretensions evince more than a little self-mockery.

But, although sometimes he seems like a scientist from a different era, he is also accomplished in the registers of theoretical biology, so distinct in tone and ambition, and he can wield them to address a different set of abstractions. In 1965, for example, he completes *The Dance Language and Orientation of Bees,* the summary statement of his research. Forced by the occasion to confront the ontological question in its fullness, he uses the preface to affirm unequivocally the limits of analogy: "Many readers may wonder whether it is proper to call the communication system of insects a 'language.' The use that is made here of this word must not be misunderstood, as though what bees inform one another of were to be regarded as the equivalent of human speech. In its wealth of concepts and its articulate mode of expression the language of man stands on quite a different plane." The language of the bees, he concludes in his clearest statement on the matter, though "unique in the whole animal kingdom," is actually a "precise and highly differentiated sign language."[59]

But this may be less restrictive than it at first appears. Von Frisch was writing at a moment when sign language promised a key to the otherwise inaccessible nonverbal mind. In this spirit, he introduces to the hive a wooden bee—his own prosthesis—and manipulates its movements, hoping that if he speaks their language, his bees will respond. The object's followers express curiosity, but they are not fooled. "The model," von Frisch acknowledged, "evidently lacked some significant characteristic without which it could not be taken seriously."[60] The bees know it is an alien. They attack and sting it repeatedly.

Meanwhile, across the Atlantic, the psychologists R. Allen Gardner and Beatrix Gardner, preoccupied by the evolution of cognition, were preparing to welcome Washoe the chimpanzee into their Nevada home, to raise her as their human girl child and teach her American Sign Language. In an attempt to render vulnerable to empirical investigation Wittgenstein's insight "If a lion could talk, we could not understand him," the Gardners reversed von Frisch's procedure and set out to prove that nonverbal animals can acquire human language and use it to communicate with one another and with their trainers.[61]

But Wittgenstein's lion, as the animal philosopher and trainer Vicki Hearne pointed out, is not without language; he is just "not talking."[62] His muteness proposes an irreconcilable difference, an indifference that refuses to be tamed, a fullness, not a lack; a "consciousness that is beyond ours," Hearne called it.[63] And yet this phenomenological abyss is exactly what von Frisch dared to cross—though less by code breaking than by the projection of his (and Lindauer's) most intimate longings. Because when forced to succumb to the language of science, to surrender the language of bees, he, too, was reduced to speaking in code.

Honeybees, like Wittgenstein's lion, don't talk to us. Instead, von Frisch taught us how to eavesdrop on them. And—in a whisper—he told us, too, that even if their "dance language" exhibits the automatic quality of the code, we should not assume that those signals we can access encompass their communicative world.

Of course this isn't merely a struggle over what the animal means; it is a struggle over the meaning of the animals themselves. And it is a battle long fought on the terrain of language. Though no philosopher, von Frisch understood this only too well. Language—the absence of language—continues to define the subordination (rather than simply the difference) of the animal in post-Enlightenment Western philosophy, a tradition remarkably Cartesian on this question.[64] Could von Frisch be clearer? This "dance language" is restitutive, an appeal to an ethic of mutuality and recognition, a call for respect for the nonhuman animal—for the animal in general and the astonishing honeybee in particular.

"It took some ten years of patient observation," wrote Jacques Lacan in the wake of the Brunnwinkl experiments, "for Karl von Frisch to decode . . . [the bees'] message, for it is certainly a code, or system of signaling, whose generic character alone forbids us to qualify it as conventional."[65] As code is to language, Lacan wants us to understand, so nature is to culture and animal is to human. Hardwired, hard-pressed, the bees stand for a programmed, mechanical nature in vivid contrast to the complex spontaneity of human culture.[66] Indeed, they enable this line between animal and human, between nature and culture, to be drawn with some severity.

The argument is not new: animals can sign, but they cannot lie. They can react, but they cannot respond.[67] They can communicate, but they cannot participate in the second-order metacommunication so familiar to humans. They cannot signify about signifying, think about thinking, and nor, for that matter, can they "dance about dancing."[68]

It is a conventional claim, this humanist insistence on language lack in the animal. And its framing in such irreducibly human terms makes it impossible to disprove (though not to dispute: in the cooperative setting of the hive, for example, it is difficult to imagine why a bee should be moved to dissemble about the location of a feeding site, and, anyway, wasn't it the bees' "honesty" that so appealed to Lindauer?).

But the point is not to make the bees speak, to have them tell us their secrets as the Gardners would have liked poor Washoe to tell them hers. Nor is it to imagine that the little honeybees are somehow just like us, that their world somehow corresponds to ours, that to be a bee is somehow equivalent to being a human equipped with a different sensory apparatus. That somehow our shared evolutionary origins, our intertwined deep histories, provide us also with a shared ontology.

Instead, can it be enough to point out that the honeybees' repertoire exceeds functional explanation and biochemical predictability, that the more researchers find out about honeybee cognition and behavior, the less appropriate and effective is the metaphor of the machine? In this instance, at least, it seems that language (or its absence) is an inadequate marker of interiority. And it seems that the assumption that language, human language, is "an unprecedented inferential engine" is itself a product of linguistic circularity—a product that tells us more about the making of the animal in language than about the living animal that is the ostensible subject of science.[69]

What, in such terms, can we make of the bees' "spasmodic dance," which is "more the expression of a dancing mood than an effective signal"? Or of the "trembling dance," which according to von Frisch "tells the bees nothing" yet manifests in times of stress and appears to mark some kind of "neurosis"? Or of the "jerking dance" that he considers "an expression of joy and contentment"?[70] Or, indeed, of the nest dances described by Lindauer, each of which intervenes in a larger social process of decision making?

But these are murky waters. Like von Frisch, I prefer to avoid this treacherous and much-debated question of language and cognition. The terms are too literal. The cards too stacked. The conflation of difference and deficiency too pervasive.

Like so many others, Lacan holds fast to the promise of that boundary between code and language, the promise of escape, a way to leave behind the animal to arrive as a thoroughly human subject. And in the inclusive corner, Griffin's cognitive ethology, with its principled determination to restore dignity, agency, and consciousness to the animal through methodological and theoretical humility, arrives at a troubling humanism of its own, a "giving speech back," conferring minority rights on the animal as on the thinking child, an uncanny recapitulation of the history through which colonial hierarchies were made.[71]

Such is von Frisch's dilemma. He knows his bees do not speak as humans; he knows their "language" is less but also more than his own. And he knows his new discipline allows space only for the less. Where within the rationality of his science could he find a language to express the profound commonality of life and the irredeemable fact of shared mortality? Where could he find its double, a language to communicate a difference for which no words exist? And where could he find a language in which to understand the absence of language as something other than a lack?

(Pity the animal that lives only as a shadow of the human, the animal forced to react rather than respond, the animal whose task is to give flesh, spirit, and meaning to the human, the animal whose melancholy fate is to be humanity's other.)

6.

"There is really no reason to suppose," says W. G. Sebald's Austerlitz, "that lesser beings are devoid of sentient life."[72] Remembering childhood nights, he wondered, Do moths dream? Do they know they are lost when, misled by the flame, they enter a house to die?

What was von Frisch's question: Can the honeybee speak? No, that wasn't it. First he thought, There is really no reason to suppose that honeybees are devoid of language. And then he asked, My little comrade, what does she say?

Pity the honeybees. Pity and protect them. In this, too, their indifference is of no avail. So trapped in language. The honeybees and us, held together, pushed apart. Even von Frisch, even Lindauer, who loved them so dearly, who found in them redemption from the brutish horrors of their times . . . Well, do you remember what they'd do to prove their little ones' capacities?

But enough paradox. To give them language was simultaneously to celebrate their difference and to doom them to impossibility, to condemn them to the merely imitative, at which they could only fail, to (mis)take "linguistic self-referentiality [as] the paradigm for self-referentiality generally."[73] But of course the failure is human (a specific scientific human, perhaps, but human nonetheless), this failure of being able only to imagine sociality and communication through something language-like and to grant ourselves its apogee. What foolishness to judge insects—so ancient, so diverse, so accomplished, so successful, so beautiful, so astonishing, so mysterious, so unknown—by criteria they can never meet and about which they could not care! What silliness to disregard their accomplishments and focus instead on their supposed deficiencies! What pitiful poverty of imagination to see them as resources merely for our self-knowledge! What sad, sad, sad sadness when language fails us.

My Nightmares

The thing most feared in secret always happens.

CESARE PAVESE, August 18, 1950

For a long time I thought only of bees. They crowded out all the others, and this book became just for them. A book of bees in all their bee-ness. All the physical capacities, all the behavioral subtleties, all the organizational mysteries, all the comradeship. All that golden beeswax lighting up the ancient world. All that honey sweetening medieval Europe. All those bees, timeless templates for the most diverse human projects and ideologies. Bees took over.

But then a plague of winged ants invaded my living room, and after they left I began thinking of locusts and then beetles—all those beetles!—and then caddis flies and crane flies and vinegar flies and botflies and dragonflies and mayflies and houseflies and so many other flies. Then one thing led to another, and I came across field crickets and mole crickets and Jerusalem crickets, and then Jessy sent me a weta from New Zealand. And then the seventeen-year cicadas emerged in Ohio, and I discovered the thrips and the katydids, remembered the aphids on California roses and the summer wasps drowning in water-filled jam jars, and then termites and hornets and earwigs and scorpions and ladybugs and praying mantises sold dry in packets in garden-supply stores. And then there were the mosquitoes with long legs and the mosquitoes with short legs and far too many butterflies and moths of all kinds. And I remembered what we all already know: that insects are without number and without end, that in comparison we are no more than dust, and that this is not the worst of it.

There is the nightmare of fecundity and the nightmare of the multitude. There is the nightmare of uncontrolled bodies and the nightmare of inside our bodies and all over our bodies. There is the nightmare of unguarded orifices and the nightmare of vulnerable places. There is the nightmare of foreign bodies in our bloodstream and the nightmare of foreign bodies in our ears and our eyes and under the surface of our skin.

There is the nightmare of swarming and the nightmare of crawling. There is the nightmare of burrowing and the nightmare of being seen in the dark. There is the nightmare of turning the overhead light on just as the carpet scatters. There is the nightmare of beings without reason and the nightmare of being unable to communicate. There is the nightmare of their being out to get us.

There is the nightmare of knowing and the nightmare of nonrecognition. There is the nightmare of not seeing the face. There is the nightmare of not having a face. There is the nightmare of too many limbs. There is the nightmare of all this plus invisibility.

There is the nightmare of being submerged and the nightmare of being overrun. There is the nightmare of being invaded and the nightmare of being alone. There is the nightmare of numbers, big and small. There is the nightmare of metamorphosis and the nightmare of persistence. There is the nightmare of wetness and the nightmare of dryness. There is the nightmare of poison and the nightmare of paralysis. There is the nightmare of putting the shoe on and of taking the shoe off. There is the slithering nightmare and the one that walks backward. There is the squirming nightmare and the squishing nightmare. There is the nightmare of the unwelcome surprise.

There is the nightmare of the gigantic and the nightmare of becoming. There is the nightmare of being trapped in the body of another with no way out and no way back. There is the nightmare of abandonment and the nightmare of social death. There is the nightmare of rejection. There is the nightmare of the grotesque.

There is the nightmare of awkward flight and the nightmare of clattering wings. There is the nightmare of entangled hair and the nightmare of the open mouth. There is the nightmare of long, probing antennae emerging from the overflow hole in the bathroom sink or, worse, the rim of the toilet. There is the nightmare of huge blank eyes. There is the nightmare of randomness and the unguarded moment. There is the nightmare of sitting down, the nightmare of rolling over, the nightmare of standing up.

There is the nightmare of the military that funds nearly all basic research in insect science, the nightmare of probes into brains and razors into eyes, the nightmare that should any of this reveal the secrets of locusts swarming, of bees navigating, or of ants foraging, the secrets will beget other secrets, the nightmares other nightmares, the pupae other pupae, insects born of microimplants; part-machine, part-insect insects; remote-controlled weaponized surveillance insects; moths on a mission; beetles undercover; not to mention robotic insects, mass-produced, mass-deployed, mass-suicide nightmare insects.

These are the nightmares that dream of coming wars, of insect wars without vulnerable central commands, forming and dispersing, congealing and dissolving, decentered, networked; of netwar, of network-centric warfare, of no-casualty wars (at least on our team), dreams of Osama bin Laden somewhere in a cave. These are the nightmares of invisible terrorists, swarming without number, invading intimate places and unguarded moments. The nightmares of our age, nightmares of emergence, of a hive of evil, a brood of bad people, a superorganism beyond individuals, "swarming on their own initiative—homing in from scattered locations on various targets and then dispersing, only to form new swarms."[1] The nightmare of language. The language of bees. Nightmare begets nightmare. Swarm begets swarm. Dreams beget dreams. Terror begets terror.

Where are the bees now? Collapsing in their colonies, gliding through their plastic mazes, sniffing out explosives, sucking up that sugar water, getting fat and weak on corn syrup, locked in little boxes at airports, sticking out their tongues on cue. Who knew the tiny critters were so smart, said the journalist. Fuzzy little sniffers. Buzz, buzz, buzz. Keeping us safe. Helping us sleep easy at night.

Nepal

And then, on waking one morning, as if in a dream, I left London with my friend Greg, headed for north India and Nepal. We planned to travel together for several months, but Greg returned after just a few weeks and I went on to Nepal with another friend, Dan, who, like me, had earned his ticket money as a porter in the local hospital. In all, I was away for six months but am surprised to realize now that I have no photographs from that trip and not many memories. Perhaps this is what happens when you travel without purpose, or at least when the only purpose is a hazy sense of adventure derived from a hazy sense of privilege. I do remember that Dan liked his drugs and that once he arrived, the two of us smoked more or less continually from the time we woke up until bedtime. We lived in a state of sensuous, if not analytic, clarity.

In those days, the town of Pokhara was little more than a main street, at one end of which the breathtaking mass of Annapurna rose vertiginously above all else. When the clouds cleared, it felt as if the mountain would topple over and bury everything. We stayed there in a sort of workers' dormitory for one or two nights and then decided to go to the hills. Somehow, I'm not sure how, we made a Nepalese friend of about our age who agreed to accompany us, and we set off walking. I have no photographs, letters, or journals of any of this, but if I fix on an object and move from there to another and then to the next, I create memories. A plunging waterfall in the side of a cliff and our bodies afterward covered in black leeches that we burned off with cigarettes. A woman killing a chicken for our dinner and our embarrassment because it was too big a thing and she wouldn't take payment. A wooden house on a hillside where, after dinner, a young boy tried to sell me his sister for the night.

Fried bread and salted buttered tea. Broad stony valleys. Strings of flapping Tibetan prayer flags. When I first saw the breathtaking opening scene of Werner Herzog's *Aguirre, Wrath of God*, I remembered the mule trains we passed picking their way along the sides of the mountains. When I heard on the BBC that the Maoists had finally entered Kathmandu and national government, I remembered the women who pleaded with us for money for their sick babies, who explained that the health post was closed, who showed us their children, listless, potbellied, and covered in sores, who made us feel helpless, stupid, ignorant, and out of place, as we were, who made me swear to myself I would never do this again.

Tonight, thirty years later, sitting near the back of the M5 bus on Seventy-second Street in Manhattan as the driver turned onto Riverside Drive and we sped along the darkened road with its grand doorman buildings on our right and the shadows of the park on our left, with the river and the highway below and out of view, I suddenly remembered, I can't say why, the completely different feeling of rounding a curve on the brightest of mornings, high in the mountains, the three of us striding carelessly along the gravelly path, the valley stretched below us, the peaks rising around us, the snows of the Himalaya so crisply unreal above us, and a group of children tumbling, laughing, along the road toward us, on their way to collect wood, we guessed, and a girl, maybe ten years old, I remember, the biggest of the little group, stopping in front of us, her arm outstretched, holding out her closed fist, palm-side down, telling me to hold out my palm under hers and all the while giggling so hard that we were giggling too without really knowing why, until she opened her hand and dropped into mine a ball, a closed-up living ball, something multicolored and alive that sat there still as stone, hiding in that sharp, sharp light, its segmented shell like a rolled-up sea creature or a special jewel, something very rare, and after I'd looked at it a few moments without comprehending what it was or why it was there in my hand, she plucked it back, still curled tight, and giggling still, swung her arm in the widest arc, and before I could get the words out, she had flung it high and far, causing it to spiral off the side of the mountain into the thin air and down, dizzyingly down into the gray-brown valley below, and had run off laughing, twirling around but staying upright, little friends, carrying their bundles, laughing and not looking back.

On January 8, 2008, Abdou Mahamane Was Driving through Niamey . . .

1.

On January 8, 2008, Abdou Mahamane, the managing director of Radio et Musique, Niger's first independent radio station, was driving home through Niamey, the country's capital. Around 10:30 p.m., as he entered Yantala, a suburb on the western outskirts of the city, his Toyota hit a land mine hidden in the unpaved road. The radio announcement was blunt: "Our colleague was torn to pieces." A woman passenger survived, but with serious injuries.

Karim and I had just got off the bus in Maradi, 415 miles to the east, and were watching the news report along with three or four other guests in the dimly lit hotel bar. "That's the road I take home every night," Karim said, shaken. On the large flat-screen TV, a silent crowd stared down at a floodlit crater and the mangled carcass of the journalist's car. In the studio, seated in front of what looked like someone's cell-phone photo of the blazing vehicle, a government spokesman was denouncing the Mouvement des Nigériens pour la justice (MNJ) and calling on loyal citizens to root out the evil in their midst. For its part, the MNJ, the Tuareg movement that has been in armed rebellion in the north of Niger since February 2007, accused President Mamadou Tandja's regime of setting the mines itself to feed the spiraling insecurity and violence and of further entrenching this latest phase of a decades-long conflict by refusing to negotiate.

In the hotel bar, it was doubt, counterdoubt, and pensive silence. This was the first attack in the capital, but just the previous month two people had been killed by anti-tank mines here in Maradi, and four others had been wounded in the town of Tahoua. The month before that, a bus loaded with passengers had been hit outside Agadez, the major city of the north. There was no uncertainty about government hostility to independent journalists—two Nigerien and two French reporters were being held incommunicado for nosing around in the militarized rebellion zone. But who could say whether Abdou Mahamane had been targeted or was simply a chance victim? And in either case, who could be certain of the killers' loyalties? People are "walking around on tip-toe," reported the radio, everyone is "afraid of being blown apart."

Still, as Nigeriens well know, there are many ways of being blown apart and many sources of insecurity and dread. These mines and this fear were just two of the routes by which the unrest was coming home. The first time we met, Karim had given me a concise introduction to Nigerien politics. Welcome to Niger, he said, a large country with a small population, a poor country rich in resources, a weak country with powerful neighbors.

A couple of days before the explosion, the two of us had taken a taxi over the U.S.-funded Kennedy Bridge, which spans the Niger River in Niamey, and walked through the lively campus of the Université Abdou Moumouni. Karim had studied law here until 2001, when the university was closed by student strikes. After that, he left to continue his schooling in Nigeria and Burkina Faso. He has many friends here still, and we stopped frequently to exchange greetings. Groups of young men were gathered in the sunshine outside their dormitories, listening to the radio, talking politics, getting haircuts. Young women strolled past arm in arm.

In a book-filled office on the ground floor of the two-story red-brick Faculty of Science building we met Mahamane Saadou, professor of plant biology. Karim had patiently explained to me how the political instability in the north generated random violence and psychic perturbation, how it held back the national economy by preventing the exploitation of subsurface wealth (uranium and oil), and how it increased the opportunities for geopolitical mischief by France, the colonial power, as well as by Libya and other neighbors. Professor Saadou listened as I described my ideas for this book and Karim explained that we were spending two weeks together talking to people in Niamey, Maradi, and the surrounding countryside about locusts—what these insects do, what is done to them, what they mean, and what they have created here in Niger. When we finished, Professor Saadou told us that one thing created by both land mines and locusts was terror and that they did it not only separately but together.

Because of the political standoff and the proven danger of kidnapping, Professor Saadou said, the internationally funded anti-locust teams in Agadez, close to the mountainous Aïr region and the advancing sands of the Sahara, rarely leave their bases. When they do, he continued, it is only for short visits to the field. They can't carry out their work, and—because a chain is only as strong as its weakest link—neither, therefore, can the elaborate trans-Sahelian locust-monitoring network, the early-warning system designed to give protection to those adjacent to what is not just a zone of conflict but also a zone of distribution, a point from which the *criquet pèlerin*, the most destructive of the Sahelian locusts, swarms west and south into the agricultural regions.

In fact, the professor went on, if you examine the desert locust atlas and look closely at the maps of the insect's recession area—the zone in which it breeds and aggregates, the zone from which the swarms set out for pastures wetter and greener, a zone that covers about 6 million square miles in a broad belt that runs across the Sahel and through the Arabian Peninsula as far as India, and the only zone in which there is perhaps some slim chance of controlling the animal's development—you'll see clearly that many of the most important sites are in places commonly rendered inaccessible by conflict: Mauritania, eastern Mali, northern Niger, northern Chad, Sudan, Somalia, Iraq, Afghanistan, western Pakistan. It's an extensive, familiar, and in this context, deeply disheartening list.

Across campus, in the Faculty of Letters and Human Sciences, Professor Boureima Alpha Gado told a similar story. A historian, Professor Alpha Gado is a leading expert on the famines of the Sahel and the author of an authoritative text on the subject.[1] He described how he had used manuscripts from Timbuktu, the ancient center of Islamic and pre-Islamic learning, to determine occurrences of *"calamités"* dating to the mid-sixteenth century. For twentieth-century disasters, he collected oral histories from villagers, constructing a chronology of the major famines and identifying the critical factors—primarily drought, locusts, and changes in the agricultural economy—and their shifting interactions.

Professor Alpha Gado's research revealed a rural society grappling with deeply founded insecurities, vulnerable to the vicissitudes of rainfall, human and animal epidemics, and upsurges in insect life. His work invigorated the truism that "natural disasters" act on already-existing social vulnerabilities and inequalities and that "nature" itself (driven in this case by desertification and climate-change-induced drought) is far from innocently natural. He carefully detailed the local social dimensions of these events: the colonial and postcolonial policies that increased the susceptibilities of people in the countryside to famine and reduced their resilience to insect invasions and disease. Notwithstanding the small number of all-too-brief interludes of relative prosperity, he described an everyday state of attrition interrupted by periods of catastrophe, in which the number of deaths has been "incalculable." Like Mahamane Saadou, he painted a picture of overlapping terrors, of a persistent teetering on the brink, more a condition than an event, a condition with its own rhythms, histories, and enduring effects.

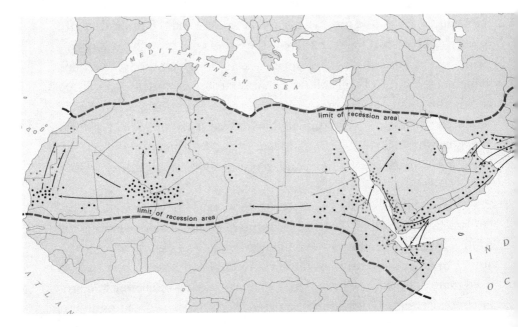

2.

Locusts appear twice in *Things Fall Apart*, Chinua Achebe's famous 1958 novel of British colonialism's explosion of rural life in the late-nineteenth-century Niger Delta. The first time, "a shadow fell on the world, and the sun seemed hidden behind a thick cloud." The village of Umuofia stiffens in anticipation of the darkness engulfing the horizon. Or does it?

Okonkwo looks up from his work and wonders if it is going to rain at such an unlikely time of year. But almost immediately a shout of joy breaks out in all directions, and Umuofia, which has dozed in the noonday haze, bursts into life and activity.

"Locusts are descending" is joyfully chanted everywhere, and men, women, and children leave their work or their play and run into the open to see the unfamiliar sight. The locusts have not come for a very long time, and only the old people have seen them before.

At first, there are not so many, "they were the harbingers sent to survey the land." But soon a vast swarm fills the air, "a tremendous sight, full of power and beauty." To the entire village's delight, the locusts decide to stay. "They settled on every tree and on every blade of grass; they settled on the roofs and covered the bare ground. Mighty tree branches broke away under them, and the whole country became the brown-earth colour of the vast, hungry swarm."[2] The next morning, before the sun has a chance to warm the animals' bodies and release their wings, everyone is outside filling bags and pots, gathering all the insects they can hold. The carefree days that follow are filled with feasting.

But Chinua Achebe's story is a tale of destruction. Joy becomes unrelenting historical pain. The cloud still looms, and its shadow falls over Umuofia's future. Pleasures are bound fast to their fatal opposites. Everyone in the village is happily enjoying the unexpected harvest when a delegation of elders arrives at Okonkwo's compound. Solemnly, the elders decree the killing of the beloved child who is Okonkwo's ward, a killing that corrodes his family. Years later, when the locusts reappear, Okonkwo is in exile.

It is his friend Obierika who visits him with the news. A white man has appeared in a neighboring village. "An albino," suggests Okonkwo. No, he is not an albino. "The first people who saw him ran away," says Obierika. "The elders consulted their Oracle and it told them the strange man would break their clan and spread destruction among them." He continues, "I forgot to tell you something else the Oracle said. It said that other white men were on their way. They were locusts, it said, and that first man was their harbinger sent to explore the terrain. And so they killed him."[3]

They kill him, but it is too late. The vast swarm of white men would soon arrive. There's no ambiguity in this story. The pleasures are quickly excised. It's all flat, the flatness of history foretold. The flattening of everyday life among the locusts. Hard to think past these terrors, you might say (with reason). A vast swarm would soon come, and nothing would again be the same.

3.

Mahaman and Antoinette are such good hosts! We're sitting in their luxuriant tropical yard in Niamey talking about *les criquets*. We're trying to specify the exact category of food in which they belong. Everyone agrees they're a special food. But they're a special kind of special food, different from the special crispy honey cakes Mahaman just brought back from Ethiopia and insists that Karim and I eat more of. *Criquets* are a social food, Antoinette says. Sort of like peanuts, but not a party food. Hmmm. A short silence. Well, texture is important: They're crunchy! And they're spontaneous, too. How so? Well, we shop in the open-air markets here, not in the supermarket, so we shop every day. It's an every-day economy. We see *criquets* on the market and maybe we think, I'm going to buy some of them! We bring them home and cook them with oil, chilies, and plenty of salt. Sooo *delicious!* It's a spontaneous treat. It's a food for fun, a fun food, a personal, friendly treat. Friends, family. Social food. It's the kind of food you eat just because you feel like eating it.

It's a Nigerien food, adds Mahaman. When our daughter is at school in France, she always asks us to send her *criquets*. It's the thing she misses most, the strongest taste of home. Yes, Karim agrees, it's what everyone misses; we sent packages to my sister when she was in France as well. And don't you remember, he asks me, that's what the guy this morning selling those rust-colored, crunchy-looking insects on the sleepy market just past the university said too? Fry some in salt and take them back to New York, he said; share them with a homesick Nigerien and make him very happy!

Talking like this, we quickly establish that—like so many foods—*criquets* satisfy spiritual as well as physical hungers. Eating them is one of those things that makes someone Nigerien. They eat them in Chad too, says Karim, but the quality is not so good. And no one eats them in Burkina, although Nigerien students bring packages from home across the border, and people in Ouaga are starting to get a taste for them. But Tuaregs don't eat them, someone says, further complicating the national question. And, entering right on cue, closing the garden gate behind him with a broad smile, the director of LASDEL, the research institute that is hosting my stay, says yes, that's right, we Tuaregs don't eat small animals at all!

A special food, we all agree, and in the markets in Niamey and Maradi, this is obvious. The United Nations calculates that 64 percent of the population of Niger lives on less than the equivalent of U.S. $1 per day. The regime struggles to maintain its position at the helm of the state. How can the administration capture the resources it needs to maintain its popular base when 50 percent of its potential annual budget goes directly to the international development organizations? The government disputes the U.N. figures, as well as the 2008 human development index score of 0.370, which placed Niger 174th out of the 179 countries measured, as well as the Save the Children Mothers' Index of 2009, which ranked the country 158 out of the 158 countries surveyed and cited 44 percent of its children as malnourished, the life expectancy of its women at fifty-six years, and a figure of one in six for the number of its infants expected to die before their fifth birthday. In the media, those numbers are taken to be both a national shame and—more assertively—an expression of international hostility.[4] Yet, however you look at it, in this situation the rhetoric of crisis does not work to the government's advantage. Some of those figures may be debatable in a largely rural and far from straightforwardly cash-based economy. But it's abundantly clear that few people outside development workers, successful merchants, and the political class have much income to circulate.

Nonetheless, in January 2008 traders in Niamey's many markets were selling enamel basins of dried *criquets* for 1,000 CFA each, well over double the United Nations' estimate of most people's daily income.[5] *Criquets* are a special food. And an expensive one, too.

January is not a good month in this business. With Eid al-Adha falling in early December this year and then Christmas and the celebration of the new year, there's little extra cash for *criquets,* and people buy only in small amounts, just fractions of the enamel *tia* measuring bowl. It's not only money that's tight. There aren't many insects in circulation either. January turns out to be a long way from September, when supply peaks at the end of the rainy season and the markets are full of locust sellers and the price falls as low as 500 CFA. Now, as we soon find out, *criquets* are scarce in the villages, and in another month no one will be bringing them into town.

We talked to all the insect-selling stallholders we could find in

Niamey. Some of them buy their stock in nearby market towns like Fil-
ingué and Tillabéri, some buy from traders on larger markets in Niamey,
and some simply buy wholesale from neighboring stalls in the same
market. Most, though, said their *criquets* come from Maradi, and all of
them told us to go there. That's where these animals are sent from,
that's where you'll find the collectors out in the bush early in the morning, that's where the big suppliers are based.

I'm enjoying running around Niamey with Karim. There's so much
to see and learn here. I love the markets, discovering with a shock that I
recognize only a tiny proportion of the vegetables. These plants got here
through an evolutionary history I can't begin to imagine! And then there
are products for sale that might equally be animal, vegetable, or mineral
for all I can tell. I can't come close to guessing their purpose until Karim
explains that these neatly stacked mottled-glass marbles are globules of
tree resin, which make a superior chewing gum; that those dark, craggy
tennis balls are crushed and compressed peanuts used for sauce; that
those bottles of murky liquid are full of contraband gasoline smuggled
in from Nigeria.

Karim and I keep each other busy visiting the markets, the university,
and government offices, meeting all kinds of interesting people, not just
scholars and traders but state officials, development workers, insect scientists, insect eaters, and talkative fellow passengers in communal taxi-
cabs. We make the most of Mahaman and Antoinette's hospitality. But
this can't last. After just a few days, we find ourselves huddling in the
crowded bus station at 3:30 a.m. We're cold, sleepy, and a little bad tem-
pered, and it feels as though the bus to Maradi will never arrive.

4.

We spent those first few days in Niamey chasing after Achebe's paradox:
How could these animals bring both feast and famine? How could they
be harbingers of both life and death, bearers of both pleasure and pain?
Our contacts and our conversations multiplied, and as they did, our
questions changed. Soon, we were wondering if—as Boureima Alpha
Gado had tactfully suggested—this was less a paradox than a confusion,

if maybe there were more animals here than we realized, if perhaps they weren't the animals we thought they were, if maybe we weren't always talking about the same ones, if perhaps some of this was a problem of translation. In French, everyone called them *criquets*. In Hausa, they were *houara*. We'd thought we were talking to people about locusts, but now we weren't quite so sure.

AGRHYMET, an agricultural research organization sponsored by Africa's nine Sahelian countries, has offices and a library in Niamey, just past the university. The helpful and generous staff members gave us a set of attractive pocket-size paperbacks, including the *Vade-Mecum des criquets du Sahel* by My-Hanh Launois-Luong and Michel Lecoq, a field guide to more then eighty regional species. Some of these, such as the *criquet pèlerin,* the *criquet migrateur,* the *criquet nomade,* and the *criquet sénégalais,* are famously destructive and have long been the object of intensive research and control measures. Others, listed by their Latinate species names, are included simply because they're abundant or, conversely, because they're unusual.[6]

The *Vade-Mecum* identifies nearly all the *criquets* of the Sahel as members of the Acrididae family, the short-horned grasshoppers. Among the approximately 11,000 known species of grasshoppers, 10,000 are in the Acrididae family, including all the locusts (about 20 species). What is it that makes the locusts special? Biologists distinguish them from the other acridids by their ability to change form in response to crowding. *Schistocerca gregaria*—the *criquet pèlerin,* the desert locust, the eighth plague of Egypt—is perhaps the most characteristic of all. The harmless solitary insect is thought to be stimulated to enter a gregarious phase by the increased contact that accompanies high population density, a density which results from two coinciding but not unusual factors: higher than average rainy seasons, which encourage the insects to reproduce, followed by dry periods, which shrink its habitat, limit its food resources, and encourage it to travel.[7] In phase transformation, the rapid and reversible changes in the animal's morphology (wider head, larger body, longer wings), life history (earlier reproduction, reduced fecundity, more rapid adult maturation), physiology (higher metabolic rates), and behavior are so radical that for a long time insects in the two phases were thought to be distinct species.

The gregarious nymphs—the hoppers—form into bands of thousands or even millions of individuals and begin to march. As they make their way across the desert, other hopper bands arrive and merge with the original column. They can cover tens of miles heading in a straight line, and as they march, they pass through their five instars, stopping their journey only when they finally molt to become the adult insect.

At a critical density, the adult locusts take to the air. Until recently, it was thought that the Sahelian swarms were carried along the intertropical convergence zone to areas of rainfall favorable for reproduction. It's now clear that rather than being passively transported on the current, the animals control their route and direction: they navigate, altering their course and orientation both collectively and individually, often flying against the wind rather than with it and stopping at attractive feeding areas as they go. It has also become clear that swarming is principally a foraging activity rather than a migratory one and that long-distance migration is more commonly undertaken by solitary adults flying huge distances at night. It is this complex combination of talents—rapid reproduction and aggregation, long-distance flight, mass foraging, and individual migration—that allows the *criquet pèlerin* to find and exploit temporary patches of favorable habitat in an overall highly marginal environment.[8]

The scale of the swarm is well-known but still hard to comprehend. The *University of Florida Book of Insect Records* (a wonderful project!) describes one in Kenya in 1954 that contained about 50 million insects in each of the seventy-five square miles it covered, a total of 10 billion animals.[9] These are vast numbers and vast appetites. One locust can consume the equivalent of its own body mass in vegetation every day; only 0.07 ounces perhaps, but multiply that by 10 billion and calculate the consequences. Somewhere on the BBC website, I read the impressive statistic that one ton of locusts, just a small patch of a swarm, eats the same amount of food in twenty-four hours as 2,500 people (but which people, we might wonder?). It's obvious but still worth stating that the impossibly high numbers are compounded by the huge distances the insects travel (up to 2,000 miles in a season) and the destruction they bring over this enormous area, as well as by their willingness and capacity to eat almost anything, not only crops but plastics and textiles. Only subground crops—tubers, for instance—are safe.

In English, the linguistic distinction between locusts and other grasshoppers is emphatic.[10] *Locust* conjures up a tight set of referents linked to rapaciousness, fear, and suffering. By contrast, *grasshopper*—at least outside the anti-acridian literature—is rarely menacing. Think of David Carradine in *Kung Fu* or of Keats's little friend who "takes the lead / In summer luxury" and is "never done / With his delights."[11]

There's nothing in the popular use of the word *grasshopper* that calls up the *ravageurs*. But there should be. Fearsome as they are, locusts do not have a monopoly on terror in the Sahel. Even on insect terror. The other most-dreaded *criquet* in Niger is a grasshopper, *Oedaleus senegalensis*, the *criquet sénégalais*. Described as a nongregarious grasshopper because it does not change phase, it nonetheless forms hopper bands and loose adult swarms and can migrate more than 200 miles in one night.[12] The *criquet sénégalais* has been responsible for devastating invasions of Nigerien farmland and pastureland on a scale comparable to that of the *criquet pèlerin*. Like the desert locust, this grasshopper is a continual threat to Sahelian farmers. Unlike the locust, it breeds in areas close to cropland and has a development cycle tightly coordinated with that of millet. It's a persistent, debilitating presence, rarely absent from the fields. Indeed, it's often argued that the use of pesticides to control insect outbreaks has increased grasshopper populations by removing their predators. "Grasshoppers," wrote the entomologist Robert Cheke in 1990, "afford a much greater long-term and chronic menace to agriculture than do the classic locusts."[13] People in the countryside told us that even when the *criquet sénégalais* and its allies aren't swarming, there's terror in the slow death caused by their constant undermining of everyday life and future horizons.

Yet, it is still the case that the bulk of research and management funding for securing crops against agricultural pests is aimed at the *criquet pèlerin*. It's partly a taxonomic disorder—a question of naming and its consequences—that grasshoppers, some of whom are identical to locusts in all significant respects, have been cast into the shade. Whereas the swarming of the *criquet pèlerin* has long provoked the full-blooded apparatus of humanitarian intervention, until quite recently farmers' losses in their struggles with the Sahelian grasshoppers were understood only as part of the cost of growing food under marginal conditions.[14] This is also partly a problem of temporality. And of vision and visibility, too. A long-term war of attrition hardly lends itself to the campaign politics of disaster relief. An upsurge of locusts is a crisis, with all the international media and aid-agency mobilization that a crisis entails. It is a "plague," driven by the locust's perverse glamour, its charisma and celebrity, generating spectacular news and both the obligation for governments to be seen combating an iconic foe and the opportunity for international agencies to step in to the administrative void.

The two most common Nigerien terms for this animal are expansive. Both *criquet* (in French) and *houara* (in Hausa) describe a motley community of insects whose commonalities far exceed their differences. Karim and I never systematically mapped this community's boundaries, nor did we map differences between the terms, but each comfortably enfolded all the insects we were talking about: the ones eaten at parties, the ones collected in the bush, the ones caught up in children's games, the ones sold in markets, the ones sent to homesick relatives, the ones that swarm and ravage spectacularly, the ones that don't swarm but still ravage, the ones with polymorphic phases, the ones without, the medicinal ones, the magical ones, the ones that offer a glimpse of financial possibility, the locusts and the other grasshoppers.

One morning in the village of Rijio Oubandawaki, a dusty three-hour drive north of Maradi, a crowd of men and boys came up with the names of thirteen different *houara* in just a few minutes. As it's women who collect these animals, who knows how many more we'd have learned if they'd been back from the fields. Eleven of those thirteen *houara* were edible. Three of them were considered especially dangerous to crops. Only one was a swarming insect. Some of the men in this big village, with its clusters of low adobe houses, its narrow lanes bordered with woven fences, its open sandy plazas, and its large concrete schoolhouse, remembered the arrival of those swarming *houara* in their youth. How could they forget? The insects stripped the fields, invaded the houses. Could they have been the *criquet pèlerin?* Or perhaps the *criquet séné-galais?* Or perhaps it was the *criquet migrateur,* once a source of terror in this region but now largely neutralized by environmental changes in its outbreak zone in Mali. It would depend on when the animals appeared. From 1928 to 1932, it was the *criquet migrateur;* from 1950 to 1962, the *criquet pèlerin;* from 1974 to 1975, the *criquet sénégalais.*[15] Whichever it was, they told us categorically, those particular *houara* have never been here since.

The biologists we met in the cities couldn't match the animals' lively names—chief's knife, from the kalgo tree, sorcerer *houara*, radada (an onomatopoeia)—with their French or Latinate equivalents. They couldn't even help us identify the dark ones called *birdé* that everyone in Rijio Oubandawaki loves to eat, which eats all the medicinal plants so is itself a strong medicine, but whose appearance in the fields is nonetheless a source of dread. Of all the *criquets* we encountered, *birdé* is the one that seems to conform most closely to Achebe's paradox. We suspected it was *Kraussaria angulifera,* a well-known swarming grasshopper that combined with the *criquet sénégalais* in massive outbreaks across West Africa in 1985 and 1986 and AGRHYMET's *Vade-Mecum* describes as among the most dangerous *ravageurs* of millet in the entire Sahel. Flanked by pesticide posters in his office at the anti-acridian section of the Maradi Direction de la protection des végétaux, Dr. Mahaman Seidou gave it a second life as one of the two most popular insect food species in Niger.

Nonetheless, we were starting to think of the *houara* as more protean than paradoxical: many selves, many beings, many lives. Still, here and now, in this place, at this moment, its identity seemed profoundly fixed. Locusts or not, swarming or not, food or not, income or not, they cast a shadow on the land. The facts, even if not completely precise, were unavoidable. Approximately 20 to 30 percent of the Nigerien agricultural crop, some 450,000 tons, a total greater than current estimates of the country's food deficit (the difference between what the population eats and what it grows), is lost annually to insects and other animals, mostly birds. Here in the Maradi region, where conditions are even more favorable to insects than elsewhere in the country, that figure is closer to 50 percent.[16]

Perhaps, though (we had to wonder), it wasn't only the weight of the facts that cast this shadow over our conversations. Perhaps the depth of the shadow was also an artifact of our interest and of the resources we embodied in a country dependent on and habituated to international aid workers. That day in Rijio Oubandawaki, life's pleasures and the *houara*'s possibilities—the food, the games, the cash in hand, the knowledge—slipped quickly out of sight. In other circumstances, it might be satisfactions that come to the surface. But with such a brief visit, with so little earned intimacy, with just the appeal and the desire on all sides, the life most visible was the obvious—the *houara* most visible was the obvious—the one that multiplied the manifold insecurities of a profoundly hard-scrabble human existence.

"I have a question," one man said to me as we were leaving. "Can you tell us some techniques we can use to control these *houara* and protect our millet?" How could I respond? "I'm afraid I'm not really an expert in that kind of thing," I said awkwardly, adding that when I returned to Niamey the following week, I would immediately visit the central office of the Direction de la protection des végétaux and tell the officials about the problems people here are facing. Everyone fell silent. The men with whom we'd been talking thanked me courteously but said I should understand that there was really no point in doing that.

Fifteen years ago, the questioner explained, a team of agricultural-extension workers had come to the village. They trained people to use pesticides and left a supply for the residents' use. Everyone applied the chemicals as instructed and was happy to see that they worked: insect

damage was significantly reduced, yields increased, and there seemed to be no harmful effects on crops, people, or other animals. Soon, though, the chemicals ran out, and fifteen years later the stock has still not been replenished. Nowadays, he continued as we all listened attentively, the only people who use pesticides in this village are the rich farmers, those with more than twenty-five acres, who can afford to buy chemicals privately. The *houara* avoid their fields and concentrate their appetites on the rich men's less fortunate neighbors. Every year the insects and birds (those terrible birds!) eat our millet, our sorghum, and our cowpeas; sometimes they eat half our crop or more. We stretch wire for the birds, and we set fire to the *houara*. We burn the birds, too. But none of it helps. He lapsed into quiet and another man in the group spoke. Actually, he said, you *should* go to the ministry. When you do, if you look hard enough, you'll find thick folders of paperwork about this village. You should go, but you shouldn't bother talking to anyone about us. You shouldn't imagine they're not aware of the situation here. Whatever else is going on in the capital, it's not ignorance.

5.

The bus arrives and we clamber aboard. With the hugest red sun rising ahead of us, we're soon barreling out of Niamey and across the baked landscape, its flatness punctuated by low rounded hills and sharp lateritic escarpments. For the next few hours, the two-lane highway is lined by ocher villages filled with family compounds of rectangular mud-brick houses. Graceful onion-shaped granaries overflow with sheaves of millet from the recent harvest. People sit outside their homes or at stalls along the road. Men build and renovate walls and fences, repair the granaries, hoe fields. Women thresh tall heaps of grain, pound millet for porridge, gather around village wells, carry large bundles of firewood or millet stalks, their dazzling cotton cloths billowing as they walk. Children collect wood too, or tend other children or herds of goats. We stop briefly to buy food in the crowded bus station at Birni N'Konni and then continue east, ignoring the turning that cuts north to Tahoua, Agadez, and the uranium town of Arlit. From this point on, everything feels a little greener, a bit more prosperous: large herds of long-horned cattle, flocks of camels, their front legs loosely bound to stop them from straying too far too fast, droves of donkeys, more granaries, more fields, and the startling dark splash of irrigated onion patches.

Maradi hums with commercial energy, but its position at the hub of Niger's economic life dates only from the end of the Second World War. Because of its geographic location and an inability to secure its supply lines, the town was excluded from the great trans-Saharan caravan routes that for centuries linked Algiers, Tunis, Tripoli, and other Mediterranean ports first to Zinder, Kano, and destinations close to Lake Chad, and then to the rest of Africa. This trans-Saharan trade supplied the eighteenth-century Hausa city-states, commercial powerhouses that in turn supplied gold, ivory, ostrich plumes, leather, henna, gum arabic, and, most lucratively, sub-Saharan slaves to Tuareg and Arab traders, who carried them north, returning from the coast with firearms, sabers, blue and white cotton cloth, blankets, salt, dates, and the multi-purpose mineral natron, as well as candles, paper, coins, and other European and Maghrebi manufactured goods.[17]

By 1914, the British rail network through Nigeria had reached Kano, close to the border with Niger. It was now both cheaper and safer to send goods by train to Lagos and the other Atlantic ports than to ship them north on the cross-desert camel trains. Taking advantage of the decline of the caravans and the sudden access to transportation, the French administration pushed aggressively to provide the Maradi Valley with the initial capital and infrastructure needed to cultivate groundnuts for the colonial oil market. By the mid-1950s, Maradi was competing as a regional center for a crop that had been strongly commercialized by the French in Senegal and elsewhere in their West African colonies but until then had barely taken hold in Niger. Forced to pay colonial taxes in cash—and drawn to the new European trading houses selling imported goods—Maradi's farmers brought more and more land into groundnut cultivation and initiated two dynamics that would prove devastating during the extended drought and famine that lasted from 1968 to 1974: the undermining of already-fragile food security through the large-scale substitution of groundnuts for staple crops, especially millet, and the encroachment on and effective privatization of grazing areas used by

Tuaregs, Fulanis, and other pastoralists, who, pushed with their animals onto increasingly marginal lands, would make up the significant majority of famine victims.[18]

The border that split Hausaland between French-ruled Niger and the British Protectorate of Northern Nigeria was fixed in a series of conventions agreed to by the two colonial powers between 1898 and 1910. Insecure about the transborder loyalty of their Hausa subjects, the French funneled their patronage to the Djerma of western Niger, moving the capital from Zinder to Niamey in 1926. "While roads, schools, and hospitals were gradually introduced [by the British] into Northern Nigeria," writes the anthropologist Barbara Cooper, "the French permitted Maradi to languish as a neglected backwater in a peripheral colony, where infrastructure developed fitfully if at all."[19]

The effects of these policies were, predictably, not quite as intended. Even though precolonial Hausaland had been riven by violent rivalries, the common experience of colonial exaction under both British and French rule, plus the persistence of cultural, linguistic, and economic connections, created powerful cross-border identifications that continue to this day. One mark of this linkage is the emergence in Maradi of the *alhazai* (from the Islamic honorific Alhaji—he who has completed the hajj, the pilgrimage to Mecca), powerful Hausa merchants who began their careers in the groundnut industry and the European trading houses but rapidly diversified to exploit the opportunities for commerce, licit and illicit, offered by the border. As Cooper notes, it was the ability of the *alhazai* to capitalize on British investments in northern Nigeria— such as the rail link to Kano—that propelled them to prominence and allowed them to weather such crises as the famine of 1968–74 (from which many profited handsomely) and the devaluations of the Nigerian naira in the 1990s.

The *alhazai* are also lively participants in the global Islamic geography that links Maradi to Egypt, Morocco, and other sites of higher education, and to Abu Dhabi, Dubai, and other centers of big capital. And they are conspicuous in the resurgent Islamic networks that tie the city to the twelve sharia-governed states of northern Nigeria. Recalling his experience as a leftist student activist confronting the rise of a newly politicized Islam in the university, Karim predicts that the young urban intellectuals leading the Islamist organizations will take power in Niger within twenty years. Their discipline, probity, and commitment has a powerful appeal, modeling a future radically distinct from the remoteness and opportunism—the lack of ideology, as Karim puts it—of the politicians in Niamey and the debilitating combination of ineffectuality and neo-colonial authority that has come to characterize the aid organizations.

Discourses of political and moral decadence easily merge. The riots that shook Maradi in November 2000 were led by Islamist activists protesting the Festival international de la mode africaine, a fund-raising fashion show backed by the United Nations that drew leading designers from Africa and overseas. Demonstrators denounced single women as prostitutes, targeting them in the streets and in a refugee village to which many had fled from prior Islamist violence in Nigeria. Rioters torched brothels, bars, and betting kiosks. They invaded Christian and animist compounds.[20]

People in Niamey point to signs of change in public culture: stores that just a couple of years ago stayed open during Muslim prayers now shutter; large numbers of women on the university campus now wear veils. Maradi is in the vanguard of this complex struggle among "reformist" and "traditional" Muslims, evangelical Christians, and secular Nigeriens. Karim tells me it's a very different place from when he lived here in the 1990s. Even so, one evening we're taken by surprise in the city's giant open-air movie theater when our undubbed, unsubtitled Hindi-language Bollywood gangster film cuts without warning into cheap hillbilly porn that someone has spliced into the pirated DVD. A thick sexual silence descends on a theater that moments before had almost as much life in the all-male audience as it had on-screen. But the surreal effect soon wears thin, and we head off to our hotel on the back of zippy motorbike taxis under starry black skies. When we arrive, Karim tells me that (despite the theater) the Islamists are the future now. With international development and its version of modernity discredited, with the nation in tatters, with no alternatives in sight, time is on their side. When I reply that I didn't come all this way to write a lament for Africa, he offers a quote he attributes to Lenin: The facts, he says, are unavoidable.

6.

January is as slow a month for *criquets* here as in Niamey. Yet, passing through the fortresslike gate of the Grand Marché, we're right away in conversation with a friendly young guy who sells some *houara* here but mostly exports to Nigeria. The Nigerians look for insects from Maradi because they know that farmers in this area don't use pesticides, he tells us. We ask where he gets his animals and he calls to a man sitting chatting at the back of the stall. Hamissou is a supplier with whom the owner of this stall has a long-term contract. He shyly describes how he's been traveling through the villages north of Maradi on his motorbike for ten years buying millet, *bissap* (hibiscus flowers), and *houara*.

Two days later there are four of us: Karim, Hamissou, Boubé (who usually drives for Médecins Sans Frontières), and me. We're heading fast but cautiously—because of land mines—out of Maradi along a red dirt road so straight it seems it will never end. Hamissou is next to me in the backseat, dressed all in white, his cotton scarf thrown across his face against the dust.

Visiting villages with Hamissou was a pleasure. Everyone was excited to see him. His arrival generated laughter and excitement. Men jumped up to playact wrestling with him. They affectionately made fun of his shyness. His trade was a happy, relaxed affair with no economy of distrust.

That morning he took us into the bush to meet women collectors. They'd left their village after the 6 a.m. prayers, and when we caught up with them four hours later, they were far from home. They showed us where they find the *houara* under low shrubs, how they poke at them with millet stalks, catch them in one hand with swift, sure movements, snap the back legs of the lively ones to stop them from jumping, and secure them in a cotton pouch. If this were September, they said, they'd be collecting pounds every day, making 2,000 or 3,000 CFA from Hamissou and still having a good quantity left to eat. *Houara* replace meat, they said, reminding me of the conversation in Mahaman and Antoinette's yard in Niamey. They're full of protein and—also like meat—they're not something you eat every day (or, if you want to avoid vomiting and diarrhea, too much of). They're delicious fried with salt or ground up to make a sauce for millet. In September, there are so many out here in the fields that we bring the children with us to hunt. But now, in January, it's too cold in the mornings for children, and there aren't any insects anyway. Look at this sad collection: it takes two days to fill this pouch, and it sells for just 100 CFA. Even the higher price this time of year doesn't compensate for the poor supply.

If the returns are so low, why spend all these hours in such back-breaking work? I asked, stupidly. An older woman responded, not troubling to hide her scorn: Because we're hungry. Because we have no money. Because we have to buy food. Because we have to buy clothes. Because we have to stay alive. Because in one month we won't have even these few insects. Because there's nothing else we can do to make money at this time. Because it's something, and doing something is better than sitting at home doing nothing.

She continued: Sometimes there are years when the *houara* don't arrive at all. But when they do, they help us build capital. With the proceeds from collecting, we can buy cooking oil, plastic bags, and everything else we need to sell *masa*, deep-fried millet cakes. With the proceeds from that, we can save a little more, buy our children things they need, create a little security. There are years when so many *houara* come to the village, she added, that we can even buy a cow. But what we can't do is store the surplus against the times of hunger. They keep—that's not the problem—but we can't do without the cash.

She turns back to catching insects under the shadeless sun. The rest of us follow suit and are soon scrambling around chasing *houara* in the dust. And what I remember best about this is that Boubé was really good at it, that he kept going long after Karim and I had given up, that he really didn't want to leave, and that in no time at all the rest of us were standing out there under that everlasting blue sky watching him digging in the bushes and laughing at his success.

A few days later, there were again four of us passing through the police roadblocks and bouncing along the red road north from Maradi. This time, Hamissou was busy elsewhere, and we were accompanied by Zabeirou, an energetic presence in the front seat next to Boubé, explain-

ing in a stream of Hausa, French, and English how he had become the largest *criquet* merchant in Maradi, if not in the entire country.

From 1968 to 1974, a savage drought and famine, compounded by outbreaks of *Schistocerca gregaria,* destroyed Niger's groundnut economy. Hunger forced farmers to abandon export cropping and return land to subsistence foods, the displacement of which had so undermined their security. Across the Sahel, between 50,000 and 100,000 people died. In Niger, groundnut production plummeted from 210,541 tons in 1966 to 16,535 tons in 1975.[21]

But by the mid-1970s, some of the world's largest deposits of uranium, discovered by the French atomic energy commission in the Aïr region, were filling the fiscal void. At its height, uranium provided well over 80 percent of the country's export revenues and stimulated a national economic boom. But by the early 1980s, following the meltdown at Three Mile Island and the success of the anti-nuclear movement in Europe and the United States, the price of uranium began its long fall, a slump from which it is only now emerging.[22] Production of uranium in Niger collapsed along with the price, once more throwing the economy into a revenue crisis and even further on the mercies of the multilateral donor agencies and their punishing financial prescriptions.

At the beginning of this cycle, the uranium enterprise SOMAIR—a subsidiary of the French nuclear conglomerate COGEMA—built a new mining town out in the desert 150 miles north of Agadez. This was Arlit, called Petit Paris for its expat-focused amenities, such as supermarkets stocked directly from France. It was here that Zabeirou had worked as a laborer until 1990, when he left with a payment of 150,000 CFA (something like $550 in those days). He moved back to Maradi and, once there, started to study the markets. He quickly saw that there was a high demand from women for *criquets* and that—unlike other popular goods—there were no big operators working the trade. The *alhazai* of Maradi had failed to step in, and business was dominated by petty entrepreneurs.

As he tells it, Zabeirou moved decisively to become Niger's first serious *criquet* merchant. Armed with his Arlit capital, he built up his stock by buying all the animals he could from rural collectors. Once he'd cornered the market, he slashed his price deep enough to force out the competition. With his monopoly in place, he raised his prices again and soon recovered his losses.

Nowadays, the competition is more serious and Zabeirou's business more elaborate. He has a network of informants scattered in towns and villages around Niamey, Tahoua, and Maradi and across the border in northern Nigeria whose job is to seek out *houara* in times of scarcity. He also has buyers, each with a budget of 300,000 CFA, whom he sends out from Maradi and Niamey to procure in villages and markets. It's a wary world. Zabeirou keeps his sources secret. Often, he keeps his own location hidden too, moving around clandestinely, letting people think he's in Maradi checking on supply when he's actually doing business in Niamey. It's a wary world, but it pays off: there have been times when he has made 1 million CFA in a week.

When he is in Maradi, Zabeirou is most likely to be at Kasuwa Mata, the Women's Market, a mostly wholesale market on the northern edge of the city dominated by women traders. Kasuwa Mata is a staging area for goods arrived from the countryside. From here, they go to the Grand Marché and other outlets in town, to markets elsewhere in Niger, and to buyers in Nigeria. Zabeirou has a well-stocked stall here, a destination for middlemen like Hamissou and for women collectors arriving from their villages with *houara* for sale.

He has four resale options: he can retail directly from his stall; he can wholesale to traders in Kasuwa Mata and elsewhere in Maradi who then resell in the local markets; he can send sacks by truck for his employees to sell in Zinder, Tahoua, or Niamey; or he can take the *houara* to Nigeria. At this time of year, a time of high prices and scarce supply, many of his customers are women who prepare the animals for their preteen children to sell from metal trays balanced confidently on their heads. It's a popular spicy snack, tiny packs of five or six insects for 25 CFA that other children buy outside their elementary schools or bigger packs for 50 CFA that the drivers of *kabu-kabu,* motorbike taxis, stand crunching as they wait for their next fare.

Zabeirou led us to a storage facility behind his stall and showed us some of his stock. Sacks and sacks of *criquets,* several months' supply, 2 million CFA worth, he said. He would add to them over the next few weeks—until there were no more in the countryside and the price started to rise. Then he'd release them to the market. Good business, we all agreed.

Three wives and ten children. A large house with a walled yard close to Kasuwa Mata. Zabeirou's prosperity was matched by his expansive manner. Karim and I were cautiously pleased that he'd decided to adopt

us. After a couple of hours on the road, we stopped in the market town of Sabon Machi, where he insisted on buying us a breakfast of *masa* and sweet tea. Another couple of hours and we arrived in the village of Dandasay.

Zabeirou's brother Ibrahim is one of the three schoolteachers here. He has a quiet and gentle manner quite different from that of his older sibling. As we talk, I'm thinking what a sympathetic teacher he must be. He is telling me that parents in the village have so little cash that he is scared when he sometimes has to ask them for 10 CFA for supplies. He introduces me to his colleague Kommando, a strikingly tall, thin man with a similarly kind demeanor. Karim figures out that Zabeirou hasn't been here before. Off-road on the last stretch of the journey to Dandasay, we'd been forced to stop for directions more than once. As we pulled into the village, he'd ordered the children who raced to greet us to run and tell their mothers that he's here to buy *houara*.

It turns out to be a complicated day. Assuming the twin roles of tour guide and impresario, Zabeirou has decided we need to see *houara* being prepared for sale. He begins to organize the performance but has barely started rounding up likely women when he discovers that the collectors have yet to come back from the bush and no one here has any fresh *criquets*. In the meantime, women alerted by their children have emerged from their houses with small bags of insects. Normally, they take these to the nearby market in Komaka or to Sabon Machi, bigger and further away, or, on a Friday, to Maradi, much bigger and further still. Normally, Zabeirou would have buyers waiting for him in those markets. But today is a special day, and he sets up shop behind our truck and starts to deal.

He hasn't got very far when a group of men arrives to invite us to a *cebe*, a baby's naming ceremony. It's on the far side of the village, so Zabeirou suspends operations, and we make our way through the narrow sandy lanes to where the first row of chairs has been vacated in front of a thatched patio beside a small house. The imam takes his place on a mat among a group of senior men, and the audience watches, periodically joining in to recite the blessings, as the dignitaries move through the solemn ceremony. It's calmly meditative, and everyone is focused on the chants with a quiet intensity. But as the service proceeds, I gradually become aware of what sounds like a spirited debate going on behind us.

I turn around, and there's Zabeirou in position again at the back of the truck, bargaining with a line of women waiting to sell their *houara*.

We're treated too well here. After the ceremony, the father of the child invites us all to eat first, before his other guests. Karim, Boubé, Zabeirou, Ibrahim, and I enter a small round building and are served an elaborate meal of millet and meat. We reemerge to hear that the collectors have returned from the bush. A fire is hastily lit outside a nearby house, and a young woman (decidedly unimpressed) begins heating a large pot of water under the gaze of what is by now a sizable crowd. As the scene develops, Zabeirou offers detailed *National Geographic*–style commentary for our benefit and repeatedly cautions me not to miss the opportunity to take photos. When the *houara* arrive, he dumps them in the boiling water, takes the young woman's stick, and not letting up his patter, shoves the flailing animals deep into the pot. The women who perform this mundane operation on a daily basis are shut out of the circle and wander off to more compelling things. The men take turns poking at the pot, closely watching something that they, too, must have seen untold times but takes me entirely by surprise: as they churn in the roiling water, the tan-colored insects rapidly turn pink, resembling nothing so

much as cooked shrimp and, in that moment, opening an unlucky door into other universes of possible fates.

The insects boil for thirty minutes. Meanwhile, Ibrahim and I chat with the *maigari*, the headman of this large village, and with a few other men. They tell us that the *criquet pèlerin* was here sixty years ago but has not been back since. These older men remember the destruction but— like the men in Rijio Oubandawaki—it's not something they dwell on. Rather than this once-in-a-lifetime apocalypse, it's the less exotic *houara* like the *birdé*, with their grinding away at everyday food security, that preoccupy them.

Kommando is part of this conversation, too. As it ends, he tells me that he used to work in a village about sixty miles north of here called Dan mata Sohoua. We should visit, he says. The chief there can tell us about the locust invasion of 2005. It's quite a story. Just then I spot Zabeirou across the crowd. He has a *tia* and is using it to measure out the women's insects. To the sellers' dismay, he piles the animals high, mounding more and more until there must be as much as 40 percent extra heaped on the basin, which he then tips into his sack. As I watch, I recall how he always gives an additional "social payment" when he sells in Kasuwa Mata, how he piles on varying amounts depending on the status of the buyer (a widow, for instance, may get more), so that the *houara* spill over the lip of his *tia* in a gesture of generosity that is, however, somewhat more modest than the one he's managing today.

The drive back to Maradi is uneventful. Before we leave, the woman who had begun boiling the *houara* is called back to spread them on a blue tarpaulin so we can watch them dry in the sun. Zabeirou declares himself satisfied with the day's program. As we approach the city, he asks if I'll be back soon. I can't offer a date, and we all slip into our own thoughts. When we reach Zabeirou's house, his demeanor changes abruptly. Eschewing conventional sentimentalities, he demands payment for his services, apparently forgetting that our outing was conceived under the banner of international friendship and that he has already done rather well from the women of Dandasay. Karim is infuriated, and we enter into testy negotiations, Zabeirou refusing to let us leave until an unhappy compromise is reached.

The three of us drive back across town feeling irritable. But the mood doesn't last long. Our sense of purpose returns when we decide to follow

Kommando's advice and head out early the next morning for Dan mata Sohoua.

7.

According to the World Bank, the invasion area of the *criquet pèlerin* extends over 20 percent of the earth's farm- and pastureland, a total of 11 million square miles in sixty-five countries. Control measures, primarily surveillance and chemical spraying, focus on outbreak prevention and elimination in the recession area, the drier central zone of this region, the 6 million square miles within which the animals mass. The reasoning is simple: once the hopper bands have undergone their final molt to become winged adults and the swarm has taken to the air, the only option is crop protection through upsurge elimination on-site, an option with very low rates of success. Crop protection in the village, Professor Mahamane Saadou had told us, is a mark of the failure of prevention in the recession area. It means villages are saturated with pesticides—some that are banned in Europe and the United States—placing in jeopardy both the members of the village brigades who apply the chemicals (often

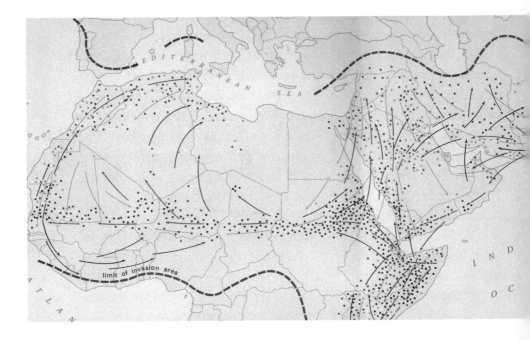

limit of invasion area

without protective clothing or adequate training) and the community's food chain and water supply.

As Kommando had promised, the chief of Dan mata Sohoua was keen to tell the story. The locusts arrived from the west, he said. It was October, just after the rainy season. The millet was fully ripened, but the harvest had not yet begun, and the grain was still on the plants. The timing could not have been worse.

At first there were only a few, the harbingers—as Chinua Achebe has it—sent to survey the land. They appeared around midday. The children came running from the fields to raise the alarm. But none of the adults went to look. They knew it was already too late. By the time darkness fell, the swarm had arrived.

The next morning the village was overrun. The *houara* covered the ground. They covered the bush. You couldn't see the ground. You couldn't see the millet. People tried to chase them away. They used tools, they used their hands, they set fires. They tried to save the millet by picking it from the plant. What could they do but heap the seed heads on the ground? By the time they turned back, the insects were all over them.

On the morning of the second day, the *maigari* and a group of senior men went to Dakoro, the nearest town, to alert the Agricultural Service. Normally, the *maigari* told us, the Agricultural Service paid no attention to the problems here. But that day they came. After inspecting the fields, they advised people to pray. There was nothing else for it, they said.

Nonetheless, later that day a plane arrived to spray the area with pesticides. As it flew overhead, the *houara* took off. At first it seemed as if they were leaving the village, but instead they took aim at the plane. They flew straight for it, enveloping the cockpit, swarming over the wings, trying to force it up and away from the village. The pilot changed tactics. He couldn't come in low. Instead, he tried to spray alongside the insects, but they scattered and the chemicals had little effect. The animals were disciplined and organized. It was as if they had a commander and were following orders.

As if they had a commander. Every day, they started work at exactly 8 a.m. No, not because it was cold before then. That's what everyone thinks, that they were waiting for the heat to warm their wings. But, no, it was because they had their workday. Like white people. They started at 8 a.m., never earlier. As it got close to 8, they became restless and ready to fly. The commander gave the order, and they began. When they took off, they flew low, scouring the ground for food, always ready to land. At 6 p.m., they stopped. Like an army with a commander. These animals were intelligent. It was as if they had binoculars. If they left anything, they turned around and came back for it. If one of them was injured, they turned around, came back, and ate their fallen comrade rather than leave it on the road.

There were people who set fire to them in the mornings as the *houara* massed there waiting for the order. It was a mistake. It was just a provocation. If they managed to kill a sackful like that, they could be sure that double that number would soon arrive to take their place. Everyone stopped going to the fields. When they went outside, they had to cover their faces. Adults stopped children from going into the bush.

On the third day, the locusts left. There was no more millet. They'd taken it all. But they'd left something of their own. Two weeks later, the eggs hatched, and the hoppers emerged from the ground. This time was far worse than before.

A small girl walked across the sand to where we were seated under a generous shade tree. The afternoon air was hot and still. In the distance, we could hear the rhythmic thuds of women pounding millet. The *maigari* sold the girl a few bouillon cubes. A thin-faced man seated behind a tabletop sewing machine picked up the story as the rest of us, six men and two women, listened.

We'd never seen these *houara* before, he said. Even people 100 years old had never seen them. We called them *houara dango*, destroyer crickets. They were bright yellow on the outside, black inside. The yellow came off like paint if you touched them. They were so strange that at first we thought they'd been invented by white people. The old people told the children not to touch them. The goats that ate them aborted, the chickens died. Not from the pesticides, as you might think, but from some tiny insects that lived inside the *houara*. The chickens and goats weren't safe to eat. We had to destroy them. The *houara* entered the wells. They poisoned the water. Not even the cattle could drink from that water. Someone in another village ate them, and he was sick, vomiting for days. We couldn't eat them. If we could, there were so many we'd be eating them still.

Now everyone was talking. There was no doubt that the second wave was even more devastating than the first. The Agricultural Service sprayed the hatchlings, but the survivors ate the corpses. There was nothing left in the fields. Whatever the hoppers could eat in the village, they ate. This time, they stayed for three weeks, working their way systematically through the village, consuming everything in their path, even their own dead; yes, that's right, they left nothing, not even their own dead.

With no millet in the granaries and no harvest to look to, people in Dan mata Sohoua were completely dependent on emergency food aid. Fueled by emotionally charged reporting on the BBC, the situation in Niger and across the Sahel became international news. The specter of famine coupled with plagues of locusts prompted high-profile public appeals in the donor countries. These in turn generated dismayed reaction from the administration of Mamadou Tandja, who watched as this media-driven internationalization gave carte blanche to the nongovernmental organizations to act on behalf of a humanitarian global public, further undermining the state's already-limited capacity.

For a few weeks, the Médecins Sans Frontières feeding center in Maradi "received more media attention than anywhere on the globe."[23] And, indeed, although it is unclear how severe the situation was in other parts of Niger, for residents of the countryside around Maradi (and for pastoral people in the north), things were significantly more difficult than normal. Oxfam stepped in to Dan mata Sohoua with 400 bags of rice, which arrived just as everyone was debating whether to abandon the village. Dan mata Sohoua became a center of food distribution for people who arrived from all around to collect their ration. Oxfam promised three full consignments, but for reasons unknown to people here, the second delivery was much reduced and the third simply didn't materialize.

That year of the *houara dango*, farmers in Dan mata Sohoua had planted seed lent by development organizations as an advance against their crop. When the millet failed, they had few options. One was to appeal to local merchants—from a position of extreme weakness—to convert donated rice to cash to meet their debt. But the rice never came, so the debts deepened (and people were unable even to sell their food aid, a practice that, although reviled by the aid agencies as profiteering, can have its own compelling logic).

Two harvests later, people told us, they still hadn't repaid the loans. Nor had they paid their taxes since 2005. Just as the Nigerien state is caught in its chronic international dependencies, so people in the countryside around Maradi struggle to access whatever resources might come their way.[24] In the long days of hunger after the invasion, farmers in Dan mata Sohoua joined with NGOs in the region to start a *banque céréalière*, taking grain (rather than seed) on loan and repaying the loan after the harvest. Even in the best of times, the harvest provides little surplus, so the obligation to give some of it away is not a welcome one. But at least in this arrangement there is no need for cash—or for a Zabeirou. Perhaps, says someone wistfully, if the harvests are good, if no more swarms arrive, we'll be out of this hole in another two years.

8.

On the bus back from Maradi, Karim and I found ourselves sitting with a group of agronomists headed to Niamey for a conference on insect-pest management. They shared with us their ridged sheets of *tchoukou*—tangy crispy-chewy cheese—and when we all got down to stretch our legs at Birni N'Konni they insisted on paying for sodas. We talked about their work with resistant strains of millet, and I thought back to the conversation Karim and I had a few days before with an enthusiastic young researcher at the Maradi Direction de la protection des végétaux who is developing a biological control of the *criquet pèlerin* using pathogenic fungi as an alternative to chemical pesticides.

The next morning we went back to the university to visit Professor Ousmane Moussa Zakari, a prominent Nigerien biologist critical of the U.N. Food and Agriculture Organization's efforts at pest control. The FAO has never successfully predicted an invasion of the *criquet pèlerin*, Professor Zakari said. He calculates that there have been thirteen major locust outbreaks in Niger since 1780, and although the local effects can be overwhelming, the aggregate is less so. Like many of the researchers and farmers we talked to, he regards current control efforts as a failure. The recession area is too large and too inaccessible, the insects are too adaptable, capable of withstanding extended drought and responding rapidly to favorable conditions. He argued that the hundreds of millions of dollars spent on eradication would be better spent elsewhere, helping farmers draw on their own knowledge of pest control, for example, and working with them to develop new techniques, such as interrupting the development of the *criquet sénégalais* by delaying the planting of the first of the two annual crops of millet.

That same day, as if in a reminder of the complex fragilities with which Nigeriens struggle, a French aid worker was caught in a carjacking in Zinder. She had stopped her vehicle for two men who appeared to need help at the side of the road. They bundled her out of the car and drove off. No one was hurt, but unfortunately for everyone involved, the men had left without realizing that the woman's toddler was still in the vehicle's backseat.

I think it was also that day that Karim told me about catching *houara* when he was little. I think it was that day—although it could have been earlier, as the bus worked its way into the sunset across the plains from Maradi, or it could have been in a taxi at another time altogether, as we drove onto Kennedy Bridge past the U.N. billboard that celebrates the "Rights of the Child," or it might even have been before we left Maradi, driving back from Dan mata Sohoua along the only road in Dakoro, a road lined with signs for international development agencies (just as the main drag in a U.S. town is lined with signs for motels and fast-food restaurants). Anyway, it was on one of those occasions that Karim told me about catching *houara* when he was little. It was in the village close to Dandasay where he grew up. It was a favorite game. All the children played. They'd make a light to draw the insects and catch as many as they could, the more the better. There was no shortage, and the winner was the one who caught the most. It was a simple game but a happy one, he said.

Il **P**arco delle Cascine on Ascension Sunday

1.

In Japan, the crickets sing in fall, giving voice to the season's transience and its reassuring melancholies. But in Florence, writes the folklorist Dorothy Gladys Spicer in her *Festivals of Western Europe*, the cricket arrives in spring as a symbol of renewal, and its song is the soundtrack to lengthening days, to life lived outdoors, and on Ascension Sunday in the Parco delle Cascine, the city's most important public park, to its very own festival.

It's not clear whether Dorothy Spicer actually witnessed the *festa del grillo* herself, but she describes it vividly anyway. On the forty-third day of Easter, a warm Sunday in late May or early June, she writes, "parents pack generous lunch baskets, gather up the children, and flock to Cascine Park." In earlier times, children hunted the crickets themselves; nowadays (this is 1958), they buy them on the festive market. It's all so colorful: "hundreds of brightly-painted wicker or wire cages imprisoning hundreds of crickets caught in the Park, dangle from vendors' stalls." Traders sell all kinds of food and drink. There are red, green, orange, and blue balloons. There is music. And there is plenty of ice cream. It is, she comments drolly, "one of the happiest and gayest spring events for everyone—except the *grilli!*"[1]

The Parco delle Cascine is no more than a thirty-minute walk along the shadeless northern bank of the Arno from the historic center of Florence. But especially in summer, it's a very different urban space, a world away from the tourist crush of the Ponte Vecchio, the Duomo, and the Piazza delle Signoria, the iconic splendor of the Fra Angelicos, the Giottos, and the Michelangelos. The famous treasures truly are stunning individually and overwhelming in their abundance. It's no mystery that the English and other visitors have been spellbound ever since the eighteenth-century Grand Tour made the city an obligatory destination for any of the upper class in need of an education. For good reason, the paintings, statues, and historic buildings of Florence were recognized as emblems of Western civilization centuries before UNESCO, with true Enlightenment spirit, declared the city center a World Heritage Site.

Still, even when Dorothy Spicer wrote, the intensity of cultural consumption was not what it is today. I know this because just a few years before Spicer wrote her book, my parents—young Jews abroad and somehow at ease in postwar Europe—found themselves stranded in Florence on their honeymoon after rapidly running through the £50 in cash that the British government allowed travelers to take out of the country. Those were the days before credit cards, but they got by, happily eating picnics in the hills around Fiesole, overlooking the tranquil sea of red roofs punctured by the soaring cupola of the Duomo.

Florence then was still much more the city beloved of Ruskin, Shelley, and Henry James than the one recently tagged by a jaded *New York Times*

travel writer as a "Renaissance theme park."[2] Today, the historic center is still an extraordinary place, but now it's part museum, part playground, and wholly commercial. Everyone browses, and so do we. The line for the Uffizi Gallery is a three-hour wait, and like Goethe—though perhaps with more regret—Sharon and I end up being bad tourists. In October 1786, early in his travels through Italy on his own version of the Grand Tour, the great writer-scientist-philosopher "took a quick walk through the city" to visit the Duomo and the Battistero. "Once more," he wrote in his diary, "a completely new world opened up before me, but I did not wish to stay long. The location of the Bobboli Gardens is marvellous. I hurried out of the city as quickly as I entered it."[3]

2.

Tucked away among the stores selling handmade gelato, handmade paper, and handmade shoes, there are shops that offer another Florentine specialty: wooden Pinocchios. Some of them are giants, far taller than the puppet-boy in Carlo Collodi's much-loved morality tale. Collodi was born in Florence and worked there as a civil servant, journalist, and writer of children's stories his entire life. His madcap adventure story, serialized from 1881 to 1883 in the weekly children's magazine *Giornale per i bambini*, is a box of tricks that takes fairy tales (Collodi translated French ones) as well as oral narrative (he was an editor of an encyclopedia of the Florentine dialect) and the Tuscan short story, and turns them inside out to give his readers something new, something sharp and darkly funny, full of unexpected twists, and, beneath the pyrotechnics, deeply serious.

One of Collodi's most memorable creations is the talking cricket, the *grillo parlante*, a rather minor character that Walt Disney Productions transformed into Jiminy Cricket. It seems significant that Florence's most famous modern novel gave the world its most famous cricket, but I can't say to what extent this *grillo* was a product of local or, more broadly, Italian lore. The Florentine fascination that produced the *festa* might well be just an expression of a larger national or even regional (southern European? Mediterranean?) insect intimacy.

People have kept crickets here for centuries. Little cages similar to the ones sold at the Florence festival were even found painted on the walls of houses unearthed in Pompeii. And there is plenty of linguistic evidence that noisy insects have chirruped their way far into Italian life. The connections between talking insects and human speech are audible in the many terms that *cicala*, the cicada, has spawned for frivolous or convoluted human chattering (*cicalare, cicalata, cicaleccio, cicalio, cicalino*).[4] Evidence like this tells us something about the place of crickets today but only confuses their cultural location in the past. After all, modern Italian is derived in large part from the Florentine dialect nationalized by Dante, and I'm not sure that it's possible to know precisely where this particular etymological cluster originated. Perhaps there *is* something unique about Florence and its crickets. Either way, the great early-nineteenth-century poet and philologist Giacomo Leopardi dignifies the notion that insect sounds are empty chatter when—along with that other southern European philosopher-poet and insect lover Jean-Henri Fabre—he explains that crickets and cicadas, like birds, sing for the joy of it, the pleasure of it, the sheer beauty of it.[5]

The European tradition of hearing only silliness, vanity, and a source of irritation in the cricket's song is ancient and survives in Italy in the phrase *Non fare il grillo parlante*, which translates as something like "Don't talk nonsense!" This isn't the only tradition, of course, as these insects played an entirely different role as fixtures of the classical idyll, but it's nonetheless the theme of the two fables of Aesop's in which crickets appear. Collodi, who achieved fame, if not fortune, despite having grown up in profound nineteenth-century poverty, revels in subverting expectations, and his talking cricket's words are unmistakably meaningful. Yet—and this, too, is surely biographical—the *grillo parlante* has a much harder time of it, a much more grittily realistic time of it, than Disney's chirpy Jiminy Cricket. Nightmarish as the classic American remake can sometimes be ("Pleasure Island," where kidnapped little boys are encouraged to throw off their inhibitions, was sufficiently lurid to be invoked during Michael Jackson's pedophilia trial), Collodi's original is altogether darker, and Pinocchio, initially a spectacularly selfish puppet-boy with no sense of the ordeals he inflicts on his destitute father, Geppetto, suffers a range of exemplary tortures, which include burning, frying, flaying, drowning, forced confinement in a dog kennel, and the more traditional transformation into a donkey.

Disney's *Pinocchio* was released in the bleak February of 1940, with the shadows of war and mass unemployment darkening all horizons. Jiminy—"Lord High Keeper of the Knowledge of Right and Wrong, Counselor in Moments of Temptation, and Guide along the Straight and Narrow Path"—burst from the opening credits, a tireless spirit of can-do energy and well-judged humility who sings one of Hollywood's most enduringly democratic lyrics, a lyric that brilliantly captures the emptiness, naïveté, and consolations of the American dream. (I wanted to quote from the song—"When You Wish Upon a Star"—but the copyright holder wanted way too much money.) Collodi's *grillo parlante* was no less a virtuous insect. He urges Pinocchio to honor his father, to go to school, to work hard and practice thrift, to learn the values needed to survive in modern society. But he has tougher words for a tougher puppet, a working-class puppet in a harsh world who would have finished the story swinging by his neck from the Big Oak at the end of chapter 15 but for the outpouring of protest from appalled readers and the intervention of a savvy editor.[6]

The outrage saved Pinocchio, but it was too late for the cricket. As Giuseppe Garibaldi, the Hero of Two Worlds, lay dying on Caprera, off the coast of Sardinia, the *grillo parlante* faced his own mortality. The ailing Garibaldi, the Sword of Italian Unity, was also the founder of Italy's first animal-protection society and a man who, as death neared, gathered his family to listen to a songbird perched on his windowsill above the crystalline Tyrrhenian Sea. Collodi, a patriotic volunteer in Garibaldi's wars of independence and, like the father of the new nation, a critic of political corruption, social inequality, and clericalism, departed at this point from the author of the maxim "Man created God, not God man." Perhaps it was Collodi's disillusionment with the failure of unification to bring with it social transformation. Perhaps it was life in a hardscrabble, topsy-turvy world of insecure income and rapid social change. Or maybe he just couldn't resist an occasion for slapstick violence. In Collodi's universe, everyone fights for his crumbs without the privilege of species. It's a dog-eat-dog, dog-eat-puppet, puppet-eat-dog, boy-become-donkey world in which it's never quite clear who needs protecting from whom or even who is who. It is the scoundrel fox and the ne'er-do-well cat who string Pinocchio from the oak. By the end, Pinocchio has chewed off the blinded cat's paw, and the starving fox has sold his own tail. And the talking cricket? With the story barely under way, in another scene that didn't make it into the Disney movie, the *grillo parlante* finds himself, with scant warning, "stuck, flattened against the wall, stiff and lifeless"— speechless, too, flat as a pancake beneath the petulant puppet's flying mallet.[7]

3.

Maybe there's something in the coexistence of Disney and Collodi that helps explain a confusion surrounding the *festa*. Crickets have long been visible enough here to attract their own feast day; it's just not clear whether the event exists to celebrate or demonize them—just as it's not quite clear whether this region loves them or hates them.

For some people, the *festa del grillo* has a precise moment of origin: July 8, 1582, in San Martino a Strada, in the parish of Santa Maria all'Impruneta, not far from Florence. According to Agostino Lapini's *Diario fiorentino* (a detailed eighteenth-century history of the city), on that day the parish organized a force of 1,000 men to save the crops from devastation by field crickets. Lapini describes a state of emergency. For ten days a crowd in the most resolute mood swarms over the fields, hunting down every cricket it can find. It *fare la festa*—"makes merry," we might say—with the animals killing all it can in a feast of killing, a festival of killing, a carnival of killing. Yet no matter the many ways of killing—even mass live burial and death by drowning—"the smallest ones remained rather well," recounts Lapini, "and because of the great heat went below ground and there made their eggs."[8]

Two more crickets. The bad cricket: insect of plague and retribution, feared by the farmer. The good cricket: symbol of spring and good fortune, loved by the children. How do we get from the mob scene of 1582 to the family outing described by Frances Toor in her *Festivals and Folkways of Italy*, the same event that Dorothy Spicer would write about five years later? Crowds pack the Cascine; there are balloons, an abundance of food and drink, cages in all shapes and sizes; the songs of crickets fill the air; it is a day that children remember their entire lives, "the whole *festa* is an authentic one of color . . . everything is bright." The cricket is a "harbinger of spring as it used to be for the races before them," writes Toor, meaning for the Etruscans, the Greeks, and the Romans.

> In Florence they say if the *grillo* you are taking home sings soon, it means good luck. My friends selected for me two males, recognized by a thin yellow stripe around the neck, because they sing most, and one of mine sang all the way home. Freeing also brings luck. I did not know that but let mine loose in the garden immediately. The happy one jumped away singing, the other silent one seemed to have been hurt but he also limped away as if pleased to be free.[9]

Freeing brings luck? I can't find a convincing narrative that ties these two scenes together. Instead, there is Lapini's blood fest of 1582 and then nothing for an entire century, no record of anything cricket related. (Were there no more plagues of crickets in the Tuscan countryside? Did those eggs never hatch? Was there no local commemoration of the mass expedition?) When crickets do reappear, it is the late seventeenth century, they are in the Cascine, and, like so much else in Florence during this period, they are firmly within the orbit of the Medicis.[10]

In the 1560s, Cosimo I, first Grand Duke of Tuscany, undertook the initial landscaping that created the Parco delle Cascine. He added groves of oak, maple, elm, and other shade-giving trees. The long, narrow park beside the Arno was subsequently used by the nobility as a promenade, hunting ground, and venue for outdoor entertainment—including, according to some accounts, cricket catching. Following the decline of the Medicis and the accession of the house of Habsburg-Lorraine in 1737, the park became state property. At what point the public gained full access is not clear, but open events—including perhaps the *festa del grillo*—were commonplace during the late-eighteenth-century rule of Pietro Leopoldo, the "enlightened" grand duke who was also the Holy Roman Emperor Leopold II (and the brother of Marie-Antoinette) whose modernizing enthusiasm is evident in his sponsorship of Florence's science museums and in the superb collections of scientific intruments that they house, collections that include both the bony middle finger of Galileo's right hand ("This is the finger, belonging to the illustrious hand / that ran through the skies, / pointing at the immense spaces, and singling out new stars," runs Tommaso Perelli's inscription) and his telescope, perhaps the very one he used to sketch those washes of the moon's phases that so inspired Cornelia Hesse-Honegger.

There is little doubt that by the end of the nineteenth century a *festa del grillo* was securely fixed in the spring calendar. It was a popular event, open to all and packed with picnicking families. The aristocratic tradition of the parade of the notables continued, although now led by municipal officials and culminating in the formal blessing of the city. Already it appears that rather than collecting the insects in the park, people were acquiring their crickets by buying them (along with the painted cages) from vendors who hunted up on Monte Cantagrilli (Singing Cricket Mountain) and the other surrounding hills. This shift fully into consumption sounds urban. And so does the festival's unambiguous celebratory tone (spring renewal, good fortune, long life, and so on), a tone that also continues the aristocratic tradition of the *festa* as treasure hunt. Where is the uncertainty of peasant life? Where is nature, wild and dangerous? The *grillo parlante* has arrived. Jiminy's on his way. The locusts are no more. Crickets are our friends.

4.

I first learned about Garibaldi's feelings for birds and other creatures in a short book published in Rome in 1938 by the National Fascist Organization for the Protection of Animals. The architect of the Risorgimento appears in a trinity of animal lovers along with Saint Francis of Assisi and Benito Mussolini, who is quoted as urging a congress of veterinarians— apparently without irony—to "treat animals with kindness, because they are often more interesting than human beings." Feliciano Philipp, the book's author, explains that the new Italian state has a rational attitude toward animals, neither sentimental nor cruel. "It has instilled into every child the idea of duty towards those who are younger or weaker," he writes. Its aim is to foster "that indulgence which is due to inferior beings."[11]

Given that the Nazis' enthusiasm for animal welfare and environmental conservation is well known, it wasn't surprising to discover that their Axis allies also professed compassion for animals. But it was still startling to think of twentieth-century European fascists indulging, rather than exterminating, those they considered inferior. This seems like a paradox, but perhaps it results from a particular clarity about the distinction between humans and other animals. It was, after all, an area in which that giant of Western thought, Martin Heidegger, was able to offer his Nazi sponsors valuable philosophical support. Humans and others, he wrote, are separated not merely by capacity but by an "abyss of essence."[12] The difference is fundamentally hierarchical: "The stone is *worldless;* the animal is *poor in world;* man is *world-forming.*"[13]

Heidegger talks only in terms of *the* animal, but the encounters of everyday life are with animals in the plural and in their many guises. A greater difficulty for the fascist policy makers lay with the subhumans, those beings whose inferiority was of a different order from that of the compassion-eliciting nonhuman animals. The special problem of the

Jews, the Roma, the disabled, and the rest, lay in their capacity to confuse categories, to be unnervingly proximate despite their enormous distance, to be both corrupting from within (parasitic) and threatening from without (invasive). These are beings for whom, as we know, neither of the fascist states legislated protection or indulgence. These are beings who take their place among the outcast animals as the lives not worthy of life, the vermin of both kinds.

There are other histories of animal protection. One that has always seemed significant is the convergence between the animal-welfare movement that emerged in Europe in the early nineteenth century and the abolitionist movement that campaigned in the same period to free enslaved people in the United States. The two often combined organizational resources and individual activists, and—along with the twentieth-century fascists—they shared the belief that certain forms of superiority demanded paternalist responsibility. To many members of the two campaigns, there was little distinction between transplanted Africans and domestic animals. Both elicited liberal sympathy and action. Both needed care and, perhaps, indulgence. Neither had the capacity to speak for or represent themselves. Both deserved the opportunity to labor with dignity.[14]

None of this is to suggest that animal-welfare advocates are still hostage to these pasts. But genealogies haunt, and unresolved dilemmas persist, and at the least, they imply caution in assuming that a caring attitude toward other beings brings with it access to moral high ground. Maybe it's the condescension inherent in the notions of care, protection, and welfare that needs reviewing. There is much to the argument made by Isaac Bashevis Singer and many others that cruelty to animals is morally corrosive and leads readily to similar brutality toward people. Obviously, though, there is no reason to assume that kindness to animals leads equally to compassion toward people. It can just as directly cultivate the ability to discriminate between lives worth protecting and lives not worth living.

Mussolini's state put in place an array of legislation to guarantee the security and humane treatment of a range of animals—the standard elite of pets and native species whose legal protection had already become a mark of modernity. Among the regime's initiatives were the Fascist Act for the protection of wild animals and Article 70 of the Public

Safety Act, which prohibited "all spectacles or public entertainments involving torture of or cruelty to animals."[15] This last prohibition has a particular significance for our story. Public events featuring animals are widespread in Italy, and among them is the *festa del grillo*. Article 70 marked the opening of a new chapter.

During the 1990s, Florence found itself a target in the nationwide drive to stop the incorporation of live animals into religious and other festivals. "No holy spirit or expression of sincere devotion gives people the right to crucify a dove in Orvieto or sacrifice an ox in Roccavaldina or slit the throat of goats in San Luca," said Mauro Bottigelli of the Lega anti-vivisezione, a leader of the campaign.[16]

In Florence, activists attracted influential support. The famous *scoppio del carro*—the dramatic explosion of a large cart of fireworks in the Piazza del Duomo on Easter Sunday—was reworked so that the live dove bound to a flaming rocket that traditionally sparked the conflagration was replaced by a mechanical bird. Then, in 1999, the administrative district of Florence passed a law banning all commerce in wild or "autochthonous" (native) animals, a move targeting the sale of *grilli* on Ascension Sunday. (Did the deputies think of themselves as continuing the labors of Il Duce? I suspect most imagined a more benign lineage. If the thought did congeal, they might have drawn comfort from knowing that the fascists had no interest in crickets. Feliciano Philipp's only reference to insects in his book is a rather dubious calculation of the quantity eaten by a pair of nesting swallows and their young in one day—6,720—a figure designed to show the birds' importance to agriculture and public health rather than the insects' importance to the health of the birds.)

The battle for the soul of the cricket festival took shape as a struggle between the *animalisti* and the traditionalists. The harm involved was perhaps less self-evident than that in the case of the *scoppio*—though not, I think, because the pain of a bird is more accessible than that of an insect. The question was more subtle because the relationship between Florentines and their *grilli* was more intimate.

All of the parties competing in this drama considered themselves pro-cricket.[17] In their eventual resolution of the problem, the district government took the most pro-cricket position of all, protecting the living animals and promoting the mythical ones. Vendors were prohibited from trading in live crickets, and anyone caught selling them was to have his or her cages confiscated and the animals released to "roam freely through the hills of Florence." But the sale of cages wasn't banned, and the cages were not to be sold empty. To keep the cage makers in business and to retain the cultural and historical form (if not the precise content) of the event, the city provided the cricket vendors with two approved native species. One, especially handsome, was made of terra-cotta and based on a design by Stefano Ramunno, a local artist; the other, more noisy, was battery operated and produced a recognizable, if not quite authentic, "cri-cri." You can see what the politicians were thinking: the livelihood of the local artisans was protected and even enhanced, the crickets—the live crickets—were free to roam all day and sing out without fear of capture and confinement, and the public, the cricket-loving people of Florence, could celebrate their affinities, their culture, and their history free from bad faith.

As might be expected, there soon appeared a black market in crickets, fueled by parents determined that their children would experience the pleasures of selecting a fanciful cage and its tiny occupant, carrying home their new chirping friend, releasing it in their backyard, and if they were lucky, feeling its companionship as it sang for them throughout the summer. These were deeply felt pleasures of which people were reluctant to let go. But those deputies who supported the change didn't simply reject such tradition; they saw themselves as embracing a dynamic conception of its possibilities, a conception in which intimacies with these animals were anachronistic, archaic. Somehow, in this official pro-cricket vision, the crickets themselves, the crickets as living beings, were so incidental to the *festa del grillo* that there was no question that it would persist without them, as a celebration of their absence and as a celebration of the enlightened thinking which made that absence possible. "Freeing the crickets we leave behind an aspect of the past that doesn't reflect modern sensibility, without subtracting anything from the flavor of the event at the Cascine," Vincenzo Bugliani of the local Green Party, the deputy with responsibility for the environment, told the national press. "The tradition," he asserted, "evolves and improves."[18] "The *animalisti*," shouted a headline in *La Repubblica*, "have won."

The new *festa* made its debut on Ascension Sunday 2001, along with a high-profile public-education campaign encouraging students to understand, honor, and respect the *grilli*.

Exactly five years later, full of anticipation, we left our *pensione*, crossed the Ponte Vecchio, and walked out eagerly along the bank of the Arno to the Parco delle Cascine and the *festa del grillo*, excited to know what kind of event it had become. A cricket festival without crickets. The river gleamed, placid as a pond under the bluest Tuscan sky.

5.

It was hot and humid. The air was thick and still. We'd been wandering around the park for hours. There was not a cricket in sight or earshot. Terra-cotta, mechanical, or even alive. And there weren't any of Dorothy Spicer's painted cages either. Were we in the right place? Had we got the date right?

As promised, there were plenty of vendors. They just weren't selling crickets. There were toys, food, clothes, belts, caps, housewares. There were plenty of fake designer watches but not even one fake cricket. There were two long lines of stalls, tightly packed along the park's main thoroughfare. Right in the middle, attracting the biggest crowd of all, was a large stand with sad-looking caged animals, dogs, cats, exotic birds—none wild, autochthonous, or illegal.

We walked up and down the strip yet again, then cut out to cover the park more systematically in case the cricket action was elsewhere. We stumbled upon the Fonte di Narciso, where Shelley (who elsewhere wrote of insects as his "kindred") composed "Ode to the West Wind," and we puzzled over a mysterious overgrown pyramid, which, we later found out, was one of the Cascine's famous icehouses. We found the amusement park and the handsome eighteenth-century façade of the School of Agricultural Science, in which Italo Calvino studied briefly before joining the partisans. And we saw the "no thoroughfare" signs beside the market that read "Divieto di Transito per Festa del Grillo," the sole indication that this was the event for which we'd come all the way to Florence.

But it must be somewhere, surely. We must be somehow missing it, surely. And simultaneously, we both remembered a hazy afternoon more than twenty years before when we'd stood on the terrace in front of Sacré-Coeur in Montmartre, looking out over the soothing gray panorama of Paris and trying without success, for a full ten minutes, to locate the Eiffel Tower until, all of a sudden, as if clouds had cleared, the city's most prominent structure suddenly appeared soaring high above the landscape in the very center of our view and we couldn't imagine how we'd failed to see it. And as that memory surfaced, we discovered that the man who runs the immaculate public restrooms in the middle of the Cascine was Brazilian, from Fortaleza, in Ceará; that he was a great conversationalist; that he was delighted to talk in Portuguese; that he had arrived in Florence thirty years ago after passing through Paris; and that, unlike the Eiffel Tower two decades earlier, the *festa del grillo* would not be appearing miraculously from the ether that afternoon.

So here was Seu Edinaldo from Fortaleza, full of life and energy, with just a touch of the melancholy of exile. I don't know if he and his wife lived in the building, but they'd turned it into a tropical home, the most beautiful restrooms you can imagine, magical restrooms, all beaded curtains, whitewashed walls, cutout magazine photos of birds and landscapes, floors so burnished you could take your reflection as a dance partner. Seu Edinaldo's family is in Rio and São Paulo, but it's too late to go back. Oh, the *saudades,* the longing, the absence.

The crickets? A few years ago they changed the law and banned the sale of live crickets at the *festa,* he said. And since then, well, it's not really the *festa del grillo* anymore. It used to be such a special day; at one time

tens of thousands of people came out for it, grown-ups, children—it filled the park. Now . . . he gestured toward the market and the sparsely occupied lawns. On the other hand, he continued, seeing our disappointment, if you're lucky, if you search carefully in the stalls, you might find one of the little battery-operated insects they've been selling for the last few years. And maybe you'll find one of the cages, though it's been a while since I've seen one, he added.

So we did look again, and this time we saw a T-shirt with a bee on it, and some painted clay ladybugs, and a diamanté (or maybe cubic zirconia) butterfly pin, and some plastic Chinese singing birds in green and gold cages that just for a second we thought held crickets, and one table with some very blond dolls and a few Tamagotchi, the lovable-egg virtual pets that were such a phenomenon in Japan in the late 1990s and which in that moment, on that table, made perfect sense as reincarnations of the *grillo parlante*, returned from the dead, just as he returns, without explanation, at the end of Collodi's masterpiece.

Why so perfect? Because through the Tamagotchi—its fans claimed—young people could learn to care for other creatures, could grow to appreciate the needs of beings apart from themselves, could acquire an early intimacy with mortality and the uncertainties of life, could gain a practical knowledge of the connectedness, the pleasures, and the sadnesses of life. And it seemed serendipitous to see them here at the new

festa del grillo because these claims for the Tamagotchi are exactly the same as the claims for crickets advanced by their admirers, that is, by those cricket lovers who love being around crickets, who love having a cricket as a personal friend to talk to, to listen to, to play with, to feed, and to share their house with for the summer of its life. These are the claims they used against those other lovers of crickets who are so determined to save crickets from that kind of possessive love and the confinement and loss of freedom that is its gift, who see themselves as the selfless lovers, the pure lovers, the lovers who can love without demanding anything in return, whose theme song might well be Sting's "If You Love Somebody Set Them Free."

But that battle was over, at least for now. There were no more crickets in the Parco delle Cascine on Ascension Sunday, and there were no more cricket intimacies to serve as the stuff of moral education and future nostalgias. There were only the Tamagotchi. And no one seemed to be buying them anyway.

The Quality of Queerness
Is Not Strange Enough

1.

Have a look at this photograph. It was taken in Rondônia in the southwest Brazilian Amazon on March 15, 1991, by George O. Krizek, a psychiatrist and amateur entomologist from Florida. On the left is a butterfly of the genus *Dynamine;* on the right, a rove beetle.[1]

Dr. Krizek was observing the beetle when the butterfly showed up. He or she (the article doesn't specify) landed on the left-hand leaf, extended its proboscis, and right away began exploring the beetle's raised anus.

Krizek whipped out his camera. But by the time he'd adjusted the focus, the sheepish-looking butterfly—maybe not wanting to be caught at such an intimate moment—had withdrawn. Still, it's not hard to imagine what this picture would have looked like had the doctor moved a bit faster.

2.

Who knows what Dr. Krizek witnessed that day in Rondônia? Let's suppose it really was some casual interspecies ass play (I'm sorry, I can't think of a more polite term). And let's suppose, as Krizek suggests, that the two animals had no ulterior motives: the beetle wasn't a mantis trying to lure the butterfly for a next meal; the butterfly wasn't an ant tailing an aphid for sugary anal exudates. Let's suppose, instead—as Dr. Krizek supposes—that these were just two little animals enjoying a little action, getting to know each other, and feeling pretty good about it.

Krizek had no doubt about what he saw. Both insects were "calm" throughout their six or seven seconds of intimacy. (Calmer than he was, in fact.) All signs were that their interaction was consensual. If this cross-species "orogenital contact" had occurred between a human and another mammal, he said—and as a practitioner in the field, he spoke with some authority—it would have been instantly recognized as a "sexual paraphilia," that is, a fetish.

But, Krizek adds, international psychiatric terminology is restricted to humans, so this interaction needs another name. He suggests *zoophilia*. He must know that this is the current term for the activities of people who enjoy sex with animals of other species, the term that even the animal lovers themselves now use for what was once bestiality. Could his just-too-late photo be an open invitation to sexual explorers of all species to launch their brave new world of truly diverse diversity?

3.

In "Beasts Are Rational," one of the liveliest of his famous *Moralia*, Plutarch, writing in the early second century A.D., pointed to the absence of homosexuality among animals—as opposed to among "your high and mighty nobility, to say nothing of the baser sort"—as definitive proof of the superior virtue of animals compared with people.[2] Ever since, researchers seem to have had difficulty recognizing carnality in male-male, female-female, and mixed-group animal encounters. Even so, there's now simply too much evidence to ignore. As the neuroscientist Paul Vasey and the evolutionary anthropologist Volker Sommer recently wrote, it's "increasingly difficult to discount all sexual interactions in animals among members of the same sex as exceptions, as idiosyncrasies, or as pathologies."[3]

It's not just the famously flexible bonobos. A diverse sexual repertoire has been documented among a large number of species, from geese (male-male pair bonding) to dolphins (solo and mutual masturbation, oral sex, and "petting"), lizards (voyeurism and exhibitionism), American bison (male-male and female-female coupling), and plenty in between. As long ago as 1909, the Italian entomologist Antonio Berlese reported that the silkworm *Bombyx mori* was only one of many insects prone to what he described as "homosexual perversion."[4]

For a long time, animal scientists simply explained away the queerness (homosexual and otherwise) they stumbled onto, not thinking to take it seriously. At first, as if it were gay sex in prison, they dismissed it as the corrupting effect of domestication or of confinement in laboratory cages. Later it became apparent that animals "in nature" often choose same-sex partners even when opposite-sex ones are available. These creatures, the scientists decided, were either deviant or, more commonly, mistaken. They simply didn't realize they were fooling around with a partner of the same sex.

By the 1970s, there was increasing acceptance among biologists that despite its apparent transgression of the fundamental evolutionary imperative to procreate, homosexual and other nonreproductive behavior could make evolutionary sense. Rather than denying its significance, researchers (particularly those influenced by sociobiology and evolutionary psychology) started to develop explanations that brought this superficially anomalous activity within the frame of natural selection. If queer sex existed, they reasoned, it must, like all behavior, have an adaptive function. They identified nonreproductive sexual interactions such as butterfly-beetle ass play as "sociosexual behaviors"—social in function, sexual in form.

Yet even before biologists observed the behavior, even before they saw what it was, even before they had even recorded its existence, they believed they already knew its purpose. Like all behaviors, they maintained, same-sex sex functioned to make possible "some sort of fitness-enhancing social goal or breeding strategy" for the parties involved.[5] Understood like that, it resembled a crossword puzzle in which the answers are known but the questions are blank—only, unlike a puzzle, there is no guarantee (beyond the faith of the researchers) that the answers and questions are connected by the same rules. In more orthodox analytical procedures, wouldn't the theory be open to revision by the data?

Not surprisingly, explanations derived in this way could be tortuous. Male-male sex among adolescent fruit flies is commonly understood as training or practice for future heterosexual adventures.[6] The "feminine" behavior of male rove beetles—which avoid bigger and more aggressive males by doing the things that females do, such as foraging dung and having sex with males—is a strategy of these weak males to gain access to otherwise unavailable food and females.[7] The bisexual "promiscuity" of male creeping water bugs, who forgo courtship and jump on any other water bug they encounter, makes sense because "the costs of time and energy expended in copulatory attempts with other males are exceeded by the benefits of never failing to inseminate every potential mate."[8] The two-hour postcoital embrace of male and female Japanese beetles, *Popillia japonica,* is a result of the polygamous and homosexually inclined male beetle's determination to protect its "genetic investment" from other males who might want to impregnate the female before she deposits her eggs. On the other hand, the same-sex mountings of both male and female *P. japonica* are the "misdirected behavior" of "sexually aroused individuals."[9] Bisexual female grape borer weevils mount females three times more often than male grape borers mount other males. Nobody knows why, but researchers are confident that this behavior has a "biological function" that will be discovered soon.[10]

All function and no fun. So much for the joy of sex. Predictably, I have my own unscientific hunch: I suspect that if good sex hasn't been found among the insects, it's because no one—except perhaps George Krizek— has been out there looking for it.

Because the fact is that biologists studying other animals have found that sex—"nonreproductive" and otherwise—is often all about pleasure. And inevitably, they've moved swiftly to assign a function to that, too. Good sex, many say, is a social lubricant. The enjoyment and affection it generates ease group tensions. It is a tool of reconciliation. It is part of the intimacy that enables social bonding.[11] We could, of course, make that same argument about the function of sex among humans. And who knows; it might even be true. Even if it were, though, it would also be the case that it explained very little, that it was just the tiniest raggedy edge of one of life's most complicated stories.

4.

Must queer animal sex always have an evolutionary function? It seems too obvious a point, but just as it is for people, might not sex itself be reason enough for animals to get together?

In some species, at least, the answer is clear. Among the female Japanese macaques studied by Paul Vasey, relationships are based on "mutual sexual attraction."[12] Vasey and his co-workers have spent years watching female macaques stroking themselves with their tails and rubbing each others' clitorises. In Vasey's opinion, none of this female-female sex play has any adaptive function. Rather, he says, it originated as a by-product of heterosexual sex and now has a lively and pleasurable existence all of its own.

In arguing that pleasure and desire are sufficient explanation for same-sex encounters, Vasey and others have drawn on work by the evolutionary biologist Stephen Jay Gould that dates back almost thirty years. In a series of groundbreaking and controversial papers, Gould argued that adaptation was drastically overemphasized in U.S. evolutionary theory. Instead, he pointed to traits that were not directly selected but were instead functionless by-products ("biological spandrels") of other adaptations.[13] Such traits were often evolutionarily neutral, causing no disadvantage to those involved and so not subject to negative selective pressure. Lesbianism among Japanese macaques is one example. Vasey speculates that it originated when females mounted apathetic males in an effort to rouse them to intercourse. Once the females discovered they enjoyed rubbing up against male bodies, it was a short step to finding out that it was even better with their girlfriends. The originary hetero sex had an evolutionary function; the queer sex was just more fun.

Who knows if Vasey is right about these gay monkeys. At the very least, he's got a good story, a better story than the one that says they're doing it because they can't tell the difference.

5.

We need better stories about queer insects too. Entomologists, start writing! It's so frustrating to have to deal with mechanistic models all these centuries after Descartes. We need to bring back pleasure and desire. Even deep, dark, complicated paraphilic praying mantis pleasure-desire. Especially deep, dark, paraphilic praying mantis pleasure-desire.

We need more queerness! We should remember the bees. The supposedly sexless sisterhood of the bees. Sipping and sucking in the darkness of the hive. Touching and taking, rubbing and writhing. That liquid world of intimate intensities.

Who knows what George Krizek witnessed that day in Rondônia? It's nice to think it really was a little interspecies ass play. Two little animals enjoying a little action and feeling good about it. But it doesn't matter if it wasn't. It could have been. And if not at that moment, then at some other time. The possibilities are vast. We should be paying attention. Who knows what we'll find? Who knows what we'll learn? Who knows how much more interesting this world could be?

The Deepest of **R**everies

If you get down from the Hankyu Railways train at Minoo, a spa town that begins just where the densely populated Kansai Plain rises sharply into the thick greenery of the surrounding mountains, if you leave the station and walk up the narrowing, winding road lined with small stores selling pickled radishes, seaweed teas, inflatable animals, handmade pottery, freshly battered maple-leaf tempura (a specialty in a town famous for its fall colors), as well as other goods that might attract older, health-conscious, nature-loving people and young families on days out from Osaka, if you resist the pull of the twenty-story elevator ready to whisk you in an instant to the slightly faded but still appealing hot-springs resort complex perched high on the hillside and instead bear right with the roadway as it narrows to follow the stream so clear below that you can count the fish rooting in its bottom, and if you keep walking, slowly because of the intense summer humidity, past the pretty, open-sided pavilion festooned with red holiday lanterns and past the delicately bowed wooden bridge, then soon, as the path curves back around the foot of the mountain, you will see a small space open beside the river and three wooden benches that someone has placed—with the care and attention given to everything here—to overlook the thickly wooded hillside that rises from the far bank of the stream.

We stopped, drank some water, nibbled on sweet tempura leaves, and soon, without talking, fell into the deepest of reveries, immersed in sound, resonating in sound, the sound of cicadas, surrounded by cicadas, a summer symphony of cicadas. A man sat at the next bench and removed his shoes. He rested his feet on the fence and closed his eyes. And as we sank deeper into sound, the wall of cicadas ebbed and flowed, its rhythms changed, its notes found a clarity—or, rather, we found the clarity in them—virtuoso musicians took their solos (I don't know how else to describe it), a monkey shrieked, a child ran laughing behind us, and the pulsating thickness of melody and tone wove itself around the gurgling of the stream passing over the rocks below. "Have you got your recorder?" Sharon whispered, and I found the digital recorder I use for interviews and placed it upright on the fence. And now we have that sound to play whenever we need to be back in that place, with those trees, that river, those animals, that man. A soundscape of Minoo Park, Osaka Prefecture, Japan, August 1, 2005, in the heat of the early afternoon.

Sex

1.

In September 1997, Keith Toogood, described in the British press as a forty-four-year-old factory worker and father of two, was arrested at his home by customs officers who had seized a suspect item at a London mail-sorting office. The package originated in New York with a mail-order company called Expressions Videos and contained ten films, including *Clogs and Frogs*, *Barefoot Crush*, and *Toad Trampler*. Appearing eleven months later at Telford Magistrates' Court, Mr. Toogood pleaded guilty to importing obscene material and was ordered to pay a fine of £2,000 plus costs. A customs spokesman, Bill O'Leary, commented that officers with twenty-five years' experience "thought they had seen everything before they came across this." The videos, he said, "are too grisly to describe." Mike Hartley of the West Midlands Royal Society for the Prevention of Cruelty to Animals agreed. These so-called crush videos, he told a reporter for *The Scotsman*, "are as sick and depraved as you can get."[1]

2.

Four years earlier, with Toogood's arrest and all that would follow still unimagined, Jeff Vilencia was living and making movies in his mother's garage in Lakewood, a suburb south of Los Angeles. He was enjoying the unexpected art house success of two short films: *Squish*, which features a woman squishing grapes, and *Smush*, which involves a different woman smushing a large number of earthworms. Both movies had screened at film festivals, some of them prestigious, and with his surfer looks and easy smile Jeff was proving an engaging interviewee, charming, articulate, and disarmingly direct. "A crush freak," he patiently explained to the rather uncertain host of a Fox daytime talk show, "is one who desires himself tiny, insect size, bug-like, and then stepped on and squashed by the feet of a woman."

"I've always been a pervert!" he merrily replied to an audience member's question about how long he'd felt like this. If he was going to be a freak, he'd be his own freak. He was poised and relaxed, enjoying confounding expectations. This wasn't some guy who had trouble getting girls—unlike the timid-looking Pie Man with whom he shared the stage. ("Sexuality has power in it," Jeff pointed out, his tone somewhere between sex ed and a laundry-liquid commercial, "and we're bound by humiliation—especially the Pie Man and myself.")[2]

Jeff passed on the opportunity to treat the studio and TV audience to a full description of what he meant by humiliation. He explained, instead, that since he'd made his first movie, in 1990, he'd become the linchpin in an international brotherhood of 300 crush freaks ("all gentlemen, by the way, very intellectual people"). Interested individuals could contact him at Squish Productions, a mail-order business he ran out of his home in Lakewood, from which they could purchase his videos or a copy

of *The American Journal of the Crush-Freaks*, the first of two books that he wrote and published as a way to build the crush community.

The *Journal* bursts with compressed energy, its pages packed with information and opinion: extended discussions of the fetish (its histories, its pleasures, its variations); a lengthy interview with Jeff in the foot-fetish magazine *In Step* (Jeff on his movies: "We have life, and the origin of life is sex, or the sexual act, and we have death which is the very final, very frustrating, very dark unknown thing. Somehow, occasionally these two things collide in some type of an orgasmic imagery"); a demographic analysis based on letters Jeff received after the interview was published ("A large concentration of the Crush-Freaks hail from the north and east coast, with a large amount of foot fetish people coming from New York"); reproductions of those letters ("I've read your interview in *In Step* and was very happy to learn that I am not the only one that has the fantasy of being stepped on by a Giant Woman!"); a helpful list of phrases guaranteed to excite a crush freak ("I'm going to squish you through my toes"); a review section highlighting gardening and entomology books that contain scenes of insect killing and are ranked from one ("Eeeeh") to five pumps ("Thru the roof! Obviously the author herself has the crush fetish and this is her way of expressing it"); an extended interview with Ms. J, crush mistress, about her craft ("I do not step on the little spindly legged spiders 'cause they're my friends. But when it comes to bugs, I mean they're just icky little creatures so I can't think of why they shouldn't be stepped on!"); casting notices and responses ("I'm a model and commercial actress with a theatrical background. I have exactly what you want, BIG FEET. Enclosed is my modeling comp—read sizes carefully"); and much more. Interspersed among all this—some of it playful, some of it funny, some of it a bit scary, some of it a bit sad, all of it in his take-me-as-I-am, straight-from-me-to-you writing style—are Jeff's crush fantasies, his stories and reminiscences that deploy what he identifies as the three key narrative elements of the crush fetish: power, sex-violence, and voyeurism.

Rei, Jeff's girlfriend, has placed him in a small jar. She's poked four or five airholes in the lid. She is on her way out for the evening with a couple she met through an ad in a foot-fetish magazine. As she leaves, she switches out the light. Jeff dozes off in the jar.

Rei comes home. The couple tie her up and lick the soles of her feet. ("She knows that I am helpless and can do nothing but watch. . . . I like to watch! I like to be bug-sized and trapped and forced to watch.") Next thing he knows, Rei is shaking the jar like a bottle of hot sauce. His head smashes against the glass; he thinks his arm could be broken, his skull might even be fractured. She unscrews the lid and pours him out onto the carpet, flicks him over with her big toe. "Hey, you guys, look what I found, a squirmy little bug!"

The three of them tower over him. He tries to move but feels glued to the floor. "I must look like a tiny, squirmy silverfish or an oversized white worm or maggot." He squirms helplessly. Rei peers down: "Look, there on the floor, you guys, it's my boyfriend. I know it looks like a strange insect but it's him." One of her new playmates makes to fetch some tissue. "Why bother," says Rei. "Let's just step on him!"

It all happens in super-slow motion, the way we might guess that time occupies another scale for tiny short-lived beings, the way time drifts to a

near halt in moments of extremity. "She raises up her huge foot. I try to lift my head but it is no use. I can't move. I hear her speak one last time. 'Squish that bug!' "[3]

And now it all converges. As he lies there immobilized, willing the foot toward him, begging it toward him, the foot descending toward him, the giant foot right over him, he spontaneously ejaculates and, right then, exactly then, the sticky foot crushes down on him.

> My guts gushed out of me as my eyeballs popped out of their sockets. My inner matter came squishing through every orifice of my body! . . . My sides split open, and all of my intestines smushed out like a half-flattened grape. I became a tiny bloody mess under the ball of the foot. The warm foot twisted back and forth to make sure I was smashed. Half of my tiny body was broken up into bits and ground into [the] carpet. The other half of me was stuck to the bottom of the foot like to the skin of a squished grape.[4]

Perhaps these words speak to you only if you're already inside this story and captive to its call. Perhaps different writing could better measure this orgasmic collision of death, sex, and submission. Or perhaps the question is meaningless because these stories are functional, not educational. But *Squish* and *Smush*—Jeff's art films—somehow manage to create experience for all kinds of viewers, not only the already committed. Maybe that says something about the difference between print and film, the modes of attention they create. Or maybe just about the inescapability of these particular movies, compressed and compact, distilled down to just pure idea, inexorable and unambiguous.

These are short films, five and eight minutes only, shot in high-contrast black-and-white. Erika Elizondo, the star of *Smush,* appears in a dark dress on a bright white background. She's right there in extreme close-up over and over, her cute baby-fat face, her mobile expression, a little innocent, a little knowing, a little flirty, a little unpredictable, a little inaccessible, her pedicured feet, the fleshy soles soon soiled with bloody mess of worm.

"I weigh one hundred twenty-two pounds and have a size eight-and-a-half shoe," she begins, striking a few exaggerated runway poses. "I love to smush worms. I love to tease them by pressing down softly at first." She talks like Betty Boop, her voice high-pitched with lots of echo. She's talking to *you*, she knows what you like, and she's going to give it to you. She's not judging you, she's playing with you, and she's toying with you too. She's giggling, but she's in charge. She wrinkles her nose in mock disgust. "It's fun to pretend that the worms are little men under my feet. Even better I like to pretend that they are old boyfriends and this is my revenge." The amplified squelch of worms underfoot sounds like squealing. Eight minutes feels very long as she teases the animals, laughs, poses, switches into black pumps. ("These pumps belong to my mother. I decided to use them because she didn't want me to be in a foot-fetish film!") She stamps her bare feet on the flailing animals, and their intestinal fluids shoot from their anus like an orgasm, like the orgasm Jeff has the instant before Rei's foot crushes him into messy oblivion. "You're just a grease spot," Erika Elizondo tells the worms as she grinds them into the bright white butcher paper.

Crush freaks loved the movies, which quickly became genre classics. You still come across people on fetish discussion boards trying to locate

copies. But critics and festival audiences were unsure how to react. "It fascinates, but . . . pushes the limits of tolerance," said a spokesperson for the Helsinki International Film Festival. It's a "humane society horror show," wrote Charles Trueheart in *The Washington Post*.

For Jeff Vilencia, the movies, the books, and the TV appearances were a celebration, an assertion of the right to live fully. "I love myself and my fetish and I won't trade places with another fetish, ever! I love girls' feet (sizes 8, 9, 10 and up!). I love to lick the soles and suck on their toes. I love to fantasize about being a bug and having her step on me and squish me! I masturbate about this two times a day," he declared in the *Journal*. "We must be free to talk about sexuality and feelings," he continued; "then all taboos will vanish. . . . We must move forward with teaching sexuality, and teach every child that sex and fantasy and fetishes are good things that can create a happy, healthy sex life which in turn will nourish a better relationship between partners. The world will be a better place through an understanding of sexuality and the meaning of this life experience. Many happy fantasies to you all whatever your kink may be. *We are the Crush-Freaks—Step On Us!*"[5]

3.

Keith Toogood's arrest was just the beginning, Jeff told me as we sat talking in the afternoon sunshine outside a Starbucks in suburban Los Angeles.[6] The British animal activists alerted the Humane Society in Washington, D.C. That organization, in turn, directed the district attorney's office in Ventura County to Steponit, a video production company operating in its jurisdiction. On viewing the tapes, the L.A. cops reacted with the same disgust as the U.K. customs officers, but they were unable to build a case: the participants in the films were unidentifiable, visible only from the legs down; Steponit had already gone out of business; and it was unclear whether the videos had been produced within the three-year statute of limitations stipulated by the California animal-cruelty laws, the legislation that the D.A.'s office decided offered the best chance of a conviction.

Frustrated, law enforcement took the operation undercover. Calling herself Minnie, Susan Creede, an investigator with the Ventura County D.A.'s office, signed on to the Crushcentral discussion board and, in January 1999, made contact with Gary Thomason, a local producer and distributor of crush videos. Soon they were chatting online, and Minnie told Thomason how much she enjoyed stomping on mice with her size-ten feet in her boyfriend's garage and, more important, how she had ambitions to star in a video. Thomason, whose productions till this point had been restricted to smaller animals—worms, snails, crickets, grasshoppers, mussels, and sardines—was taken aback by Minnie's uncommon enthusiasm but was nonetheless intrigued. They met in person in early February, and with Minnie's encouragement, Thomason felt emboldened to try something new. As he explained to *California Lawyer* magazine's Martin Lasden, "Mice are very popular to at least 30 percent of the crush community, which makes them well worth the effort."

Lasden reported that communication cooled off for a while. Then, in late May, Thomason wrote to tell Minnie about a new movie he'd completed, in which an actress had crushed two rats, four adult mice, and six baby mice, known as pinkies. He sent Minnie a clip, to which she responded, "Nice work."

Three weeks later, Minnie, along with her friend Lupe—a Long Beach police officer named Maria Mendez-Lopez—arrived as scheduled at Thomason's apartment. Thomason headed out to the pet store. Minnie asked him to pick up some guinea pigs, but when he returned thirty minutes later, the five boxes he was carrying each contained a large rat, sold to him as food for snakes. The guinea pigs, he explained, were too expensive.

From then on, it was all over pretty fast. Thomason closed the blinds and locked the front door. With some difficulty, he secured a reluctant rat by taping its tail to the top of a glass table—a valuable prop in that filmed from below, it affords a last-gasp point-of-view shot of the woman's bloody soles. Lasden reconstructed what followed:

Thomason and his associate, Robert, raise their cameras.
MINNIE: I wish that was my ex-husband.
LUPE: Yeah, he was a real jerk.
A loud knock on the door.

THOMASON: Who's there?
Police.
Panic. Thomason tries to free the rat. Before he succeeds, the door crashes in and eight plainclothes cops, guns drawn, rush the apartment.
Police! Police! Get on the ground.

"They were the most vicious cops you've ever seen," Jeff told me. "They broke all his stuff. They stole his coin collection. They answered his phone when one of his relatives called: 'Yeah, we know Gary. Did you know Gary was a fuckin' pervert?' "

The police let Robert go but charged Thomason with three felony counts of cruelty to animals carrying a possible three years' jail time. Bail was set at $30,000. Rifling through his confiscated computer, they found files identifying the actress in his previous rat movie. When they caught up with Diane Chaffin in La Puente, California, she still had the guilty shoes.

The section of the California Penal Code dealing with the inhumane treatment of animals was written in 1905, when the animals uppermost in legislators' minds were farm stock. It defines an animal as any "dumb creature" and sanctions any person who "maliciously and intentionally maims, mutilates, tortures, or wounds a living animal, or maliciously or intentionally kills . . . [one]." The defense lawyers in *People v. Thomason* sought to limit the reach of this clause by citing the Health and Safety Code's injunction that California residents have an obligation to exterminate rodents in their homes "by poisoning, trapping, and other appropriate means."[7] In the abstract, it seemed plausible to argue that mice and rats were excluded from protection (along with invertebrates, whose killing excited no legal controversy) and, moreover, that the approved methods of extermination also involved mutilation and torture. In practice, however, the prosecution had only to show the judge a few brief clips of Diane Chaffin in character for legal niceties to lose their traction. ("Hey, pinkie," the court heard her tell the baby mouse, "I'm gonna teach you a lesson. I'm gonna teach you to love my heel.")[8]

"You can kill animals all day long," commented Tom Connors, the Ventura County deputy D.A. overseeing the case. "They do it in slaughterhouses. What matters is *how* you kill [them]."[9] Nonetheless, Chaffin was charged in only three of the deaths. The D.A. was uncertain he could demonstrate cruelty in the cases of the other nine animals. What this meant in reality, Jeff Vilencia explained, was that the struggling of the adult rats was visible whereas the death throes of the tiny babies were not. "Isn't that the most convoluted thing you ever heard in your life?" Jeff asked me.

4.

Squish and *Smush* are just two of Jeff Vilencia's many crush-movie credits. The other films were released in his *Squish Playhouse* series of fifty-six titles, which he sold via mail order, mostly by word of mouth and through ads in porn magazines. None of these videos made it onto the film-festival circuit, nor were they intended to. "They were made for private masturbation," Jeff told me, "for guys who had the fetish."

The *Squish Playhouse* movies are in color and are much longer than the art films, lasting for at least forty-five minutes. They might involve crickets, snails, and pinkies as well as worms. They feature Jeff as an off-camera master of ceremonies and interviewer. And they employ plot conventions familiar to viewers of low-budget "amateur" porn, in which a premium is placed on the ordinariness of the women involved and the production of a fantasy of normality, the fantasy that these events could happen anywhere, anytime, that right now your doorbell might ring and a girl show up who'd love to do all this just for you, too.

It all happens in what looks like Jeff's apartment. He starts out by interviewing the actress, his voice disembodied, deep and strong, like that of a friendly radio host. It's low-budget but professional, though he laughs a lot, nervous laughter, and it's clear he's excited. He's set this up and is running things, but there's uncertainty in the air.

The actress sits in front of a white drop sheet. "How tall are you?" he asks her. "How old are you?" "How much do you weigh?" "What's your shoe size?" He wants to hear fetish talk: "What drew you to the bug-squishing ad?" he asks. Elizabeth, the tall, dark-haired star of *Squish Playhouse 42*, dabs at her runny nose with a tissue and responds without hesitation. "Money!" she says, and they both laugh.

The woman might be shy. Jeff coaxes her into talking about how they met—in a parking lot!—asks what she knows about the fetish, how she feels about insects, about squishing insects, what her mom would think about her doing this, what she thinks of the guys who get off watching her do this. He elicits embarrassed giggles and a few insect-killing anecdotes. ("What kind of shoes were you wearing?") He teases her. ("You *are* a monster!") She goes to work.

It's basic: a large square of white paper, a change of shoes, a few small animals. She might be wary, like Elizabeth, or she might be enthusiastic, like Michelle in *Squish Playhouse 29*. ("What did that feel like?" "It felt artistic.") She pushes the animals around with her toe. He coaches. She pushes some more. The camera pulls in and focuses on the action. She crunches a few, grows in confidence, maybe gets angry with them, threatens them, mocks them, laughs at them, laughs at the situation, plays with them with her foot, pretends they're her ex-boyfriend. ("You're an asshole, you're a prick, you fucked me over, you fucked my best friend, you humiliated me, you deserve to die, you need to die painfully, you need to have a very horrible, painful, excruciatingly, horrifically painful death," Michelle says in a strangely uninflected voice.) She lets them escape a little, catches them again, kicks them around, applies more pressure, less pressure. Jeff pulls in for an extreme close-up on a cricket's head sticking out from under her shoe. ("Look at him squirming, that's cool, they suffer more that way," Michelle observes.) They take a break to discuss the mess on the sole of her shoe. They start again: new paper, new animals, sometimes a whole new outfit.

There's no slick editing, no effects, no pretense. It's homemade, it's right here, it's happening in real time with real people. But what is happening? With the camera fixed on Michelle's blushing face, Jeff prompts her to explain:

JEFF: The guys who are gonna watch this tape, you know what they're gonna do, right? What are they gonna do?
MICHELLE: They're gonna get off on it. (*Embarrassed laugh.*)
JEFF (*also laughing*): How are they gonna get off on it?
MICHELLE: They're gonna jack off! (*Both laugh.*)
JEFF: So they're gonna fantasize that *you* are crushing them. And they're gonna get a hard-on and jerk off. What do you think of that?

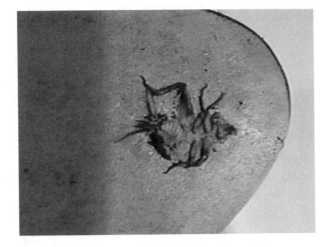

MICHELLE: They're gonna picture themselves as a bug. *(Camera moves closer.)*

JEFF: Yeah, and then what happens? . . .

MICHELLE *(very quietly)*: I don't know, I guess . . .

JEFF: Well, they picture themselves as a bug . . .

MICHELLE: Well, yeah . . .

JEFF: And then what happens? . . .

MICHELLE: And then I crush them, and it's like I'm crushing *them* and not the bug . . .

JEFF: Wow! Can you believe this! Did you tell any of your friends about this fetish?

Michelle tells Jeff that she prepared for her role by watching his movies and dipping into the two volumes of *The American Journal of the Crush-Freaks*. Jeff tells me that these scenes were never rehearsed.

I know where Michelle got this idea that the men picture themselves as the bug. I've read the same books, watched the same movies, and I'd guess I've had some of the same conversations with Jeff Vilencia. It seems straightforward: "picture themselves" as a gentle shorthand for that intense identification at a moment of wildly disorienting arousal. But what exactly are Jeff and his fellow crush freaks identifying with?

At first, I pictured some kind of *becoming*, some kind of cross-species melding of two beings into something new, a bug-guy/guy-bug, something attainable by the triggering of ecstatic moments in the detailing of the fantasy. I imagined that this momentary bug-guy somehow felt himself to be occupying the psychic and physical lifeworld of the insect. And I liked that idea, because it opened the possibility of this being an unusual struggle to escape the limits of being human, rather than that more familiar human struggle for fulfillment and expression. It seemed utopian, in an unusual, messed-up kind of way.

But then I noticed that in Jeff's fantasies—or at least in his fetish stories and movies—the woman always knows that the bug-guy is no bug. She knows that the bug-thing writhing on the carpet is Jeff. Sometimes— actually, quite often—she'll have her big, strong boyfriend (often called Sasha) crush him for her, and Sasha might not know he's crushing Jeff until she tells him afterward, or sometimes she might never tell him and Sasha might never know. But the woman always knows, and it's the woman, the arbiter and architect of punishment, who matters in these stories.

Remember Jeff's fantasy of being ground into the carpet by Rei and her friends, one story among many, a large number of stories, a small number of plots? Jeff is tiny, he's squirmy, he's disgusting, he's worthless. He is good for nothing but crushing. He has the characteristics of an insect and deserves to be treated accordingly, with cruelty, without mercy. The players in this drama are quite clear on this point. Jeff is *like* a bug. But he's *not* a bug. He's not *part* bug. He's not *in-between* bug. He's definitely not *trans*-bug. He's not even passing as a bug. He's *bug-like*. Everyone knows that it's Jeff down there on the carpet getting

stomped: he knows it and Rei knows it and that couple licking her feet know it too. Remember what Rei said? "Look, there on the floor, you guys, it's my boyfriend. I know it looks like a strange insect but it's him."

So even though Jeff likes to sign off as Jeff "The Bug" Vilencia, his aspiration is really quite modest: he just wants what a bug's got—worthlessness, repulsiveness, vulnerability, squishiness. It's not a huge transformation. He already has most of this. And he's managed to find a positive value in it, discovered that, for him, humiliation is the fulfillment of desire. He can pay women to walk on him. But he needs more. He needs his bug-like nature to be made visible, and he needs to be forced to suffer the consequences—again and again and again.

And that's why I'm guessing he's not really a guy-bug/bug-guy, because, by necessity, none of this suffering and humiliation produces empathy or sympathy for the insect. How could it? Because suffering is pleasure and because the insect is just a container for all that dark pleasure, nothing more. The insect is the dark place that sucks up society's disgust. It is the anonymous dark place that enables relentless repetition. Squish, squish, squish. Like a baby throwing its bottle to the ground again and again, every time it's picked up, again and again, trying to figure out something that's all at once obscure and vacant. Again and again. Nothing more.

Are you feeling it? That's what counts here. Don't worry about why they're doing this, even though crush freaks themselves—cursed with the explanatory burden of a "minority sexuality"—have little choice but to fret about that all the time. Bastard child of foot fetishism, reject infant of giantessism, downcast cousin of trampling, alienated half sibling of zoophilia, evil twin of the messy thing.[10] Everyone traces it to childhood, to an unanticipated glimpse of an unfortunate episode: mother, insect, foot. In that blink of a wide-open eye, something gets made forever, something gets lost forever.

To Freud, fetishism is a disavowal, "an oscillation between two logically incompatible beliefs."[11] The impossibility of resolution produces the constant return—to the foot, to the insect, to the explosive death, to the moment long ago before that bad thing happened. To the absent female phallus. Or maybe not. It doesn't seem wholly serious when you write it down like that.

Still, it's not just crush freaks who need to know. As we'll soon see, everyone wants an origin story, everyone from Fox TV to the D.A.'s office to the Humane Society to the Judiciary Committee of the U.S. House of Representatives. Why this need to unravel causation? To make sure it doesn't happen again? To develop a cure? To nullify, justify, pathologize, normalize, criminalize? There's agreement on all sides that this stomping is a symptom of something gone wrong. The only symptoms no one feels compelled to explain are the ones revealed in these inescapable demands for explanation.

Like most of us, Jeff is thoroughly inconsistent. Unlike most of us, he is highly quotable. "At this point in my life," he wrote in the *Journal*, "I am more interested in the thing itself rather than its origin."[12] The bug gets squished. The man gets off. That's what counts. Maybe you're not feeling it. Jeff is feeling it.

5.

Georges Bataille begins his inspiringly unapologetic picture book, *The Tears of Eros,* in the voice of the utopian manifesto. "We are finally," he announces, "beginning to see the absurdity of any connection between eroticism and morality." Morality, he tells us later, "makes the value of an act depend on its consequences."[13]

With the arrival of *People v. Thomason* in the summer of 1999, Jeff Vilencia, America's only telegenic crush freak, found himself back in the media spotlight. But this time, everything was different. It wasn't only hapless Gary Thomason who was making headlines. Crush freaks were also keeping cops busy in Islip Terrace, a suburb of Long Island. Acting on a tip from Thomas Capriola's ex-girlfriend, the police raided the twenty-seven-year-old's bedroom and found a half dozen semiautomatic firearms, a poster of a Nazi storm trooper, a fish tank full of mice, a pair of high heels coated in dried blood, and—the items that disturbed them most of all—seventy-one crush videos, which, Suffolk County prosecutors claimed, Capriola was selling through his Crush Goddess website and ads in porn magazines.[14]

Suddenly, America was in a pincer grip. Seeping across the map like the red tide in a cold war animation, crush freaks were advancing on the heartland from both coasts. Someone had to stand and fight. Michael Bradbury, the Ventura County district attorney, held a press conference along with representatives of the Doris Day Animal League. On a sunny day in Simi Valley, in front of large-format images of insects, kittens, guinea pigs, and mice being squashed under women's feet, they launched the campaign to fast-track House Resolution 1887, a federal bill designed to criminalize the production and distribution of crush videos.[15] The sponsor of the bill was Representative Elton Gallegly, a seven-term California Republican known for his energetic support of the citrus and wine industries' campaign to eradicate the glassy-winged sharpshooter leafhopper (as well as a record on immigration so hawkish that it led to his induction into the U.S. Border Patrol Hall of Fame).[16] Gallegly described the fetish as "one of the sickest and most demented forms of animal cruelty that I've ever been exposed to."

The campaign presented crush as a "gateway fetish." Just as cannabis leads inexorably to crack, its spokespeople argued, fetishists might begin innocuously enough with grapes and worms, but—step by step—they will be drawn up the ladder of Creation, until, in Bradbury's lurid scenario, it won't be long before someone "pay[s] $1 million to have a kid crushed."[17] To underline the point, one of his deputies testified to having seen a video in which a baby doll was trampled underfoot. Seventy-eight-year-old former child star Mickey Rooney piped up. "Put a stop, won't you, to crush videos," he begged. "What are we gonna hand our children? This is what we're going to hand down, these videos, crush videos? God forbid."[18]

As the bill headed to Congress, Jeff became the go-to guy for the entire media. For a few intense weeks, he was inundated with requests from radio stations, magazines, and newspapers. Perhaps seduced by that peculiarly American brew of idealism, exhibitionism, and celebrity seeking, he ignored the advice of a lawyer friend. Perhaps naïvely, he made himself available to all requests. ("I thought, Well, that's not fair because, first of all, we didn't do anything wrong. . . .") Still, for a while at least, he was able to give himself some cover. In interviews, he declared that he had ceased production of videos until all legal questions were resolved, and he drew a sharp line between the "vermin" featured in his own movies—specifically insects—and the mammals with which Bradbury, Gallegly, and Rooney were especially preoccupied. He didn't believe crush videos of domestic mammals actually existed, he said, but if they did, he certainly had no interest in them. I at first assumed this demarcation was a legalistic maneuver Jeff was using to protect himself in the midst of a dangerous moral panic. But then I realized it was a distinction fundamental to his fetish. Of course, he maintained, he had no interest in stomping on domestic pets. Even rodents, he told the Associated Press, are "too furry, too animal-looking."[19]

Jeff's argument was the same now as it had been on the talk show circuit in 1993. He took aim at those like Tom Connors, the Ventura County deputy D.A., who claimed it was the method, not the fact, of killing animals that was at issue. In Jeff's view, it was the very fact of killing animals that was wrong. The method was irrelevant. His critique was systemic. ("Look," he told me, "America's seventy-five percent grossly obese—you don't think they got there eating fuckin' vegetables?") Killing animals was endemic to capitalist society. What was at stake in the fight over crush videos, he argued, was the hypocrisy of a society that turned a blind eye to the daily mass slaughter of all kinds of animals but threw up its arms in horror when a tiny number of people killed for sexual pleasure. Jeff, it turned out, was a vegan and an animal rights activist.

"What about the fur industry, what about fishermen, what about the cattle industry?" he asked the BBC. "You can kill anything you want, basically, in any manner you want if it's for food or for sport or for fashion, but you cross the line when you do it for sexual gratification."[20] And anyway, he added, if we're honest, don't we all know that the excitement of the bullfighter and the thrill of the hunter is a sexual thrill, a sexual excitement. They're getting off on killing. The problem here is that crush freaks don't pretend otherwise. "I thought," Jeff told me, "I'm going to tell the world it might be reprehensible and gross, but it's not anything worse than what everybody does on a day-to-day basis." Or as he put it in a live encounter with Elton Gallegly on Court TV: "Our fine Congressman says there's a humane way to kill vermin. That's a colloquialism. Killing is killing. You kill them fast, you kill them slow. I wonder if the Congressman has ever seen a sticky trap or a snap trap. There's nothing humane about them."[21]

Gallegly's bill sailed through Congress by a vote of 372–42 in the House and unanimous acclaim in the Senate. Nonetheless, there was significant unease about the law's First Amendment implications. This was a bill written to criminalize content—"the depiction of animal cruelty"—and before it reached the floor of the House, it was substantially revised in the Judiciary Committee's Subcommittee on Crime to allow exceptions "if the material in question has serious religious, political, scientific, educational, journalistic, historic, or artistic value."[22]

Despite that, a number of representatives, most notably Robert Scott (D-Va.), argued strongly that the bill was still too broad ("Films of animals being crushed are communications about the acts depicted, not doing the acts") and failed to demonstrate compelling government interest (a test established by the Supreme Court in 1988 for First Amendment cases).[23] On this point, it was clear from the Supreme Court's upholding of the rights of the Santería church of Lukumí Babalu Aye in 1993 against a Hialeah, Florida, city ordinance banning animal sacrifice that, despite the arguments of animal rights activists, the welfare of animals was not recognized in law as sufficient grounds to restrict First Amendment speech.[24]

So what might constitute the compelling state interest in crush videos? Representative after representative rose in support of Gallegly's bill to secure the link between violence toward animals and violence toward people. They invoked spousal abuse, elder abuse, child abuse, and even school shootings. Congressman Spencer Bachus (R-Ala.) summarized the logic of this animal protection legislation most succinctly of all: "This is about children," he informed the Speaker of the House, "not about beetles."[25]

Still, the real headline grabbers were the celebrity serial killers. What did Ted Bundy, Ted "the Unabomber" Kaczynski, and David "Son of Sam" Berkowitz have in common? Gallegly had the answer: "They all tortured or killed animals before they started killing people."[26]

It made good copy, but I doubt even the politicians believed this link between crush videos and mass murder. After all, many of them had already listened to Susan "Minnie" Creede, the D.A.'s undercover investigator, as she testified before the Subcommittee on Crime about the psychology of the crush fetishist. After almost a year in the Crushcentral chat room, Creede was an expert witness.

"They spoke about their fetishes and how they developed," she told the committee.

For many of them the fetish developed as a result of something they saw at a very early age, and it usually occurred before the age of five. Most of these men saw a woman step on something. She was usually someone who was significantly in their lives. They were excited by the experience and somehow attached their sexuality to it.

As these men grew older, the woman's foot became a part of their sexuality. The power and dominance of the woman using her foot was significant to them. They began to fantasize about the thought of being the subject under the woman's foot. They fantasized about the power of the woman, and how she would be able to crush the life out of them if she chose to do so. Many of these men love to be trampled by women. Some like to be trampled by a woman wearing shoes or high heels. Others like to be trampled by women who are barefoot. They prefer to be hurt and the more indifferent the woman is to their pain, the more exciting it is for them.

I have learned that the extreme fantasy for these men is to be trampled or crushed to death under the foot of a powerful woman. Because they would only be able to experience this one time, these men have found a way to transfer their fantasy and excitement. They have learned that if they watch a woman crush an animal or live creature to his death, they can fantasize that they are that animal experiencing death at the foot of this woman.[27]

Congressman Gallegly also heard much the same thing from Jeff Vilencia during their encounter on Court TV. "The viewer identifies with the victim," Jeff stated flatly in an attempt to counter Gallegly's alarming claim that crush freaks were dangerous sadists. The fetish "starts in childhood, when the child observes an adult person, usually a woman, stepping on an insect," he continued, echoing Creede, his legal nemesis. "He becomes sexually aroused, sort of by happenstance, and as he becomes an adolescent, he eroticizes his behavior in his sexuality, and it becomes a part of his love map—" ("His *love map?*" interrupted the host incredulously.)

Without an origin story, how else can Jeff refute Gallegly's fantasies of the crush freak as the proto–serial killer and the insect as the proto-baby? There's no space for refusal. At the center of a frighteningly unstable public debate (TV host: "Jeff Vilencia, are you a tiny bit afraid you're going to be prosecuted? You're the one producing these films"), explanation is Jeff's only option. He has to explain that his fetish has a specific history that ties it to specific objects, that it is masochistic, and that masochism—as the philospher Gilles Deleuze argues in his famous discussion of Sacher-Masoch—is not a complementary form of sadism but part of an entirely distinct formation. A "sadist could never tolerate a masochistic victim," writes Deleuze, and "neither would the masochist tolerate a truly sadistic torturer." The distinctions abound: the masochist demands a ritualized fantasy, he creates an anxiety-filled suspense, he exhibits his humiliation, he demands punishment to resolve his anxiety and heighten his forbidden pleasure, and—quite unlike the sadist and with Sacher-Masoch as the locus classicus—he needs a binding contract with his torturess, who, through the contract (which, in truth, is no more than the masochist's word), becomes the embodiment of law.[28]

But if only it really were that straightforward. When, in a reflective moment, Jeff tells me that the one thing he learned from all of this was that "women are really cruel, just really evil, man," and he says it bleakly, with not a hint of teasing, I see that I haven't quite got the hang of this, and I'm not sure that Deleuze has either. Isn't the point that cruelty is

part of a compact, that there is agreement, tacit or explicit, about boundaries and needs? Isn't that what all Jeff's banter with Elizabeth and Michelle is probing? Admittedly, at the end of Sacher-Masoch's *Venus in Furs,* Wanda lets loose her Greek lover on Severin with the full force of his hunting whips. It's horrible, and unexpected too. But it's also a momentous effort on her part to finally break his dependency, to enforce that break by unambiguously stepping outside the contract. Wanda strains for the gesture that will free them both without the death of either. Under this assault, writes Sacher-Masoch, Severin "curled up like a worm being crushed." All the poetry is whipped out of him. When it is finally over, he is a changed man. "There is only one alternative," he tells the narrator, "to be the hammer or the anvil." Henceforth, he'll be the one doing the whipping.[29]

But could this be what happened to Jeff too? Only differently? Did the furies of Fox News strip him of his pleasures? Was that tense but playful self somehow swept away in the storm of disgust that poured down on him? The wrong kind of suffering. Game over, lights on. Cruelty is suddenly just cruelty, Michelle is just Michelle, stomping on animals and maybe actually enjoying it. No longer a goddess, no longer exciting. Just mean.

Such a long road to get here. A road paved with explanation. Explanation was straightforward for investigator Susan Creede. Her task before the House subcommittee was to manufacture an object that could be acted upon by the law. Think of her as the forensic expert narrating the corpse. But it's so much more complicated for Jeff Vilencia. It's not simply the demands of the moment that force him to speak Creede's language. Among the DVDs, videos, books, audiotapes, unpublished writings, and press clippings he sent me when we first talked was an unexpected item: a three-page article he'd written called "Fetishes/ Paraphilia/Perversions." The essay begins programmatically: "Perversions are unusual or important modifications of the expected pattern of sexual arousal. One form is fetishism, of which crush fetishism is an example." It goes on to describe seven theories of fetish formation ("oxytocin theory," "faulty sexualization theory," "lack of available female contact theory," and so on) and includes as an appendix a discussion of the seventeen "possible stages of fetish development basic to the modified conditioning theory" which both Jeff and Susan Creede used to explain the birth of the crush freak to Congressman Gallegly.

At the time I didn't understand why Jeff wanted me to have this essay. Nor did I understand why he had dedicated *Smush* to Richard von Krafft-Ebing, the pioneering nineteenth-century Viennese sexologist whose *Psychopathia sexualis* documented "aberrant" sexual practices as medical phenomena. But then I got to the second volume of *The American Journal of the Crush-Freaks*, published in 1996, which is subtitled: "Just where do we fit in, in all of this?" In the introduction, Jeff writes:

> Imagine all of the shame you would feel having no one to talk to about your desires. It is as alone as one could feel. You might as well be stranded on an island someplace.
>
> Well those dark days are behind us now. As we move towards the 21st century, and as various sexual groups have come out over the years, I cannot see any reason that people should feel shame any more. . . .
>
> There are more choices today than there ever were. When I was a kid, I was a crush-freak, only I didn't know what to call myself. Today, I know who I am, and more important, I know *why* I am.

It was that *why* that mattered: "As a child I had a knack for getting in trouble. As an adult I look forward to telling the world my sexuality. I am willing to take all my critics on. I have appeared on television and radio, major newspapers, and adult fetish magazines. I have spoken at four different universities in Southern California. I also produce videotapes that I sell to my fellow crush-freaks for masturbation purposes. Trouble comes to town and his name is Jeff Vilencia!"[30]

6.

When Bill Clinton signed H.R. 1887 into law on December 9, 1999, he issued a statement instructing the Justice Department to construe the act narrowly, as applicable only to "wanton cruelty to animals designed to appeal to a prurient interest in sex."[31] In the years since, perhaps wary of the legislation's frailty, prosecutors have used it only three times. On each occasion—and contrary to Clinton's directive—they wielded it against distributors of dog-fighting videos. In July 2008, a federal appeals court struck down the law, agreeing with Robert Scott that the First Amendment does not allow the government to ban depictions of illegal conduct (as opposed to that conduct itself). In October 2009, the Supreme Court heard an appeal from the government backed by animal rights groups.[32]

No matter the fate of H.R. 1887, for Jeff Vilencia there is no going back from those few hot weeks in the fall of 1999. Jeff tells me how his radio and TV interviews were edited to make him monstrous, how he tried to play the unedited tapes for his family but they believed only the broadcast versions. He tells me how his niece—in the name of her new baby—led his mother on a tour of websites that featured crush videos or specifically targeted him. "I lost friends, my brothers and sisters . . . I mean, it was just a horrible ordeal. I was almost isolated. I mean, I had no friends, no one wanted to talk to me, you know, and I just thought . . . you know . . ." He trailed off. He tells me how he quit video making entirely. "I just got to the point of giving up on life." He tells me how it's since been impossible to find a job because these days employers automatically Google their applicants.

So here we are on the featureless patio outside that suburban Starbucks, and he's telling me that he learned two things from all this: that women are "really cruel bitches" and that "perversions are best left in the closet, buried in the dark." He's telling me about the men who were inspired by his example to come out to their girlfriends and wives and how in all cases their lives fell to pieces. And he's telling me that he needs love too and that now he has someone who gives it to him but doesn't want him talking about all this anymore. And he checks my watch nervously, leans back in his chair, looks out across the parking lot, sighs, and says softly: "Seems like a dream, man . . ."

7.

Go to YouTube, search for "crush videos," and see what you get. There's a lot up there. Short, poor-quality home videos of women stepping on crickets, worms, snails, lots of squishy soft fruit. Some of the clips have had tens of thousands of views, most have a few thousand, one has a couple of hundred thousand. It's a long way from the underground trade of expensive Super 8 film in the 1950s and '60s and even from the back-of-the-porn-mags sales in the '80s and '90s. If YouTube doesn't meet your need, it's easy to find longer and more professional product on the many specialist websites that are trading entirely openly despite Gallegly's legislation.

Gallegly himself allowed for this future. At one point in the debate on H.R. 1887, he took the floor to clarify a crucial point. "This has nothing to do with bugs and insects and cockroaches, *things* like that," he told his colleagues. "This has to do with *living animals* like kittens, monkeys, hamsters, and so on and so forth."[33] For a moment, there's something on which everyone can agree. There are animals that matter, and there are things that don't. And then Gallegly draws breath, and before you know it, he's off again about Ted Bundy, the Unabomber, and the safety of our children.

Temptation

1.

It was August 1877, and Baron Carl Robert Osten-Sacken, a Russian aristocrat recently retired as the czar's consul general in New York, had stopped for a few days at Gurnigel, "the well-known watering-place near Bern."[1]

The baron was forty-nine years old and at a turning point in his life. He would spend a year traveling in Europe before arriving in Cambridge, Massachusetts, where, once more in the New World but freed from imperial service, he would settle at Harvard's famous Museum of Comparative Zoology, and spend the rest of his days pursuing his passion for flies. Some thirty years later, his obituarist would describe him as "the *beau ideal* of a scientific entomologist," citing his mastery of relevant languages, his independence of means, his elevated social rank, his prodigious memory, exceptional observation skills, "almost perfect" library of works on the Diptera, and naturally, his impeccable manners.[2]

Strolling one morning in the Alpine woods behind his hotel, the baron's eye was caught by something quite new to him, something he suspected was "unique in entomology." It was not yet ten o'clock, but the sun was already high in the sky. Above his head, zigzagging among the shafts of light slicing through the shadows of the fir trees, were swarms of tiny flies. "What attracted my attention," he wrote that October in an enthusiastic note from Frankfurt, was "the uncommonly brilliant white or silvery reflection which they gave in crossing the sunbeam."

The baron gave chase with his net, caught one with his forceps, and was "astonished to find a much smaller fly than I had expected, and without anything silvery about it." The insect he held was dull gray and thoroughly unremarkable looking.

Tiny things can be slow to reveal their secrets. But Baron Osten-Sacken's exceptional observation skills yielded a clue: "I perceived on the gauze of my forceps, not far from the fly, a flake of opaque, white film-like substance, oval, about 2 mm. long, and so light, that the faintest breath of air could lift it." He thinks of the fine silk spun by ballooning spiders preparing for takeoff. "But for its much lesser weight, it might also be compared to the petal of a small white flower." He catches another, then another, and each time pulls from his net a male fly clutching under its body the same diaphanous structure. He concludes that "these bits of white tissue, which they waved like flags behind them," are the source of the brilliant reflection. But he has no idea what they are or why the flies carry them.

2.

The baron was the first entomologist to encounter balloon flies, as these insects came to be known. But he was by no means the last. In the decades following his discovery, more and more of these animals were described. All turned out to be male. All carried an object of some kind. And all of them belonged to the Empididae, the so-called dance flies, famous for their huge flittering swarms.

In 1955, Edward Kessel, associate curator of insects at the California Academy of Sciences, wrote a definitive paper on the balloon empidids in which he suggested that the baron and his successors had been unlucky enough to have stumbled upon a limit case.[3] It was as if, knowing only European painting of the late nineteenth century, these gentlemen entomologists had wandered into the art museum and met a wall of Mark Rothkos. They had come upon an abstraction, an inscrutable object that betrayed no trace of the original from which it was distilled. Really, encountered like this, these flakes of white tissue could have been anything, anything at all, even the "aeronautical surfboards" proposed by Josef Mik in 1888.

But over time, Kessel wrote, observers noticed that the male balloon fly always presented his substance to a female fly and, soon after, the two of them had sex. Rather coyly, entomologists called these objects "nuptial gifts," a euphemism still widely used today. Some of the gifts consisted simply of an unadorned dead insect, in others the corpse was bound in frothy or silky tissue (sometimes casually, sometimes carefully), and in some there was no body at all, the elaborate wrapping itself being the offering.

Kessel created an evolutionary history of the empidid gift. He described a hierarchy of species defined by their gift-giving habits, from the primitive to the urbane, the crude to the refined. It was an eight-stage history in which the object in question evolved from something obvious in the most material way (food) to something subtle, recondite, and arguably immaterial (a symbol).[4]

Empidids are predatory carnivores, and much as it is for praying mantises and many spiders, their sex life is a fraught affair. The way Kessel tells it, the males have become calculating cynics, the females capricious and, as luck would have it, easily distracted. His males—no surprise here—do just about anything for sex; his females, material girls all the way, do whatever it takes to get the bauble. It's very mid-1950s, very *Gentlemen Prefer Blondes*, very film noir too, except that instead of taking place in a nightclub, this is all happening in what biologists call a lek, an arena where the males perform for attention and the females get to pick from the assembled "eligible bachelors."

The stakes are high. Kessel's males are cocky and cunning, but edgy and anxious too. They're calibrating for optimum mileage, making sure their temptations cost as little as possible but still do the job. They're really good dancers. They're constantly watching their backs. Kessel was right that Osten-Sacken could never have figured this out.

Kessel found species of empidids for each of his eight evolutionary stages. From the most primitive, in which "the male does not bear a wedding gift for his bride," to a second stage, in which he carries "a wedding present in the form of a juicy insect," to a third, in which "the prey has become the stimulus for mating," to a fourth, in which "the prey is more or less entangled in silky threads."

Kessel and his wife, Berta, found the fifth stage in Marin County, north of San Francisco, and named it *Empis bullifera* for the sticky bubbles it uses to make its container. They spent the summer of 1949 observing mating pairs "drifting in lazy flight, first in one direction and then in another, back and forth within the clearing under the trees, their glistening white balloons producing flashes whenever they penetrate a

sunbeam." They watched the animals meet in the air, watched them embrace, and watched the males present the females with balloons containing a midge, a spider, or a tiny psocid. Then they wrote an article together announcing the new species, which they published in 1951 in the *Wasmann Journal of Biology.*

In the sixth and seventh stages, the male has sucked the prey dry before giving it to his partner. All she receives is an inedible husk. Nonetheless, the familiar sequence unfolds: the flies embrace, the balloon changes hands (well, legs actually), and sex ensues. The eighth, and final, stage was the one witnessed by the baron. Among *Hilara sartor* and a few other species, the enigmatic gift contains no prey at all, not even the withered shell.

Kessel emphasized distinctions among species. So do contemporary biologists, but they also recognize a good deal of within-species variation. They describe dance fly species in which males offer both large and small presents and others in which they offer both edible and inedible ones. They also describe males whose prey gifts are hunted from their own species and others who eschew insect prey altogether to gather entirely different gifts—flower petals, for example. Despite this variety of behavior, the small number of researchers who study these little flies still closely follow Kessel's account of an evolutionary *Diptera economicus,* in which males do everything they can to minimize their energy output and maximize their reproductive return, relentlessly downgrading their gifts in the effort to get cheaper and cheaper sex.

This substitution of "empty gifts" for nutritious ones has become a famous case of "male cheating," an idea that doesn't require just the males' shrewd duplicity but also relies on the females' slowness.[5] Even when the gifts are "worthless," even when they're just the cheapest gimcracks—plain cotton balls provided by biologists, for example—the researchers describe the foolish female fly giving the fake-gift giver what he wants, or at least the researchers see the female taking so long to catch on to the phoniness of her reward that she's given her partner what he wants before she realizes she's had nothing in return. Tricked. Deceived. Fucked. Over and over and over.

Or so the story goes.

3.

Writing about Ellis Island, the French novelist Georges Perec found himself haunted by what might have been, by what he called "potential memory."

"It concerns me, it fascinates me," he wrote, "it involves me, it questions me." Broken by the deportation of his mother from Paris to Auschwitz when he was six years old, Perec kept running into histories that could have been his own, a boy who veers down a monochrome side street half a block ahead, "a life-story that might have been mine," "a probable autobiobiography," "a memory that might have belonged to me," books full of absences, a novel without the letter *e,* a novella that lacks the other vowels: *a, i, o,* and *u.*[6]

These fictive histories aren't just imaginative games. They're hard facts of existence that weigh down the present with paths not taken. We all have them: the discarded negatives of decisions whose weight only later becomes clear, the psychic resonances that complete the life we do have, the life that does get made. When Sharon shivers without warning, she says, "Someone just walked over my grave."

Kessel saw that Osten-Sacken's flies flittered not only in the open forest but also in a narrative vacuum. How could the baron and those who followed him take these inscrutable flakes—like petals but so much less substantial—and build a story when there was no history? What could they do when none of the signs signified, when all they had was gossamer? The beauty touched them. But that just made it worse. Without even potential histories, how could they understand what might be, what might have been, and what now was?

But the opposite problem is equally real. The problem of too much history. How can one understand what might be, what might have been, and what now is when confronted by a history so potent that it makes different or simply more expansive stories so hard to imagine?

Of course, it is possible that male empidids are cheats and that female empidids are dopes. But it's also possible that male and female dance flies are not constantly at war with each other and are not always caught up in relationships drawn straight out of daytime soaps.

"Perhaps animals do lie to each other now and then," writes the evolutionary biologist Joan Roughgarden, "but biologists have yet to catch them in a lie."[7] She presumes that animals are honest until proven devious and that they have capacity until proven incapable. What if, like her, we assume that those female flies know what they are doing? What if those empty balloons actually are gifts—but gifts whose value we don't understand? Perhaps these tiny structures possess an ecstatic tactility. Perhaps they're seductively comforting. Perhaps they trigger memories or appetites. Perhaps they're symbolically precious, full of affect and meaning. Perhaps the flies just like them.

How do we avoid turning the empidids into one of Stephen Jay Gould's evolutionary just-so stories, stories that can't be validated or falsified because they begin from the conviction of a mechanism—in this case, sexual selection driven by sexual conflict—and shoehorn whatever data emerge from experiment into a preexisting argument? What, for instance, if we leave open the possibility that there is a diversity of relationships among these flies that corresponds to the diversity of behaviors that biologists have already observed? What if we assume that the willingness of many female flies to accept cotton balls indicates that rather than being "worthless," the objects have qualities unknown to us? Is it too obvious to point out (again) the hazards of presuming what an object is and what it does for beings whose ways of being are so different from our own?

4.

It is August 1877, and Carl Robert Osten-Sacken stands among the trees behind his hotel in Gurnigel, shading his eyes as he gazes up into the dappled sunlight and marvels at the dazzling flashes of *Hilara sartor* dancing in and out of the sunbeams.

It is summer 1949, and Edward and Berta Kessel keep impossibly still in Marin County, California, so as not to disturb the mating *Empis bullifera* and especially not the female exploring her delicately wrapped present.

It is May 2004, and on a farm in Fife, Scotland, Natasha LeBas uses her forceps to prize a dead insect from the clutch of a female *Rhamphomyia sulcata* and, hoping against hope not to interrupt the flies' coitus, carefully swaps the prey for a cotton ball.

It is mid-2010 or further into the future, and here we are again, caught between the unavoidability of comparison and the awareness of fundamental difference. Here we are still, caught in that imperative to understand, bearing our various tools for analysis and interpretation, trying to locate both the objective principles and the lived life in the enigmatic clues of observed behavior. Here we are again, caught somewhere between the reduction that makes things fathomable and the generosity that gives them fullness. Here we are, caught looking yet again, still looking, this time at tiny flies and their shiny gifts.

The Unseen

1.

Sometimes late at night I hear rustling. I work here, upstairs in my room, writing this book at the top of the building, perched on the roof, thinking about insects and all the things they make and do, sitting at my desk in this squat box coated black with pitch to protect against the city rain.

There are grilles on the windows. But there's also a sliding door, and if you step outside onto the squishy silver-coated tar and look to the left, the sweep of the Hudson will catch your breath, especially in winter, when the trees are bare and the lights of New Jersey glitter in the river's laquered blackness.

In the daytime, white egrets and red-tailed hawks fly past on their way to Central Park. Cardinals, finches, blue jays, squeaky mourning doves, and raggedy pigeons perch on our railing. At dusk, the sparrows go crazy in the trees below. A little later, Sharon and I head downstairs into Riverside Park, down past the Amtrak tunnel where Brooklyn (six years in the Marines, twenty-four on the streets) sleeps with her cats and raccoons, and where we watch the urban wildlife forage garbage in the gloom of the streetlamps.

It's peaceful upstairs in this blanket of quiet. Night falls, and one by one the lights go out in the surrounding apartment buildings. The rush of traffic on the Westside Highway subsides. The last planes pass overhead. The quiet deepens, and we all head into the darkness.

Up here, at the top of the building, I turn my desk light down. I lower the brightness on my laptop. My eyes struggle against the dimness, then relax. Everything slows.

Sometimes in summer, when it's hot and humid, the night is interrupted by rustling. It's not the mice in the drywall or the squirrels in the guttering. It's not the hairy centipedes that scamper into the corners. It's not the mosquitoes or bluebottles or those erratic crane flies. It's not the ladybugs or winged ants that arrive each year en masse without warning and just as abruptly disappear. It's not the building stretching in the breeze. It's not the leaves blowing up against the windows. It's not a mystery. I know what it is. It's the big water bugs, the American cockroaches, come to scratch along the walls, doing what they do, going from place to place, up from the drains, not really wanting to be here, a bit lost, looking for something.

Kikuo Itaya, the twentieth-century Zen Buddhist short story writer, lived among cockroaches, refusing to harm them, allowing them to share his home. But he was unusual, even in Japan. I think of him when I kill them. I have to kill them because Sharon is phobic; she freaks out when she sees one: she hides, she shakes, her body goes into spasm. Once she's seen one, I can't just pretend to have killed it. If I do, it will only break cover again, and everything will be worse than before. And anyway, she knows when I lie.

When I hear the scratching, I turn the lights down even further. My skin crawls in anticipation. If she doesn't see it, if I don't see it, if it remains unseen . . . I don't want to know it's there.

But sometimes the scratches are too insistent. One night, distracted and without thinking, I swiveled around. A healthy-looking water bug was sitting on a pile of books behind my shoulder. We locked eyes. Its head extended like a turtle's. Its face was angular and inquisitive. Really, as Karl von Frisch once remarked, it had "the lofty brow of the philosopher."[1] Our eyes met as in an animal movie. An understanding beyond words. But I must have moved too suddenly, and it took off and I took off after it, grabbing a broom—everything all of a sudden kinetic—trapping it in a cluttered corner, its legs a whir of mad scrambling, and caught up in the moment, I beat it and beat it, until I realized I was trembling and disgusted and confused and it was just a smush of fat and chitin on the wooden floor. "Just a grease spot," as Erika Elizondo would say.

I keep the lights low and the shadows deep. I know it's there, but I can't see it. If I don't see it, we're safe. The night protects us both. When the rustling begins, I don't turn around. If all goes well, eventually it stops, and not long after, the birds start singing, just a few at first, then more, and louder, until, as the dawn rises and the sun fills the room, they come louder still.

2.

But then, this morning actually, something new happened. I was in the shower, daydreaming as usual under the soothing warm water, thoughts rambling around the chapter of this book I'm trying to finish—the one about queer insects and the queer things they like to do—when, out of nowhere, a three-inch water bug dropped from the bathroom ceiling and landed at my feet.

I admit it: I screamed. Wouldn't you? I shut off the water. It took a moment to get over the surprise. And then there we were, the water bug and I, trapped and defenseless and covered in soapsuds. And we both stayed very still until that very big little animal, a female animal, I noticed, climbed swiftly up onto the towel rack and stopped there at eye level a few inches away, her handsome and intelligent face cocked at a philosophical angle, giving me a funny, quizzical look up and down as if amused by this unexpected situation and intrigued to see what would happen next. One of us was very calm. One of us—it was the bathroom, after all—began carefully to groom her antennae. I won't go into the details of what happened next. I'm not sure even Erika Elizondo would have felt good this time.

Vision

1.

Academy Studios, an exhibition design and fabrication company based in Novato, California, created these interactive stations for the Arthropod Zoo at the North Carolina State Museum of Natural Sciences. They built a seven-foot praying mantis and a dragonfly with a twelve-foot wingspan—both anatomically accurate!—but it's these masks that get the most attention, spooky-looking sci-fi helmets that, as Academy's promotional materials put it, "give visitors a chance to see life through a bee's eyes."

Robert Yagura, then Academy's creative director, told me that they used hexagonal pieces of Lucite to mimic the facets of a bee's compound eye and bonded them to a curved form to produce a fractured image. But even with that prosthetic, Robert told me, the visitor does not see like a bee. For a start, a bee's sensitivity to the electromagnetic spectrum is shifted significantly to wavelengths shorter than those visible to a human. At the low end, below 380 nanometers, bees are able to make out ultraviolet light invisible to us; at the high end, they're red-blind, red appearing to them as an empty blackness, the absence of light.

The little-remembered zoologist Charles Henry Turner shares credit with Karl von Frisch for providing the first glimpse of the world through the eyes of a bee.[1] Turner, the first African American to receive a Ph.D. from the University of Chicago and the author of more than fifty research papers, published his account in 1910, at the beginning of a long career as a science teacher in public high schools. Von Frisch completed his studies in 1913, well before he became director of the Institute of Zoology at Munich and witnessed the honeybees' dances. He was already driven by the impulse to demonstrate the capacities of his tiny friends that would eventually win him the Nobel Prize. Despite the extravagance of floral color and the intricate economies of codependence that tie insects and angiosperms across the millennia, before Turner and von Frisch had given the matter their attention, it was commonly thought that insects were entirely color-blind.

Von Frisch's refutation is famous—and characteristically and elegantly low-tech. He set out a series of dishes on cards. In just one square, the only blue card in a field of varying grays, the dish contained sugar water. He began by training his bees to visit this card and dish. Then, over several hours, he varied their position in the matrix. Next, he removed all the cards and dishes, replacing them with a new set of identical materials, only now leaving the dish on the blue card empty. As he expected, the bees returned to the blue card, attracted by color rather than odor or location.[2] As von Frisch explained, this behavior demonstrated the bees' "true color sense," not simply their ability to distinguish among light intensities. If their vision were monochromatic, he pointed out, they would have found at least some of the gray cards indistinguishable from the blue.[3]

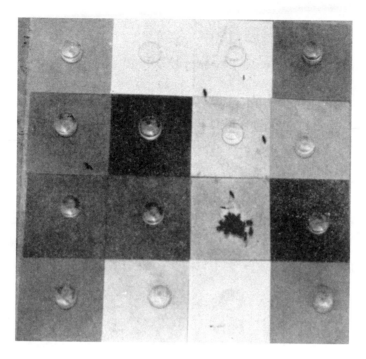

There's little argument nowadays that most insects see in some form of color. Through electrophysiologic experiments on photoreceptive cells, researchers can readily demonstrate the capacity for color vision. They know, for example, that bees, like humans, are trichromatic, possessing three types of photosensitive pigments that absorb maximally in different parts of the spectrum (though in green, blue, and ultraviolet rather than our red, green, and blue). And they also know—though there are few ways of conceiving what it might actually mean—that dragonflies and butterflies are often pentachromatic, possessing five types of pigments. (They also know that mantid shrimp have receptors sensitive at *twelve* different wavelengths!)

It is one thing, however, to demonstrate that animals possess the capacity for color vision, quite another to show that the world through which they move glistens and glimmers, as does ours, in multiple hues. For this, researchers rely on behavioral studies, and they still use the techniques pioneered by Turner and von Frisch, training their animals to respond to food rewards and colored patches.

But insects can be recalcitrant research subjects, and so far this type of work has been carried out only among honeybees, blowflies, and a few species of butterflies.[4] Given the distinctive absorption spectra of these animals' photoreceptors, we can be fairly certain that objects will appear quite different to them than they do to us. Many flowers, for example, look quite different when viewed through an ultraviolet filter. These black-eyed susans (*Rudbeckia hirta*) display a bull's-eye pattern that seems to guide bees, wasps, and other pollinators to their target; other flowers have a characteristic runway pattern leading to the same destination.

This is so simple yet so intriguing. There are invisible worlds all around us, parallel worlds. Familiar objects have secret identities, some of which we can access through straightforward mechanical tricks, like Lucite fractals and UV filters, but others of which remain inaccessible, even to our imagination (*twelve* pigments?). We pass through not just purblind but encumbered by the everyday assumption that the world we see is the world that is. In this respect at least, our perception is rather shallow, though I admit it's unlikely bees or butterflies are any more decentered.

Nonetheless, at the very least, the natural world's indifference should make us wary of assuming too quickly that flowers that draw our eye are similarly seductive to a pollinator. Such hidden truths make visible one important fact about vision (our own and that of other beings): it is a property not only of the viewer and the object but also of the relationship between them.[5]

2.

The closer we look, the more we see. Bee masks and UV photos are not just intriguing; they're beguiling. If we could only re-create an insect's visual apparatus, they promise, we could see what it sees, and if we could see *what* it sees . . . why, then we could see *as* it sees, too. But I doubt many of us, including scientists and exhibit designers, believe this. Vision is so much more than mechanics.

The Soviet entomologist Georgii Mazokhin-Porshnyakov drew attention to this long ago: "When we talk about vision," he wrote in the late 1950s, "we imply not only that animals are able to distinguish objects visually (i.e., the stimuli), but also that they are able to recognize them."[6] Photoreception, on its own, he suggested, is of little value to an organism; what counts is the ability to identify an object and make some sense of it. Reception presupposes perception. Insects see with their brain, not their eyes.

In this respect, an insect's vision is identical to that of a human. Like ours, an insect's vision is a complex sorting procedure, a way to filter and hierarchize objects in the world, one sense among several interdependent senses, one entangled element of perception.

Frederick Prete, a biologist at DePaul University who studies the visual universe of praying mantises, points out that until quite recently the standard scientific assumption was that insect vision operated by exclusion, that bees, butterflies, wasps, mantises, and similar creatures were designed "to ignore all but some very limited, specific types of visual information . . . [such as] a small, moving, fly-shaped spot just a few millimeters away . . . [or] yellow flowers of a certain size." Instead, Prete and his colleagues demonstrate, mantises and many other insects deal with sensory information in ways not dissimilar from those of humans: "they use categories to classify moving objects; [and] they learn and use complex algorithms to solve difficult problems." Prete describes human processing of visual information as a type of taxonomy:

> We filter sensory information by recognizing and assessing certain key characteristics of the events and objects around us, and we use that infor-

mation to identify an event or object as an example of a general class of events or objects. For instance, you would not reject a meal . . . because it did not look like a specific, idealized plate of food. You would assess its characteristics (odor, color, texture, temperature), and if they all met certain criteria, you would take a bite. In this case, the novel meal is an example of the category "acceptable meal." Likewise, we can learn that a particular task—mending a ripped curtain, for instance—is an example of the category "sewing material together." So, when attempting to mend a curtain for the first time, we apply the rules that we learned are successful in other, analogous mending tasks. In other words, we have acquired and employ an algorithm, or "rule of thumb" for solving specific problems of this general type.[7]

A mantis, write Prete and his colleague Karl Kral, is confronted by a large number of potential meals in the course of a day, and like us, it both creates and deploys a relational category ("a theoretical, perceptual envelope") that corresponds to the thought "acceptable meal." To evaluate an object, the animal draws on experience—learned from past events and encounters—to assess a series of "stimulus parameters" that include the object's size (if it is compact), its length (if it is elongated), the contrast between the object and its background, the object's location in the mantis's visual field, the object's speed, and the object's overall direction of movement.[8] A varying number of these criteria must be met for the mantis to strike. Yet, rather than a reaction being triggered by the meeting of a specific threshold, the mantis takes into account the relationship among different data in each parameter. Kral and Prete call this calculation a "perceptual algorithm" (and make the not-unreasonable point that if it were described in primates, it would be considered abstract reasoning).

Along with a small number of other invertebrate scientists who integrate behavioral and neuroanatomical studies in what is sometimes called psychophysiological research (that is, research on the connections between the psychological and physiological aspects of behavior), Kral and Prete write un-self-consciously of the complexity of insect behavior, of the correspondence between the ways insects and vertebrates (including humans) make sense of the world, and of the insect's *mind*.

But maybe these insects are just a little too calculating, modeled a little too much on the rational actors of classical economic theory (who we know from our own experience don't really exist). Maybe they're not lively and spontaneous enough. How do we know they always calculate solely according to the logic of the hunter? Might they have other desires? Or maybe this is exactly how mantises are even if we don't have to assume that butterflies, say, or fruit flies proceed in this way too. No matter; this is thought-provoking work: there is a cognition here, say Kral and Prete, that is dependent on but somehow not reducible to physiology. Yet, if cognitive processes are irreducible to electrochemical function, what exactly are they? Nobody seems very sure.[9]

It's worth noting that these questions are central to contemporary neuroscience, the interdisciplinary field concerned with the study of the nervous systems of animals. Neuroscience is dedicated to physiological explanation but is nonetheless deeply preoccupied with questions of mind, with such indeterminate phenomena as consciousness, cognition, and perception, with material solutions to what many might consider ontological or even metaphysical problems. In neuroscience, it is axiomatic that the brain is the center of all animal life—"the key philosophical theme of modern neural science is that all behavior is a reflection of brain function" begins a standard reference work.[10] "Higher-order" brain functions, such as metacognition (thinking about thinking) and emotion, tend to be understood as functional outcomes of brain anatomy and physiology.[11]

Yet the model of perception that overlies this straightforward if controversial principle is formidably elaborate. Perception is conceived as a set of dynamic, interactive brain functions that integrate cognition and experience and include filtering, selection, prioritization, and other forms of active and flexible information management in the context of previously unimagined neuroplasticity. One example might be the interplay between the brain and particular visually salient objects, such that the objects instantly and without conscious registration are isolated within a saturated and nonhierarchical visual field. Such ideas are fully congruent with the type of perceptual algorithm developed for insects by Kral and Prete (and others; see, for example, the two decades of work on honeybee cognition carried out by Mandyam Srinivasan and his team at Australian National University). Yet this parallelism between people and invertebrates would, I suspect, seem foolish to many neuroscientists, for whom the marvelous size and complexity of the modern hominid brain—specifically the number of its neural connections—is the decisive marker of human exceptionalism.

Kral and Prete are likely to find still less support in the social sciences and humanities, though for different reasons. Research on vision here emphasizes the role of culture and history in mediating between the human eye and the world.[12] For cultural analysts, physiology often provides little more than a set of possibilities for a complex human perceptual engagement with the world. How humans see and what we see are understood as profoundly shaped by social and cultural history. Vision, and perception more generally, are neither unchanging in time nor constant across cultures.[13] They have history—several histories, in fact, as the character of perceptual understanding is understood to be shaped by regional and national aesthetic cultures. Key moments of transformation are tied to the emergence of specific visual technologies. In the West, for example, among other moments, scholars have drawn attention to the invention and dissemination of linear perspective in the fifteenth century and the shift in the nineteenth century to a preoccupation with surface morphologies: the preoccupation with the superficialities of objects and bodies with which we still live.[14] In these accounts, vision—the ways in which we observe people and things, the forms of categorization that are embedded in our own ways of looking, and the technologies through which we, in turn, are seen, surveilled, classified, assessed—is central to the ways in which we understand ourselves and are understood by others; it is a source of culture-history-society as well as its outcome.

Such a different vision of vision! Unlike the isolated neurobiological brain, the social brain is immersed in a world that is itself overflowing with meaning, is deeply part of a universe in which even so-called natural phenomena are always simultaneously both biophysical and cultural-historical, so that colors, for example, are always at the same time both measurable wavelength and shimmering story (in which we can't escape knowing that pink—whether it works for us or not—is cuter than navy blue). In this vision, people *learn* to see, and the form and content of that learning are specific to time and place. A man blinded years before recovers his sight and must be taught to recognize perspective in culturally effective ways; a woman leaves the closed forest in which she has spent her life and has to make radical, even traumatic adjustments before understanding the spatiality of the urban landscape that is now her home.[15]

Yet history, politics, and aesthetics—the central categories employed by cultural theorists to explore vision—are by definition exclusively human, are, in fact, definitively, classically, human. Though their proponents may disagree about almost everything else, when it comes to human exceptionalism, there is an emphatic alliance between the social brain, with its immersion in culture, and the neurobiological brain, preoccupied as it is with size and physiological complexity. And the differences on which these competing visions converge are surely not trivial. How can we hold on to them and at the same time refuse their implicit hierarchy?

3.

"The best of the [insect] eyes," wrote the optical-instrument maker Henry Mallock in 1894, "would give a picture about as good as if executed in rather coarse wool-work and viewed at a distance of a foot." Indeed, Mallock continued, a compound eye with the resolution of a human eye would itself be a spectacle. Mallock estimated its diameter at more than sixty feet.[16] Why so monstrous? Because to adequately counter diffraction—the tendency of light to spread out and blur as it passes through a narrow opening—each lens in every one of the many facets of the compound eye would require a diameter of 0.08 inches, the size of a human pupil—small, perhaps, but an eightyfold increase for a bee.[17]

Mallock's fantastic notion—the insect head: outsize, outrageous, but not horrific, not Cronenberg's fly—makes me want to climb back into one of those Lucite masks! Even though I know that they don't really work, that there's far more to vision than this, the urge to see through another's eyes isn't easily suppressed. And I'm far from alone. So many people have been driven to try it, the more scientifically minded concocting ingenious ways to record the view directly, delicately scraping out the eye's internal structures, removing the retina, cleaning the cornea, experimenting with light, microscopes, cameras, the product less immersive than a mask but more objective seeming, more authentic feeling. This impulse to capture the vision of another being is potent, and I believe I'm right in thinking it derives its power from the unusual coincidence it creates between the two visions of vision we're caught in here: the promise of the natural sciences (that is, the revelation of how things work, a revelation of structure and function that is often ultimately rather unrevealing) and the inaccessible dream of the human sciences (the utopian dissolution of ontological difference, the impossible yearning to enter another self). The most recondite mysteries are resolvable, the impulse tells us. Everything can be illuminated.

Anton van Leeuwenhoek, the discoverer of bacteria, sperm, and blood cells, of the mouthparts and stings of bees, of animal motion in a droplet of water, and of many, many other microbiological phenomena, was the first to see the gleam in a compound eye. Shining a candle through an insect's cornea, he used one of the gold and silver compound microscopes of his own invention, one of the microscopes sold by his family after his death and now lost, one of the microscopes that Robert Hooke copied to access the unimagined and deeply disturbing world he laid bare with his draftsman's precision in *Micrographia*, the volume that includes his famous engraving of a dragonfly's head—its diabolical masklike face made visible for the very first time—and in which he recorded his disbelieving observation that reflected perfectly from each of the facets of the animal's compound eye was "a Landscape of those things which lay before my window, one thing of which was a large Tree, whose trunk and top I could plainly discover, as I could also the parts of my window, and my hand and fingers, if I held it between the Window and the Object."[18]

Hooke wondered aloud about the optics of his "drone-fly" ("How exceeding curious and subtile must the component parts of the medium that conveys light be, when we find the instrument made for its reception or refraction to be so exceedingly small?"),[19] but it was van Leeuwenhoek—thirty years later—who first realized that the image transmitted to the fly's brain was fractured, that each facet of the eye captured its own image. Van Leeuwenhoek recorded his account in a

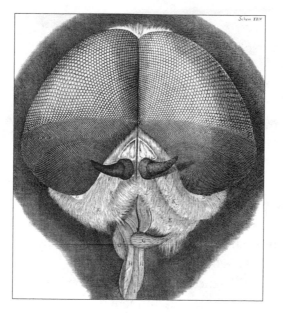

breathless letter to the Royal Society of London, published in 1695, an age when the arts and sciences were still negotiating their formal separation. "What I observed by looking into the microscope," he informed his colleagues, "were the inverted images of the burning flame: not one image, but some hundred images. As small as they were, I could see them all moving."[20]

Almost exactly two centuries later, Sigmund Exner, the eminent physiologist who would guide his young nephew Karl von Frisch in setting up the family natural history museum on the shores of Lake Wolfgang, was completing *The Physiology of the Compound Eyes of Insects and Crustaceans,* the first authoritative account of insect vision and a groundbreaking monograph whose claims survive intact to this day.[21] Exner was an assistant to Ernst Brücke, the professor of physiology at the Institute of Physiology in Vienna who persuaded Sigmund Freud to reject neuroscience for neurology. Exner and Freud were colleagues at the institute, both under the mentorship of Brücke, and like Freud, Exner was at the same time subject to the compulsion of vision and fascinated by its mechanics. With great care and labor, he succeeded in taking a photograph through the compound eye of the firefly *Lampyris,* but the image he saw was quite different from van Leeuwenhoek's.

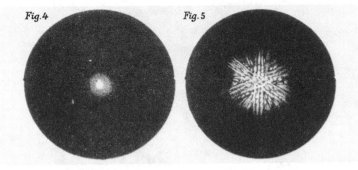

How could the multiply-fractured compound eye, with its numerous facets, produce only one image, and how could that image be erect rather than inverted, like the image that travels to the brain from the eye of both the fly and the human being?

Although the difference is not externally evident, Exner knew that there are two distinct types of compound eyes. The compound eye of the fly examined by van Leeuwenhoek is made up of multiple light-gathering units, called ommatidia, each of which is itself a single, independent eye that collects light from just a narrow section of the animal's field of view. Exner discovered that in this type of compound eye—called an apposition eye—light passes through the hexagonal facet lens into the crystalline cone, with its sheath of pigmented cells that block ambient light from adjacent ommatidia, down the cylindrical light-sensitive rhabdom, which houses the eight photoreceptive retinal cells, and all the way to the nerve cells that transmit the image 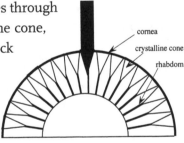 to the optic ganglion and into the brain, where the inverted mosaic produced by the retinal cells is turned into a single erect image.

But Exner also knew that like moths and many other insects that fly at twilight and after dark, the firefly, whose retinal image he reproduced in his 1891 monograph, is nocturnal and possesses what is called a superposition eye, an instrument 100 times more light sensitive than the apposition eye of diurnal insects.

Rather than being separated into individual ommatidia, the retina of the superposition eye is a single sheet, and it lies deep in the eye, above a clear zone across which light is focused. We might say that in the superposition eye the ommatidia cooperate: the image falling on its retina at any point is the product of multiple lenses.[22]

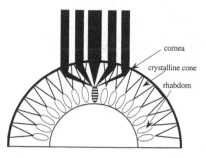

cornea

crystalline cone

rhabdom

But the real puzzle was how such optics succeeded in producing an erect image. And it was Exner, working on this problem throughout the 1880s without tools for definitive demonstration, who figured out that the rhabdom of the superposition eye functions as a two-lens telescope, redirecting the rays of light so they cross each other within the cylinder and reverse the image. "Clearly," says the biologist Michael Land, "we are dealing here with something quite out of the ordinary."[23] The views below, taken by Land and Dan-Eric Nilsson, demonstrate the difference between the images produced by the two types of compound eyes. The inverted apposition view, on the left, was photographed through the cornea of a robber fly; the rather blurry image (of Charles Darwin) on the right is seen through that of a firefly.[24]

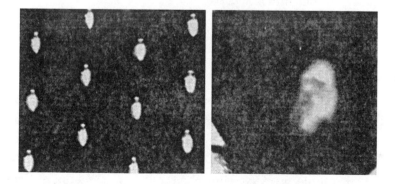

The number of ommatidia in a compound eye varies enormously, from single digits in some ants to more than 30,000 in some dragonflies. As we might expect, the more ommatidia that are present, the better the eye's resolution. But even the best compound eyes cannot focus, and cannot move in their sockets (and so demand that the insect swivel its entire head to shift its view), and, except at very close range, compound eyes have relatively very poor acuity. Where insect eyes do excel, as anyone who's tried to snatch a fly or squish a mosquito knows very well, is in their sensitivity to movement. Flying insects in particular often have an extraordinarily wide field of vision, as great as 360 degrees in those dragonflies whose eyes meet at the top of the head.

But this is not the insects' only basis for motion detection. To compensate for the animals' accelerated flicker-fusion frequency—the rate at which a moving image appears as one continuous flow rather than a series of discrete events like those on the pages of a flip-book—a movie designed for (or by) a fly would run five times faster than the standard twenty-four frames per second. Flies, this suggests, live in a world that moves much faster than ours. They are born and they die within days, weeks, or months, not decades. They occupy a different plane from us. Not only is it a plane in which acuity, pattern, and color are distinctive, but it is also one in which space-time is lived in another register. If we think of our senses as mediating our relationship with the world around us, we might wonder about the perceptual, intellectual, and emotional lives of beings, including human beings, whose sense organs differ from our own. Some of this mystery can be captured by blurry pictures and plastic masks. Some of it should be allowed to throw our own perceptual certainties into relief.

4.

This thought leads to one more view from an insect's eye. And this time it's not a photograph. It's a different kind of re-creation, and it was made in the 1930s by the great Estonian biologist-philosopher Jakob von Uexküll. In the forests through which von Uexküll wanders, all sensate beings are subjects, occupying their own *Umwelt*, an environment defined by the limits and possibilities of their senses.[25] All beings live in their own time worlds and space worlds, too, distinct worlds in which

both time and space are subjectively experienced through sense organs
that differ radically among beings and produce radically different experiences. "The subject sways the time of his own world," von Uexküll
writes. "There is no space independent of subjects."[26]

Above is a room as sensed by a housefly. Von Uexküll divides it into
"functional tones." Everything except the plates, the glasses, and the
lamp is a "running tone," a surface on which the fly can run. The heat of
the light pulls the animal in; the food and drink on the table hold fast its
taste-bud-equipped feet. I don't believe that the universe of a fly is quite
this bland, but nonetheless there is an important insight here. Remember the black-eyed susans? "There can be no doubt," von Uexküll writes,
"that a fundamental contrast prevails everywhere between the environment which we see spread around animals, and the *Umwelten* that are
built up by the animals themselves and filled up with the objects of their
own perception."[27]

Parts of these alien *Umwelten* arise from simple motor responses, the
kind of thing that Jean-Henri Fabre called instinct. But others are the
result of trial and error, of judgment, of "repeated personal experiences."
These are "free subjective products," and like time and space, they are
experiential and individualized.[28] This concept doesn't seem too hard to
grasp: that the world is multiple and is different for different beings; that

our world is our world and theirs is theirs; that when we meet, it is across and between distinct, intersecting realities. Actually, isn't this the road we began to travel when we donned the Lucite mask? And now that we're here, doesn't it look as if these masks are finally less about the promise of communication and communion, about seeing as the animal sees, than they are about the fact of unbridgeable difference?

Well, continues von Uexküll, hammering his point home, although things exist objectively in the physical world, they never appear in any being's *Umwelt* as their objective selves. All animals, ourselves included, know these objective things only as perceptual clues with functional tones—and "this alone makes them into real objects, although no element of the functional tone is actually present in the original stimuli." And so he continues, on and on, getting deeper and deeper into the flow of his argument (so deep, in fact, that it is hard not to keep quoting him), "we ultimately reach the conclusion that each subject lives in a world composed of subjective realities alone, and that even the *Umwelten* themselves represent only subjective realities."[29] All of us, all the people and all the animals, live in worlds of our own making, more or less complex, more or less stimulating, similarly subjective.

And then, as if he hasn't traveled quite far enough, von Uexküll takes an unexpected turn. The worlds of animals and men, he says, are often governed not by logic but by magic. The intricate boring of a bark beetle beneath the surface of a tree is a magical phenomenon. The owner of a dog is a magical figure to the animal. The unlearned routes of migratory birds are similarly beyond understanding. He shows us how an oak tree is many different things to the many different animals that live in and around it. He shows us how sound waves are a different entity to the physicist who studies radio frequency than they are to the musician. ("In the one there are only waves, in the other only sounds. Yet both are equally real.")[30] I think of Annmarie Mol's atherosclerosis, that gesture of covering the corpse's face; I think of those strange fighting fruit flies with their poor ground-up heads. "So it goes on," says von Uexküll. And so we follow him into a universe saturated with signs, a semiotic universe of subjective responses and near-limitless human and animal subjectivities.

Of course I like this. But it makes me nervous. Like a plunge into the void. There is so much possible between seeing and perceiving. And a world of signs is also a world of communication. Senses combining, working together, overlapping, contradicting. So what's this I'm hearing? Magical sounds from unearthly sources? Sounds? Noise? Music? It's very loud. And it's very strange. It's on my headphones. It's coming from New Mexico . . .

The Sound of Global **W**arming

1.

Listen. It's the sound of global warming. It's getting even louder . . .

2.

Close your eyes. We're in another world. A wet world, watery, echoey, a jungle of pipes perhaps. Or a subterranean cave. We could be in that cathedral of a cave where the Princess's crippled ship crash-lands in Hayao Miyazaki's *Nausicaä of the Valley of the Wind* (his ecofantasy anime of "The Lady Who Loved Worms"), an oversize underground tropical lagoon, an oasis of mysterious life in a prophetic poisoned land.

We could be anywhere.

What are these unearthly noises? High-pitched squeaks and deep groans, the long, low creak of huge doors (that can't be doors), the electric crackling of rapid-fire static. High-pitched chirps, more chirps, that grating sound, which suddenly fades, that rush of liquid like a wave rolling up the beach. Something drumming, something fizzing, something gnawing, something splashing, something squeaking . . . something orchestrated. Over there: a detonation. Close by: something heavy raises itself to its feet with a querulous bellow. There are animals in here. What kinds of animals? What are they doing? Polyrhythmic, polyphonic animals chirping in counterpoint, call-and-response. So much activity in here. So much motion. So much rhythm. More clicks, more chirps, more squeaks, more splashes, more echo.

Where are we?

3.

We're inside a tree. A piñon pine (*Pinus edulis*). We're in its vascular tissue, just beneath the outer bark, inside the phloem and cambium. We're enclosed in a rich sound-world, a world audible only on David Dunn's CD *The Sound of Light in Trees,* the one that's on my headphones.[1]

The tree we're inside could be thirty feet tall. That's big if you're tiny, no larger than a grain of rice, like the piñon engraver beetles (*Ips confusus*) that arrive by the thousands to lay their eggs and hatch their larvae in these tough, slow-growing trees, with their much-loved seeds and aromatic wood, that dominate the harshly beautiful pine-juniper landscapes of northern New Mexico.

The piñon engravers are bark beetles, members of the Scolytidae, one of only a very small number of insect families whose adults are able to pierce the outer bark of woody plants. Until a few years ago, they seemed to have reached a kind of compact with the piñons. Attracted by signals from pioneer males, the female beetles gathered on weak and dying trees to bore their tunnels and lay their eggs. Their incursions through the bark interrupted the upflow of fluids and nutrients. The blue-stain fungus they carry further clogged the system. The weak trees capitulated. Their demise thinned the forest yet also strengthened it, the pine population benefiting from the easing of intraspecific competition for light, water, and nutrients. But only 10 to 15 percent of the male beetles' dispersal flights ended in successful reproduction, and healthy trees had little trouble resisting their advances. The trees pumped resinous sap to seal the wounds in their bark, forcibly ejecting the intruders or trapping them in stickiness. Scented monoterpenes, volatile essential oils dissolved in the resin, neutralized the fungi.[2]

But the droughts that swept the southwestern United States in the first years of this century introduced a new dynamic. Stressed by lack of water, the piñons produced less resin and found that the increasing sugar concentrations in their cells served only to bring more beetles. Higher levels of monoterpenes in the sap extruded from the engravers' entry holes attracted even more insects. Cavitation—the collapse of xylem tissue induced by the formation of vacuum bubbles under drought conditions—increased to such an extent that for some trees the acoustic emissions produced by the bubbles' implosions became "an almost continuous ultrasound signature," a soundtrack to which, as we will see, the beetles may have been paying close attention.[3]

While the trees struggled, the unusually warm temperatures helped the beetles (and the fungi) raise their reproduction and general activity rates. The convergence of weakened trees and hyperactive beetles led to a catastrophic die-off of piñon pines in the region. In 2003, the peak year of the crisis, over 770,000 acres of New Mexico forest were affected. Millions of trees died, and no effective ideas emerged in response. Using aerial surveys taken by the U.S. Department of Agriculture Forest Service and studies of a piñon-juniper forest plot at the Los Alamos National Laboratory, researchers from the University of Arizona calculated a 40 to 90 percent mortality of piñons across New Mexico, Colorado, Utah, and Arizona in 2002 and 2003.[4] Assuming no similar events occur, it could take centuries for the landscapes to recover.

But everyone knows that similar events, and others unimagined, will occur. And as immediately devastating as was the loss of the piñons to local people and to animals such as the pine-nut-eating piñon jay, the death of the trees is felt most painfully in its etching on the landscape of a new sense of foreboding. The collapse earned its place among the spectacular "natural" events of recent years, whose rawest member is still Hurricane Katrina. The now-famous images from New Orleans revealed a cluster formed from race, class, bureaucratic incompetence, government indifference, and climate. The piñons' fateful convergence acted on insects, fungi, trees, the insufficiency of expert knowledge, and again, climate. Both events made it starkly apparent that new formations in the age of climate change are unlikely to produce linear outcomes. The future is deeply marked by the inevitable eruption of nonpredictable phenomena on startling scales.[5] Forget "homeland security." Time itself has changed. We know catastrophes are coming, and we know they'll take us by surprise.

4.

We're inside a piñon pine in northern New Mexico. All around are engravers, other bark beetles, beetle larvae, and carpenter ants. That drumming is the ants, David Dunn tells me when I call him in Santa Fe. The detonations are cavitation events. That creaking is the tree swaying in the wind.

The Sound of Light in Trees is a soundscape, a "sonic environment."[6] It aims to tune us in to the aural dimension of our everyday world, to create what the anthropologist and soundscape pioneer Steven Feld calls "a sonic way of knowing and being in the world."[7] The piñon environment is not one we can ordinarily perceive through sound. We need transducers—human and mechanical—to convert these inaudible-to-the-human-ear low frequency and ultrasonic emissions into vibrations within our acoustic range.[8] Knowing we need transmutation and translation heightens the strangeness of the recording, as does knowing that even with such mediation this world remains deeply inaccessible. There is an unusual, somehow troubling quality to this soundscape, immer-

sive and alien all at once, able to convey both the proximity and the indifference of the natural world, to capture that uneasy paradox at the core of the new realities of global warming.

Entering the piñon arouses dormant senses. I close my eyes to isolate the sounds and discover that listening to these insects might not be so different from collecting them. For me, the listening experience resonates with the Japanese neuroscientist Yoro Takeshi's persuasive argument about the visual experience of finding, capturing, and studying insects. Yoro says that the Japanese conservationists who are trying to ban insect collecting are destructively shortsighted, that it is through collecting that people, particularly young people, learn what it means to sympathize with others and to live among other beings. Like many of the insect people we've met in this book, Yoro and his fellow collectors argue that the close attention demanded by this engagement with another life, another *tiny* life, develops unfamiliar ways not only of seeing but also of feeling, that the close focus on detail disrupts scale and hierarchical certainty, and that these experiences transmute into ethics. The focused attention on another life creates patience and sensitivity in the collector, Yoro claims, an awareness of subtle variations and other temporalities (change can be very slow, movement very fast, lives very short), and leads to an appreciation of differences, perhaps to a new way of being in the world.

This is seeing rather than merely looking, just as the piñon soundscape cultivates listening rather than merely hearing. Within these trees, among these animals, people "shift their thinking about the centrality of humans in the physical world," David Dunn tells me, and I realize that unlike Yoro, he's not looking for insect love but for something closer to appreciation or understanding. He doesn't exclude the possibility that getting up close to insect sounds might also generate anxiety and reinforce antipathies.[9] After all, the insects are not the heroes of this New Mexican story.

Two years of recordings compressed into one hour. Sounds from many different trees edited together. Not just a recording but a composition that takes, remakes, and rearranges nonhuman sound. Even though it's a self-conscious artifact, this kind of soundscape breaks from its precursor tradition of *musique concrète,* in which found sounds are explicitly manipulated to emphasize and express human intervention.[10] David tells me that the accent in his work is on "the inherent nature of these things," that the task is "to reveal aspects in time and space that are inherent in the materials" and to explore through sound the larger phenomena that these beings—the trees, the insects, the people—create and are a part of.

Thirty-five years as an avant-garde musician and sound artist, theorizing, composing, publishing, performing, collaborating, and of course, recording. There are still few ready-made tools. He uses open-source transducer systems of his own design to make low-frequency vibrations and ultrasonic emissions audible. He sends the contraptions to beetle specialists as far away as China. He runs workshops to show children how to make them.

Like many people in the Southwest in those years, David sat and stared at the piñons near his home. He watched their green needles turn to reddish brown, then drop. He thought about "the materiality of their world," the wood, the impedance, the possibilities. He took the piezo-electric transducer disc from a Hallmark greeting card, glued it to a gutted meat thermometer, pushed the apparatus into the bark of the dying piñon, and angled it to pick up the vibrations. One per tree. Less than $10 each.

5.

Technology can bring us closer to the world, David Dunn tells me. Perhaps, he continues, the rich and complex soundscape accessible through a pair of headphones approximates the sensory experience of other forms of life, with their distinctive ambient sensitivities.

Among the best known of his numerous recordings is "Chaos and the Emergent Mind of the Pond," a twenty-four-minute composition that discovers in the sounds of aquatic insects in North American and African ponds "a sonic multiverse of exquisite complexity."[11]

Listening to the pond with two omnidirectional ceramic hydrophones and a portable DAT recorder, he hears a rhythmic complexity altogether greater than that in most human music, patterns comparable only to the

most sophisticated computer compositions and the most complex African polyrhythmic drumming.

The sounds can't be arbitrary, he decides. These animals are not simply following their instincts. "The musician in me cannot help but hear more." In fact, the musician in him understands human music as a parallel expression to these sounds, as the expressive modality that brings people closest to the ways in which other forms of life communicate. Music suggests organization, not simply sound, and he hears the pond "saturated with an intelligence emergent from the very fullness of interconnection." He begins to hear the pond as a kind of superorganism, a transcendent social "mind" created from the autonomous interaction of all the life within it, terms not dissimilar to those used by complexity theorists to describe the nest colonies of the eusocial insects (ants and termites, some bees and wasps, some aphids and thrips).

As I read these ideas in the liner notes for "Chaos and the Emergent Mind of the Pond," I start to understand that the soundscape is more than a recording, more even than a composition. It is also a research method, one that flows easily from a principle of wholeness. The soundscape encounters its piece of the world as a totality. In this, it's quite unlike scientific investigations that begin their search by isolating individual elements. The method is different, and not surprisingly, the outcome is different too. Something else surfaces. Let's not stay deaf to its music.

6.

"For a long time," David Dunn told me, "that was enough." He composed soundscapes to sensitize his audience to the acoustics of the natural world, to stimulate the recovery of older, lost sensitivities, and to offer more intimate relationships with other life-forms. But climate change changed that too. The dying forests posed the question of responsibility with new urgency. Like many in the midst and wake of disaster, he found himself wrestling with the desire to do something effective, something, as he put it, "to diminish my own sense of tragedy and depression."

The piñon die-off was no anomaly. As temperature zones have shifted in the past decades, insects have shifted with them. Swift, numerous, and astonishingly adaptive, beetles, mosquitoes, ticks, and others have taken advantage of new conditions and newly expanded habitat ranges with spectacular results. One widely publicized effect is the unwelcome appearance of insect-borne diseases in unexpected latitudes and altitudes (Lyme disease in Sweden and the Czech Republic; West Nile virus in the United States and Canada; dengue fever as far north as Texas; malaria in the East African highlands).[12] Another is the unprecedented deforestation that's struck the boreal forests of Siberia, Alaska, and Canada, the coniferous forests of the southwestern United States, and the temperate forests of the Midwest and Northeast.

The details vary, but the dynamic is well established. Confronted by regional increases in winter and summer temperatures, decreases in precipitation, and the reduction in the duration of freezes, plants and insects have fallen out of step—despite often having co-evolved for millennia. The animals adapt at a rate far more rapid than that of the trees. The beetles accelerate: they eat more; they develop faster (some species move to adulthood in one year rather than two); they reproduce quicker and survive longer. Their numbers explode.

The same conditions of higher temperature and lower rainfall stress the trees. As drought intensifies, their metabolism breaks down, and their defenses weaken. Their established strategy—the migration of populations out of the higher temperature zones over generations—is simply too slow. Temporalities are out of joint. The forest comes apart. The trees are overwhelmed long before they can escape to a place less hospitable to the insects.

The result has been a catalog of destruction. Since the early 1990s, spruce bark beetles have caused the death of 4.4 million acres of Alaskan boreal forest. In the same period, the mountain pine beetle has moved into 33 million acres of forest in British Columbia and caused major

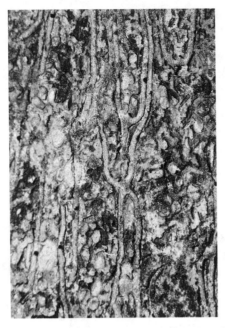

damage in Montana, northern Colorado, and southern Wyoming. Long-term predictions are suitably apocalyptic. One North American scenario envisions a continent-wide invasion of bark beetles radiating from British Columbia to Labrador and down into the forests of eastern Texas.[13]

David and his collaborator, the University of California physicist James Crutchfield, an expert in nonlinear complex systems, describe the mechanism at work here as a "desynchronization of biotic developmental patterns."[14] They investigate it in a new project imagined through the logic of the soundscape, a scientific inquiry symbiotic with *The Sound of Light in Trees* that doesn't so much look at climate change as listen to it.

For several decades, research on insect behavior has been dominated by chemical ecology, the study of the effect of chemical cues on ecological interaction. In his fascinating account of a life among insects, Thomas Eisner, pioneer and undisputed giant in the field, documents the discoveries: the bombardier beetles that spray scalding benzoquinones when threatened; the female *Photuris* fireflies, which procure defensive chemicals by consuming male fireflies of a different genus; the beautiful female moth *Utetheisa ornatrix*, which discriminates among sexual partners according to the finest calibrations of pheromonal scent; the defensive toxic-vomit response of sawfly larvae and grasshoppers. The stories seem infinite, and so, too, Eisner makes clear, do the opportunities for further research.[15]

Chemical ecology has proved to be an overwhelmingly fertile field for insect studies. In particular, tremendous energy has been funneled into work on three classes of compounds: pheromones, which influence the behavior or physiological development of members of the same species (for example, in mating or aggregating); allomones, which act on members of a different species to the advantage of the producer (for example, defensive toxins, such as the bombardier's spray); and kairomones, which affect members of a different species to the advantage of the receiver (for example, those monoterpenic pine resins that inadvertently attract parasites or predators to a wound).

The explanatory power of chemical ecology is unquestioned. Its descriptions of the intricacies of insect life are quite amazing. Nonetheless, David Dunn tells me, it has done little to slow the advance of bark beetles through the northern forests. Its primary pest-control tools— pheromone traps (which decoy the beetles or disrupt their behavior) and pesticides—have proven ineffectual or impractical. Despite hundreds of research papers and untold millions of dollars in research funds, the beetles march on.

7.

Listen. They're coming through loud and clear. Those squeaky chirps are the piñon engraver beetles. The female has a small, hard comb (the *pars stridens*) on the back of her head, which she grates against a scraper (the plectrum) located under the front edge of her prothorax. The male makes sounds too, but no one is sure how.

The range of sound-making organs in bark beetles is substantial. And so are the uses to which all the noise is put. Think of the Scolytidae as social insects. Not in the same way as eusocial insects, like the honeybees, with their elaborate nests and sharp divisions of labor. Social in a looser sense: they live in groups; they coordinate mass arrivals on target trees; they arrange spacing to ensure that they don't settle too densely; some occupy their nests collectively. Such complex cooperative behavior presumes communication.

Research on bark beetle interaction has focused largely on chemical signaling; sound has been regarded as ancillary.[16] Symptomatically, there is still nothing published on how bark beetles hear or what kinds of auditory organs they possess.[17]

But what if—as Dunn and Crutchfield propose—bark beetles are attracted to vulnerable trees not only by the aggregation pheromones of the male pioneers and the kairomones released in the wounded trees' resin but also by bioacoustic cues, such as the internal explosions of gas bubbles during cavitation events? Could we provisionally assume that, like many butterflies, moths, mantises, crickets, grasshoppers, flies, and Neuroptera, bark beetles, too, may have hearing in the ultrasonic range? The rich ultrasonic sound-world of the piñon pine suggests as much, as do recent studies indicating that hearing among insects is far more widespread than previously assumed.[18]

Indeed, after spending time inside the piñon alongside the animals and scaled to their world, it becomes more and more inconceivable that so little research is being done on beetle bioacoustics and that the intensely interactive sounds inside the tree are arbitrary. Reviewing the piñon soundscape, Dunn and Crutchfield discover that "a very diverse range of sound signaling persists well after the putatively associated behaviors—host selection, coordination of attack, courtship, territorial competition, and nuptial chamber excavations—have all taken place. In fully colonized trees," they write, "the stridulations, chirps, and clicks can go on continuously for days and weeks, long after most of these other behaviors will have apparently run their course." What does this mean? Their inference is careful but important: "These observations suggest that these insects have a more sophisticated social organization than previously suspected—one that requires ongoing communication through sound and substrate vibration."[19]

Recent research by Reginald Cocroft and his associates at the University of Missouri at Columbia raises yet another question. Cocroft has shown that the low-frequency and ultrasonic airborne sounds recorded by David Dunn are actually only one element of an insect's sound-world. In huge numbers, it seems, insects that live on plants also communicate by the nonacoustic vibration of their living substrate. "Vibration-sensitive species," write Cocroft and Rafael Rodríguez, "can not only monitor vibrations to detect predators or prey but also introduce vibrations into structures to communicate with other individuals." By vibrating the leaves, stems, and roots of plants, insects send meaningful signals across significant distances (up to twenty-six feet in the case of stoneflies). Unconstrained by the physical limitations of airborne communication, they can deter predators by producing low-frequency signals that mimic far larger animals. Some, such as leaf-cutter ants, vibrate to call their comrades to a high-quality food source. Others, such as larval tortoiseshell beetles, exchange vibrational signals that coordinate the formation of defensive groups. Still others, including thornbug leafhoppers, generate collective distress signals to summon their mothers when they are under threat. And needless to say, predators eavesdrop on vibrations to locate their prey (a practice that accounts for "vibrocrypticity," by which some insects "move so slowly and generate so little vibration in the substrate that they can walk past a spider without eliciting an attack"). The diversity of vibrational signalers and signals is "fantastic."[20]

Let's reimagine the landscape of the soundscape. Let's begin with all that busy, noisy, musical energy and open our senses wider still. And let's assume not only multimodality but cross-modality—that, like our own, these senses make sense in combination rather than in isolation.

Yes, the world of insects is a noisy world, a constant whir of acoustics: drumming, clicking, squeaking, chirping.

Yes, it's also a vibrating world, so sensitive that even gentle winds can disrupt it and a rainstorm can cause it all to dry up or be drowned out.

Yes, it's a chemical world, too: a nonstop, impossibly complex, wildly inventive molecular maze of attractants, repellents, potions, poisons, and disguises.

And yes, as we know from von Frisch's honeybees, it's a world of direct physical intimacies—touching, palpating, and substance sharing—and a world of visual cues, too.

It's an intensely interactive world, a landscape across which animals of the same and different species connect and communicate.

Listen. Can you hear it? With the soundscape we take tentative steps into a wider, richer world.

8.

But more than just the sound of life in trees, the soundscape is the soundtrack to an epidemic. These noisy beetles are not merely symptoms of global warming, say Dunn and Crutchfield; they are also its cause. Dunn and Crutchfield see forest dynamics as a cybernetic feedback loop accelerating under conditions of climate change. With their relentlessly successful adaptive population dynamics, the insects drive the system past equilibrium. Decisive in felling the forests and so releasing carbon stored in tree biomass and captured during tree growth, bark beetles become the accelerating motor of what Dunn and Crutchfield call "entomogenic climate change."[21]

It is an intriguing insight. But in practice it is likely to make little difference to the Scolytidae and their bark-piercing allies. Already there is

 little hesitation from any quarter in holding beetles responsible for the deforestation overwhelming so many North American forests, in understanding their behavior as "infestation" and "invasion" (folding these anxieties into persistent fears of human immigration), and in working to eradicate them.

Listen. These sounds provoke complicated responses. The beauty of that rich interior life, the music of the phloem—it is self-contained, indifferent, the soundtrack to catastrophe. These beetles live fully communicative lives, their *Umwelt* is thoroughly social. These are not the enemies we ought to choose. The biosecurity state, with its traps, its pesticides, its arborists, its public-education programs, and its quarantined counties, is largely powerless. It was Mao Zedong, apparently, who said that where there is repression, there is resistance. He wasn't thinking of insects. But we should be. As far back as twenty-five years ago, 7 billion beetles were caught in pheromone traps during a campaign to repulse an invasion of European spruce bark beetles in Norwegian and Swedish forests.[22] Seven *billion*, and still they kept coming. Repression is futile. Somehow, we will have to cohabit. Somehow, we will have to make friends.

Ex Libris, Exempla

Excess

December 26, 1934. A famous episode in the history of Surrealism. In a Paris café, André Breton and the up-and-coming writer Roger Caillois quarrel over two Mexican jumping beans.

* * *

Three years later, Caillois founded the Collège de sociologie with two other dissident Surrealists, Georges Bataille and the anthropologist Michel Leiris. (He also participated, halfheartedly, in the charismatic Bataille's Acéphale [Headless] group, a secret society whose few members, the story goes, having reached agreement on the radical gesture of a human sacrifice, found plenty of volunteers among themselves to play the victim but none to perform the execution.)[1] Two more years passed, and Caillois left France to sit out the Nazi occupation in Argentina. Nine years after that, he began a career as a cultural bureaucrat at UNESCO. Twenty-three years later, he was elected to the Académie française. Along the way, he wrote a series of erudite, idiosyncratic, and barely remembered books on unusual topics, among which insects—and in particular praying mantises, lantern flies, and other masters of mimicry—held a special place.

* * *

Sometime on December 27, 1934, perhaps nursing a hangover (he was twenty-one), Caillois sent a letter to Breton in which he declared his break with Surrealism. "I had hoped," he wrote, "that our two positions were not as deeply divided as they turned out to be during our conversation yesterday evening."[2]

* * *

The enigmatic beans sat in front of them on the table. Why did they jump like that? Were those irregular twitches a symptom of some strangely suspenseful life force? Caillois took his knife to break them open. Breton, nearly twice his age, recently  expelled from the Communist Party, the author of the Surrealists' founding manifestos, a prominent figure in French intellectual life, made him stop.

They knew that each bean contained a larva of the *Laspeyresia saltitans* moth and that its spasms were the creature's movements inside its hollowed shell. But Breton didn't want this type of confirmation. "That would have destroyed the mystery, you said," wrote Caillois.[3]

* * *

Caillois described the dispute as between poetry and science. But his science was distinctively poetic even then. He threw himself into the "utter confusion" that he identified as the hallmark of inquiry in a contemporary world characterized by "the *debacle of the evident*."[4] Like any good scientist, he saw confusion as a provocation to systematic inquiry. But he was developing his idea of "diagonal science," "the science of what exceeds knowledge," a science that would encompass "what science doesn't want to know." He was in search of "an order that will allow disorder itself to enter into the order of things."[5] Revealing the larva inside the bean would hardly end the mystery, he wrote to Breton: "Here we have a form of the Marvellous that does not fear knowledge but, on the contrary, thrives on it."[6]

* * *

The natural world is full of marvels. Maria Sibylla Merian came across one in Suriname. The lantern fly, *Laternaria phosphorea*, she discovered, creates enough light by which "to read a book printed with the same type as that used for the *Gazette de Hollande*."[7] Actually, she was mistaken; the lantern fly creates no phosphorescence—an odd, uncanny mistake that affixed itself to the insect for more than 100 years and lives on in its Linnaean name. Caillois suggests that the appearance of this creature so surprised Merian that she unconsciously made sense of it by the substitution of a different, unrelated strangeness, the strangeness of animal luminosity.

And *L. phosphorea* is a startling animal. Like the praying mantis, it fills the world around itself with myth, storytelling, and legend. Henry Walter Bates, the British naturalist who lived eleven years in the Amazon basin and discovered, among many other things, a form of butterfly mimicry crucial to Darwin's theorization of natural selection, retold stories that circulate in the region about lantern flies that attack and kill men on the rivers. In Amazonia, Bates says, the insect is known as the crocodile head because of its long, snoutlike proboscis.[8] This empty box extends from its face and "imitates an alligator's head exactly," writes Caillois (who was not really one for biogeographic precision); "color and relief combine to simulate the savage teeth of a powerful jaw." The effect is "absurd, even ridiculous," but undeniable.[9] How strange that a small fly that lives among the trees should have this resemblance and, accordingly, such power to intimidate.

* * *

There is, Caillois proposes, "a repertoire of frightening appearances," a set of prototypes in nature upon which both the crocodile and the lantern fly draw. Mimicry is not about disappearance, about hiding in plain sight. It's more often the capacity to reappear, to induce panic by the sudden substitution of one appearance by another, like a Haida shutter mask. Out of nothing, out of empty space, the praying mantis abruptly rears up over its prey, revealing its intimidating eyespots, emitting sinister sounds; its victim is rooted, paralyzed, hypnotized, incapable of fleeing its presence, and the mantis "seems supernatural, unrelated to the real world, coming from the beyond."[10]

And so does the lantern fly. Behind its reptilian "false head, dwarf and giant at the same time," Caillois makes out another head, "the tiny head of the insect," with its "two bright, black, almost microscopic points— the eyes."[11] The crocodile face is a mask, a mask that corresponds in its effect and method of use to the mask of the human shaman. The lantern fly "behaves like a spell-binder, a sorcerer, the wearer of a mask who knows how to use it."[12]

* * *

Caillois was a dedicated collector of rocks and stones. Toward the end of his life, he published *The Writing of Stones*, a lavishly illustrated guide to the highlights of his collection, in which he describes each stone with his singular combination of biological reason and analogical poetics. He finds the same kinds of correspondences in stones as those that draw him so relentlessly to insects. Just as insect mimicry shares the decisive characteristics of sorcery, just as the animal's mimetic ornaments are equal in practice and effect to the shaman's mask, just as the alarming eyespots on the wings of the *Caligo* butterfly call to mind the evil eye ("The eye is the vehicle of fascination in the whole animal kingdom"), so the gorgeous stones of Caillois' collection—"and not only they but also roots, shells, wings, and every cipher and construction in nature"— share, along with the human arts, a "universal syntax," a connection to the "aesthetics of the universe."[13]

If categorical segmentation is always the first step in scientific reasoning, this is a world that at all times exceeds its compartments. It is the dissolution of boundaries—self, other, body, animal, vegetable, mineral. The dissolution into space. At the end of one of his most famous essays, Caillois quotes the final ecstasy from Flaubert's *The Temptation of Saint Anthony*, "a general spectacle of mimicry to which the hermit succumbs":

"Plants are no longer distinguished from animals. . . . Insects identical with rose petals adorn a bush. . . . And then plants are confused with stones. Rocks look like brains, stalactites like breasts, veins of iron like tapestries adorned with figures. . . ."

Anthony, writes Caillois, "wants to split himself thoroughly, to be in everything, 'to penetrate each atom, to descend to the bottom of matter, to *be* matter.'"[14]

The inky-smoky-vibrant polished surfaces of jasper and agate can take Caillois there. A riled hawk moth can take him there. A rearing mantis can take him there. A lantern fly can take him there. "No one," he writes, "should say it is nonsense to attribute magic to insects."[15]

Exaction

Writing from what is now Mexico City, the Franciscan chronicler Juan de Torquemada described how, after Hernán Cortés had taken Moctezuma II prisoner in the Aztec ruler's own palace in 1520, the conquistador gave his men free rein to explore the royal compound. Among the Spaniards' discoveries, wrote Torquemada, were a number of small bags, which they at once assumed were filled with gold dust.

When they cut the bags open, the Spanish were dismayed to find that instead of gold, they were filled with lice. In Torquemada's story—a story he attributes to two of Cortés's lieutenants—the lice were an expression of the profound sense of duty that even the poorest of the emperor's subjects, those with nothing else to offer him, felt toward their sovereign.[16]

Torquemada credited the discovery of the bags to Alonso de Ojeda, the notoriously brutal governor of Urabá who accompanied Columbus on his second voyage to the Indies. But Ojeda had died five years earlier, in Santo Domingo, following a rout by Indians at Cartagena and a subsequent shipwreck. If Torquemada, writing nearly a century after the event, was wrong about Ojeda, perhaps he was mistaken about other details too?

* * *

In another version of this story, the lice made their way to the palace through the efforts of elderly people conscripted for the task by Moctezuma. Incapable of more onerous duties, these men and women were charged with visiting their neighbors' houses, delousing the occupants, and delivering their bounty to Tenochtitlán as tribute. Given that the earliest medical text from the Americas—the Aztec codex of 1552 (unearthed in the Vatican in 1931)—lists indigenous herbal treatments for head lice, phthiriasis (eyelid lice infestation), and "lousy distemper," it could be that this tribute was an initiative of imperial public hygiene.[17]

* * *

Far to the southwest, the Inca ruler Huayna Capac was touring the limits of his empire. Arriving at Pasto, a frontier outpost close to today's border between Colombia and Ecuador, he supervised the building of defenses and pointed out to the leaders of the district that as a consequence of the empire's investment in their welfare, they were now in his debt. According to Pedro de Cieza de León, one of the most important Spanish chroniclers of the Incas, the local notables replied that they were entirely without the means to meet new taxes.

Resolved to teach these lords of Pasto the reality of their situation, Huayna Capac issued instructions that "each inhabitant should be obliged, every four months, to give a rather large cane full of live lice." Cieza de León says that the lords laughed out loud when they heard this command. Soon enough, though, they learned that no matter how diligent they were in collecting, they were unable to fill the designated baskets. Huayna Capac provided them with sheep, writes Cieza de León, and it wasn't long before Pasto was providing Cuzco, the Inca capital, with its full complement of wool and vegetables.[18]

* * *

Further south, the Urus retreated to floating reed islands in Lake Titicaca in an effort to stave off Inca conquest. (These artificial islands and the few people who live on them are today one of the area's principal tourist attractions.) The chroniclers report that the Incas regarded the Urus as so lowly that the word with which they named them meant "maggot." The same accounts explain that the Incas levied the Urus' tribute in lice simply because they considered them unfit to pay in any other currency.[19]

* * *

Nothing like this is documented for the Wari, the Maya, the Mixtec, the Zapotec, or the other great pre-Columbian empires. Often the records are just too scant. However, it is known that in battle the Maya were able to create a formidable panic among their enemies by bombarding them not with lice, but with missiles constructed from live wasps' nests.[20]

Exile

From a remote district of mountainous Guangxi Province, the renowned Tang-dynasty poet and philosopher Liu Zongyuan described the character of owl-fly larvae.

* * *

Owl-flies are ancient creatures. They have been identified in amber from the Dominican Republic that is more than 45 million years old.[21] The adults resemble dragonflies, but the larvae look like the larvae of ant lions: they have dark brown oval armored bodies about an inch long, with powerful pincer-shaped mandibles. Unlike ant lion larvae, which set a shallow trap in sandy soil and lie in wait for ants and other prey to drop in, owl-fly larvae camouflage themselves by pulling debris over their bodies. Only the outsize mandibles remain uncovered. When an insect wanders too close, the large jaws snap shut, and the larva sucks the pinioned body dry.

* * *

In A.D. 805, Liu Zongyuan was banished from the cosmopolitan imperial capital of Chang'an (present-day Xi'an) for his involvement in a failed reformist coup. Chang'an, says Liu's biographer Jo-shui Chen, was "the 'hometown' to which he dreamed of returning" but never would.[22]

In "My First Excursion to West Mountain," one of the eight short essays he completed between 809 and 812 that are "considered to have inaugurated the genre of the lyric travel account," Liu wrote:

> I have been in a state of constant fear since being exiled to this prefecture. Whenever I had a free moment, I would roam about, wandering aimlessly. Every day I hiked in the mountains accompanied by friends with similar fates. We would penetrate into the deep forests, following the winding streams back to their source, discovering hidden springs and fantastic rocks—no spot seemed too remote. Upon reaching a place, we would sit down on the grass, downing bottles of wine until we were thoroughly drunk. Drunk, we would lean against each other as pillows and fall asleep. Asleep, we would dream.[23]

Liu died in 819 at the age of forty-six. More than 500 years later he would be recognized as one the eight masters of Tang and Song dynasty prose.

The year he died, in A Record of Fu Ban, he described how, when an owl-fly larva catches its prey, it carries it "forward with its chin up."

> Its load is getting heavier and heavier. Though very tired, [the larva] does not fall down as it cannot rise to its feet once it has stumbled. Some people take pity on it and lift off the load so the insect can continue walking forward. However, it soon takes on its burden once again.[24]

* * *

Elsewhere during these years of exile, in a meditation on the nature of heaven and human responsibility, Liu Zongyuan asks: "Were someone to succeed in exterminating the insects that eat holes in things, could these things pay him back? Were someone to aid harmful creatures in breeding and proliferating, could these things resent him?"

No, of course not, he says. The fact of the matter is that "merit is self-attained and disaster is self-inflicted." He is near the end of his time in this melancholy place. "Those who expect rewards or punishments are making a big mistake. . . . You should just believe in your [principles of] humanity and righteousness, wander in the world according to these principles, and live [in this way] until your death."[25]

Extermination

After the defeat of the Nazis, Karl von Frisch returned to Munich to resume his work as director of the Institute of Zoology. In 1947, he published *Ten Little Housemates,* a small book for nonscientific readers in which he tried to show that "there is something wonderful about even the most detested and despised of creatures."[26]

* * *

He begins with the housefly ("a trim little creature") and moves on to mosquitoes (which, he admits, "can never be pleasant"), fleas ("An adult man wanting to compete with a flea would have to clear the high-jump bar at about 100 metres and his long-jump would have to measure about 300 metres. . . . At one jump he could leap from Westminster Bridge to the top of Big Ben"), bed bugs ("We must remember that all living creatures are equal in the eyes of the great law of life: men are not superior to mice nor bugs to men"), lice ("With its forefeet alone a louse can carry up to two thousand times the weight of its body for a whole minute. This is more than the strongest athlete could ever hope to do; it would mean holding up a weight of 150 tons in his hands!"), the cockroach ("a community that has come down in the world"), silverfish ("*Lepisma saccharina*—the sugar guest. . . . They are entirely harmless housemates"), spiders ("It is astonishing how little the inborn [web-making] skill of these animals is bound to a rigid system, how greatly their actions differ in detail according to local conditions and according to the weaver's character"), and ticks ("As there is good reason for the female's bloodthirstiness, we cannot blame her. Anyone who has to hatch out a few thousand eggs can do with a good meal").

* * *

Von Frisch devotes one of his longer chapters to his tenth housemate, the clothes moth. He begins with the caterpillar. Like the dung beetle, it turns out to be an essential scavenger, feeding off the planet's suffocating mountains of surplus hair, feathers, and fur. Like the caddis fly larva, it fashions itself a protective case, spinning a tiny silken tube, a minute padded sock, which it covers with trimmings from the keratin-based world around it. To eat, it peeks its head out of the tube and nibbles the landscape beside the opening. When everything within reach is gone, it explores by extending its case further into the underbrush.

Soon the caterpillar is fully grown and leaves its tube. Awkwardly, it makes its way to a new location, from which the moth will easily be able to take to the air. Maybe it's the surface of your grandmother's fur coat or perhaps your favorite winter sweater. Once it arrives, the caterpillar spins itself a new home, gussies it up as before, and prepares for pupation.

* * *

Like many lepidoptera, the adult clothes moth cannot eat or drink. In its few weeks of life, it exhausts the energy stores it accumulated as a caterpillar, losing 50 to 75 percent of its body weight in the process. The female, heavy with up to 100 eggs, is reluctant to fly and spends her days hiding in the dark. Von Frisch is irritated by uninformed violence. "When a lively moth flies around the room," he says, "there is no point in the whole family chasing it. It is only a male. There are plenty of male moths, actually about double the number of females. So the birthrate will not be affected if a few more or less are killed."[27]

* * *

Von Frisch's little housemates are extraordinary and, in their own ways, exceptional. He explores the extremes of their existence, explains their extravagances, examines their exuberances, and excluding exaggeration, exalts in their extravagations. With his characteristic exactitude, he examines his own experiments and expands on his experiences. In extensive and exhaustive excurses—often external to the exegesis—he extends excuses and extenuations for their excesses. Still, each of his chapters ends with recommendations for his little housemates' extirpation, that is, for their extermination.

Houseflies should be trapped on flypaper or poisoned. Clothes moths are susceptible to naphthalene and camphor. Silverfish can be controlled with DDT (which "does not harm human beings or domestic animals if it is used in reasonable quantities and according to the instructions"). Lice should be mass-killed by fumigation with prussic acid and its derivatives ("one useful product of the war"). Mosquitoes require more drastic measures: you should drain their wetland habitats, flood the area with petroleum, or introduce predatory fish into their breeding pools. DDT should also be used against cockroaches.

"It is doubtful whether insects feel pain at all as we do," says von Frisch. And he tells a story to demonstrate his claim. He goes back to his beloved bees, the little comrades to whom he devoted his adult life. "If you take a pair of sharp scissors," he begins, "and cut a bee in two, taking care not to disturb it while it is taking a drop of sugary water, it will go on eating."[28]

Von Frisch's even, good-natured tone doesn't change. Roger Caillois encountered something like this too, something that brought death, pleasure, and pain into one claustrophobic space. But Caillois, conscripted by a different type of science, found himself bound and subject to his animal: "I am deliberately expressing myself in a roundabout way," he wrote as he tried to explain the peculiar power of the praying mantis, "as it is so difficult, I think, both for language to express and for the mind to grasp that the mantis, when dead, should be capable of simulating death."[29]

But the bee just keeps on drinking. It doesn't seem to raise questions beyond the experiment. It appears to have lost its magic. Its "pleasure—if it feels any—is even considerably prolonged," von Frisch observes. "It cannot drink its fill, for what it sucks trickles out again at the rear, and hence it can feast on the sweetness for a long time before it finally sinks dead of exhaustion."[30] Ex-animal, ex animo. He extends, exhibits, and exanimates. It excretes, exhales, and expires.

But let's not forget: just as there are forms of the marvelous that thrive on knowledge, there is knowledge that despite itself adds to the marvelous; just as there are those who underestimate the lowly multitude, there are people who understand only too well its many-sided power; just as there are those who subject the animal to the steel of experiment, there are those who take pity and lift off its load, even though it soon takes on its burden once again.

Yearnings

1.

Kawasaki Mitsuya sells live beetles on the Internet. My friend Shiho Satsuka found his site and, knowing it would get my attention, sent me the link. A few weeks later, I was in the suburbs of Wakayama City, outside Osaka, with my friend CJ Suzuki, sitting in Kawasaki's insect-filled living room and talking about *ookuwagata*, the Japanese stag beetles in which he trades.

Kawasaki Mitsuya recently gave up his job as a hospital radiographer, but there's no money in stag beetles, he tells us. He opens some jars and explains that he does this for love. He fills his website with his poems. Some are silly, some are cute, some are abruptly bitter, even angry. Most are melancholy laments that contrast middle-aged male disillusion with the innocent openness of youth. ("He looks at the sky and the blue stays in his eyes. / The eyes of a child are like glass balls that truthfully reflect the world. / The eyes of the grown man have lost their light, / His eyes are cloudy like stagnant pools.")[1]

Kawasaki tells us that his mission is to heal the family. He wants to open the hearts of men and bring them closer to their sons. Fathers have become cold; their hearts are hard and dry. Their lives are deadening. They have no interest in their children. They don't feel the connection. On his website, he offers to lend stag beetles at no charge. Perhaps insect friends will bring families together. He remembers the love he felt when he was a boy hunting beetles in the mountains around Wakayama. "I want to nourish their hearts," he says.

Online, Kawasaki Mitsuya calls himself Kuwachan, a sweet name that a parent might give a child who is fond of insects: *kuwa* from *kuwagata*,

or stag beetle, and *-chan* a common diminutive suffix. Across the top of his home page is a brightly colored cartoon of a small boy in full insect-collecting kit. It is Kuwachan as he remembers himself in the 1970s, white hat, hiking boots, water canteen and collecting box slung around his neck, a butterfly net grasped like a flag in the breeze, its pole thrust into the earth. Kuwachan the insect-boy, high on a hill, back to the viewer, face upturned to the blue of the sky, arms thrown wide to the world and its possibilities.

A few days earlier, CJ and I had spent the day in Hakone, a popular spa town in the hills southwest of Tokyo. We were visiting Yoro Takeshi, neuroanatomist, best-selling social commentator, and insect collector. Like Kuwachan, Yoro welcomed us into his home and filled the day with wide-ranging conversation. Yoro is in his late sixties, but he pursues his insects with youthful energy, augmenting his enormous collection with expeditions to Bhutan, chasing weevils as well as the more extravagant elephant beetles. When CJ and I arrived at his house, he was examining a set of burnt-orange penises from type specimens on loan from the Natural History Museum in London, using his state-of-the-art microscopes and monitors to reveal species-defining morphological differences that made me wonder about human limitations that had never previously crossed my mind.

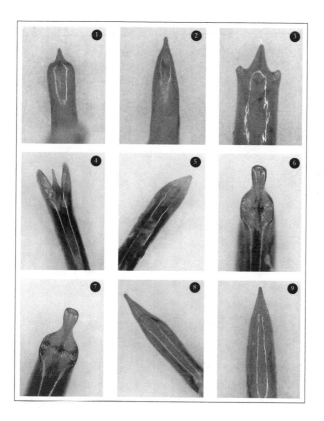

Like Kuwachan, Yoro has loved insects since he was a child. Like Kuwachan, he told us that they affected him profoundly. After collecting for so many years, he now has *"mushi* eyes," bug eyes, and sees everything in nature from an insect's point of view. Each tree is its own world, each leaf is different. Insects taught him that general nouns like *insects, trees, leaves,* and especially *nature* destroy our sensitivity to detail. They make us conceptually as well as physically violent. "Oh, an insect," we say, seeing only the category, not the being itself.

Shortly after returning to Tokyo, CJ and I came across this photograph, evidence that Yoro, like Kuwachan, was once an insect-boy, a *konchu-shonen.* There he is on the right, resolutely setting off into the hills of Kamakura soon after the Second World War, a time of devastation and hunger, but a time nonetheless of adolescent exploration and freedom.

We met Yoro at his newly built weekend home, a quirky barnlike construction designed by the "Surrealist architect" Fujimori Terunobu that—with its strip of meadow sprouting from the apex of the roof—suggests both *Anne of Green Gables* and *The Jetsons.* The house reminded us of those out-of-joint structures that populate *Spirited Away, Howl's Moving Castle,* and other epic animations by Hayao Miyazaki, structures that fill an elaborate universe that is somewhere and some when unknown but still somehow instantly familiar.

The connections were not accidental. It emerged that not only are Yoro Takeshi and Hayao Miyazaki close friends but that Miyazaki, too, cultivates a passion for insects that began with a childhood as a *konchu-shonen.* What's more, it seems Miyazaki also enjoys collaborating with avant-garde architects. He and the artist-architect Arakawa Shusaku have drawn up plans for a utopian town whose houses are not unlike the one in Hakone to which Yoro gets away from the city and in which he keeps his insects. Theirs is a distinctly hippie vision of social engineering, motivated by some of the same worries about alienation and some of the same yearnings for community that preoccupy Kuwachan. Theirs is a town where children can escape what all of these men see as the profound estrangement of Japan's media-saturated society and where they can rediscover a golden childhood of play, experimentation, and exploration in nature, where children—and adults too—can learn (again) to see, feel, and develop their senses.[2]

Kawasaki, Yoro, and Miyazaki were only the first of many insect boys that CJ and I encountered in Japan. It seemed that wherever we went, we met *konchu-shonen*, both large and small. We came across a famous one in Takarazuka, the home of the celebrated all-women theater company, with its long-lasting idols and mass following of devoted female fans. We couldn't get tickets to a performance, but no matter. We were in town for another attraction, the Tezuka Osamu Manga Museum, a perfect small museum dedicated to the life and work of the acknowledged god of manga (and innovator in anime), who died in 1989.

If Miyazaki is the current superstar of anime, Tezuka was the artistic genius who used the narrative techniques of cinema to transform the printed page, creating a dizzyingly kinetic comic-book form that accommodates every conceivable subject matter and emotion. He, too, was a passionate insect collector, so passionate that he named his first company Mushi Productions, incorporated a cute version of the Sino-Japanese character for the word *mushi* into his signature, and populated his stories with butterfly-people, erotic moths, beetle robots, and endlessly varied metamorphoses and rebirths. Sure enough, there was Tezuka fully decked out as Insect Boy in the museum's introductory video, ready for adventure, an early intimation of Astro Boy, the android superhero who is still one of Tezuka's most marketable creations (and who, in the intricate, multiauthored ways of such creativity was, Tezuka recalled, inspired by Walt Disney's Jiminy Cricket—a different kind of insect-human).

"This place was a space station, a secret jungle for explorers to discover," Tezuka's text reads; in the background melodic harpsichords and the chirps of birds and crickets. It was "an infinity where imagination could expand forever." The sky is a dreamlike azure; the boys are in sepia. As the images floated by, CJ translated: "I was bullied as a child and thrust into war. I cannot say everything was great, and I don't want

to dwell in the past. But looking back now, I'm grateful to have been surrounded by so much nature. My experience of running freely in mountains, rivers, and meadows and of the insect collecting in which I was so absorbed gave me unforgettable memories and imbued in me a feeling of nostalgia as a deep part of my body and my heart."

Tezuka won't dwell in the past, but he won't give up that longing either, the sweet-sad pleasure that feeds on the impossibility of erasing the distance between me then and me now. It's an absence easy to reproduce: easy as an azure sky and two sepia boys. It's an absence easy to fill, too, if not with a mail-order *kuwagata* then with an afternoon spent *mushi* hunting.

CJ and I shade our eyes as we step out of the insect museum in Minoo Park, the same park where Tezuka the *konchu-shonen* first collected insects with his sepia friends. Here, all around us, under the bluest sky, are living families, here in the here and now, fathers and sons (and a few women and girls also, although they rarely show up in the memories or longings of *konchu-shonen*). Here they are in the bright afternoon sun, fully equipped *konchu-shonen*, spread out along the shallow river, searching for bugs—water striders, water boatmen, crabs, too—serious but happy, balanced on rocks, dipping toes into the cool water, splashing around, emptying nets, showing their grown-ups what they've found (not much, as it's too early in the summer).

The children are collecting specimens for their school summer projects, and their fathers are there to help them, also in shorts and hats, also holding the nets and buckets, which they got for ¥2,000 (U.S.$20), a price that includes a lab session at which anything they find can be pinned, ID'd according to the full-color *zukan* (field guide), and turned into a specimen. It's a sunny day of *kazoku service*, family service. A day to fulfill the promise of Kuwachan's poems, a day for boys to use their nets to catch the memories for a lifetime and men to learn again how to be fathers as they relive what it felt like to be a son.

And speaking of fathers and sons, here is one more insect-boy. He's standing with the inflatable rhinoceros beetle that his father just bought for him at the summer festival. They're on their way home, late at night outside the Minowa metro station in northeast Tokyo, a boy and his father under the streetlights, stopping to chat with a stranger and pose for a photo.

That's just camera shake during a long exposure. But it's as if he's hardly there. The little boy with his giant *kabutomushi*. He's melting into the lights, already inaccessible, already an object of desire, longing, and regret.

2.

CJ and I were here in Japan to find out about the two-decade-old craze for breeding, raising, and keeping stag beetles and rhinoceros beetles. We'd prepared in the usual way: by spending too much time Googling Japanese insect sites (of which there are many) and by talking to friends and reading the books and articles they recommended. By the time we met up in Tokyo, we knew that as well as generating widespread excitement, these big, shiny beetles so reminiscent of the chunky Japanese robot toys that swept the United States in the mid-1980s were also creating considerable anxiety among ecologists and conservationists and in Japan's venerable insect-collecting community.

But what we hadn't realized was the extent to which this beetle boom was part of a much larger phenomenon. Those *konchu-shonen* were a symptom. In our three weeks traveling in Tokyo and the Kansai region around Osaka, both of us were openmouthed at the abundance and diversity of human-insect life. Returning to Tokyo after four years in California, CJ—my research friend, translator, and up-for-anything traveling companion—confessed that although he must have lived most of his life in the midst of this insect world, he'd never really seen it before.

Because insects were everywhere! It was *insect culture,* something I'd never imagined. Insects had infiltrated a vast swath of everyday life. CJ and I pored over super-glossy hobby magazines with their beetle glamour spreads, spoof advice columns, and colorful accounts of exotic collecting expeditions. We studied pocket-size exhibitions and read xeroxed newsletters from suburban insect-lovers' clubs. We visited the geek-tech-culture *otaku* stalls in Akihabara, Tokyo's Electric City, and found pricey plastic beetles on sale alongside maid and Lolita fetish figurines. We ducked under low-hanging subway-car posters for *MushiKing*, Sega's warring-beetle trading-card and videogame phenomenon, and we watched kids battling one another with controlled intensity at the *MushiKing* consoles in city-center department stores. We bought soft drinks in convenience stores hoping for the free Fabre collectibles that came with them. We explored some of the scores of insectaria throughout the country and gaped at the glass-and-steel grandeur of the butterfly houses, monuments of the 1990s' bubble economy but also testament to a popular passion. We sat in smoke-filled coffee shops and on air-conditioned bullet trains reading the insect-themed serials in the biweekly mass-circulation manga anthologies (*Insectival Crime Investigator Fabre*, *Professor Osamushi*), a legacy not only of Tezuka's insect obsession but also of other manga pioneers, including Leiji Matsumoto, famous for his hyper-detailed drawings of future technology (cities, spaceships, robots—insects made metal). We YouTubed *Kuwagata Tsumami*, a cartoon for young kids about the super-cute mixed-species daughter of a *kuwagata* father and a human mother (don't ask!). We visited the country's oldest entomological store, Shiga Konchu Fukyu-sha, in Shibuya, Tokyo, which sells professional collecting equipment of its own design—collapsible butterfly nets, handcrafted wooden specimen boxes—of a quality to rival any in the world. We read about (but couldn't get to) the officially designated *hotaru* (firefly) towns, whose residents strive to capture the charisma of bioluminescence, to build a local tourist trade, and to pull in conservation funding as riverine habitats decline and firefly populations dwindle. (And, if we forgot the allure of the firefly, we were reminded every evening by the strains of "Hotaru no Hikari," "The Light of Fireflies," broadcast at closing time in stores and museums, a song about a poor fourth-century Chinese scholar studying by the light of a bag of fireflies, a song that every Japanese person seems to know, set to a tune—"Auld Lang Syne"—that every British person knows too.)

Of course, we took any opportunity we could to talk to people in the neighborhood insect pet stores, which were packed to the rafters with live *kuwagata* and *kabutomushi* in Perspex boxes and with the numerous products marketed for their care (dry food, supplements, mattresses, medicine, and so on), often in cute *kawaii* packaging depicting funny little bugs with big, emotion-filled eyes acting out in funny little poses. And we also saw the much sadder boxes in department stores crammed with too many too-agitated big beetles and skinny *suzumushi* bell crickets, all on sale at rock-bottom prices. One late night we stumbled upon a display of live beetles in a glass box in the lobby of a suburban train station, an encounter made surreal by the silence of the hour, the insistent sound of the animals' scratching, and the realization that they, we, and the battering moths were the only living beings on hand. Should we liberate them? We wanted to visit a *mushiokuri* festival to see how the driving out of the insects from the rice paddies—banned by the Meiji government in the early twentieth century as anti-scientific superstition—was being revived as a rural tradition in an ever-urbanizing, ever-reflective nation, but the closest event (at Iwami, overlooking the Sea of Japan in Shimane Prefecture) was just too far, given everything else we were cramming in, and the *mushiokuri* became another of those items we failed to cross off our to-do list.

Knowing our interests, everyone was keen to tell us about Japanese insect love. Look around you! Where else are fireflies, dragonflies, crickets, and beetles so esteemed? Did you know that the ancient name for Japan, Akitsu-shima, means "Dragonfly Island"? Have you heard "Aka Tombo," the Red Dragonfly song? Did you know that in the Edo period, the time of the Tokugawa shogunate, people would visit certain special places (Ochanomizu, in downtown Tokyo, was one) just to bask in the songs of their crickets or the lights of their fireflies? Did you read the classical literature? The eighth-century *Man'yo-shu* has seven poems about singing insects. The great classics of the Heian period, the *Pillow Book* of Sei Shonagon and Murasaki Shikibu's *Tale of Genji* contain butterflies, fireflies, mayflies, and crickets. Crickets are a symbol of autumn. Their songs are inseparable from the melancholy of life's transience. Cicadas are a sound of summer. Do you know haiku? Basho wrote, "The silence; / The voice of the cicadas / penetrates the rocks."[3] Do you know "The Lady Who Loved Worms"? She was the world's first entomologist. A twelfth-century entomologist! You know she was the inspiration for Miyazaki's famous Princess Nausicaä? Do you know Kawabata Yasunari's beautiful story of the grasshopper and the bell cricket? It's just a wisp of memory held together by two tiny insects. Have you read Koizumi Yakumo's writings on Japanese insects? Maybe you know him as Lafcadio Hearn? He had a British father but worked in America as a journalist. He became a Japanese citizen and died here in 1904. In his famous essay on cicadas, he wrote, "The Wisdom of the East hears all things. And he that obtains it will hear the speech of insects."[4] (And a few days later, over coffee in downtown Tokyo, Okumoto Daizaburo, literature professor, insect collector, and Fabre promoter, paraphrases his own book and rather sourly, though perhaps not unfairly, says of Hearn, the unashamed Japanophile and Orientalist who was also the translator of the definitive version of Flaubert's *Temptation of Saint Anthony*, "No one can find in others what they lack in themselves.") Please go to Nara! You must visit the Tamamushi-no-zushi shrine in the ancient Horyuji Temple. It was constructed in the sixth century from 9,000 scarab beetle carapaces!

These last suggestions came from Sugiura Tetsuya, an erudite and energetic docent volunteering at the Kashihara City Insectarium not far from Nara and its many ancient temples. In his younger days, Sugiura told us, he collected butterflies in Nepal and Brazil. Recently, he had donated his specimens to the insectarium in which he worked, where, as he pointed out, he was able to see them whenever he wished. He would, he said, have preferred to send them to a bigger and better-attended facility, like one of the Tokyo zoos—Ueno or, more likely, Tama, with its huge butterfly-shaped insectarium—but neither, disappointingly, had the capacity to accept donations.

It turned out it was Sugiura Tetsuya himself who had suggested the insect museum and butterfly house to the mayor of Kashihara when the plan for an aquarium turned out too expensive. He was kind enough to spend the entire afternoon explaining the museum's extensive collection to us and later sent a package to me in New York with a selection of Hearn's insect writings along with articles on many ancient items of interest, including one describing an elaborate insect box and other objects finished with lac—the resinous secretion of scale insects—that had been placed in the Shosoin, the Imperial Repository, near the Todaiji Temple in Nara in A.D. 756 and immaculately preserved to this day.

In the final room of the museum, after our exhaustive tour, Sugiura-san stopped at a case documenting the insect cuisine of Thailand and told us how Japanese visitors, schoolchildren especially, are disgusted by

this display and how they exclaim over the primitive habits of the Thais. I remember quite clearly, he continued with no change of expression, how I used to go into the mountains with my classmates after the war to collect locusts, which we would bring back to school and boil with shoyu. We also ate boiled silkworm larvae in those days, he said, and stopped only when the silk industry declined in the 1960s and the supply of insects dried up. It was hard-times food, but it was good food. It was part of our cuisine, but you would never know that now. It was the culture of the popular classes, he said, a culture rarely recorded and always forgotten.

3.

Sugiura Tetsuya had his doubts about the fashion for *kuwagata* and *kabutomushi*. He was happy to see so many children and families coming to Kashihara; he knew their enthusiasm was sparked by pet beetles and the runaway success of *MushiKing*, and he didn't want to discourage them. But like most collectors and insectarium people we met, he was anxious.

Yes, he agreed, the excitement over stag beetles and rhinoceros beetles was an expression of (and a stimulus to) the national enthusiasm for insects. But it brought problems all its own.

Nearby, at the Itami City Insectarium in Hyogo Prefecture, CJ and I stumbled onto an "insect carnival." Upstairs in the nature-study library, a crowd of high-spirited children and adults was creating some impressively complicated insect origami. We stopped at the "Befriend a Cockroach" table to learn how to handle the large live animals (stroke their backs gently, then pick them up carefully between thumb and forefinger and set them in your palm). All around, the walls were papered with exhibits by local insect-lovers' clubs: spreads from their newsletters, illustrated reports of environmental challenges met and often overcome, photos from field trips that showed smiling club members (varied in their ages but united in their enthusiasm).

Downstairs, the staff had given pride of place to *kuwagata* and *kabuto-mushi*. But they had also set free their psychedelic imagination. CJ read off the titles from the cases: "Wonderful Insects of the World," "Strange Insects of the World," "Beautiful Insects of the World," "Ninja Insects of the World." And across the room, "Surprising Insects of the Kansai Region." The Beautiful Insects formed an intricate mandala; the Ninja Insects (characterized by skillful camouflage) disguised themselves as a tiki mask; in one display, two tiny leaf bugs were dressed up in paper kimonos; in another, a host of gorgeous blue morpho butterflies floated between glass, spotlit to magnify their irridescence. Hard not to love this place, we agreed. Part science center, part art museum, part amusement park. A place to celebrate our inner insect.

Just before "Hotaru no Hikari" rang out for closing time, we bumped into a museum guide and a curator in the hallway. They talked the same language as Sugiura, found themselves caught in the same contradictions. The emphasis on the spectacular imported insects made them uneasy. But they felt compelled to promote those big foreign species even though they believed that doing so placed Japanese beetles in peril.

Some backstory is in order here. The right person to tell it is Iijima Kazuhiko, who works at Mushi-sha, the largest and best known of Tokyo's many insect stores. Most of these are pet stores, overflowing with beetles and the paraphernalia needed to keep them. Most cater to ele-

mentary school boys, their indulgent (or perhaps long-suffering) mothers, and a smaller
number of middle-aged men who buy the
more expensive animals. Most of the stores
have appeared since 1999, the year the current
beetle boom really took off.

But Mushi-sha, Iijima Kazuhiko explained,
doesn't quite fit this profile. It reaches across
two insect worlds, joining the preteen *Mushi-
King* fans to the scholarly collectors like Sugiura Tetsuya and Yoro Takeshi. Since it opened
its doors, in 1971, the store has continually
published *Gekkan-mushi* (*Insect Monthly*), a
respected entomology journal, and has sold
specimens, boxes, and collecting tools. In those early days, its customers
were serious amateurs and professional entomologists, *konchu-shonen*
old and young who were building collections primarily by catching their
own insects.

It was in the 1980s that Mushi-sha began selling live animals. Back
then, Iijima told us, it was *ookuwagata,* the large Japanese stag beetles that
Kuwachan breeds, that were in demand. They had become difficult to find
in urban areas but were still easily available in the countryside, and it was
commonplace there for children to keep them as pets. Some stag beetles
lived in the mountains, mostly in Osaka, Saga, and Yamanashi Prefec-
tures. But most made their homes close to villages, in *satoyama,* the
patches of forest that people managed for mushrooms, edible plants, timber, compost, and charcoal, among other useful goods.[5] Over time, the
burned and coppiced charcoal trees came to look like dark knobs, Iijima
said, and it was in the holes in those trees that the *kuwagata* lived. *Kuwagata* were at home in *satoyama,* he told us, because they like being close to
humans.

Iijima explained that the *kuwagata* and *kabutomushi* boom of the
1980s was stimulated by an increased supply of insects to the cities at a
time of high disposable income, before the collapse of the bubble economy. Recognizing the signs of urban demand and developing more
effective trapping techniques, villagers brought beetles to Tokyo from

the countryside, selling them to department stores and pet shops. Some urban enthusiasts went the other way, deepening their hobby by traveling to the country to catch beetles themselves (and plant the seeds of the informal network of rural inns that now advertise their services as beetle-hunting bases). Others became interested in breeding beetles. Both larvae and adult beetles were available to buy and hobbyists started investing their time in developing techniques for raising bigger animals. This shift to breeding was a significant innovation, said Iijima. Even though back then no one managed to raise beetles as large as the ones found in *satoyama* or the mountains, many people took up the challenge. Not surprisingly, it was in these years of growth—both in the economy and in the passion for beetles—that most of the country's insectaria opened.

The real estate boom that swept Japan in those years transformed the countryside. As demand for charcoal fell and brick replaced timber in home construction, the maintenance of managed forest declined; as housing developments expanded, *satoyama* retreated. By the early 1990s, it was challenging even for local people to find large stag beetles in the wild. For most visitors from the city, it was far harder. Prices of wild insects soared. Yet by this point there was a thriving subculture of beetle breeders throughout the country—amateur experts like Kuwachan who succeeded in mapping the life cycles and habits of the popular species and in developing and circulating sophisticated yet easily replicated techniques for raising large animals from eggs.[6]

It was a complex story, but Iijima Kazuhiko was a patient narrator. Like everyone we met in Mushi-sha, he was young, friendly, knowledgeable about all aspects of the business, and serious about insects. We were standing at the back of the store, in front of a large, indexed cabinet full of high-quality specimens from around the world and beside tall stacks of *Gekkan-mushi, Be-kuwa!, Kuwagata Magazine,* and other glossy and expensive specialist publications. On all sides were shelves of Perspex containers holding male and female *kuwagata* and *kabutomushi* of varying sizes and prices. From behind the counter Iijima pulled out a large foam-lined case. Inside—huge, soft bodied, and defenseless, motionless on its back—was a metamorphosed beetle pupa. It was a male *Dynastes hercules,* the largest of the rhinoceros beetles, recorded as growing to just over seven inches, and worth well over U.S. $1,000. A small group of admiring customers gathered to look.

In the 1990s, continued Iijima after returning the case, there were three types of enthusiasts. There were those who went to the mountains to hunt beetles; they were working in the tradition of the old-time collec-

tors, but it was, of course, much harder now for them to find insects. Then there were those, usually schoolboys, who purchased inexpensive live beetles and kept them as pets. Finally, there were those who bought larvae or adult pairs and bred

them as a hobby or for sale, often trying to set the record for the largest individual of the particular species. Indeed, he said, by that point it was much easier to breed *kuwagata* and *kabutomushi* than to catch them.

Despite (and because of) the decline in wild beetles and the destruction of their habitat, beetle keeping and raising was thriving. Mushi-sha was at the center of a lively entrepreneurial culture serving both a new generation of insect fans and an aging but rejuvenated cadre of experts. When CJ and I met Okumoto Daizaburo a few days later, he readily took on the task of explaining why it was that all this insect love existed here in Japan. Professor Okumoto used arguments we had heard from other insect people, arguments that described a uniquely caring Japanese relationship with nature and drew on *nihonjinron,* the persistent ideology of Japanese exceptionalism, which, like many nationalisms, is based on a belief in a unified national population possessing a unique transhistorical essence.[7]

The beetle boom, Okumoto said, was just one piece of a special national affinity for nature. He talked about the high species endemism of the country's island ecosytem and how this unusual variety of animals and plants, and of insects in particular, produced an exceptional sensitivity among the human population. He talked about earthquakes and typhoons and how these too-familiar events created a visceral awareness of the surrounding environment. He talked about the role of animism, Shintoism, and Buddhism in creating an intimate environmental ethic that still pervades Japanese daily life despite the decline in overt religious practice. He talked about the audiologist Tsunoda Tadanobu's controversial research in the 1970s, which suggested that Japanese brains are singularly attuned to natural sounds, including cricket song.[8] He talked about the extraordinary expressions of high cultural attachment to insects in literature and painting. And borrowing my notebook, he drew a diagram—a schematic representation of an ideal Japanese life, which CJ later annotated for me.

It was an ideal man's ideal life, timeless but classical, the ideal life of a scholar or nobleman. Professor Okumoto offered it as a sketch of enduring national tradition, an elegantly simple capsule of a complex ideology. He depicted three ages of man in an arc from youth to dotage, from carefree friends chasing dragonflies and goldfish to the sunset years of meditative solitude; he described how each stage has objects and activities appropriate to the correct forms of self-cultivation (from *kabutomushi* and fireflies through *ka-cho-fu-getsu*—flower-bird-wind-moon, the contemplation of the subtleties of nature—to the care of chrysanthemums); and he explained that these simple practices can (even in such an elementary version) create a meaningful Japanese life.

As the professor talked, it struck me and CJ that these forms of play, culture, and contemplation were an aspiration, a promise of contentment and fulfillment that tied together many of the insect people we had met. His sketch reminded us of the yearning for emotional purity at the heart of Kuwachan's insect poems. It was a framing for the stories of insect love as a formative stage in the making of a whole person. Antithetical to urbanized, bureaucratized modern life, unattainable by most people even in childhood, as a model for a form of life, its role was largely critique. It was part of that family of utopian insect stories that included Miyazaki's hippie town, Tezuka's secret jungle, Kuwachan's poetry, and those hopeful weekends of *kazoku* service. And, like those stories, it helped explain some of the emotional burden that Japanese insects were asked to assume and some of the desires that they seemed so readily to bear.

4.

Before 1999, most Japanese insect lovers knew foreign stag and rhinoceros beetles through magazines, television, and museums. These animals were often bigger and more spectacular than the local species; many had longer horns and antlers, larger bodies, and showier coloring. But under the Plant Protection Act of 1950, it was illegal for private collectors to bring them into Japan. There was, however, no penalty for owning or selling restricted animals once they were in the country, and that anomaly enabled a lively black market, extravagant prices, and a profitable smuggling industry reputedly controlled by the *yakuza*. Still, the number of animals involved was relatively small and the well-heeled collectors involved were a select set.

The Plant Protection Act compiles lists of animals considered "detrimental" to native plants and agriculture. However, it has an unusual precautionary protocol: all species are classed as detrimental until authorized for entry at a plant protection station. In 1999, under pressure from collectors eager to know which beetles were permitted, the Ministry of Agriculture, Forestry, and Fisheries published a list on its website of 485 stag beetles and 53 rhinoceros beetles considered "nondetrimental."[9] Within two years, 900,000 live *kuwagata* and *kabutomushi* had been imported.[10] Even so, in succeeding years the ministry added more species to its list until, by 2003, 505 species of stag beetle had been authorized out of a worldwide total of around 1,200 described species. As the entomologists Kouichi Goka, Hiroshi Kojima, and Kimiko Okabe commented drily, "The habitat maintaining the highest biodiversity of stag beetles is Japanese pet shops."[11] In 2004, they estimated the value of the import trade at ¥10 billion (about U.S.$100 million). Large individuals of desirable species were selling in Tokyo for upward of U.S.$3,300.[12]

The scale of the growth in live-insect imports was completely unexpected. Iijima Kazuhiko told us that the Ministry of Agriculture, Forestry, and Fisheries ignored warnings from the Ministry of the Environment but, nonetheless, the government had no idea what it was unleashing. However, he added, there were high-profile precedents that should have been cause for hesitation: animals such as the black bass, the raccoon, the small Indian mongoose, and the European bumblebee *Bombus terrestris*, which are infamous in Japan for adapting too successfully to their new environment. But when it came to beetles, policy makers and scientists were confident that foreign *kuwagata* and *kabutomushi*, most of which come from subtropical and tropical Southeast Asia and Central and South America, would be unable to survive the harsh Japanese winter. Only later did they realize that many of those animals' home ranges were at high altitudes in cooler temperatures.[13]

The import boom crested quickly. By 2001, the number of beetles entering Japan had fallen significantly from its height, and as the supply increased, the prices for all but the rarest (and largest) slumped too.[14] But even with reduced quantities, it was evident that the boom had radically expanded the breadth of the trade. New insect shops had opened their doors, and existing pet stores had retooled. Large department stores were carrying imported species. For a while, live beetles were available from vending machines. All kinds of products that made rais-

ing and caring for the animals simpler and more appealing were brought to the market (individual servings of food in jelly form, "fungus jars" of habitat medium, deodorizing powders, cute carrying cases). Most significantly, an unknown but anecdotally vast number of people had taken up beetle breeding. Between 1997 and 2001, seven glossy specialist magazines were founded that offered advice to breeders, ran competitions, featured stories of intrepid collectors, shaped a sense of beetle aesthetics, and nurtured the emerging communities of enthusiasts.[15]

Struggling to account for the surging appeal of pet insects, the author of the insect section of the Japan External Trade Organization's *Marketing Guidebook for Major Imported Products* for 2004 pointed out that beetles "require little time and energy to take care of. They do not need to be fed anywhere in particular, and their pens take up only a small amount of space on top of a desk. . . . [They] do not make noise and they do not have to be taken outdoors for exercise."[16] This seemed like an uncontroversial if superficial explanation, but the correlative claim that much of the market expansion was due to twenty-something urban women attracted to low-maintenance companion species was more dubious. Despite the apparent democratization of the hobby, despite the eager participation of some schoolgirls in summer insect projects, despite the success of insect-loving female role models such as Miyazaki's Princess Nausicaä, and despite Sega's girls-only *MushiKing* events, Iijima Kazuhiko—in line with other people CJ and I spoke to—estimated that even if the total number of female insect lovers was growing, only 1 in 100 of the enthusiasts who shopped at Mushi-sha were women, a proportion that had changed little over the years. Most of the women entering the store, he said, were chaperoning their sons. Instead, insect-loving women and girls were rare enough to warrant a satirical column in *Be-kuwa!* purportedly written by a beetle-crazy dominatrix-ish *Sex and the City*–ish girl-about-town (the continuing joke being the incongruity of the glamorous Ms. Shoko's passion for insects).

Yet there was absolutely no question that the overall base was rapidly increasing. Professional insect specialists found themselves yearning for the calm old days. The stern price discipline reputedly enforced by the *yakuza* no longer seemed so grim. Stories circulated of families, tired of pet keeping or sorry for the animal cooped up in its plastic box, driving out of town and releasing their *kuwagata* in the woods. Reports surfaced of large caches of imported beetles discovered in the countryside: surplus stock abandoned by breeders and store owners who had fallen victim to too-rapid expansion. ("It's only the people like me, who were in this for love rather than money, who have survived," Kuwachan told us.)

More embarrassing, a series of high-profile cases involving the arrest of Japanese nationals caught smuggling quantities of prohibited beetles out of Taiwan, Australia, and various Southeast Asian countries revealed that the incentives and possibilities for trafficking had only increased with liberalization. Similarly, surveys of Japanese insect stores found a substantial number of beetles on sale that were not only prohibited for collection in their countries of origin but also prohibited in Japan under the Plant Protection Act and, in some cases, listed under CITES, the Convention on International Trade in Endangered Species.[17]

The environmental impact of the expanding Japanese market on the countries of origin was one concern for conservationists. But they also found three issues closer to home to worry about.[18] Adult stag and rhinoceros beetles are vegetarians, living on tree sap and plant juices. The larvae and imagoes are important in the early stages of forest decomposition, mechanically breaking up decayed wood and creating the conditions for microorganisms to do their work. Beyond this, though, not much is known about their ecology. The obvious possibility was that powerful newcomers that liked similar niches would outcompete local species for food and habitat, threatening both the Japanese beetles and their food source. Goka and his colleagues were also concerned that the foreign beetles would bring unknown parasitic mites, which could undermine local beetle populations—in the same way that the varroa mite, exported from Japan with commercial hives, has devastated the European honeybee. And they worried, too, about the reduction of genetic diversity through interbreeding. Back in the lab, they created a "Frankenstein stag beetle," successfully mating a female Sumatran *Dorcus titanus*—a popular pet—with a male from one of Japan's twelve endemic subspecies. The sex wasn't pretty, with the Indonesian female using what the scientists called "violent cruelty" to force herself on the reluctant Japanese male. But the resulting larvae grew into large fertile hybrids, similar to other hyphenated Japanese beetles that the scientists later collected in the wild, making real the troubling specter of genetic introgression.[19]

In 2003, just as the beetle craze seemed to be cooling off, Sega launched *MushiKing*. Targeted at elementary school children, it was exciting, addictive, and elegantly simple, efficiently bringing together its audience's passions for big beetles, obsessive collecting, competitive gaming, and souped-up graphics. Very soon it was Japan's biggest-selling game franchise since *Pokémon* (and was doing quick business in Korea, Taiwan, Malaysia, Hong Kong, Singapore, Indonesia, Thailand, and the Philippines, too).

Sega rolled out a ruthlessly effective promotional campaign. They staged hundreds of thousands of tournaments and demonstration matches. They set up banks of console machines in department stores and hypermarkets. They flooded the country with ads. In 2005, they announced versions of *MushiKing* for Nintendo DS, Game Boy, and other handheld devices. That year Sega began a spin-off anime series on Tokyo TV. In 2006, they released the anticipated blockbuster movie.

There was no question that *MushiKing* added value to the commercialization of stag and rhinoceros beetles. Nor that in doing so it intensi-

fied the paradoxes. Its mention provoked resigned smiles from the curator and docent in the hallway of the Itami City Insectarium, just as it did
in similar conversations elsewhere. This was the summer of 2005, the
height of the phenomenon, and it was obvious that the game had crys-
tallized many insect people's ambivalence about the form the beetle
boom was taking. Keen as they were to inspire the public, happy as they
were to see the excitement with which children entered their museums
and stores, they had little enthusiasm for the game's elevation of beetle
belligerence and worried about the narrowing of these animals' identities to their most mechanical aspects, worried that children would think
of them as tough toys, not living creatures.

But Sega anticipated the unease. As if to mock both fears and hopes,
they wrapped *MushiKing* in a package that compounded the ironies. The
game wasn't just an intensification. It was an environmental parable,
and its plot was the same classic story that the insect people themselves
were trying to tell.

MushiKing described the destruction of Japan's indigenous fauna by
an invading army of fugitive imported beetles. And it enlisted Japanese

A long time ago, there was a lush, green forest.
Many beetles lived in peacefully in the forest.

However, a terrible thing was happening
in this peaceful forest.
Beetles that humans had brought from countries
far away had escaped from their cages, and entered
into the forest.

children in the fight to save the nation's endangered species. It was an apocalypse story in the tradition of the monster movies and TV shows that first made *kuwagata* and *kabutomushi* popular in the mid-1960s. It lifted its instantly recognizable plotlines from pop media, and it revealed that the scientists were drawing on those sources too. Sega and the entomologists were telling the same story. They were telling it to the same audience. And as was obvious, Sega was telling it much more seductively.

5.

Before *MushiKing*, before the Plant Protection Act, before Mushi-sha, before inflatable *kabutomushi* in summer festivals, before insect figurines in Akihabara, before the "Befriend a Cockroach" table at the Itami City Insectarium, before Kuwachan quit his salaried job to sell *kuwagata* full-time, before Sugiura Tetsuya came home from Brazil with butterflies, before Miyazaki turned the Lady Who Loved Worms into Princess Nausicaä, before Tezuka turned Jiminy Cricket into Astro Boy, before Yoro Takeshi and his school friends hiked the mountains of Kamakura, before all of that—though after so much else—Yajima Minoru, still a *konchu-shonen*, a fourteen-year-old boy stumbling through a dark nightmare of personal and collective trauma, stood on the lip of a water-filled crater among the smoldering remains of wood-frame Tokyo—a city all but obliterated in the firestorm ordered up by Robert McNamara—and there, on the rim of the bomb crater, as all around him people scrabbled in the ruins for the remnants of their lives, he watched a dragonfly settle on a floating shard of wood and, as if nothing were any different, lay her eggs in the stagnant water. "That dragonfly didn't care about all the corpses," he wrote fifty years later, the image still vivid in his mind. "In the midst of that terrible reality, in spite of everything that was going on around her, she was alive and strong."[20]

Yajima-san survived the war, but only just. He writes of what he witnessed as if from a dream, a trauma-dream with all its strange infoldings of linear time. The thousands of burned and rotting corpses. The young woman alone in a charred field cradling two bundles: under one arm her colorful kimonos, under the other the blackened body of her child. Tokyo is a "sea of fire." Outside the factory in which he was working, he watches shrapnel explode as if in slow motion. He sees people dig useless shallow trenches in the ground for shelter, uncomprehending of the power of the B-29s. After the night of the Great Tokyo Air Raid, in which more die than even at Hiroshima, he watches the survivors gather up the piles of burned bodies. At a train station, caught in a stampeding crowd strafed by an American aircraft, a man, shot dead, falls on top of him.

Yajima-san was a sickly child. In the years leading up to the war, he came down with jaundice and spent a long time at home unable to attend school. Every day on the radio, he heard news of the successes of the Japanese military. Around him, the excitement mounted. In middle school, the students were told they were no longer children. Military exercises were compulsory. His classmates craved the honor of sacrificing themselves for the nation. His sickness, they said, was evidence of a weak mind. When he again fell ill, he was not permitted to be absent from school. As militarism increased, his health deteriorated further.

After the war, he contracted lung disease. His uncle, shell-shocked in the air raids, had moved to Saitama, in those days outside Tokyo and a place of rural calm. Here, exploring the countryside, Yajima Minoru recovered his connection to the natural world, to the dragonflies, tadpoles, ant lions, and cicadas he'd played with while in elementary school. In the fall, he helped supplement the household's diet of poor-quality American relief bread and corned beef with locusts from the rice fields. If you observe locusts closely, he says now, you see that their eyes are really *kawaii,* and—just as cute—you see that when people approach, the animals move around to the opposite side of the rice stalk. In those days, though, it was all hunger all the time, and he thought of the insects only as food, doing his best to trap as many of them as possible.

In 1946, his doctor ordered a year of rest. Yajima moved back to Tokyo and discovered Osugi's translation of Fabre's *Souvenirs entomologiques.* He was fascinated by the way Fabre looked so closely at his animals and by how he reasoned from analogy. He was deeply impressed that the Insect Poet asked his questions of the living creatures he saw around him at l'Harmas; he was moved by Fabre's curiosity and the vigor of his writing, and by the way he took you into the insects' world, a world Yajima so badly needed at that moment.

Inspired, he spent five months studying the natural history of the swallowtail butterflies near his home. Just a short time before, a train full of students had been massacred on this spot by a U.S. plane. Often, he just sat and stared at the animals fluttering over the scene, immobilized by their life force and beauty, just as he was by the dragonfly in the bomb crater during the war. Looking back now, he sees his immersion in the swallowtails as the therapeutic compulsion that released him from the weight of the war and its afterlife.

Perhaps, as it does me, this story makes you think of Cornelia Hesse-Honegger, Li Shijun, Joris Hoefnagel, Karl von Frisch, Martin Landauer,

Jean-Henri Fabre himself, and of other people for whom an insect universe provided an often-unexpected refuge. Perhaps it brings to mind people who, to put it another way, entered the world of insects and were, in turn, entered by it, who at times were swallowed up by it and who at other times found their bearings inside it, such that the normal scale of existence—the standard hierarchies of being—in which we know small things because they are physically smaller than we are and we know lesser things because they lack our capacities, was no longer a basis for either action or meaning, and such that the enormity of the circumstances that bound their lives could assume another proportion and a different place in their world, such that the world itself could become immeasurably larger and unconfining.

At some point during the solitary months spent observing swallowtails, Yajima Minoru made the decision to dedicate his life to studying insects. It was almost sixty years later when CJ and I met him for lunch in a cafeteria in the Tocho, Tokyo's monumental two-towered city hall. By then he was one of Japan's most eminent biologists, the creator of the world's first butterfly houses, a maker of popular nature films, a leading conservationist, the pioneering developer of numerous insect-breeding protocols, and a science educator committed especially to sharing his love of insects with children. He was full of energy, telling us eagerly about his newest project, Gunma Insect World, which includes a spectacular butterfly house (designed by the architect Tadao Ando) and a substantial area of community-restored *satoyama*. It was due to open the next day, and we were all disappointed that CJ and I wouldn't have time to visit. Yajima-san was kind, unassuming, generous with his time, and infectiously positive. We talked for a long while and afterward posed for photographs, tiny as ants in front of the colossal municipal building.

6.

The destruction of Tokyo was also the destruction of a thriving commercial insect culture centered in the city. "We were back to the beginning," wrote the historian Konishi Masayasu, referring to the *mushi-uri*, itinerant sellers of singing insects who had first appeared in Osaka and Edo (Tokyo) in the late seventeenth century and who reappeared after the war to hawk their cages in the ruins of the capital.[21]

It's not difficult to imagine the special importance at that moment of these animals, with their bittersweet songs of melancholy and transience, their cultural intimacy, and their unconditional companionship. But the *mushi-uri* were not walking the streets by choice. The bombings had destroyed Tokyo's insect stores, and although the traders soon managed to set up roadside stalls in the Ginza shopping district, even then they were still back at the beginning: their breeding infrastructure had collapsed, and like the original *mushi-uri*, the postwar traders were simply selling animals they trapped in the fields.

Japanese insect traders had known how to breed *suzumushi* (bell crickets) and other popular insects by the late eighteenth century. They had also discovered that by raising larvae in earthenware pots, they could accelerate the insects' development cycle and increase the supply of salable singers, inventing techniques that are still in use today (among cricket breeders in Shanghai, for instance). Konishi describes a florescence of insect culture under the Tokugawa shogunate, that long period of relative isolation, from 1603 to 1867, when the possibility of external travel for Japanese people was strictly limited and the only point of entry for foreigners was through the port of Nagasaki. He notes the existence of clubs for the study of animals and plants in Nagoya, Toyama, and elsewhere; he describes the biennial residence in Edo of the daimyo, the feudal lords, during which the notables and their intellectual allies spent their leisure time collecting, identifying, and classifying insects; and he discusses the long-standing scholarly interest in and gradual incorporation of *honzo*, Chinese materia medica, a healing corpus that includes not just plants and minerals but insects and other animals.[22] Rather than making specimens in the manner of the European naturalists, these insect lovers, the *mushi-fu*, preserved their collections in paintings annotated with observations, dates, and locations. Prominent artists such as Maruyama Okyo (1733–95), Morishima Churyo (1754–1810), and Kurimoto Tanshu (1756–1834), whose *Senchufu* is one of the incomparable treasures of the period, painted from life to produce portraits of insects and other creatures that not only were outstanding in their delicacy and precision but also were organized serially in a way that prefigured the arrangement of the *zukan* guides used by insect collectors today.

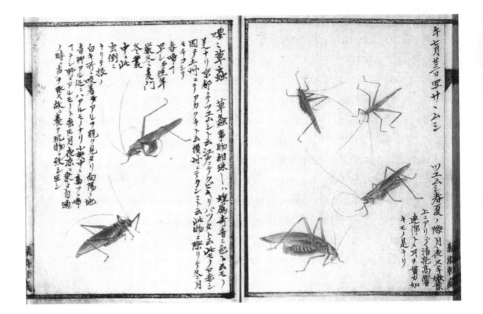

Konishi calls the Tokugawa shogunate the "larval stage" of Japanese insect studies. Despite their commitment and ingenuity, without sustained interaction with Western naturalists the *mushi-fu* were merely incubating their passion, he says, awaiting the external stimulus that would trigger its transformation. To Konishi, it was only through the energy unleashed in the Meiji period (1868–1912), with its eager embrace and importation of Western knowledge, that Japanese insect love entered the modern world and found its adult form. That moment of modernity can be dated to 1897 and the response of the Meiji government to the invasion of the national rice harvest by *unka* leafhoppers. In Japan, as in Europe and North America, entomology—the study of insects according to Western scientific principles—was tied from the beginning to pest control and the management of human and agricultural health.

This journey from enthusiasm to entomology is a standard narrative of Japanese science and technology, late on the scene but quick to play catch-up. As an account of a passage from darkness to light it closely parallels the conventional narrative of the scientific revolution in Enlightenment Europe two centuries earlier. But as many scholars have pointed out, these histories not only rather take for granted the Enlightenment/ Meiji belief in the superiority of science over other forms of knowledge but also assume too easily the distinction between them, underestimating the continuities that tie earlier ways of understanding nature to those that come to count as modern, and overlooking the fact that enthusiasms and instrumentalities persist together side by side and often without contradiction or conflict, in the same pet store, in the same magazine, in the same laboratory, even in the same person.[23]

On the other hand, there's little doubt about the surge of energy in Meiji Japan that resulted in insect love being recast in entomological terms and supported by an array of institutional innovations. Konishi describes the "fever" for beetles and butterflies that took hold among biology students at the newly formed Tokyo University (1877); the groundbreaking publication of *Saichu shinam* (1883), a handbook of advice on collecting, preserving specimens, and breeding (drawn largely from Western sources) by Tanaka Yoshio, the founder of Tokyo's Ueno Zoo; and the opening of three stores in Yokohama selling Okinawan and Taiwanese butterflies to sailors and other foreign visitors.

Half a century later, the descendants of the first patrons of those butterfly stores would bomb the emergent industry back to its eighteenth-century beginnings. Somehow, Japanese insect culture recovered with the same alacrity that had allowed it to seize upon Western science in the years following the Meiji Restoration. Somehow, the survivors of the destruction of 1945 drew strength from trauma. Yajima-san meditates on the life force of the dragonfly laying her eggs in the flooded bomb crater. Shiga Usuke, the founder of the country's most eminent insect store, describes how he buried his precious supply of specimen pins in one of those shallow Tokyo bomb shelters and how, returning after the war to find them rusted and useless, set about designing more durable equipment, succeeding many years later in manufacturing instruments from stainless steel.

7.

Shiga Usuke was born in 1903 into a family of landless peasants in the mountains of Niigata Prefecture, northwest of Tokyo.[24] Like Yajima Minoru, he was a sickly child who spent much of his time confined to his home—in Shiga's case because of malnutrition. When he was five, he went blind after a simple cold turned into a fever. Each week, his father carried him three and a half miles to the nearest doctor. Eventually, Shiga-san regained the vision in his right eye but not in his left.

Despite his poor health and having to work to help his family, Shiga-san was an outstanding student and, as a result, was sent to Tokyo for high school. Unlike the insect men whom CJ and I encountered, he was never a *konchu-shonen*. In fact, he writes, he had little awareness of his environment and no memory of ever hunting insects as a child. He explains this as an effect of poverty and sickness and his preoccupation with work, but quickly interjects a doubt: are these simply excuses for the insensitivity he once had to nature, an insensitivity, he adds, that was normal among those around him?

High school was uneventful. He worked in his headmaster's household and graduated at fifteen. It was then that he found a position at the Hirayama Insect Specimen Store in Tokyo, one of only a very few businesses in the city that made specimens for collectors.

Hirayama employed two workers. One was assigned to the store and one to the household. Shiga-san was the household servant, tasked with cooking, shopping, and cleaning. Despite this, he soon began to take notice of the store's collection. Surrounded by insects, he started to see things he'd never seen before. He looked closely and observed differences, details of color, shape, and texture. He found himself looking more carefully, finding the specimens more interesting, excited by their unexpected beauty. Very quickly he determined to make a life as an insect professional. Soon he was bribing the store apprentice with candies to show him how to collect—at that time, houses in the city were surrounded by green space, and it was easy to find insects—and how to prepare specimens. But even as he became fascinated by all the variety, it also overwhelmed him. How could he ever hope to master this field? Hirayama carried no books or good-quality *zukan* in which to explore, and the store owner had no interest in furthering Shiga's ambitions. Thrown back on his own resources, he stole time to study the shop's collection, memorizing the names of species and matching them with the number and patterns of wing spots and the size and shapes of the markings.

Among Hirayama's insects, he was in a dreamworld. Seen through a hand lens, every specimen was astounding, especially the butterflies. But back in the world of men, things were different. People were constantly reproaching him: why did he waste his time on this dross? Their contempt was intimidating and oppressive. Even his father—an open-minded man who supported his impoverished family by fixing umbrellas, making balloons, giving massages and acupuncture, and telling fortunes, and who was gaining a reputation as a midwife (an occupation forbidden to men)—was hostile to his work. People judged insects only according to whether they were useful or dangerous. It was acceptable to eliminate them but not to collect them. Away from Hirayama, Shiga-san remembers, he felt that he, too, was just a *mushi*.

In those days, insect collecting was confined to a small section of the social elite. Hirayama's customers were drawn largely from the *kazoku*, the Meiji hereditary peerage. Rather than following the Tokugawa daimyo in catching the animals themselves, these men ordered their insects from the specialist stores. They coveted specimens as cultural capital in what they considered the manner of the European aristocracy, displaying them alongside other high-value objects in the guest rooms of their houses. At the same time, the formation of boys' insect-study associations across the country was a sign that the government's support of scientific entomology was stimulating a wider interest. However, with boxes imported from Germany and nets made of silk, the essential tools for collecting remained prohibitively expensive.

In 1931, Shiga Usuke left Hirayama to start his own store. He was motivated both by the need to escape his exploitative situation and by a determination to make the world of insects available to everyone, not just the wealthy. And like Yajima Minoru, he wanted especially to reach out to children. He states his belief clearly: if people care for insects when they're young, they grow up with an ethic of care that extends not only to nature and the smallest creatures but also to all beings—human and otherwise—that surround them. He named his new business Shiga Konchu Fukyu-sha, Shiga's Insect Popularization Store, signaling both his modernity and his pedagogical intentions with the scientific term *konchu* rather than the idiomatic *mushi*.

Shiga-san threw all his creative energies into his new enterprise. To draw passersby, he placed tables on the sidewalk outside the store and staged demonstrations of specimen mounting. Not satisfied with the size of his audience, he struck a deal with Tokyo's four leading department stores—sophisticated, contemporary venues that captured the spirit of the new science he was promoting. He and his friend Isobe would spend a week in the stationery section of each store answering questions at special insect-inquiry booths and demonstrating Shiga's proprietary collecting tools: the low-cost collapsible pocket-insect-collecting net and new copper, nickel, and zinc pins, all of his own design. The demonstration sessions quickly became popular. Children flocked to the events, eager to ask questions. Seeing them staring so intently at his hands as he worked, Shiga-san recognized himself in his first days at Hirayama's store and felt happy.

This was 1933. That year a new magazine, *Konchukai* (Insect World), started to publish field reports from middle school students around the

country. About the same time, Shiga Usuke began to receive orders for mounted specimens from schools (orders he refused, deciding that students would learn more by preparing their own specimens than by viewing ready-mades). Those years saw the establishment of insect stores, magazines, entomology clubs and associations, networks of professional and amateur collectors, and university departments of entomology— and not only in Tokyo, Osaka, and Kyoto but also in small towns and in many parts of the country. The rising popularity of insect study was clear, as was the maturing of its culture and infrastructure. Indeed, these were the years in which that density of people and institutions came into being which enabled insect commerce to recover so rapidly from the ravages of military defeat.

But for Shiga Usuke, this prewar growth of insect culture did little to displace the elite character of insect collecting. There may have been more children handling more specimens than ever before, but so far as he could see, they all still came from exclusive schools and wealthy families. Rather than the story of the essential national affinity for insects CJ and I heard from Okumoto Daizaburo and others, Shiga Usuke describes class-based practices of insect love and insect hostility that are selective in their objects (crickets, jewel beetles, *kuwagata*, dragonflies, fireflies, houseflies) and vary across time. Some of those practices, such as chasing dragonflies and listening to crickets and cicadas, have appealed both to the connoisseur and to a wider public. Some, such as the use of insects for food, have long been restricted, as Sugiura Tetsuya pointed out, to poorer people in now-gone times and places. Some, such as the use of insects in healing (cockroaches for chilblains, frostbite, and meningitis, for instance), became less widespread as *kampo* medicine, based on Chinese materia medica, was first banned in the Meiji era and then rehabilitated in the limited form of complementary, primarily herbal therapies alongside allopathic medicine. Collecting, the scholarly activity to which Shiga, Yoro, Sugiura, and Okumoto are committed (the activity that places them in the august aristocratic tradition of the daimyo and the more ambivalent aristocratic tradition of the European colonial naturalists, as well as in the satisfyingly iconoclastic lineage of Jean-Henri Fabre), begins to generalize from its origins only with Japan's postwar economic expansion, the rise of pop-culture media, and the creation of a new middle class equipped with surplus income and the leisure time in which to enjoy it. Other practices, most obviously the breeding and raising of *kuwagata* and *kabutomushi*, arrive as something new and unsettling, attracting a new type of *konchu-shonen* with new experiences, new insect equipment—manga, anime, inflatable beetles!— and newly complicated ideas of what an insect might mean in their and their families' lives.

As well as expendable income, the unprecedented economic growth of the postwar era brought the unforeseen shock of environmental disaster, most famously with the mercury poisoning at Minamata, in Kumamoto Prefecture, in 1956 and again in Niigata in 1965. A growing sense of national dystopia contributed to the emergence of new forms of nature appreciation and protection. The first *mushi* boom, a combination of new consumerism and new environmentalism, arrived in the mid-1960s. Inspired, as we have seen, by the stars of the *kaiju* (strange-beast) movies—especially the very popular Mothra, a butterfly-moth monster who uses her powers for good—and "special effects" TV series like *Ultraman*, as well as by the insect creations of Tezuka Osamu and other manga pioneers, it fixed on butterflies, *kuwagata*, and *kabutomushi* as its objects of desire. For the first time, the big beetles, considered ugly for centuries, were in greater demand than the *suzumushi* and their singing comrades.

These years saw the publication of affordable insect encyclopedias, high-quality field guides, new collectors' magazines, and in 1966, the opening of the butterfly-shaped insectarium at Tokyo's Tama Zoo (one of Yajima Minoru's first major projects). Perhaps most tellingly, these were the years when the summer collecting assignment became a fixture of the elementary and middle school curricula.

These were also the years when Shiga Usuke—who would soon receive an award from Emperor Hirohito for his collecting tools, an award, he said, that for the first time made him feel accepted in his profession— petitioned the Ministry of Education to stop department stores from selling live butterflies and beetles. They were, he said, encouraging students to cheat on their summer projects: teachers were unable the tell the difference between store-bought and wild animals. Actually, Shiga-san added, teachers were giving higher marks for the purchased ones because they were in better condition. How could students learn anything from insects if they were just one more commodity? The ministry agreed, and the stores went back to selling specimens and Shiga-san's innovative and beautiful collecting instruments. It was only in the 1990s, with the rise of the insect pet shops, the liberalization of imports, the heightened commercialization of the *mushi* trade, and Shiga's rearguard action long forgotten, that the stores once more began stocking their shelves with beetles.

8.

Soon after Sega released *MushiKing*, the Ministry of the Environment began hearings on a major new piece of conservation legislation. The Invasive Alien Species Act was designed to remedy the gaps in the Plant Protection Act that had allowed the black bass, the European bumblebee, and other unwelcome immigrants to slip across the nation's borders. Like most such debates, this one was immediately caught in the rhetoric of exclusion and belonging that the language of *native* and *invasive* incites—the same rhetorics that led Kouichi Goka and his colleagues to identify so closely with the reticent male *Dorcus* that they forced into sex with its cruel Indonesian cellmate. Given that Japanese nature is often taken as a defining element of national and personal identity, it is easy to see why the debate over this legislation was so fraught.

One of the more controversial questions was whether *kuwagata* and *kabutomushi* would be listed on the act's roster of prohibited species. Conservationists lobbied for inclusion, concerned about both the continuing effects of beetle imports and the logic of collecting more generally. They had long argued that collecting was harming native species through damage to habitats from tree felling and other indiscriminate methods, through the removal of breeding populations from the wild, and through the impact of released foreign animals.

Representatives of insect commerce were well organized. After all, they were the ones with the most to lose. Tokai Media, the publisher of *Be-kuwa!*, sponsored a nonprofit organization, the Satoyama Society, which worked to enlist the industry in a preemptive campaign of conservation education that included articles in the specialist magazines, lectures, posters, flyers promoting more careful management of beetles, and the formation of local collecting clubs. The Satoyama Society promised their beetle-industry colleagues that the education campaign would generate lecture fees and new customers.

People from Mushi-sha gave expert testimony at the hearings. They estimated a core of 10,000 to 20,000 amateur breeders, another 100,000 beetle-keeping adults (mostly middle-aged men), and millions of children raising insects from eggs. They argued that with estimates of up to 5 billion non-native beetles in circulation inside Japan, it made no sense to talk about import controls. The real danger was not from animals entering the country but from those already here. Controls would only undermine the educational and moral value of collecting. Instead, like their allies in the Satoyama Society, they proposed to manage the situation with a campaign to educate their customers about the consequences of abandoning their animals.

By the third public hearing, it was clear that the industry and its allies had won the day. Few beetle species were included in the final document, and those that were appeared under the nonrestrictive "organisms requiring a certificate" column.[25] However, conservationists were involved in a larger struggle that didn't solely target the commercial collectors. Many also disliked what they saw as the unnecessary destruction behind the vast private collections of scholars like Yoro Takeshi. They worried about the moral effects that the sanctioned killing of animals had on children. For a number of years, and with success in Tokyo and elsewhere, they had worked to stop schools from assigning the summer entomology projects.

My first thought on hearing this was for Kuwachan and his dream of fathers, sons, *kuwagata,* and *kazoku service.* But collectors such as Yoro Takeshi and Okumoto Daizaburo were forced on the defensive too. Aren't we, they argued, like Fabre, both scientists and insect lovers? Don't we, too, have reservations about the beetle boom? Aren't we, perhaps even more than the conservationists, committed to fostering a world of sensitive and creative nature loving, especially among children?

It was true that the commercialization of *kuwagata* had been highly damaging, they agreed, although the decline in numbers was due as much to loss of habitat through real estate development as to overharvesting. But in general, collecting had no effect on other insects: their populations were simply too large and reproduced too rapidly to be affected. The more serious question was about killing. For Yoro-san and

his friends, a truly deep relationship with other beings results from interspecies interaction, not separation; it results not from abandoning communication in the name of paternalist stewardship but from the radical change in consciousness that comes with developing those hard-to-acquire "*mushi* eyes." To find insects, you have to understand them, you have to find a way into their mode of existence. The focused attention that is needed to enter their lives is a form of training, philosophical as well as entomological. It brings a knowledge of nature that is inseparable from an affection for nature and an expansion of the human world. Killing insects is painful, but it is also meaningful. Echoing Cornelia Hesse-Honegger, Yoro-san told us that he had enough insects now. He had stopped killing them. Okumoto-san told us he never killed them but collected live specimens and pinned them only after they had died a natural death.

Shiga Usuke also experienced this unease. One year, on the anniversary of the opening of his store, he invited a Buddhist priest to come to Tokyo from the mountains and perform *kuyou* to console the souls of the departed. Instead of photos of the dead, he arranged specimens. Instead of favorite human foods, he arranged insect food. This was more than seventy years ago, in the 1930s. The sense of guilt about other beings, he writes, the sensibility that killing living things is wrong, is far from new.

He tries not to care about this, but he can't escape it. He often wonders which is better: to live as a mayfly for only one day or to survive as a specimen for hundreds of years.

I'm happy that I've known insects, says Yajima Minoru. Shiga Usuke feels the same way and adds that it's easy to get to know them. All you need is a magnifying glass and a net (maybe one of his inexpensive folding pocket nets).

As you observe tiny insects, writes Shiga-san, you'll grow more interested in nature and you'll find more pleasure and more satisfaction in the world around you. There is really nothing better than getting to know insects. The relationship between human beings and nature starts with insects and ends with insects, he says. And then he adds: my life has been exactly like that.

Zen and the Art of Zzz's

1.

In 1998, I was lucky enough to get a job teaching at the University of California in Santa Cruz, a beach town in northern California. I hadn't expected the offer and it came as a surprise. Both Sharon and I were raised in cities, and apart from my extended stay in Amazonia, neither of us had spent much time anywhere smaller. We were happy in our barely heated apartment in downtown Manhattan, even though the cold from the refrigerated warehouse below would often eat right through the floorboards and into our bones. But California seemed like an adventure, a whole new world. We packed up our stuff, rented a car, and set off like a couple of pioneers, trying to imagine what we'd find on the far side of the Holland Tunnel.

2.

Our favorite beach in Santa Cruz was at Wilder Ranch State Park. It's called Three Mile Beach. To get there, we would walk along the cliff tops overlooking the Pacific at the northern tip of Monterey Bay. Because it's so exposed, Wilder Ranch is usually windy and often much colder than Santa Cruz itself, which, only two or three miles away but sheltered by the bay, is a miracle of balmy weather.

The walk along the cliffs is blustery but astonishingly beautiful. We couldn't tire of it. The ocean, like all large bodies of water, never looks the same from one day to the next, and its mood always caught us unawares. Feet planted firmly on the cliff edge, high above the waves, we would look out on sea otters, seals, and sea lions far below. Sharon was the champion at spotting whales, and she'd point out gray whales and humpbacks spouting, sometimes pretty close to shore. We would tip back our necks, back, back, back into the sharp glare of the sun just as flocks of pelicans—the most inspiring of all—soared overhead, the whitest white against the bluest sky.

3.

Once we came across a dead whale. For days, we'd smelled the stench of something rotting as we drove out past the flat fields of artichokes that line the ocean side of Highway 1, a stench so strong that despite the summer heat, we rolled up the windows on our un-air-conditioned Datsun pickup and kept them up for miles. The next time we went to Wilder

Ranch, we realized that the source was nearby. As we walked out along the cliffs, the smell grew more intense until the path fell away above a narrow inlet, and below we saw a discolored hulk, something indefinite that slowly became a whale.

The animal was melting, dissolving into viscous liquid. Its mouth gaped open. Its massive penis dug awkwardly into the sand. Everything was awkward. Everything about it was wrong. Its skin peeled away in slimy blues and greens. All around it buzzed clouds of flies.

4.

When the weather was warm enough and the wind not whipping up the sand, we'd sit and read on Three Mile Beach. It was usually deserted, and sometimes I'd strip off and swim out a short distance, cautious of the crosscurrents and riptide, the icy water shocking my warm skin.

The beach is a pocket, a cove between the cliffs that slopes down gently into the ocean on one side and gives out into wetlands on the other. It has fine pale-golden sand and dotted clumps of tough marsh grass. We'd spend hours there, stretch out, breathe the sun into our bodies, the open sky above us, around us the roar of the surf as it rushed in, the tumble of smooth rocks as it poured out again.

5.

But despite all this, it was often hard to relax on Three Mile Beach. There were tiny flies, maybe the same flies that swarmed around the whale. They were fast and they were determined, too, impossible to deter. Every few seconds, one would deliver a sharp pinprick to an exposed leg or arm and then zoom off. The pinpricks hurt. They didn't leave a mark, not even any redness, but they made it difficult to sit still and even harder to sleep.

6.

Recent research suggests that insects sleep. Or at least like most other creatures, they go through regular periods of rest and inactivity, during which their responses to external stimuli are greatly reduced.[1] It would have been helpful if we'd known how to coordinate our visits to the beach with the flies' inactivity, but that just wasn't possible.

The sleep research doesn't investigate whether insects dream. That's a little too speculative for biologists right now. Perhaps the methodology isn't obvious. But what if they do . . . What do they dream of? Yet more unanswerable questions.

7.

The insects are all around me now. They know we're at the end. They're saying, "Don't leave us out! Don't forget about us!" I'm trying hard to include them all. But, honestly, there are just too many. Even the most ambitious and richly illustrated insectopedia wouldn't have room. Even Vincent Resh and Ring Cardé's monumental *Encyclopedia of Insects* had to perform some triage.

The beach flies stopped us from sleeping. Their bites were sharp stabs. They refused to leave us alone. In other ways, they were very Californian. They kept repeating the same thing, a four-part mantra: This is our beach too. Learn to live with imperfection. We're all in this together. The minuscule, a narrow gate, opens up an entire world.

NOTES

Air

1. P. A. Glick, *The Distribution of Insects, Spiders, and Mites in the Air*, U.S. Department of Agriculture Technical Bulletin 671 (Washington, D.C.: U.S. Department of Agriculture, 1939), 146.
2. For these and other examples of airborne dispersal, see C. G. Johnson, *Migration and Dispersal of Insects by Flight* (London: Methuen, 1969), 294–96, 358–59. I have drawn heavily on Johnson's classic book and on Robert Dudley's *The Biomechanics of Insect Flight: Form, Function, Evolution* (Princeton, N.J.: Princeton University Press, 2000) for this chapter.
3. B. R. Coad, "Insects Captured by Airplane Are Found at Surprising Heights," in *Yearbook of Agriculture, 1931* (Washington, D.C.: U.S. Department of Agriculture, 1931), 322.
4. Glick, *Distribution of Insects*, 87. On ballooning, see Robert B. Suter, "An Aerial Lottery: The Physics of Ballooning in a Chaotic Atmosphere," *Journal of Arachnology* 27 (1999): 281–93.
5. Johnson, *Migration and Dispersal*, 297.
6. See, for instance, A. C. Hardy and P. S. Milne, "Studies in the Distribution of Insects by Aerial Currents: Experiments in Aerial Tow-Netting from Kites," *Journal of Animal Ecology* 7 (1938): 199–229.
7. William Beebe, "Insect Migration at Rancho Grande in North-Central Venezuela: General Account," *Zoologica* 34, no. 12 (1949): 107–10.
8. Dudley, *Biomechanics of Insect Flight*, 8–14, 302–9.
9. L. R. Taylor, "Aphid Dispersal and Diurnal Periodicity," *Proceedings of the Linnean Society of London* 169 (1958): 67–73.
10. Dudley, *Biomechanics of Insect Flight*, 325–6.
11. Johnson, *Migration and Dispersal*, 606.
12. Ibid., 294, 360.

Chernobyl

1. In English, these insects, classified as a suborder of the Hemiptera, are known as the true bugs.
2. Cornelia Hesse-Honegger, *Heteroptera: The Beautiful and the Other, or Images of a Mutating World*, trans. Christine Luisi (New York: Scalo, 2001), 90.

3. Hesse-Honegger reflects on her career in a number of short published articles and, more extensively, in two books: *Heteroptera* and *Warum bin ich in Öster-färnebo? Bin auch in Leibstadt, Beznau, Gösgen, Creys-Malville, Sellafield gewesen . . .* [*Why Am I in Österfärnebo? I Have Also Been to Leibstadt, Beznau, Gösgen, Creys-Malville, Sellafield . . .*] (Basel, Switzerland: Éditions Heuwinkel, 1989). A short article that includes four good-quality color reproductions can be found in *Grand Street* 70 (Spring 2002): 196–201. Two beautifully produced exhibition catalogs also contain autobiographical accounts and useful critical essays: Hesse-Honegger, *After Chernobyl* (Bern, Switzerland: Bundesamt für Kultur/Verlag Lars Müller, 1992), and Hesse-Honegger, *The Future's Mirror*, trans. Christine Luisi-Abbot (Newcastle upon Tyne, U.K.: Locus+, 2000). My thanks to Steve Connell for all translations from the German.

4. Hesse-Honegger, *Heteroptera*, 24.

5. Hesse-Honegger, *After Chernobyl*, 59.

6. Hesse-Honegger, *Heteroptera*, 9.

7. Galileo Galilei, *Sidereus nuncius, or The Sidereal Messenger*, trans. Albert Van Helden (Chicago: University of Chicago Press, 1989), 42, quoted in Hesse-Honegger, *Heteroptera*, 8.

8. Cornelia Hesse-Honegger, "Wenn Fliegen und Wanzen anders aussehen als sie solten" [When Flies and Bugs Don't Look the Way They Should], *Tages-Anzeiger Magazin*, January 1988, 20–25.

9. Hesse-Honegger, *Heteroptera*, 94–96.

10. Ibid.

11. Hesse-Honegger discusses some of this material in the works already cited. For more detailed accounts, see, among others, Ernest J. Sternglass, *Secret Fallout: Low-Level Radiation from Hiroshima to Three Mile Island* (New York: McGraw-Hill, 1981); Ralph Graeub, *The Petkau Effect: The Devastating Effect of Nuclear Radiation on Human Health and the Environment* (New York: Four Walls Eight Windows, 1994); Jay M. Gould and Benjamin A. Goldman, *Deadly Deceit: Low-Level Radiation High-Level Cover-up* (New York: Four Walls Eight Windows, 1990); and Jay M. Gould, *The Enemy Within: The High Cost of Living Near Nuclear Reactors* (New York: Four Walls Eight Windows, 1996). On activist alliances between scientists and community groups, see, for example, Steven Epstein, *Impure Science: AIDS, Activism, and the Politics of Knowledge* (Berkeley: University of California Press, 1996); Phil Brown and Edwin J. Mikkelsen, *No Safe Place: Toxic Waste, Leukemia, and Community Action* (Berkeley: University of California Press, 1990); and Sabrina McCormick, Phil Brown, and Stephen Zvestoski, "The Personal Is Scientific, the Scientific Is Political: The Public Paradigm of the Environmental Breast Cancer Movement," *Sociological Forum* 18, no. 4 (2003): 545–76. My thanks to Alondra Nelson for directing me to Phil Brown's work.

12. For Busby's second-event theory, see Chris Busby, *Wings of Death: Nuclear Pollution and Human Health* (Aberystwyth, U.K.: Green Audit, 1995), and Busby, interview by Sunny Miller, May 8, 2004, Grassrootspeace.org, http://traprockpeace.org/chris_busby_08may04.html.

13. See, for example, the newspaper and magazine articles included in Hesse-Honegger, *Warum bin ich in Österfärnebo?*, 93–101.

14. Hesse-Honegger, *Heteroptera*, 99.

15. Ibid., 127.

16. Cornelia Hesse-Honegger, "Leaf Bugs, Radioactivity and Art," *N.paradoxa: International Feminist Art Journal* 9 (2002): 53.

17. Cornelia Hesse-Honegger, "Der Verdacht" [The Suspicion], *Tages-Anzeiger Magazin*, April 1989, 34.

18. Max Bill, *Konkrete Gestaltung* [*Concrete Formation*] in *Zeitprobleme in der Schweizer Malerei und Plastik*, exhibition catalogue (Kunsthaus Zürich, 1936), quoted in ibid., 82.

19. Max Bill, quoted in Margit Weinberg-Staber, "Quiet Abodes of Geometry," in *Concrete Art in Europe after 1945*, ed. Marlene Lauter (Ostfildern-Ruit, Germany: Hatje Cantz, 2002), 77.

20. Peter Suchin, "Forces of the Small: Painting as Sensuous Critique," quoted in Hesse-Honegger, *Future's Mirror*, n.p.

21. Hesse-Honegger, *Heteroptera*, 132.

22. Ibid.

23. Ibid., 179.

24. See especially Paul Feyerabend, *Against Method: Outline of an Anarchistic Theory of Knowledge* (London: New Left Books, 1975).

25. Cornelia Hesse-Honegger, "Field Study around the Hanford Site in the States Washington and Idaho, USA" (unpublished manuscript, Zürich, 1998–99), n.p.

26. Cornelia Hesse-Honegger, "Field Study in the Area of the Nuclear Reprocessing Plant, La Hague, Normandie, France, 1999" (unpublished manuscript, Zürich, 2000–2003), n.p.

27. Cornelia Hesse-Honegger, "Field Study in the Area of the Nuclear Test Site, Nevada and Utah, USA, 1997" (unpublished manuscript, Zürich, n.d.), n.p.

Death

1. Hans Erich Nossack, "Der Untergang," in *Interview mit dem Tode* (Frankfurt am Main, Germany: Suhrkamp, 1963), 238, quoted in W. G. Sebald, *On the Natural History of Destruction*, trans. Anthea Bell (New York: Random House, 2003), 35. Available in English: Hans Erich Nossack, *The End: Hamburg 1943*, trans. Joel Agee (Chicago: University of Chicago Press, 2004).

2. "Seen from Above," in *Miracle Fair: Selected Poems of Wisława Szymborska*, trans. Joanna Trzeciak (New York: W. W. Norton, 2001), 66. My thanks to Dilip Menon and Lara Jacob for introducing me to Szymborska's work and to this poem in particular.

3. Primo Levi, *Other People's Trades*, trans. Raymond Rosenthal (New York: Summit Books, 1989), 17.

4. Nossack, "Der Untergang," quoted in Sebald, *On the Natural History of Destruction*, 35.

Evolution

1. Jean-Henri Fabre, "The Greenbottles," in *The Life of the Fly*, trans. Alexander Teixeira de Mattos (New York: Dodd, Mead, 1913), 232; Fabre, "The Bluebottle: The Laying," in *Life of the Fly*, 316. A full-length critical account of Fabre's work is

Patrick Tort, *Fabre: Le Miroir aux insectes* (Paris: Vuibert/Adapt, 2002). See also Colin Favret, "Jean-Henri Fabre: His Life Experiences and Predisposition against Darwinism," *American Entomologist* 45, no. 1 (1999): 38–48, and Georges Pasteur, "Jean Henri Fabre," *Scientific American*, July 1994, 74–80. More often, biographers have been happy to participate in Fabre's self-fashioning while ignoring his theoretical ambitions. See, for example, Yves Delange, *Fabre: L'homme qui aimait les insectes* (Paris: Actes Sud, 1999). The "authorized biography" of Fabre was written by his friend and admirer Georges Victor Legros. G. V. Legros, *Fabre: Poet of Science*, trans. Bernard Miall (1913; repr., Whitefish, Mont.: Kessinger, 2004).

2. Fabre, "The Harmas," in *Life of the Fly*, 15.
3. Tort, *Fabre*, 64.
4. Fabre, "Harmas," quoted in ibid., 16.
5. Tort, *Fabre*, 27.
6. Jean-Henri Fabre, "The Odyneri," in *The Mason-Wasps*, trans. Alexander Teixeira de Mattos (New York: Dodd, Mead, 1919), 59.
7. Fabre, "Harmas," 18.
8. Jean-Henri Fabre, "The Fable of the Cigale and the Ant," in *Social Life in the Insect World*, trans. Bernard Miall (New York: Century, 1912), 6; Fabre, "Harmas," 24.
9. Fabre, "The Song of the Cigale," in *Social Life in the Insect World*, 36.
10. Norma Field, "Jean Henri Fabre and Insect Life in Modern Japan" (unpublished manuscript, n.d.), 6. My thanks to Norma Field for sending me this extremely helpful paper.
11. Fabre, quoted in Delange, *Fabre*, 55.
12. Jean-Henri Fabre, "The Bembex," in *The Hunting Wasps*, trans. Alexander Teixeira de Mattos (New York: Dodd, Mead, 1915), 156.
13. Fabre, "The Great Cerceris," in *Hunting Wasps*, 12.
14. Fabre, "The Yellow-Winged Sphex," in *Hunting Wasps*, 36.
15. Fabre, "The Eumenes," in *Mason-Wasps*, 10, 12, 13.
16. Fabre, "Aberrations of Instinct," in *Mason-Wasps*, 109.
17. Fabre, quoted in Legros, *Fabre*, 14.
18. Fabre, quoted in ibid., 13.
19. Fabre, quoted in ibid.
20. Tort (*Fabre*, 57) describes the two men: *"Unis par une vaste érudition, une sympathie éthique et l'expérience partagée de la douleur."* Fabre and Mill undertook a joint, never-completed project to produce a flora of the Vaucluse.
21. Romain Rolland, letter to G. V. Legros, January 7, 1910, quoted in Delange, *Fabre*, 322. The Nobel Prize that year was awarded to another great admirer of Fabre's, the dramatist Maurice Maeterlinck, a writer with an interest in entomology rather than an entomologist who was also a writer.
22. Fabre, "Harmas," 14.
23. Legros, *Fabre*, 17; Fabre, quoted in Tort, *Fabre*, 25–26.
24. Fabre, "Odyneri," 47.
25. Ibid., 46; Fabre, "Eumenes," 25.
26. See the thorough discussion in Tort, *Fabre*, esp. 205–40.
27. Fabre, "The Modern Theory of Instinct," in *Hunting Wasps*, 403.
28. Fabre, "The Ammophilae," in *Hunting Wasps*, 271.

29. Charles Darwin, *The Descent of Man, and Selection in Relation to Sex* (London: Penguin, 2004), 88, 87. See also Daniel R. Papaj, "Automatic Learning and the Evolution of Instinct: Lessons from Learning in Parasitoids," in *Insect Learning: Ecological and Evolutionary Perspectives*, ed. Daniel R. Papaj and Alcinda C. Lewis (New York: Chapman and Hall, 1993), 243–72.

30. Fabre, "Modern Theory of Instinct," 411.

31. Fabre, "Ammophilae," 269.

32. Ibid., 270.

33. Ibid., 377–78.

34. R. J. Herrnstein, "Nature as Nurture: Behaviorism and the Instinct Doctrine," *Behavior and Philosophy* 26 (1998): 83; previously published in *Behavior* 1, no. 1 (1972): 23–52.

35. Ibid., 81.

36. William James, *The Principles of Psychology* (New York: Holt, 1890), 2:384, quoted in Herrnstein, ibid., 81.

37. William McDougall, *An Introduction to Social Psychology* (London: Methuen, 1908), 44.

38. Christian Kerslake, "Insects and Incest: From Bergson and Jung to Deleuze," *Multitudes: Revue Politique, Artistique, Philosophique*, October 22, 2006, 2.

39. Henri Bergson, *Creative Evolution*, trans. Arthur Mitchell (1911; repr., Mineola, N.Y.: Dover Publications, 1989), 174. It is interesting to note that the wasps continue on this route via Bergson through the continental philosophy of the twentieth century to reach Deleuze and Guattari's *A Thousand Plateaus* in the form of the becoming animal, the wasp and the orchid that each becomes partly the other in the moment of embrace, the famous wasp-orchid that seems to have its originary spark in the Ammophila-Fabre. Gilles Deleuze and Félix Guattari, *A Thousand Plateaus: Capitalism and Schizophrenia*, trans. Brian Massumi (Minneapolis: University of Minnesota Press, 1987).

40. Bertrand Russell, *The Analysis of Mind* (London: George Allen and Unwin, 1921), 56, quoted in Kerslake, "Insects and Incest," 3.

41. Tort, *Fabre*, 232–35.

42. Fabre, "Harmas," 14.

43. My thanks to Gavin Whitelaw for his generous gift of a complete set of Fabre 7-Eleven figurines! Thanks also to Shiho Satsuka for finding a copy of Yokota Tokuo's *Konchu no tankensha Faaburu* (Tokyo: Gakken, 1978), a very popular manga of Fabre's life story. On this, see Field, "Jean Henri Fabre," 4.

44. I take this figure from Pasteur, "Jean Henri Fabre," 74.

45. Okumoto Daizaburo, *Hakubutsugakuno kyojin Anri Faburu* [*Henri Fabre: A Giant of Natural History*] (Tokyo: Syueisya, 1999), 27. All translations from the Japanese, unless otherwise noted, are by CJ Suzuki. See also Field, "Jean Henri Fabre," 18–20.

46. Osugi Sakae, "I Like a Spirit," in *A Short History of the Anarchist Movement in Japan*, ed. Libertaire Group (Tokyo: Idea, 1979), 132. Osugi's wife, the feminist Ito Noe, and their seven-year-old nephew were murdered with him in 1923.

47. Jean-Henri Fabre, *Souvenirs entomologiques* (Paris: Delagrave, 1886) 3:309, quoted in Favret, "Jean-Henri Fabre," 46.

48. Osugi was an admirer and early translator of Peter Kropotkin, who argued power-fully for mutual aid and cooperation rather than competition as the basis for evo-lution. Yet paradoxically, Osugi was also known as a social Darwinist, a philosophy widespread in Japan at the time. It was via the Spencerian disdain for cooperation and the celebration of competition as the motive force of human existence that Darwinism entered Meiji Japan, along with Western science, in the 1870s. See Field, "Jean Henri Fabre," 19 and 27n80.

49. Fabre, *Souvenirs entomologiques*, vol. 8, quoted in Favret, "Jean-Henri Fabre," 46.

50. Okumoto, *Faburu*, 189.

51. Yoro Takeshi, Okumoto Daizaburo, and Ikeda Kiyohiko, *San-nin yoreba mushi-no-chi'e [Put Three Heads Together to Match the Wisdom of a Mushi]* (Tokyo: Yosensya, 1996).

52. Imanishi Kinji, *The World of Living Things*, trans. Pamela J. Asquith, Heita Kawakatsu, Shusuke Yagi, and Hiroyuki Takasaki (London: RoutledgeCurzon, 2002); Imanishi, "A Proposal for Shizengaku: The Conclusion to My Study of Evo-lutionary Theory," *Journal of Social and Biological Structures* 7 (1984): 357–368.

53. For an attack on Imanishi that can only be described as racist, see Beverly Hal-stead, "Anti-Darwinian Theory in Japan," *Nature* 317 (1985): 587–89. And for a smart response, see Frans B. M. de Waal, "Silent Invasion: Imanishi's Primatol-ogy and Cultural Bias in Science," *Animal Cognition* 6 (2003): 293–99.

54. Imanishi, "Proposal for Shizengaku," 360.

55. Arne Kalland and Pamela J. Asquith, "Japanese Perceptions of Nature: Ideals and Illusions," in *Japanese Images of Nature: Cultural Perceptions,* ed. Pamela J. Asquith and Arne Kalland (Richmond, U.K.: Curzon Press, 1997), 2. See also Julia Adeney Thomas's fascinating *Reconfiguring Modernity: Concepts of Nature in Japanese Polit-ical Ideology* (Berkeley: University of California Press, 2001).

56. J. L. Austin, *How to Do Things with Words* (Cambridge, Mass.: Harvard University Press, 1962). See also Alexei Yurchak, *Everything Was Forever, until It Was No More: The Last Soviet Generation* (Princeton, N.J.: Princeton University Press, 2005).

57. Stephen Jay Gould, "Nonmoral Nature," in *Hen's Teeth and Horse's Toes: Further Reflections in Natural History* (New York: W. W. Norton, 1994), 32.

58. Ibid.

59. Ibid.

Generosity (the Happy Times)

1. Jia's *Cu zhi jing* is most readily accessible in Wu Zhao Lian, *Xishuai mipu [Secret Cricket Books]* (Tianjin, China: Gu Ji Shu Dan Ancient Books, 1992).

2. Quoted in Hsiung Ping-chen, "From Singing Bird to Fighting Bug: The Cricket in Chinese Zoological Lore" (unpublished manuscript, Taipei, Taiwan, n.d.), 15–16 (translation slightly amended). My thanks to Professor Hsiung for her generosity in providing a copy of this fascinating paper.

3. Ibid., 17. The entomologist Chou Io is less forgiving. "From this presentation [of Jia's activities]," he writes, "one can see how the luxurious rulers in feudal society treated the fate of the nation and people." Chou, *A History of Chinese Entomology*, trans. Wang Siming (Xi'an, China: Tianze Press, 1990), 177.

4. Isolated descriptions of insect life, often poetic, can be found much earlier, in, for

example, the *Er-ya* (ca. 500–200 B.C., a work that likely predates Aristotle's *Historia animalium* as the world's first taxonomic natural history. For a detailed history of Chinese insect knowledge, see Chou, *History of Chinese Entomology*. For historical accounts of crickets in Chinese culture, see Liu Xinyuan, "Amusing the Emperor: The Discovery of Xuande Period Cricket Jars from the Ming Imperial Kilns," *Orientations* 26, no. 8 (1995): 62–77; Yin-Ch'i Hsu, "Crickets in China," *Bulletin of the Peking Society of Natural History* III, pt. 1 (1928–29): 5–41; Berthold Laufer, *Insect-Musicians and Cricket Champions of China* (Chicago: Field Museum of Natural History, 1927), reprinted in Lisa Gail Ryan, ed., *Insect Musicians and Cricket Champions: A Cultural History of Singing Insects in China and Japan* (San Francisco: China Books and Periodicals, 1996); Jin Xingbao, "Chinese Cricket Culture," *Cultural Entomology Digest* 3 (November 1994), http://www.insects.org/ced3/chinese_crcul.html; and Hsiung, "From Singing Bird to Fighting Bug."

5. Hsiung, "From Singing Bird to Fighting Bug," 17.
6. Liu, "Amusing the Emperor."
7. Pu Songling, "The Cricket," in *Strange Tales from Make-Do Studio*, trans. Denis C. Mair and Victor H. Mair (Beijing: Foreign Languages Press, 2001), 175–87. For the ethnohistorical background to Pu's story, see Liu, "Amusing the Emperor," 62–65.
8. Seventy-two is a widely cited total, perhaps because it is both a significant number in popular Taoism and the number of Earthly Warriors in *Water Margin* (also known as *Outlaws of the Marsh*), a work first published in the sixteenth century and considered one of the four great classical novels of Chinese literature.
9. Jin Xingbao and Liu Xianwei, *Qan jian min cun de xuan yan han guang shang [Common Singing Insects: Selection, Care, and Appreciation]* (Shanghai, China: Shanghai Science and Technology Press, 1996), 114. Thomas J. Walker and Sinzo Masaki make the same point but identify different species. They write, "Even though more than 60 varieties of fighters are recognized in Chinese cricket manuals, all belong to four species (*Velarifictorus aspersus, Teleogryllus testaceus, T. mitratus,* and *Gryllus bimaculatus*)." Walker and Masaki, "Natural History," in *Cricket Behavior and Neurobiology*, ed. Franz Huber, Thomas E. Moore, and Werner Loher (Ithaca, N.Y.: Comstock/Cornell University Press, 1990), 40. There is a significant scientific literature on aggression among male crickets, although I'm not aware of studies on the relevant species. See, for example, Kevin A. Dixon and William H. Cade, "Some Factors Influencing Male-Male Aggression in the Field Cricket *Gryllus integer* (Time of Day, Age, Weight and Sexual Maturity)," *Animal Behavior* 34 (1986): 340–46, which finds that aggression is more marked among sexually mature individuals, and L. W. Simmons, "Inter-Male Competition and Mating Success in the Field-Cricket, *Gryllus bimaculatus* (de Geer)," *Animal Behavior* 34 (1986): 567-69, which concludes, rather interestingly, that "individual competitive ability was determined by . . . an individual's past experience of winning ('confidence')."
10. An authoritative list of these variables can be found at Xishuai.com (http://www.xishuai.com), a cricket-lovers' site organized by Dr. Li Shijun. See also the "Song for the Selection of Northern Crickets" in Wu Hua, *Chong qu [Insect Delights]* (Shanghai, China: Xue Ling, 2004), 168.
11. Xu Xiaomin, "Cricket Matches—Chinese Style," *Shanghai Star*, September 4, 2003. Three hundred million yuan equals about U.S. $44 million at the 2009 rate of one yuan equaling fifteen cents.

12. Li Shijun, "Secrets of Cricket-Fighting," *Xinmin Evening News* (Shanghai), September 25, 2005.

13. Wu, *Chong qu,* 165.

14. On migrant labor in Chinese cities, see Dorothy J. Solinger, *Contesting Citizenship in Urban China: Peasant Migrants, the State, and the Logic of the Market* (Berkeley: University of California Press, 1999), and Li Zhang, "Migration and Privatization of Space and Power in Late Socialist China," *American Ethnologist* 28, no. 1 (2001): 179–205. Projected revisions to the *hukou* household registration system are not slated to include Shanghai at this time.

15. On head shaking, see James Farrer, *Opening Up: Youth Sex Culture and Market Reform in Shanghai* (Chicago: University of Chicago Press, 2002), 311–12.

16. Li Shijun, *Zhongguo dou xi jian shang* [*An Appreciation of Chinese Cricket Fighting*] (Shanghai, China: Shanghai Science and Technology Press, 2001); Li Shijun, *Zhonghua xishuai wushi bu xuan* [*Fifty Taboos of Cricket Collecting*] (Shanghai, China: Shanghai Science and Technology Press, 2002); Li Shijun, *Nan pen kuan tan* [*Pots of the South*] (Shanghai, China: Shanghai Science and Technology Press, 2003); Li Shijun, *Min jien cuan shi: shang pin xishuai 108 pin* [*An Anthology of Lore of One Hundred and Eight Excellent Crickets*] (Hong Kong: Wenhui, 2008).

17. Li Jun, "Anthropologist Studying Human–Insect Relations, U.S. Professor Wants to Publish a Book on Crickets," *Shanghai Evening Post,* September 30, 2005.

18. For a useful introduction to ideas of nature in China, see Yi-Fu Tuan, "Discrepancies between Environmental Attitude and Behaviour: Examples from Europe and China," *Canadian Geographer* 12, no. 3 (1968): 176–91. My thanks to Janet Sturgeon for pointing me to this article.

19. See Ackbar Abbas, "Play It Again Shanghai: Urban Preservation in the Global Era," in *Shanghai Reflections: Architecture, Urbanism and the Search for an Alternative Modernity,* ed. Mario Gandelsonas (New York: Princeton Architectural Press, 2002), 37–55; and Abbas, "Cosmopolitan De-scriptions: Shanghai and Hong Kong," *Public Culture* 12, no. 3 (2000): 769–86. See also Andrew Ross, *Fast Boat to China: Corporate Flight and the Consequences of Free Trade; Lessons from Shanghai* (New York: Pantheon, 2006).

20. Li Shijun, "Secrets of Cricket-Fighting."

21. Li Shijun, *Fifty Taboos of Cricket Collecting,* 84.

22. Wu, *Chong qu,* 247–51.

23. I have taken this version of "The Seventh Month" from Liu, "Amusing the Emperor," 63; the original source is Chen Huan, *Shijing maoshizhuan shu* [*Mao's Edition of The Book of Songs*] (Shanghai, China: 1934), 10, 76. Discussions also appear in Hsiung, "From Singing Bird to Fighting Bug," 7–9, and Jin, "Chinese Cricket Culture."

24. Simmons, "Inter-Male Competition," 578.

Heads and How to Use Them

1. Nicholas Wade, "Flyweights, Yes, but Fighters Nonetheless: Fruit Flies Bred for Aggressiveness," *New York Times,* October 10, 2006; Herman A. Dierick and Ralph J. Greenspan, "Molecular Analysis of Flies Selected for Aggressive Behav-

ior," *Nature Genetics* 38, no. 9 (September 2006): 1023–31. See also Ralph J. Greenspan and Herman A. Dierick, " 'Am Not I a Fly Like Thee?' From Genes in Fruit Flies to Behavior in Humans," *Human Molecular Genetics* 13, no. 2 (2004): R267–R273.

2. Wade, "Flyweights."

3. Robert E. Kohler, *Lords of the Fly: Drosophila Genetics and the Experimental Life* (Chicago: University of Chicago Press, 1994), 23.

4. Anita Guerrini describes Louis Pasteur using animals "as his test tubes." "Thereafter," she writes, "bacteriological and immunological research became inextricably linked to the use of animals as culture media." Guerrini, *Experimenting with Humans and Animals: From Galen to Animal Rights* (Baltimore: Johns Hopkins University Press, 2003), 98.

5. Kohler, *Lords of the Fly*, 53.

6. Thomas Hunt Morgan, quoted ibid., 73.

7. Ibid., 67.

8. On this, see Rebecca M. Herzig, *Suffering for Science: Reason and Sacrifice in Modern America* (New Brunswick, N.J.: Rutgers University Press, 2005). The Haldane quote is from a letter to L. C. Dunn, October 19, 1932, cited in Kohler, *Lords of the Fly*, 80.

9. Erica Fudge, *Animal* (London: Reaktion Books, 2002). My thanks also to Danny Solomon at UC Santa Cruz for interesting conversations on this question.

10. Greenspan and Dierick, " 'Am Not I a Fly Like Thee?,' " R267.

11. Elias Canetti, *Crowds and Power*, trans. Carol Stewart (New York: Farrar, Straus and Giroux, 1962), 205. My thanks to Dejan Lukic for pointing me to this passage.

12. Annemarie Mol, *The Body Multiple: Ontology in Medical Practice* (Durham, N.C.: Duke University Press, 2003), 126.

The Ineffable

1. Joris Hoefnagel, *The Four Elements*, vol. 1, *Animalia rationalia et insecta* (*Ignis*), watercolor and gouache on vellum, 1582, National Gallery of Art, Washington, D.C. For this chapter, I have drawn extensively on the work of Lee Hendrix, curator of drawings at the Getty Museum in Los Angeles and authority on Joris Hoefnagel, particularly her excellent "Of Hirsutes and Insects: Joris Hoefnagel and the Art of the Wondrous," *Word and Image* 11, no. 4 (1995): 373–90. In addition, see Lee Hendrix, "Joris Hoefnagel and *The Four Elements*: A Study in Sixteenth-Century Nature Painting" (Ph.D. diss., Princeton University, 1984), and, with Thea Vignau-Wilberg, *Mira calligraphiae monumenta: A Sixteenth-Century Calligraphic Manuscript Inscribed by Georg Bocskay and Illuminated by Joris Hoefnagel* (Malibu, Calif.: J. Paul Getty Museum, 1992). See also the helpful contextualizing discussion of Hoefnagel and his son Jacob in Thea Vignau-Wilberg, *Archetypa studiaque patris Georgii Hoefnagelii, 1592: Nature, Poetry and Science in Art around 1600* (Munich, Germany: Staatliche Graphische Sammlung, 1994).

2. Thomas Moffett quoted in Vignau-Wilberg, "Excursus: Insects," in *Archetypa*, 42n14. Moffett's volume is compiled from the entomological notes of the Swiss naturalist Conrad Gesner, as well as from work by the Londoners Thomas Penny

and Edward Wotton. See Edward Topsell, *The History of Four-Footed Beasts and Serpents and Insects*, vol. 3, *The Theatre of Insects* by T. Moffett (London, 1658; repr., New York: Da Capo Press, 1967). Gesner had planned the sixth and final volume of his *Historiae animalium* to cover the insects but managed to complete only a short section on scorpions before he died in 1565. On Moffett, see Frances Dawbarn, "New Light on Dr Thomas Moffet: The Triple Roles of an Early Modern Physician, Client, and Patronage Broker," *Medical History* 47, no. 1 (2003): 3–22.

3. Topsell, "Epistle Dedicatory," in *Theater of Insects*, 6. Moffett is quoting Psalms 92:5 "How great are Thy works, oh Lord!" My thanks to Abigail Winograd for making this connection.

4. Max Beier, "The Early Naturalists and Anatomists during the Renaissance and Seventeenth Century," in *History of Entomology*, ed. Ray F. Smith, Thomas E. Mittler, and Carroll N. Smith (Palo Alto, Calif.: Annual Reviews, 1973), 81–94. For a fascinating extended discussion of Aldrovandi, see Paula Findlen, *Possessing Nature: Museums, Collecting, and Scientific Culture in Early Modern Italy* (Berkeley: University of California Press, 1994); in relation to the study of insects specifically, see Vignau-Wilberg, "Excursus: Insects."

5. Hendrix, "Of Hirsutes and Insects," 382.

6. Vignau-Wilberg, "Excursus: Insects," 39. And see, for comparison, the similar but far more ancient East Asian preoccupation with miniaturization explored in Rolf A. Stein, *The World in Miniature: Container Gardens and Dwellings in Far Eastern Religious Thought*, trans. Phyllis Brooks (Palo Alto, Calif.: Stanford University Press, 1990); see also François Jullien, *The Propensity of Things: Toward a History of Efficacy in China*, trans. Janet Lloyd (New York: Zone Books, 1995), esp. 94–98.

7. See R.J.W. Evans, *Rudolf II and His World: A Study in Intellectual History, 1576–1612* (London: Thames and Hudson, 1973), and Thomas DaCosta Kaufmann, *The School of Prague: Painting at the Court of Rudolf II* (Chicago: University of Chicago Press, 1988).

8. Thomas DaCosta Kaufmann, *The Mastery of Nature: Aspects of Art, Science, and Humanism in the Renaissance* (Princeton, N.J.: Princeton University Press, 1993), 48 (emphasis added).

9. In this sense, Hoefnagel can be regarded as an eirenist. See ibid., 92–93.

10. For an account of the ways in which epistemologies that appear contradictory to modern understandings could productively coexist in late-sixteenth-century scholarship, see Stephen J. Greenblatt's insightful discussion of John Dee in *Sir Walter Ralegh: The Renaissance Man and His Roles* (New Haven, Conn.: Yale University Press, 1973). Also, famously, Frances A. Yates, *Giordano Bruno and the Hermetic Tradition* (Chicago: University of Chicago, 1991); Yates, *The Occult Philosophy in the Elizabethan Age* (London: Routledge, 2001); and Anthony Grafton, *Cardano's Cosmos: The Worlds and Works of a Renaissance Astrologer* (Cambridge, Mass.: Harvard University Press, 1999).

11. Evans, *Rudolf II and His World*, 248 (emphasis removed).

12. Francis Bacon, *Sylva sylvarum, or A Naturall History in Ten Centuries* (London, 1627), century 7, 143. Mary Poovey has convincingly argued that Bacon's empirical "revolution" was more a question of style than substance, though no less effective for that. Poovey, *A History of the Modern Fact: Problems of Knowledge in the Sciences of Wealth and Society* (Chicago: University of Chicago Press, 1998), 10–11.

13. Lorraine Daston, "Attention and the Values of Nature in the Enlightenment," in *The Moral Authority of Nature,* ed. Lorraine Daston and Fernando Vidal (Chicago: University of Chicago Press, 2004), 100–126. For a discussion of wonder in relation to the exploration of the Americas, see Stephen J. Greenblatt, *Marvelous Possessions: The Wonder of the New World* (Chicago: University of Chicago Press, 1991). For an account of an Elizabethan England in which (un)natural events were conventionally understood in terms of portentous correspondences, see E.M.W. Tillyard, *The Elizabethan World Picture* (London: Chatto and Windus, 1943), and the early chapters of Keith Thomas, *Man and the Natural World: A History of the Modern Sensibility* (New York: Pantheon, 1983).

14. Topsell, "Epistle Dedicatory," 3.

15. Lorraine Daston and Katharine Park, *Wonders and the Order of Nature, 1150–1750* (New York: Zone Books, 1998), 14.

16. Daston and Park, *Wonders,* 167. And, among others, Oliver Impey and Arthur MacGregor, eds., *The Origins of Museums: The Cabinet of Curiosities in Sixteenth- and Seventeenth-Century Europe* (New York: Clarendon Press, 1985); Pamela H. Smith and Paula Findlen, eds., *Merchants and Marvels: Commerce, Science, and Art in Early Modern Europe* (New York: Routledge, 2002); and Findlen, *Possessing Nature.*

17. Though, as the precision of Hoefnagel's attention to morphology makes evident, it would be a mistake to imagine this break as one between new science and old superstition. For a brief and effective introduction to recent scholarship on this question, see Steven Shapin, *The Scientific Revolution* (Chicago: University of Chicago Press, 1996).

18. Such as: "In all natural things there is something of the marvellous." Aristotle, *Parts of Animals,* trans. A. L. Peck, Loeb Classical Library 323 (Cambridge, Mass.: Harvard University Press, 1937), 645a.

19. See Edward Grant, "Aristotelianism and the Longevity of the Medieval World View," *History of Science* 16 (1978): 93–106. We can extend this claim even to the alchemists, although as R.J.W. Evans makes clear, "their 'Aristotle' was a mystic sage." Evans, *Rudolf II and His World,* 203n2.

20. John Scarborough, "On the History of Early Entomology, Chiefly Greek and Roman with a Preliminary Bibliography," *Melsheimer Entomological Series* 26 (1979): 17–27. Although there is no good analogue in contemporary systematics, the Aristotelian *entomon* resembled the modern Arthropoda phylum more closely than it did the class Insecta. As well as such anomalies as the worms, it included the modern insecta, arachnids, and myriapoda (centipedes and millipedes), although it excluded the crustaceans. For overviews, see Günter Morge, "Entomology in the Western World in Antiquity and in Medieval Times," in Smith, Mittler, and Smith, *History of Entomology,* 37–80, and Harry B. Weiss, "The Entomology of Aristotle," *Journal of the New York Entomological Society* 37 (1929): 101–9. See also Malcolm Davies and Jeyaraney Kathirithamby, *Greek Insects* (Oxford, U.K.: Oxford University Press, 1986). The Linnaean shift to morphology exiled worms, spiders, scorpions, centipedes, millipedes, and others to different classes. For a detailed discussion of the taxonomic criteria at work in Aristotle and Linnaeus, see Scott Atran, *Cognitive Foundations of Natural History: Towards an Anthropology of Science* (Cambridge: Cambridge University Press, 1993).

21. Atran, *Cognitive Foundations of Natural History*, 38.

22. G.E.R. Lloyd, *Science, Folklore and Ideology: Studies in the Life Sciences in Ancient Greece* (Cambridge: Cambridge University Press, 1983), 18.

23. I have drawn on Morge, "Entomology in the Western World," for these examples.

24. In 1668, Francesco Redi carried out his famous series of experiments in which several flasks containing meat were prepared with various types of coverings. Maggots appeared only in those to which flies had access, a result that dealt a significant but not fatal blow to the theory of spontaneous generation. The question, in fact, stayed open long after the use of microscopes became widespread. It was only with Pasteur's experiments of 1859 that the basis of the dispute shifted firmly from philosophy to experiment.

25. Kaufmann, *Mastery of Nature*, 42; Vignau-Wilberg, "Excursus: Insects," 40–41.

26. Grant, "Aristotelianism," 94–95.

27. Hendrix, "Of Hirsutes and Insects," 380–82.

28. Quoted in ibid., 378; Job 14:1.

29. Michel de Montaigne, "Of Cannibals" (1578–80), in *The Complete Works*, trans. Donald M. Frame (New York: Everyman's Library, 2003), 182–93.

30. Aldrovandi's *Monstrorum historia* was published posthumously in 1642. See Hendrix, "Of Hirsutes and Insects," 377. In this respect, the González family took its place in the history of exhibition and examination visited on all kinds of non-normative others transported to Europe in the colonial period. Effective accounts of well-known examples—of which there are many—include Londa Schiebinger's discussion of Sara Baartman, the so-called Hottentot Venus, in *Nature's Body: Gender in the Making of Modern Science* (Boston: Beacon Press, 1993), and Phillips Verner Bradford and Harvey Blume's *Ota Benga: The Pygmy in the Zoo* (New York: St. Martin's Press, 1992).

31. Hendrix, "Of Hirsutes and Insects."

32. Lee Hendrix, "The Writing Model Book," in Hendrix and Vignau-Wilberg, *Mira calligraphiae monumenta*, 42.

33. Frazer distinguishes homoeopathic magic from contagious magic based on what he calls the law of contact, which works on substances—such as hair or nail clippings—drawn from the targeted body itself rather than its likeness. See James George Frazer, *The Golden Bough: A Study in Magic and Religion* (London: Macmillan, 1911), 3:55–119.

34. R.J.W. Evans explains this as follows: "The object of such a philosophy was not only to describe the hidden forces of nature but also to control them, since the initiate who understood their powers could also apply his knowledge. This pursuit was magic, yet—as its exponents never ceased explaining—the magic was 'natural' and not 'black,' for the inspiration which made it possible was divine not diabolical." Evans, *Rudolf II and His World*, 197.

35. "It is no accident that the great conquering races of the world have done most to advance and spread civilization," he wrote in a characteristic commentary. Frazer, *Golden Bough*, 3:118.

36. Frazer, *Golden Bough*, 3:55, 56.

37. Michael Taussig, *My Cocaine Museum* (Chicago: University of Chicago Press, 2004), 80; Walter Benjamin, "On the Mimetic Faculty," in *Reflections: Essays,*

Aphorisms, Autobiographical Writings, ed. Peter Demetz, trans. Edmund Jephcott (New York: Schocken Books, 1986), 333–36.

38. Kaufmann, *Mastery of Nature*, 79–99. For a very different discussion of this painting, which situates it in the history of early-modern ideas of beetles, see Yves Cambefort, "A Sacred Insect on the Margins: Emblematic Beetles in the Renaissance," in *Insect Poetics*, ed. Eric C. Brown (Minneapolis: University of Minnesota Press, 2006), 200–222.

39. Hendrix and Vignau-Wilberg, *Mira calligraphiae monumenta*.

40. Walter Benjamin, "Theses on the Philosophy of History," in *Illuminations: Essays and Reflections*, ed. Hannah Arendt, trans. Harry Zohn (New York: Schocken Books, 1969), 253–64; and Benjamin, "One-Way Street," in *Reflections*, 61–94.

41. Benjamin, "The Work of Art in the Age of Mechanical Reproduction," in *Illuminations*, 217–52.

42. Kaufmann, *Mastery of Nature*, 38–48.

Jews

1. Aharon Appelfeld, *The Iron Tracks*, trans. Jeffrey M. Green (New York: Schocken Books, 1998).

2. Heinrich Himmler, speech to SS officers, April 24, 1943, Kharkov, Ukraine, reprinted in U.S. Office of Chief of Counsel for the Prosecution of Axis Criminality, *Nazi Conspiracy and Aggression* (Washington, D.C.: U.S. Government Printing Office, 1946), 4:574.

3. In exile in Britain and the United States, Szyk worked tirelessly to publicize events in Europe. A friend of Vladimir Jabotinsky and, later, Peter Bergson (Hillel Kook), he put his work at the service of the Revisionists—whose movement was founded on the principle of a sovereign, undivided Jewish state—campaigning first for a Jewish army, then for open immigration to Palestine, and consistently on behalf of the paramilitary Irgun. See Stephen Luckert, *The Art and Politics of Arthur Szyk* (Washington, D.C.: U.S. Holocaust Memorial Museum, 2002), and Joseph P. Ansell, "Arthur Szyk's Depiction of the 'New Jew': Art as a Weapon in the Campaign for an American Response to the Holocaust," *American Jewish History* 89 (2001): 123–34.

4. Christopher R. Browning provides the rather remarkable statistic that over 50 percent of the people killed by the Nazis died in the eleven months between March 1942 and February 1943. Browning, *Ordinary Men: Reserve Police Battalion 101 and the Final Solution in Poland* (New York: HarperCollins, 1992), xv. By the time the United States acceded to the pressure to acknowledge events across the Atlantic, the fate of European Jewry had been effectively settled.

5. Both of these images are discussed in Richard I. Cohen's fascinating and comprehensive *Jewish Icons: Art and Society in Modern Europe* (Berkeley: University of California Press, 1998), 221–30. As Cohen points out, Nossig's innovation was to take an image that was widely familiar at the time and imbue it with an utterly different sensibility.

6. Jacob Döpler, *Theatrum poenarum* (Sondershausen, Germany, 1693), and Jodocus Damhouder, *Praxis rerum criminalium* (Antwerp, 1562), quoted in E. P. Evans, *The*

Criminal Prosecution and Capital Punishment of Animals: The Lost History of Europe's Animal Trials (1906; repr., Boston: Faber and Faber, 1987), 153 (emphasis added).

7. Boria Sax, *Animals in the Third Reich: Pets, Scapegoats, and the Holocaust* (New York: Continuum, 2000).

8. Alex Bein, "The Jewish Parasite: Notes on the Semantics of the Jewish Problem, with Special Reference to Germany," *Leo Baeck Institute Yearbook* 9 (1964): 3–40. See also Michel Serres, *The Parasite*, trans. Lawrence R. Schehr (Minneapolis: University of Minnesota Press, 2007).

9. Bein, "Jewish Parasite," 12.

10. Donna J. Haraway, *When Species Meet* (Minneapolis: University of Minnesota Press, 2007), 78.

11. Mahmood Mamdani, *When Victims Become Killers: Colonialism, Nativism, and the Genocide in Rwanda* (Princeton, N.J.: Princeton University Press, 2002), 13. For this type of argument in relation to the Holocaust, see Marvin Perry and Frederick M. Schweitzer, *Antisemitism: Myth and Hate from Antiquity to the Present* (New York: Palgrave Macmillan, 2002), 2–3, and Daniel Jonah Goldhagen, *Hitler's Willing Executioners: Ordinary Germans and the Holocaust* (New York: Alfred A. Knopf, 1996), 71.

12. Insectification such as this from a January 1994 article in the Hutu-power newspaper *Kangura* was a common feature of the Rwandan genocide. Quoted by Angeline Oyog, "Human Rights-Media: Voices of Hate Test Limits of Press Freedom," Inter-Press Service, April 5, 1995, and cited in Mamdani, *When Victims Become Killers*, 212.

13. Shmuel Almog, "Alfred Nossig: A Reappraisal," *Journal of Israeli History: Politics, Society, Culture* 4, no. 1 (1983):1.

14. The ZOB mainly targeted the notorious Jewish police. See Hanna Krall, *Shielding the Flame: An Intimate Conversation with Dr. Marek Edelman, the Last Surviving Leader of the Warsaw Ghetto Uprising*, trans. Joanna Stasinska and Lawrence Weschler (New York: Henry Holt, 1986), 50, and Vered Levy-Barzilai, "The Rebels among Us," *Haaretz Magazine*, February 18, 2007, 18–22. Levy-Barzilai estimates that the ghetto underground liquidated thirty-three Jews. My thanks to Rotem Geva for drawing my attention to this source.

15. Cohen, *Jewish Icons*, 227.

16. Alfred Nossig, *Próba rozwiązania kwestii żydowskiej [An Attempt to Solve the Jewish Question]* (Lvov, Poland, 1887), quoted in Ezra Mendelsohn, "From Assimilation to Zionism in Lvov: The Case of Alfred Nossig," *Slavonic and East European Review* 49, no. 117 (1971): 531.

17. *The Warsaw Diary of Adam Czerniakow*, ed. Raul Hilberg, Stanislaw Staron, and Josef Kermisz, trans. Stanislaw Staron and the staff of Yad Vashem (Chicago: Elephant/Ivan Dee in association with U.S. Holocaust Memorial Museum, 1999), 84.

18. Michael Zylberberg, "The Trial of Alfred Nossig: Traitor or Victim?" *Wiener Library Bulletin* 23 (1969): 44.

19. Arthur Ruppin, *Memoirs, Diaries, Letters*, ed. Alex Bein, trans. Karen Gershon (New York, Herzl Press, 1972), 74–76; Mitchell B. Hart, *Social Science and the Politics of Modern Jewish Identity* (Palo Alto, Calif.: Stanford University Press, 2000), 33.

20. John M. Efron, "1911: Julius Preuss Publishes *Biblisch-talmudische Medizin*, Felix Theilhaber Publishes *Der Untergang der deutschen Juden*, and the International Hygiene Exhibition Takes Place in Dresden," in *Yale Companion to Jewish Writing and Thought in German Culture, 1096–1996*, ed. Sander L. Gilman and Jack Zipes (New Haven, Conn.: Yale University Press, 1997), 295.

21. Virchow was a distinguished political liberal and a founder of German anthropology. His conclusions cut against the grain of belief in the anthropological and pathological distinctiveness of the Jews and were received with general skepticism. See John M. Efron, *Defenders of the Race: Jewish Doctors and Race Science in Fin-de-Siècle Europe* (New Haven, Conn.: Yale University Press, 1994), 24–26; George L. Mosse, *Toward the Final Solution: A History of European Racism* (Madison: University of Wisconsin Press, 1985), 90–93; and Benoit Massin, "From Virchow to Fischer: Physical Anthropology and 'Modern Race Theories' in Wilhelmine Germany," in *Volksgeist as Method and Ethic: Essays on Boasian Ethnography and the German Anthropological Tradition*, ed. George W. Stocking, Jr. (Madison: University of Wisconsin Press, 1996), 79–154.

22. Mitchell B. Hart, "Racial Science, Social Science, and the Politics of Jewish Assimilation," *Isis* 90 (1999): 275–76. For a sustained discussion of degeneration as the narrative complement to evolutionary theorizing, see Daniel Pick, *Faces of Degeneration: A European Disorder, c. 1848–c. 1918* (Cambridge: Cambridge University Press, 1989).

23. For a concise account of the politics of this debate, see Robert Proctor, *Racial Hygiene: Medicine under the Nazis* (Cambridge, Mass.: Harvard University Press, 1988), 30–38, who points out that antisemites considered Lamarckism a Jewish doctrine.

24. For the detailing of this point in relation to Germany, see Sheila Faith Weiss, "The Race Hygiene Movement in Germany," *Osiris* 3 (1987): 193–226.

25. The point here is that the logics of nineteenth- and early-twentieth-century eugenics could not only bolster anti-militarist agendas (it is the breeding stock of strong young men that is lost in war) but could also underlie welfarist social agendas based on class. On this, see Robert A. Nye, "The Rise and Fall of the Eugenics Empire: Recent Perspectives on the Impact of Biomedical Thought in Modern Society," *Historical Journal* 36 (1993): 687–700.

26. Alfred Nossig, *Die Bilanz des Zionismus* [*The Balance Sheet of Zionism*] (Basel, Switzerland: Verlag von B. Wepf, 1903), 21, quoted in Almog, "Alfred Nossig," 9.

27. I am leaving aside here the complex history of shifting relations between German Jews and "eastern Jews," in which the location of Jewish degeneracy moved gradually from the *Ostjuden* to the Diaspora more broadly and a Romantic critique of the psychopathologizing impact of modernity on the Jews of the West. For many Zionists, eastern Jews came to stand both as the expression of pathology (triply oppressed by antisemitism, poverty, and the Orthodox rabbinate) and, somewhat later, as the positive site of an authentic *Judentum* in contrast to the deethnicized modern Jews of western Europe. See Steven E. Aschheim's groundbreaking *Brothers and Strangers: The East European Jew in German and German-Jewish Consciousness, 1800–1923* (Madison: University of Wisconsin Press, 1982).

28. Though, of course, for many Jews—and not only the religious—statements such

as Marx's "The social emancipation of the Jew is the emancipation of society from Judaism" ("On the Jewish Question," 1843) and Kautsky's "The sooner . . . [Judaism] disappears, the better it will be, not only for society, but also for the Jews themselves" (*Are the Jews a Race?*, 1914) invite a form of extermination.

29. See Alfred Nossig, *Zionismus und Judenheit: Krisis und Lösung* [*Zionism and Jewry: Crisis and Solution*] (Berlin: Interterritorialer Verlag "Renaissance," 1922), 17.

30. See Israel Kolatt, "The Zionist Movement and the Arabs," in *Zionism and the Arabs: Essays*, ed. Shmuel Almog (Jerusalem: Historical Society of Israel, 1983), 1–34.

31. Almog, "Alfred Nossig," 22. Presumably, this offer was made under the Ha'avara (Transfer) Agreement, by which 60,000 Jews were able to leave Germany from November 1933 until December 1939 (that is, soon after the SS took direct control of Jewish "emigration"). The agreement permitted the transfer of part of the value of emigrants' possessions to the Jewish Agency in Palestine in the form of German goods worth an allegedly equivalent amount.

32. Marek Edelman, "The Ghetto Fights," in *The Warsaw Ghetto: The 45th Anniversary of the Uprising*, ed. Tomasz Szarota (Warsaw, Poland: Interpress, n.d.), 39.

33. Krall, *Shielding the Flame*, 15. The publication of Edelman's memoir, in 1977, was an important moment in the Polish reassessment of the Holocaust. The book sold out its initial print run of 10,000 copies in just a few days, and Edelman, who went on to become an activist in Solidarity, found himself a reluctant celebrity.

34. I take the image and its connection to Edelman from Paul Julian Weindling's magisterial *Epidemics and Genocide in Eastern Europe, 1890–1945* (New York: Oxford University Press, 2000), 3. It was Weindling who convinced me that if Himmler's conflation of Jews and lice was a commonplace among Nazi leaders, it was also both the index to a specific set of regional histories and a recognizable code that summarized a concrete array of racial policies and practices.

35. Alfred Nossig, *Die Sozialhygiene der Juden und des altorientalischen Völkerkreises* [*Social Hygiene of the Jews and Ancient Oriental Peoples*] (Stuttgart: Deutsche Verlags-Anstalt, 1894); Alfred Ploetz, *Die Tüchtigkeit unserer Rasse und der Schutz der Schwachen: Ein Versuch über die Rassenhygiene und ihr Verhältnis zu den humanen Idealen, besonders zum Sozialismus* [*The Efficiency of Our Race and the Protection of the Weak: An Essay Concerning Racial Hygiene and Its Relationship to Humanitarian Ideals, in Particular to Socialism*] (Berlin: S. Fischer, 1895). The phrase is from Procter, *Racial Hygiene*, 15. I do not want to flatten the politics of German racial hygiene by suggesting that it was a straightforwardly racist project from the outset. As all scholars of the period are at pains to make clear, eugenics was sufficiently flexible to appeal to thinkers across the political spectrum. The German variant was initially a more or less conventional eugenics movement that paralleled contemporary tendencies elsewhere in Europe in its concern with "improving" the population in general; that is, it emphasized the human race ahead of specific races. In those early years, the implications of such politics for gender (via reproduction) were more significant than they were for specific racial groups. Nonetheless, in Germany, as in Britain, there was quite clearly a subjugated Nordic tendency—both institutionally organized and theoretically emergent—present in these earliest expressions. Moreover, where Nossig emphasized

the positive role of the state in improving health care, Ploetz proposed negative policy logics, such as the withdrawal of medical support from the weak and otherwise undesirable. By 1918, the German race-hygiene movement had been captured by the conservative nationalists who would staff the Nazi medical hierarchy. For thorough accounts, see Götz Aly, Peter Chroust, and Christian Pross, *Cleansing the Fatherland: Nazi Medicine and Racial Hygiene*, trans. Belinda Cooper (Baltimore: Johns Hopkins University Press, 1994); Proctor, *Racial Hygiene*; Paul Julian Weindling, *Health, Race, and German Politics between National Unification and Nazism, 1870–1945* (New York: Cambridge University Press, 1989); Sheila Faith Weiss, "The Race Hygiene Movement"; and Sheila Faith Weiss, *Race Hygiene and National Efficiency: The Eugenics of Wilhelm Schallmayer* (Berkeley: University of California Press, 1987); in relation to German anthropology, see Robert Proctor, "From *Anthropologie* to *Rassenkunde* in the German Anthropological Tradition," in *Bones, Bodies and Behavior: Essays in Behavioral Anthropology*, ed. George W. Stocking, Jr. (Madison: University of Wisconsin Press, 1990); and Massin, "From Virchow to Fischer."

36. Many of these details are now widely available despite the increasing currency of Holocaust denial and revision. See, for example, Uwe Dietrich Adam, "The Gas Chambers," in *Unanswered Questions: Nazi Germany and the Genocide of the Jews*, ed. François Furet (New York: Schocken Books, 1989), 134–54; and Weindling, *Epidemics and Genocide*, 301–3. Of the six Nazi death camps, only Auschwitz and Majdanek—which accounted for approximately 20 percent of the Jewish deaths in the Holocaust—used Zyklon B. In the other four camps, prisoners were gassed with carbon monoxide.

37. See Etienne Balibar, "Is There a 'Neo-Racism?'," trans. Chris Turner, in *Race, Nation, Class: Ambiguous Identities*, ed. Etienne Balibar and Immanuel Wallerstein (New York: Verso, 1991), 28n8; see also Zygmunt Bauman, "Allosemitism: Premodern, Modern, Postmodern," in *Modernity, Culture, and "the Jew,"* eds. Bryan Cheyette and Lyn Marcus (Palo Alto, Calif.: Stanford University Press, 1998).

38. The principal source for this material is Weindling's exhaustive *Epidemics and Genocide*, on which I have drawn extensively for the remainder of this section.

39. Pierre Vidal-Naquet, *Assassins of Memory: Essays on the Denial of the Holocaust*, trans. Jeffrey Mehlman (New York: Columbia University Press, 1992), 13; Richard Breitman, *The Architect of Genocide: Himmler and the Final Solution* (New York: Alfred A. Knopf, 1991), 6.

40. A notion resurrected by Hitler in *Mein Kampf*; see Sander L. Gilman, *The Jew's Body* (New York: Routledge, 1991), 221.

41. Hans Zinsser, *Rats, Lice and History: Being a Study in Biography, Which, after Twelve Preliminary Chapters Indispensible for the Preparation of the Lay Reader, Deals with the Life History of Typhus Fever* (Boston: Atlantic Monthly Press/Little, Brown, 1935); Weindling, *Epidemics and Genocide*, 8.

42. Perhaps drawing on the example of the *reconcentrado* system established by Spain in Cuba in 1896, "concentration camps" became a notable feature of colonial rule in southern Africa. Surpassing Kitchener's camps for Boer civilians, from which the name originated, the most notorious example was German: the camps established for the Herero in 1906 and abolished in 1908 under pressure from liberal

church groups and the Social Democrats in Berlin. A concise account is provided by Tilman Dedering, who is careful—and I think correct—to distinguish between these slave-labor camps and the extermination camps of the Nazis, instead pointing to links between the genocidal actions of the *Schutztruppe* in Namibia (German Southwest Africa) in 1904–6 and those of the *Einsatzgruppen* on the eastern front during the 1940s. Dedering, " 'A Certain Rigorous Treatment of All Parts of the Nation': The Annihilation of the Herero in German South West Africa, 1904," in *The Massacre in History*, ed. Mark Levene and Penny Roberts (New York: Berghahn Books, 1999), 204–22. Nonetheless, the fondness of the infamous general Lothar von Trotha for the word *extermination* (*Vernichtung*) in regard to the Herero echoes the term's increasing vernacular currency through the popularization of Koch's applied biology and thickens the connections that tie Europe and Africa as sites of German genocide. For a detailed history of the Herero, see Jan-Bart Gewald, *Herero Heroes: A Socio-political History of the Herero of Namibia 1890–1923* (Oxford, U.K.: James Currey, 1999). For a similar argument that emphasizes the colonial sites of genocidal practice as a corrective to work that threatens to dehistoricize the Shoah by insisting on its sui generis European genesis, see Paul Gilroy, "Not Being Inhuman," afterword to *Modernity, Culture, and "the Jew,"* ed. Bryan Cheyette and Laura Marcus (Palo Alto, Calif.: Stanford University Press, 1998), 282–97.

43. Weindling, *Epidemics and Genocide*, 19–30.

44. See Howard Markel, *Quarantine! East European Jewish Immigrants and the New York City Epidemics of 1892* (Baltimore: Johns Hopkins University Press, 1997).

45. One example of this concern was the German campaign—in which modernizing Jewish doctors also participated—against the *mikvah*, the Jewish ritual bath. See Weindling, *Epidemics and Genocide*, 42–43. Later, however, we see this discourse shift and an emphasis placed on the vulnerability of Germans to contagion and the innate resistance of "eastern peoples," who, so the argument went, had grown up in the midst of disease.

46. Weindling, *Epidemics and Genocide*, 63–65.

47. Zinsser, *Rats, Lice and History*, 297.

48. Weindling, *Epidemics and Genocide*, 81–82.

49. Ibid., 102.

50. This reaction was not limited to Germany. The Aliens Restriction Act passed in Britain in 1919 allowed inspection and "decontamination" of arrivals. Winston Churchill's florid characterization of Soviet Russia in a 1920 speech justifying support for the Whites in the civil war offers something of the flavor of the times: anti-Bolsheviks were defending Europe against "a poisoned Russia, an infected Russia, a plague-bearing Russia, a Russia of armed hordes smiting not only with bayonets and with cannon, but accompanied and preceded by the swarms of typhus-bearing vermin which slay the bodies of men, and political doctrines which destroy the health and even the souls of nations." Weindling, *Epidemics and Genocide*, 130; Churchill quoted ibid, 149.

51. Zinsser, *Rats, Lice and History*, 299. Weindling makes the important observation that the catastrophic Russian epidemic and famine served as a vast experimental station for German tropical specialists recently deprived of colonial medical subjects. Weindling, *Epidemics and Genocide*, 177–78.

52. *The Warsaw Diary of Adam Czerniakow*, 226, 228, 236.
53. Almog, "Alfred Nossig," 22–24.
54. *The Warsaw Diary of Adam Czerniakow*, 103, 104, 226.
55. From the diary of Jonas Turkow, quoted in Zylberberg, "Trials of Alfred Nossig," 44.

Kafka

1. See David L. Wagner, *Caterpillars of Eastern North America: A Guide to Identification and Natural History* (Princeton, N.J.: Princeton University Press, 2005).
2. Roberto Bolaño, *2666*, trans. Natasha Wimmer (New York: Farrar, Straus and Giroux, 2008), 713.
3. Daniel Janzen quoted in Andy Newman, "Quick, Before It Molts," *New York Times*, August 8, 2006.
4. Jules Michelet, *The Insect*, trans. W. H. Davenport Adams (London: T. Nelson and Sons, 1883), 111, 112. My thanks to Hylon White for introducing me to Michelet's wonderful book.
5. Ibid., 111.
6. Ibid., 112.
7. In this and the next two paragraphs, I draw heavily on Lionel Gossman's excellent "Michelet and Natural History: The Alibi of Nature," *Proceedings of the American Philosophical Society* 145, no. 3 (2001): 283–333.
8. Gossman convincingly argues that financial difficulties led to Michelet's shift from history to the more popular natural history. Encouraged by his young second wife, Athénais Mialaret, Michelet authored a series of best-selling natural history titles, including *L'insecte*. The character of their collaboration is not fully clear. In Gossman's reading, it was tense and competitive with Michelet consistently asserting the upper hand and the ultimate contribution of Mialaret—who would go on after her husband's death to achieve a literary reputation of her own—reduced largely to that of a researcher.
9. Letter to Eugene Noël, October 17, 1853, quoted in Gossman, "Michelet and Natural History," 289.
10. Ibid., 114.
11. Londa Schiebinger, *Plants and Empire: Colonial Bioprospecting in the Atlantic World* (Cambridge, Mass.: Harvard University Press, 2004), 30. Having attracted considerable attention over the past few years, Maria Sibylla Merian is fast becoming the Frida Kahlo of natural history. Of the several useful accounts, I have drawn most heavily on Natalie Zemon Davis, *Women on the Margins: Three Seventeenth-Century Lives* (Cambridge, Mass.: Harvard University Press, 1995). See also Kim Todd, *Chrysalis: Maria Sibylla Merian and the Secrets of Metamorphosis* (New York: Harcourt, 2007).
12. Maria Sibylla Merian, "Ad lectorum," in *Metamorphosis insectorum Surinamensium* (Amsterdam: Gerard Valck, 1705), quoted in Davis, *Women on the Margins*, 144.
13. See "The Lady Who Loved Worms," in *Translations from Early Japanese Literature*, ed. Edwin O. Reischauer and Joseph K. Yamagiwa (Cambridge, Mass.: Harvard University Press, 1951), 186–95.
14. Charlotte Jacob-Hanson, "Maria Sibylla Merian: Artist-Naturalist," *Magazine Antiques*, August 1, 2000, 174–83.

15. Victoria Schmidt-Linsenhoff, "Metamorphosis of Perspective: 'Merian' as a Subject of Feminist Discourse," in *Maria Sibylla Merian: Artist and Naturalist, 1647–1717*, ed. Kurt Wettengl, trans. John S. Southard (Ostfildern-Ruit, Germany: Hatje, 1998), 214.

16. Michelet, *Insect*, 361.

17. My thanks to Edward Kamens for a discussion of this point. See also Michele Marra, *The Aesthetics of Discontent: Politics and Reclusion in Medieval Japanese Literature* (Honolulu: University of Hawaii Press, 1991), 66.

18. Robert L. Backus, trans., *The Riverside Counselor's Stories: Vernacular Fiction of Late Heian Japan* (Palo Alto, Calif.: Stanford University Press, 1985), 53. I have incorporated Haruo Shirane's amendment into Backus's translation; see his review of *The Riverside Counselor's Stories* in the *Journal of Japanese Studies* 13, no. 1 (1987): 165–68.

19. Maria Sibylla Merian, *Metamorphosis insectorum Surinamensium*, quoted in Schmidt-Lisenhoff, "Metamorphosis of Perspective," 218.

20. Franz Kafka, "A Report to the Academy," in *The Transformation and Other Stories*, trans. Malcolm Pasley (London: Penguin, 1992), 187, 190.

Language

1. The quotation can be found in James L. Gould's *Ethology: The Mechanisms and Evolution of Behavior* (New York: W. W. Norton, 1982), 4. Without writing directly on von Frisch, Eileen Crist has also drawn attention to this rhetorical and epistemological shift from natural history to classical ethology. My reading of von Frisch locates him as something of a transitional figure in her schema between Jean-Henri Fabre (writing in what Crist calls the *Verstehen* tradition of animal studies, a hermeneutic ethology) and the new objectivism of Lorenz and Tinbergen. See Crist, "Naturalists' Portrayals of Animal Life: Engaging the *Verstehen* Approach," *Social Studies of Science* 26, no. 4 (1996): 799–838; and Christ, "The Ethological Constitution of Animals as Natural Objects: The Technical Writings of Konrad Lorenz and Nikolaas Tinbergen," *Biology and Philosophy* 13, no. 1 (1998): 61–102.

2. An argument first elaborated by Darwin himself in *The Descent of Man and Selection in Relation to Sex* (1871) and *The Expression of the Emotions in Man and Animals* (1872). For a useful discussion, see Carl N. Degler, *In Search of Human Nature: The Decline and Revival of Darwinism in American Social Thought* (Oxford, U.K.: Oxford University Press, 1991).

3. On Clever Hans, see Vicki Hearne, *Adam's Task: Calling Animals by Name* (New York: Alfred A. Knopf, 1986). In regard to the impact of this episode on ethology, "the analysis of learning was limited to simple S-R (stimulus-response) associations; hypothesizing the existence of higher-level cognitive activities in animals was scrupulously avoided . . . until the 1960s and 1970s." James L. Gould and Carol Grant Gould, *The Honey Bee* (New York: Scientific American, 1988), 216.

4. Karl von Frisch, *A Biologist Remembers*, trans. Lisbeth Gombrich (Oxford, U.K.: Pergamon Press, 1967), 149.

5. Ibid.

6. On this, see Ute Deichmann, *Biologists under Hitler*, trans. Thomas Dunlap (Cambridge, Mass.: Harvard University Press, 1996), 10–58.

7. Von Frisch, *A Biologist Remembers*, 71.

8. Ibid., 57.

9. Ibid., 72–73.

10. James L. Gould and Carol Grant Gould, *Honey Bee*, 58.

11. In his monumental history of the early ethologists, Richard Burkhardt quotes a passage from von Frisch's *Du und das Leben* (*You and Life*), a popular biology text published in 1938 in a series sponsored by Goebbels. Burkhardt writes that von Frisch "concluded the book with a section on race hygiene, voicing there the familiar warning that the relaxation of natural selection in higher cultures was leading to the perpetuation of variations that in the wild would have been 'mercilessly weeded out.' . . . This amounted in effect, he said, to an 'encouragement of the inferior,' or, as he put it more bluntly, 'A tub of lard or a blind man finds his table as well set as any other person.' " Richard W. Burkhardt, Jr., *Patterns of Behavior: Konrad Lorenz, Niko Tinbergen, and the Founding of Ethology* (Chicago: University of Chicago Press, 2005), 248.

12. Von Frisch, *A Biologist Remembers*, 129–30; Deichmann, *Biologists under Hitler*, 45–46.

13. Von Frisch, *A Biologist Remembers*, 25.

14. Ibid., 141. See also von Frisch, *The Dance Language and Orientation of Bees*, trans. Leigh E. Chadwick (Cambridge, Mass.: Harvard University Press, 1993), 4–5.

15. Terrence W. Deacon, *The Symbolic Species: The Co-evolution of Language and the Brain* (New York: W. W. Norton, 1997), 71. Deacon provides an extended gloss on the linguistics of Charles Sanders Peirce. Although Deacon prefers to reserve symbolic reference for humans, it seems clear that the bee dances meet the particular criteria that he outlines at this point.

16. Donald R. Griffin, *Animal Minds: Beyond Cognition to Consciousness*, rev. edition (Chicago: University of Chicago Press, 2001), 190. The following account of bee "language" is drawn from a number of sources in addition to Griffin's excellent synthesis. These include three works by von Frisch: *The Dancing Bees: An Account of the Life and Senses of the Honey Bee*, trans. Dora Isle and Norman Walker (New York: Harcourt, Brace and World, 1966); *Bees: Their Vision, Chemical Senses, and Language* (Ithaca: Cornell University Press, 1950); and *Dance Language*. See also Thomas D. Seeley's excellent foreword to *Dance Language*; Martin Lindauer, *Communication among Social Bees* (Cambridge, Mass.: Harvard University Press, 1961); Axel Michelson, Bent Bach Andersen, Jesper Storm, Wolfgang H. Kirchner, and Martin Lindauer, "How Honeybees Perceive Communication Dances, Studied by Means of a Mechanical Model," *Behavioral Ecology and Sociobiology* 30 (1992): 143–50; Thomas D. Seeley, *The Wisdom of the Hive: The Social Physiology of Honey Bee Colonies* (Cambridge, Mass.: Harvard University Press, 1995); and James L. Gould and Carol Grant Gould, *Honey Bee*.

17. Von Frisch, *Dance Language*, 57.

18. Thomas Seeley suggests that it makes more sense to refer to all dances as waggle dances. Thomas D. Seeley, foreword to *Dance Language*, xiii.

19. Von Frisch, *Dance Language*, 57.

20. See, for example, Axel Michelson, William F. Towne, Wolfgang H. Kirchner, and Per Kryger, "The Acoustic Near Field of a Dancing Honeybee," *Journal of Comparative Physiology A: Neuroethology, Sensory, Neural, and Behavioral Physiology* 161

(1987): 633–43. Bee communication has actually turned out to be considerably more complex than even von Frisch imagined. In addition to this acoustical signaling, of which he was not aware, it now seems that the waggle dances are not internally consistent. When honeybees are dancing for a food source that is closer than about one mile, both the number of waggles and the direction of the straight run in each cycle show significant variation. Followers deal with this by staying with the dancer for multiple cycles, rapidly calculating a mean before flying off to the food source. James L. Gould and Carol Grant Gould, *Honey Bee*, 61–62.

21. Von Frisch, *A Biologist Remembers*, 150.

22. Von Frisch, *Dance Language*, 132, fig. 114. Von Frisch illustrates the behavior with this figure:

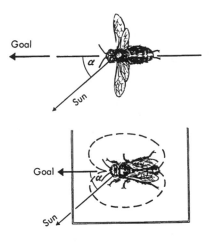

23. Lindauer, *Communication among Social Bees*, 87–111, summarizes this material.

24. I am not reviewing here the many variations that researchers have patiently documented. Lindauer (ibid., 94–96), for example, reveals that bees will compensate for side winds by altering the angle of flight, but on returning to the hive, they will indicate the optimal direction, not the actual route taken.

25. But see Christoph Grüter, M. Sol Balbuena, and Walter M. Farina, "Informational Conflicts Created by the Waggle Dance," *Proceedings of the Royal Society B: Biological Sciences* 275 (2008): 1321–27, an important paper that reports on research suggesting that the vast majority of bees observing dances do not act on the information performed, preferring instead to return to familiar rather than new sources of food. Although the authors note that bees will switch contextually between "social information" (that is, from the dance) and "private information" (that is, about an already visited plot), they propose that dance data are most often acted on by bees who have been inactive for a while or are new to foraging. In what has become a familiar but revealing trope in insect studies more generally, they conclude that further research "will most certainly reveal that the waggle dance modulates collective foraging in more complex ways than is currently assumed."

26. These findings are among those vigorously challenged by Adrian Wenner and his collaborators, who for decades—though ultimately unsuccessfully—argued that

von Frisch's claims were groundless. The controversy has generated a large literature. For a very useful account, see Tania Munz, "The Bee Battles: Karl von Frisch, Adrian Wenner and the Honey Bee Dance Language Controversy," *Journal of the History of Biology* 38, no. 3 (2005): 535–70.

27. Von Frisch, *Dance Language*, 109–29.
28. Ibid., 27.
29. Von Frisch, *Bees*, 85.
30. Von Frisch, *Dance Language*, 32, 37ff. Von Frisch's bees even "give it up on the dance floor" (265), though it's only fair to point out that—even though this is the 1970s—he's talking here about water, not the spirit of disco.
31. Ibid., 133, 136.
32. Martin Lindauer, interview by Thomas D. Seeley, S. Kühnholz, and Robin H. Seeley, "An Early Chapter in Behavioral Physiology and Sociobiology: The Science of Martin Lindauer," *Journal of Comparative Physiology A: Neuroethology, Sensory, Neural, and Behavioral Physiology* 188 (2002): 441–42, 446.
33. Lindauer, ibid., 445.
34. Von Frisch, *Dancing Bees*, 1.
35. Ibid., 41.
36. Thomas D. Seeley, *Wisdom of the Hive*, 240–4.
37. Lindauer, *Communication among Social Bees*, 16–21.
38. This, of course, is also the narrative for the robotic assembly-line hive that appears in so many variants of social theory, for example, Marx's famous fable of the architect: "What distinguishes the worst architect from the best of bees is this, that the architect raises his structure in imagination before he erects it in reality." Karl Marx, *Capital: A Critique of Political Economy*, trans. Samuel Moore and Edward Aveling (Chicago: Charles H. Kerr, 1921), 1:198. (My thanks to Don Moore for reminding me of this one.) There are only two clear examples of competition within the hive that I know of, both of which are of direct functional value to the colony. The first is the eviction of the drones, which I describe below; the second is the regulated fight for dominance among emerging queens after the nest has fissioned.
39. Klaus Schlüpmann, "Fehlanzeige des Regimes in der Fachpresse?" [Negative Reports of the Regime in Specialist Publications] in *Vergangenheit im Blickfeld eines Physikers: Hans Kopfermann 1895–1963* [History from the Viewpoint of a Physicist: Hans Kopfermann 1895–1963], Aleph 99 Productions, September 20, 2002. http://www.aleph99.org/etusci/ks/t2a5.htm.
40. Quoted in Deichmann, *Biologists under Hitler*, 43. I have taken my account of this episode from Deichmann's more detailed narrative, esp. 40–48. For additional material on von Frisch's conduct during the Nazi period and particularly his willingness to act in support of dismissed colleagues, see Ernst-August Seyfarth and Henryk Pierzchała, "Sonderaktion Krakau, 1939: Die Verfolgung von polnischen Biowissenschaftlern und Hilfe durch Karl von Frisch" [Sonderaktion Krakau, 1939: The Persecution of Polish Biologists and the Assistance Provided by Karl von Frisch], *Biologie in unserer Zeit* 22, no. 4 (1992): 218–25. My thanks to Ernst-August Seyfarth for sharing this paper with me and to Leander Schneider for translating it.

41. On Nazi sympathy for animal welfare, see Anna Bramwell, *Ecology in the Twentieth Century: A History* (New Haven, Conn.: Yale University Press, 1989), and Boria Sax, *Animals in the Third Reich: Pets, Scapegoats, and the Holocaust* (New York: Continuum, 2000).

42. Although Lorenz's involvement with Nazism was widely known at the time, it was actively forgotten postwar and effectively erased by the Nobel Committee. The extent of his commitment to the Nazi regime has only recently been documented. See particularly Deichmann, *Biologists under Hitler*, 178–205, from which I have drawn most heavily for this account. Deichmann wants to secure the link between the contemporary ethological version of instinct—derived from Lorenz—and fascist politics. See also Theodora J. Kalikow, "Konrad Lorenz's Ethological Theory: Explanation and Ideology, 1938–1943," *Journal of the History of Biology* 16, no. 1 (1983): 39–73; Boria Sax, "What Is a 'Jewish Dog'? Konrad Lorenz and the Cult of Wildness," *Society and Animals: Journal of Human-Animal Studies* 5, no. 1 (1997), http://www.psyeta.org/sa/sa5.1/sax.html; and Burkhardt, *Patterns of Behavior*.

43. Boria Sax and Peter H. Klopfer, "Jakob von Uexküll and the Anticipation of Sociobiology," in "Jakob von Uexküll: A Paradigm for Biology and Semiotics," special issue, *Semiotica* 134, nos. 1–4 (2001): 770; Ernst Haeckel, *The Evolution of Man: A Popular Exposition of the Principal Points of Human Ontogeny and Phylogeny*, 2 vols. (New York: Appleton, 1897).

44. All the more striking, then, that both von Frisch and Tinbergen stood by Lorenz following the war. Tinbergen, who was imprisoned in a concentration camp and worked actively for the resistance, wrote to an American colleague in 1945 that Lorenz "was rather nazi-infected, though I always considered him a[n] honest and good fellow. . . . It is not right," he continued, "to think that the atrocities were only committed by a minority of fanatical SS-, SD-, or Gestapo-men. Nearly the whole people is hopelessly poisoned. . . . Personally I should regret if . . . [he] would be expelled [from scientific collaboration]." Quoted in Deichmann, *Biologists under Hitler*, 203–4.

45. The only example I have come across is the brief section of *Dancing Bees* called "The Bee's Mental Capacity." Perhaps because he is forced to address this question directly, von Frisch retreats decisively from the affective burden of his corpus. "Because of its extraordinarily narrow range," he writes, "we cannot form a very high opinion of the bee's mental capacity" (162). Yet he closes his discussion more ambivalently: "Nobody can state with certainty whether the bees are conscious of any of their own actions" (164). See also Griffin, *Animal Minds*, 278–82.

46. It also provided a bridge to Jakob von Uexküll's influential phenomenology of the *Umwelt*, the sensory world through which all beings experience life. See the discussion on pages 314–17.

47. Von Frisch, *A Biologist Remembers*, 174.

48. Griffin, *Animal Minds*, 203–11. My account of swarming and nest location is drawn primarily from Griffin; Lindauer, *Communication among Social Bees*; James L. Gould and Carol Grant Gould, *Honey Bee*; Thomas D. Seeley, *Wisdom of the Hive*; and Thomas D. Seeley, S. Kühnholz, and Robin H. Seeley, "An Early Chapter."

49. Lindauer, *Communication among Social Bees*, 35.

50. Ibid., 38.

51. Ibid., 39–40.

52. James L. Gould and Carol Grant Gould, *Honey Bee*, 66–67.

53. Ibid., 67.

54. Ibid., 66.

55. Ibid., 65–66; Griffin, *Animal Minds*, 206–9.

56. James L. Gould and Carol Grant Gould, *Honey Bee*, 65.

57. Griffin, *Animal Minds*, 209.

58. Karl von Frisch, "Decoding the Language of the Bee," *Science* 185 (August 1974): 663–68.

59. Frisch, *Dance Language*, xxiii.

60. Ibid., 105. What it lacked was a response to the acoustic stop signal given by the surrounding workers. Mechanical bees have since become a staple of bee science. See, for example, Michelson et al., "How Honeybees Perceive Communication Dances."

61. Ludwig Wittgenstein, *Philosophical Investigations*, trans. G.E.M. Anscombe (New York: Macmillan, 1953), 223. See the discussion by Cary Wolfe, "In the Shadow of Wittgenstein's Lion: Language, Ethics, and the Question of the Animal," in *Zoontologies: The Question of the Animal*, ed. Cary Wolfe (Minneapolis: University of Minnesota Press, 2003), 1–57. Wolfe reminds us of Vicki Hearne's comment that Wittgenstein's aphorism is "the most interesting mistake about animals I have ever come across." Hearne, *Animal Happiness* (New York: HarperCollins, 1994), 167. Hearne was a philosopher and animal trainer who wrote insightfully on horses and dogs, among other large mammals, convincingly arguing for a human-nonhuman communicative practice that emerges from sensitivity to differential sensory abilities, a notion implicitly indebted to Jakob von Uexküll's theory of the *Umwelt*. On Washoe and the Gardners, see Donna J. Haraway, *Primate Visions: Gender, Race and Nature in the World of Modern Science* (New York: Routledge, 1989), and Hearne, *Adam's Task*, 18–41.

62. Hearne, *Animal Happiness*, 169.

63. Ibid., 170.

64. For similar assessments, see Jacques Derrida, *The Animal That Therefore I Am*, trans. David Wills (New York: Fordham University Press, 2008), Matthew Calarco, *Zoographies: The Question of the Animal from Heidegger to Derrida* (New York: Columbia University Press, 2008), and Wolfe, "In the Shadow of Wittgenstein's Lion." Derrida tracks an unhappy lineage through Descartes, Kant, Levinas, Heidegger, and Lacan. For a less unitary view, see Ian Hacking, "On Sympathy: With Other Creatures," *Tijdschrift voor Filosofie* 63, no. 4 (2001): 685–717. Hacking starts his countergenealogy with David Hume. My thanks to Ann Stoler for pointing me to this important article.

65. Jacques Lacan, *Écrits: A Selection*, trans. Alan Sheridan (New York: W. W. Norton, 1977), 84, quoted in Derrida, *Animal That Therefore I Am*, 123.

66. See James L. Gould's summary of honeybee sociality: "Everyone must be wired in exactly the same way and live by the same set of rules or social life would turn to anarchy." James L. Gould, *Ethology*, 406.

67. On this distinction, see Derrida, *Animal That Therefore I Am*, 119–40.

68. C. F. Hockett quoted in Tim Ingold, *Evolution and Social Life* (New York: Cambridge University Press, 1986), 304.

69. Deacon, *Symbolic Species*, 22. The literature on animal cognition and language is

obviously vast. For an ethological review, see Marc Bekoff, Colin Allen, and Gordon M. Burghardt, eds., *The Cognitive Animal: Empirical and Theoretical Perspectives on Animal Cognition* (Cambridge, Mass.: MIT Press, 2002); for an innovative interdisciplinary account by a biological anthropologist, see Deacon, *Symbolic Species.* Deacon argues for language acquisition and facility of use as the critical distinction between humans and other animals, including primates. It is, in his view, the distinction that enables human achievement.

70. Von Frisch, *Dance Language*, 278–84.

71. On the Aristotelian natural child as a figure in sixteenth-century European expansion, see Anthony Pagden, *The Fall of Natural Man: The American Indian and the Origins of Comparative Ethnology*, corrected ed. (New York: Cambridge University Press, 1986).

72. W. G. Sebald, *Austerlitz*, trans. Anthea Bell (New York: Random House, 2001), 94.

73. Eva M. Knodt, foreword to Niklas Luhmann, *Social Systems*, trans. John Bednarz, Jr., with Dirk Baecker (Palo Alto, Calif.: Stanford University Press, 1995), xxxi, quoted in Wolfe, "In the Shadow of Wittgenstein's Lion," 34.

My Nightmares

1. Scott Atran, "A Leaner, Meaner Jihad," *New York Times*, March 16, 2004.

On January 8, 2008, Abdou Mahamane Was Driving through Niamey . . .

1. Boureima Alpha Gado, *Une histoire des famines au Sahel: étude des grandes crises alimentaires, XIXe–XXe siècles* [*A History of Famine in Sahel: A Study of the Great Food Crises, Nineteenth to Twentieth Centuries*] (Paris: L'Harmattan, 1993). See also Michael Watts, *Silent Violence: Food, Famine and Peasantry in Northern Nigeria* (Berkeley: University of California Press, 1983), and John Rowley and Olivia Bennett, *Grasshoppers and Locusts: The Plague of the Sahel* (London: Panos Institute, 1993).

2. Chinua Achebe, *Things Fall Apart* (London: Heinemann, 1976), 39–40.

3. Achebe, *Things Fall Apart*, 97–98.

4. Souleymane Anza, "Niger Fights Poverty after Being Taken by Shame," Afrol News, January, 19, 2001, http://www.afrol.com/News2001/nir001_fight_poverty.htm; see also Frederic Mousseau with Anuradha Mittal, *Sahel: A Prisoner of Starvation? A Case Study of the 2005 Food Crisis in Niger* (Oakland, Calif.: Oakland Institute, 2006).

5. Niger is one of eight Central and West African countries that use the euro-pegged West African CFA franc as their currency.

6. Comprehensive information on *criquet* species and control can be found at the website of CIRAD (Centre de coopération internationale en recherche agronomique pour le développement), http://www.cirad.fr/en/index.php. See also Rowley and Bennett, *Grasshoppers and Locusts*, and Steen R. Joffe, *Desert Locust Management: A Time for Change*, World Bank Discussion Paper, no. 284 (Washington, D.C.: World Bank, 1995).

7. Current research also suggests that the neurotransmitter serotonin is involved. See Michael L. Anstey, Stephen M. Rogers, Swidbert R. Ott, Malcolm Burrows,

and Stephen J. Simpson, "Serotonin Mediates Behavioral Gregarization Underlying Swarm Formation in Desert Locusts," *Science* 323 (January 2009): 627–30.

8. For a more detailed account, on which I have drawn extensively here, see Hugh Dingle, *Migration: The Biology of Life on the Move* (New York: Oxford University Press, 1996), 272–81; see also the locus(t) classicus, Boris Petrovich Uvarov, *Grasshoppers and Locusts: A Handbook of General Acridology*, vol. 1 (Cambridge: Cambridge University Press, 1966).

9. The UFBIR is an ongoing online project that can be found at http://entnemdept .ufl.edu/walker/ufbir.

10. Apart, that is, from the anomalous use of *locust* in the United States to name the periodic cicada.

11. John Keats, "On the Grasshopper and Cricket" (1816).

12. Robert A. Cheke, N. D. Jago, J. M. Ritchie, L.D.C. Fishpool, R. C. Rainey, and P. Darling, "A Migrant Pest in the Sahel: The Senegalese Grasshopper *Oedaleus senegalensis*," *Philosophical Transactions of the Royal Society B: Biological Sciences* 328 (1990): 539–53.

13. Ibid., 550.

14. Michel Lecoq, "Recent Progress in Desert and Migratory Locust Management in Africa: Are Preventative Actions Possible?" *Journal of Orthoptera Research* 10, no. 2 (2001): 277–91; Joffe, *Desert Locust Management*; Rowley and Bennett, *Grasshoppers and Locusts*.

15. Alpha Gado, *Histoire des famines au Sahel*, 49.

16. Joffe, *Desert Locust Management*; Mousseau and Mittal, *Sahel*; Rowley and Bennett, *Grasshoppers and Locusts*.

17. See Emmanuel Grégoire, *The Alhazai of Maradi: Traditional Hausa Merchants in a Changing Sahelian City*, trans. Benjamin H. Hardy (Boulder, Colo.: Lynne Rienner, 1992).

18. For a detailed and insightful analysis of these colonial fiscal strategies, their long-term trajectories, and their contemporary effects, see Janet Roitman, *Fiscal Disobedience: An Anthropology of Economic Regulation in Central Africa* (Princeton, N.J.: Princeton University Press, 2004).

19. Barbara M. Cooper, *Marriage in Maradi: Gender and Culture in a Hausa Society in Niger, 1900–1989* (Portsmouth, N.H.: Heinemann, 1997), xxxv.

20. See Barbara M. Cooper, "Anatomy of a Riot: The Social Imaginary, Single Women, and Religious Violence in Niger," *Canadian Journal of African Studies* 37, nos. 2–3 (2003): 467–512.

21. Grégoire, *Alhazai of Maradi*, 11, 92.

22. The recent surge in interest in nuclear energy as a "green" fuel, the depletion of stockpiles in the United States and the European Union, and the rush to build a large number of nuclear power stations over the next decade in Asia and Europe have pushed the price of uranium up significantly, giving the Nigerien government added incentive to resolve the Tuareg rebellion.

23. David Loyn, "How Many Dying Babies Make a Famine?" BBC News, August 10, 2005, http://news.bbc.co.uk/2/hi/africa/4139174.stm. See also "Editor's Instinct Led to Story," BBC News, August 2, 2005, http://news.bbc.co.uk/newswatch/ifs/ hi/newsid_4730000/newsid_4737600/4737695.stm.

24. See Jean-François Bayart's discussion of "extraversion" in *The State in Africa: The*

Politics of the Belly, trans. Mary Harper, Christopher Harrison, and Elizabeth Harrison (London: Longman, 1993).

Il Parco delle Cascine on Ascension Sunday

1. Dorothy Gladys Spicer, *Festivals of Western Europe* (New York: H. W. Wilson, 1958), 97–98. My thanks to Gabrielle Popoff for sensitive translation and research work on this chapter and to Riccardo Innocenti for sharing his memories of the *festa*.
2. Timothy Egan, "Exploring Tuscany's Lost Corner," *New York Times*, May 21, 2006.
3. Johann Wolfgang von Goethe, *Italian Journey, 1786–1788*, trans. W. H. Auden and Elizabeth Mayer (London: Penguin Books, 1962), 117.
4. Peter Dale, "The Voice of the Cicadas: Linguistic Uniqueness, Tsunoda Tadanobu's Theory of the Japanese Brain and Some Classical Perspectives," *Electronic Antiquity: Communicating the Classics* 1, no. 6 (1993).
5. Giacomo Leopardi, *Zibaldone dei pensieri*, ed. Rolando Damiani (Milan, Italy: Arnoldo Mondadori Editore, 1997), 1:189. For an elaboration of this thinking in relation to birds, see David Rothenberg, especially his fascinating discussion of the biologist Wallace Craig. Rothenberg, *Why Birds Sing: A Journey into the Mystery of Bird Song* (New York: Basic Books, 2006), 123–28.
6. I have drawn heavily here on Jack Zipes's informative introduction to Carlo Collodi, *Pinocchio*, trans. Mary Alice Murray (London: Penguin, 2002), ix–xviii.
7. Collodi, *Pinocchio*, 14.
8. Agostino Lapini, *Diario fiorentino dal 252 al 1596 [Florentine Diary 252–1596]*, ed. Gius. Odoardo Corazzini (Florence: G. C. Sansoni, 1900), 217.
9. Frances Toor, *Festivals and Folkways of Italy* (New York: Crown, 1953), 245. As with the fighting crickets of Shanghai, it is only the males who sing.
10. For a brief background to the Cascine and the *festa*, see Alta Macadam, *Blue Guide: Florence* (London: Somerset Books, 2005), 265; Cinzie Dugo, "The Cricket Feast," http://www.florence-concierge.it; and Riccardo Gatteschi, "La festa del grillo," Coop Unicoop Firenze, http://www.coopfirenze.it/informazioni/speciali/articoli/5464.
11. Feliciano Philipp, *Protection of Animals in Italy* (Rome: National Fascist Organization for the Protection of Animals, 1938), 5, 9, 8, 4.
12. Martin Heidegger, *What Is Called Thinking?* trans. J. Glenn Gray (New York: HarperPerennial, 1976), 16.
13. Martin Heidegger, *The Fundamental Concepts of Metaphysics: World, Finitude, Solitude*, trans. William McNeill and Nicholas Walker (Bloomington: Indiana University Press, 1995), 176.
14. Karl Jacoby, "Slaves by Nature? Domestic Animals and Human Slaves," *Slavery and Abolition* 15 (1994): 89–99.
15. Philipp, *Protection of Animals*, 19.
16. Mauro Bottigelli quoted in Nicole Martinelli, "Italians Protest 'Beastly' Traditions after Palio Race Death," Zoomata: A Close-up on Italy, August 17, 2004, http://zoomata.com/index.php/?p=1069.
17. And all of them, I suspect, despite their differences, could agree with the philosopher Ian Hacking when he argues that "expanding the circle of moral concern" to include animals demands a sympathy with—rather than a sympathy for—more

than just pain and suffering; it demands a "range of sympathies" such that one can, as Hacking puts it, "resonate to the state of the animal," resonate, that is, as two tuning forks of equal pitch—even at a distance—resonate when only one is played. Hacking, "On Sympathy: With Other Living Creatures," *Tijdschrift voor Filosofie* 63, no. 4 (2001): 703. Similar arguments, more poetically rendered, can be found in several of Alphonso Lingis's brilliant essays; see, for example, "The Rapture of the Deep," in *Excesses: Eros and Culture* (Albany: State University of New York Press, 1983), 2–16; "Antarctic Summer," in *Abuses* (New York: Routledge, 1994), 91–101; and "Bestiality," in *Dangerous Emotions* (New York: Routledge, 2000), 25–39.

18. See the news articles collected by Ufficio per i diritti degli animali, http://www .comune.firenze.it/servizi_pubblici/animali/grillo2001.htm.

The Quality of Queerness Is Not Strange Enough

1. George O. Krizek, "Unusual Interaction between a Butterfly and a Beetle: 'Sexual Paraphilia' in Insects?," *Tropical Lepidoptera* 3, no. 2 (1992): 118.

2. Plutarch, *Moralia*, trans. Harold Cherniss and William C. Helmbold, Loeb Classical Library 406 (Cambridge, Mass.: Harvard University Press, 1957), 12.989 .519–20.

3. Paul L. Vasey and Volker Sommer, "Homosexual Behaviour in Animals: Topics, Hypotheses and Research Trajectories," in *Homosexual Behaviour in Animals: An Evolutionary Perspective*, ed. Volker Sommer and Paul L. Vasey (Cambridge: Cambridge University Press, 2006), 5. I have drawn extensively on Vasey and Sommer's useful essay in this section. See also the immense labor of love that is Bruce Bagemihl's *Biological Exuberance: Animal Homosexuality and Natural Diversity* (New York: St. Martin's Press, 1999). Bagemihl adopts a very generous (and therefore contentious) definition of sex that allows him to include many interactions that might otherwise be construed as nonsexually social. But he effectively demonstrates his key point: that nonreproductive sex among animals is far more varied and widespread than scientists, for various reasons, have allowed. See also Joan Roughgarden, *Evolution's Rainbow: Diversity, Gender, and Sexuality in Nature and People* (Berkeley: University of California Press, 2004), and the essays collected in Sommer and Vasey, *Homosexual Behaviour in Animals*.

4. Antonio Berlese, *Gli insetti: loro organizzazione, sviluppo, abitudini e rapporti coll'uomo* [*The Insects: Their Organization, Development, Habits, and Relationship with Man*], vol. 2 (Milan, Italy: Società Editrice Libraria, 1909), quoted in Edward M. Barrows and Gordon Gordh, "Sexual Behavior in the Japanese Beetle, *Popillia japonica*, and Comparative Notes on Sexual Behavior of Other Scarabs (Coleoptera: Scarabaeidae)," *Behavioral Biology* 23 (1978): 341–54.

5. Vasey and Sommer, "Homosexual Behaviour in Animals," 20.

6. Scott P. McRobert and Laurie Tompkins, "Two Consequences of Homosexual Courtship Performed by *Drosophila melanogaster* and *Drosophila affinis* Males," *Evolution* 42, no. 5 (1988): 1093–97.

7. Adrian Forsyth and John Alcock, "Female Mimicry and Resource Defense Polygyny by Males of a Tropical Rove Beetle, *Leistotrophus versicolor* (Coleoptera: Staphylinidae)," *Behavioral Ecology and Sociobiology* 26 (1990): 325–30.

8. George D. Constantz, "The Mating Behavior of a Creeping Water Bug, *Ambrysus*

occidentalis (Hemiptera: Naucoridae)," *American Midland Naturalist* 92, no. 1 (1974): 237.

9. Barrows and Gordh, "Sexual Behavior in the Japanese Beetle," 351.

10. Kikuo Iwabuchi, "Mating Behavior of *Xylotrechus pyrrhoderus* Bates (Coleoptera: Cerambycidae) V. Female Mounting Behavior," *Journal of Ethology* 5 (1987): 131–36.

11. See Vasey and Sommer, "Homosexual Behaviour in Animals," 20–31.

12. Vasey, "The Pursuit of Pleasure: An Evolutionary History of Female Homosexual Behaviour in Japanese Macaques," in Sommer and Vasey, *Homosexual Behaviour in Animals*, 215.

13. Stephen Jay Gould and Richard Lewontin launched their counterattack to "hyper-adaptationist" theory in the following terms: "We fault the adaptationist programme for its failure to distinguish current utility from reasons for origin . . . ; for its unwillingness to consider alternatives to adaptive stories; for its reliance upon plausibility alone as a criterion for accepting speculative tales; and for its failure to consider adequately . . . competing themes." Gould and Lewontin, "The Spandrels of San Marco and the Panglossian Paradigm: A Critique of the Adaptationist Programme," *Proceedings of the Royal Society B: Biological Sciences* 205 (1979): 581–98. See also two articles by Stephen Jay Gould, "Exaptation: A Crucial Tool for an Evolutionary Psychology," *Journal of Social Issues* 47, no. 3 (1991): 43–65; and "The Exaptive Excellence of Spandrels as a Term and Prototype," *Proceedings of the National Academy of Sciences* 94, no. 20 (1997): 10750–55.

Sex

1. David Jack, "2,000 Pound Fine for Importer of Animal 'Snuff' Videos," *Scotsman*, August 1, 1998; Damien Pearse, "Man Fined for Obscene 'Crush' Videos," Press Association, Home News, January 16, 1999.

2. *The Mo Show*, FOX TV, January 31, 1994.

3. Jeff Vilencia, *American Journal of the Crush-Freaks* (Bellflower, Calif.: Squish Publications) 1 (1993): 145–48.

4. Ibid., 1:130.

5. Ibid., 1:10, 149.

6. As well as from my conversations with Jeff Vilencia, the narrative in this section draws heavily on Martin Lasden's excellent "Forbidden Footage," *California Lawyer*, September 2000, http://www.callawyer.com/story.cfm?pubdt=NaN&eid=306417&evid=1; Dan Kapelovitz, "Crunch Time for Crush Freaks: New Laws Seek to Stamp Out Stomp Flicks," *Hustler*, May 2000; and Patrick Califia, "Boy-Lovers, Crush Videos, and That Heinous First Amendment," in *Speaking Sex to Power: The Politics of Queer Sex* (San Francisco: Cleis Press, 2001), 257–77.

7. California Penal Code and Health and Safety Code quoted in Lasden, "Forbidden Footage," 4.

8. Quoted in Kapelovitz, "Crunch Time."

9. Ibid.

10. I owe this mapping to Katharine Gates. See her *Deviant Desires: Incredibly Strange Sex* (New York: Juno Books, 2000).

11. Carla Freccero, "Fetishism: Fetishism in Literature and Cultural Studies," in *New*

Dictionary of the History of Ideas, ed. Maryanne Cline Horowitz (New York: Scribner's, 2005), 2:826–28.

12. Vilencia, *Journal of the Crush-Freaks*, 1:149.

13. Georges Bataille, *The Tears of Eros*, trans. Peter Connor (San Francisco: City Lights, 1989), 19, 70n23.

14. Edward Wong, "Long Island Case Sheds Light on Animal-Mutilation Videos," *New York Times*, January 25, 2000. See also Edward Wong, "Animal-Torture Video Maker Avoids Jail," *New York Times*, December 27, 2000.

15. Act to amend title 18, U.S. Code, to punish the depiction of animal cruelty, H.R. 1887, 106th Cong., 1st Sess., *Congressional Record*, 145, no. 74 (May 20, 1999): H3460.

16. "Hall of Fame" is Gallegly's glamorous term. Officially, he was named in the U.S. Border Control Congressional Honor Roll.

17. Lasden, "Forbidden Footage," 5.

18. "Rooney Backs 'Crush' Video Ban," BBC News, August 25, 1999, news.bbc.co.uk/2/hi/entertainment/429655.stm; Associated Press, "Activists, Lawmakers Urge Congress to Ban Sale of Animal-Death Videos," August 24, 1999; Lasden, "Forbidden Footage," 5.

19. Associated Press, "Activists, Lawmakers Urge Congress."

20. "Rooney Backs 'Crush' Video Ban."

21. Testimony of Representative Bill McCollum of Florida, speaking for an act to amend title 18 on October 19, 1999, H.R. 1887, 106th Cong., 1st Sess., *Congressional Record* 145, no. 142, H10267.

22. *Pros and Cons*, COURT TV, September 3, 1999.

23. Testimony of Robert C. Scott (D-Va.), ibid., H10268. For an incisive discussion of these points, see Lasden, "Forbidden Footage."

24. *Church of Lukumi Babalu Aye v. City of Hialeah*, 508 U.S. 520 (1993).

25. Testimony of Representative Spencer Bachus of Alabama, speaking for an act to amend title 18, H10271.

26. Testimony of Representative Elton Gallegly (R-Ca.), ibid., H10270.

27. Testimony of Susan Creede to the U.S. House of Representatives Committee on the Judiciary, Subcommittee on Crime, September 30, 1999, judiciary.house.gov/legacy/cree0930.htm.

28. Gilles Deleuze, *Coldness and Cruelty*, trans. Jean McNeil, in *Masochism*, which also contains *Venus in Furs* by Leopold von Sacher-Masoch (New York: Zone Books, 1991), 40–41, 74–76.

29. Sacher-Masoch, *Venus in Furs*, 271.

30. Vilencia, *American Journal of the Crush-Freaks* (Bellflower, Calif.: Squish Publications) 2 (1996): 12–13.

31. William J. Clinton, Statement on Signing Legislation to Establish Federal Criminal Penalties for Commerce in Depiction of Animal Cruelty, December 9, 1999, at John T. Woolley and Gerhard Peters, The American Presidency Project, University of California, Santa Barbara, www.presidency.ucsb.edu/ws/index.php?pid=57047.

32. Adam Liptak, "Free Speech Battle Arises from Dog Fighting Videos," *New York Times*, September 18, 2009.

33. Testimony of Representative Gallegly, speaking for an act to amend title 18, H10269 (emphasis added).

Temptation

1. C. R. Osten-Sacken, "A Singular Habit of *Hilara,*" *Entomologist's Monthly Magazine* 14 (1877): 126–27. All uncited quotations in section 1 are from this paper.
2. George Henry Verrall, obituary of C. R. Osten-Sacken, *Entomologist* 39 (1906): 192.
3. Edward L. Kessel, "The Mating Activities of Balloon Flies," *Systematic Zoology* 4, no. 3 (1955): 97–104. All uncited quotations in section 2 are from this paper.
4. Thomas A. Seboek discusses the symbolic qualities of the empidid gift in the context of Peircian linguistics, although largely just to emphasize its inflexibility in comparison with human symbols. Seboek, *The Sign and Its Masters* (Austin: University of Texas Press, 1979), 18–19.
5. See, among others, Natasha R. LeBas and Leon R. Hockham, "An Invasion of Cheats: The Evolution of Worthless Nuptial Gifts," *Current Biology* 15, no. 1 (2005): 64; Scott K. Sakaluk, "Sensory Exploitation as an Evolutionary Origin to Nuptial Food Gifts in Insects," *Proceedings of the Royal Society B: Biological Sciences* 267, (2000): 339–43; and T. Tregenza, N. Wedell, and T. Chapman, "Introduction. Sexual Conflict: A New Paradigm?" *Philosophical Transactions of the Royal Society B: Biological Sciences* 361 (2006): 229–34.
6. Georges Perec, *Species of Spaces and Other Pieces,* trans. John Sturrock (London: Penguin, 1998), 129, 136.
7. Joan Roughgarden, *Evolution's Rainbow: Diversity, Gender, and Sexuality in Nature and People* (Berkeley: University of California Press, 2004), 171.

The Unseen

1. Karl von Frisch, *Ten Little Housemates,* trans. Margaret D. Senft (New York: Pergamon Press, 1960), 91.

Vision

1. These discoveries are routinely attributed to von Frisch, but it seems that at least some of the experimental work was completed independently, and possibly earlier, by Turner (1867–1923), a pioneer in ethology. Despite his doctorate and his authorship of scholarly papers (including the first by an African American to appear in *Science*), Turner spent the majority of his career teaching high school— it appears that he may have turned down academic positions, preferring to teach public school because of both a sense of social commitment and the additional time it gave him to pursue his research. Turner published his demonstration of honeybees' ability to distinguish among colors in 1910. He is also credited with discovering the ability of insects to hear sounds and distinguish pitch, with recognizing the capacity of bees to utilize geographic memory, with showing that cockroaches are able to learn from experience, with documenting a characteristic

motion of ants approaching their nests ("Turner's circling"), and with developing methodology—particularly conditioning strategies—that would become basic in animal-behavior studies. See *Selected Papers and Biography of Charles Henry Turner (1867–1923), Pioneer in the Comparative Animal Behavior Movement*, ed. Charles I. Abramson (New York: Edwin Mellen Press, 2002).

2. Karl von Frisch, *Bees: Their Vision, Chemical Senses, and Language* (Ithaca, N.Y.: Cornell University Press, 1950).

3. But see the detailed critique of von Frisch's methodology in Georgii A. Mazokhin-Porshnyakov, *Insect Vision*, trans. Roberto Masironi and Liliana Masironi (New York: Plenum Press, 1969), 145–54.

4. See Kentaro Arikawa, Michiyo Kinoshita, and Doekele G. Stavenga, "Color Vision and Retinal Organization in Butterflies," in *Complex Worlds from Simpler Nervous Systems*, ed. Frederick R. Prete (Cambridge, Mass.: MIT Press, 2004), 193–94.

5. For a survey of debates on color and the problem of "color realism," see Alex Byrne and David R. Hilbert, eds., *Readings on Color*, vol. 1, *The Philosophy of Color* (Cambridge, Mass.: MIT Press, 1997), particularly the editors' lucid introduction (xi–xxviii). Further evidence of this point can be found in color constancy, the ability of humans and other animals, including bees and butterflies, to recognize the color of an object under changing light conditions. Goethe famously revealed that color was also a function of additional relationships: those between an object and its neighbors. Johann Wolfgang von Goethe, *Theory of Colours*, trans. Charles Locke Eastlake (Cambridge, Mass.: MIT Press, 1970).

6. Mazokhin-Porshnyakov, *Insect Vision*, 276.

7. Prete, introduction to pt. 1, "Creating Visual Worlds: Using Abstract Representations and Algorithms," in *Complex Worlds*, 3–4.

8. Karl Kral and Frederick R. Prete, "In the Mind of a Hunter: The Visual World of the Praying Mantis," in Prete, *Complex Worlds*, 92–93.

9. For a discussion of this problem in relation to the human mind, see John R. Searle, "Consciousness: What We Still Don't Know," *New York Review of Books*, January 13, 2005, a critical review of Christof Koch's best-selling *Quest for Consciousness: A Neurobiological Approach* (Englewood, Colo.: Roberts, 2004); and note also Koch's recent comment: "We don't understand how mind emerges out of this vast collection of neurons. We have no intuition. It's like Aladdin rubbing a lamp, and a genie appears." Quoted in Peter Edidin, "In Search of Answers from the Great Brains of Cornell," *New York Times*, May 24, 2005.

10. Eric R. Kandel, "Brain and Behavior," in Eric R. Kandel and James H. Schwartz, *Principles of Neural Science*, 2nd ed. (New York: Elsevier, 1985), 3. Indeed, much as the size of the human brain was once a measure of racial hierarchy, the marvelous complexity—and, as ever, the size—of the modern hominid brain is now a marker of human exceptionalism.

11. For a reliable popular introduction, see John J. Ratey, *A User's Guide to the Brain: Perception, Attention, and the Four Theaters of the Brain* (New York: Vintage Books, 2002). For an appraisal of debates in the philosophy of mind that is both sympathetic to neuroscientific claims of biological primacy and suspicious of their reductionism, see John R. Searle, *Mind: A Brief Introduction* (Oxford, U.K.: Oxford University Press, 2004).

12. See, for important contributions, two works by Jonathan Crary: *Techniques of the Observer: On Vision and Modernity in the Nineteenth Century* (Cambridge, Mass.: MIT Press, 1992), and *Suspensions of Perception: Attention, Spectacle, and Modern Culture* (Cambridge, Mass.: MIT Press, 2001); Martin Jay, *Downcast Eyes: The Denigration of Vision in Twentieth-Century French Thought* (Berkeley: University of California Press, 1994); and Hal Foster, ed., *Vision and Visuality* (Seattle: Bay Press/ Dia Art Foundation, 1988).

13. David Howes, ed., *The Varieties of Sensory Experience: A Sourcebook in the Anthropology of the Senses* (Toronto: University of Toronto Press, 1991); Constance Classen, *Worlds of Sense: Exploring the Senses in History and across Cultures* (New York: Routledge, 1993).

14. On linear perspective, see Robert D. Romanyshyn's rather overstated *Technology as Symptom and Dream* (New York: Routledge, 1989), and, for effective delineations of the discontinuities in and displacements of linear perspective, see Martin Jay, "Scopic Regimes of Modernity," and Jonathan Crary, "Modernizing Vision," both in Foster, *Vision and Visuality*, 3–28, 29–50. On the shift to the morphological, see Michel Foucault, *The Order of Things: An Archaeology of the Human Sciences* (New York: Vintage Books, 1994).

15. A fascinating discussion of some of the cultural components of vision along these lines can be found in Oliver Sacks's celebrated essay "To See and Not See," in *An Anthropologist on Mars: Seven Paradoxical Tales* (New York: Vintage Books, 1995), 108–52.

16. Henry Mallock quoted in Michael F. Land's excellent "Eyes and Vision," in *Encyclopedia of Insects*, ed. Vincent H. Resh and Ring T. Cardé (New York: Academic Press, 2003), 397; I have drawn substantially on that article (393–406) for this section. See also Michael F. Land, "Visual Acuity in Insects," *Annual Review of Entomology* 42 (1997): 147–77; and Michael F. Land and Dan-Eric Nilsson, *Animal Eyes* (Oxford, U.K.: Oxford University Press, 2002). Recent recalculations that take into account the poorness of human peripheral vision have reduced Mallock's calculations to a much smaller but still unwieldy 400 inches diameter.

17. Land, "Eyes and Vision," 397.

18. Robert Hooke, *Micrographia, or Some Physiological Descriptions of Minute Bodies Made by Magnifying Glasses with Observations and Inquiries Thereupon* (1665; repr., Mineola, N.Y.: Dover Publications, 2003), 238.

19. Ibid.

20. Anton van Leeuwenhoek quoted in Land, "Eyes and Vision," 394.

21. Sigmund Exner, *The Physiology of the Compound Eyes of Insects and Crustaceans*, trans. Roger C. Hartree (Berlin: Springer Verlag, 1989); originally published as *Die Physiologie der facettierten Augen von Krebsen und Insekten* (Leipzig, Germany: Deuticke, 1891). See Land and Nilsson, *Animal Eyes*, 157–58.

22. Land, "Eyes and Vision," 393.

23. Ibid., 401.

24. Land and Nilsson's choice of Charles Darwin to demonstrate the remarkable optics of the superposition eye is more than apposite. For creationists and proponents of so-called intelligent design, the eye is the Achilles' heel of natural selection. Drawing on Darwin's own uncertainties about the precise mechanisms for the evolution

of the eye and the self-evident point that each of its elements must function both independently and collectively, they assert that such a complex, integrated structure could never have evolved piecemeal through natural selection. But Nilsson and his collaborator Susanne Pelger have recently proposed a convincing 364,000-year sequence of incremental developments and pathways by which an originary patch of light-sensitive cells could evolve through extant intermediary stages into the contemporary mammalian eye. See Dan-Eric Nilsson and Susanne Pelger, "A Pessimistic Estimate of the Time Required for an Eye to Evolve," *Proceedings of the Royal Society B: Biological Science* 256 (1994): 53–58; and the clear summary in Evolution of the Eye, PBS, http://www.pbs.org/wgbh/evolution/library/01/1/l_011_01.html.

25. See Jakob von Uexküll, "A Stroll through the World of Animals and Men: A Picture Book of Invisible Worlds," in *Instinctive Behavior: The Development of a Modern Concept,* ed. and trans. Claire H. Schiller (New York: International Universities Press, 1957), 5–80.

26. Von Uexküll, "A Stroll through the World," 13, 29.

27. Ibid., 65.

28. Ibid., 67.

29. Ibid., 72.

30. Ibid., 80.

The Sound of Global Warming

1. David Dunn, *The Sound of Light in Trees* (Santa Fe, N.M.: EarthEar/Acoustic Ecology Institute, 2006).

2. John A. Byers, "An Encounter Rate Model of Bark Beetle Populations Searching at Random for Susceptible Host Trees," *Ecological Modelling* 91 (1996): 57–66.

3. Dunn, CD liner notes for *Sound of Light;* David Dunn and James P. Crutchfield, "Insects, Trees, and Climate: The Bioacoustic Ecology of Deforestation and Entomogenic Climate Change" (working paper 06-12-055, Santa Fe Institute, 2006), http://www.santafe.edu/research/publications/workingpapers/06-12-055.pdf; William J. Mattson and Robert A. Haack, "The Role of Drought in Outbreaks of Plant-Eating Insects," *BioScience* 37, no. 2 (1987): 110–18.

4. David D. Breshears, Neil S. Cobb, Paul M. Rich, Kevin P. Price, Craig D. Allen, Randy G. Balice, William H. Romme, Jude H. Kastens, M. Lisa Floyd, Jayne Belnap, Jesse J. Anderson, Orrin B. Myers, and Clifton W. Meyer, "Regional Vegetation Die-off in Response to Global-Change-Type Drought," *Proceedings of the National Academy of Sciences* 102, no. 42 (2005): 15144–48.

5. Dunn and Crutchfield, "Insects, Trees, and Climate."

6. For the foundational statement on the soundscape and acoustic ecology, see R. Murray Schafer, *The Soundscape: Our Sonic Environment and the Tuning of the World* (Rochester, Vt.: Destiny Books, 1994). Schafer defines acoustic ecology as "the study of the effects of the acoustic environment . . . on the physical responses or behavioral characteristics of creatures living within it" (271), a formulation that signals the movement's affinity with biological science.

7. Steven Feld in conversation with Donald Brenneis, "Doing Anthropology in

Sound," *American Ethnologist* 31, no. 4 (2004): 462. See also Steven Feld, "Waterfalls of Song: An Acoustemology of Place Resounding in Bosavi, Papua New Guinea," in *Senses of Place*, ed. Steven Feld and Keith Basso (Santa Fe, N.M.: School of American Research Press, 1996), 91–135.

8. For extraordinary accounts of transduction and immersion, see Stefan Helmreich's *Alien Ocean: Anthropological Voyages in Microbial Seas* (Berkeley: University of California Press, 2009).

9. See Andra McCartney, "Alien Intimacies: Hearing Science Fiction Narratives in Hildegard Westerkamp's *Cricket Voice* (or 'I Don't Like the Country, the Crickets Make Me Nervous')," *Organised Sound* 7 (2002): 45–49.

10. On *musique concrète*, see Pierre Schaeffer, "Acousmatics," in *Audio Culture: Readings in Modern Music*, eds. Christoph Cox and Daniel Warner (New York: Continuum, 2004), 76–81. A further key distinction between acoustic ecology and *musique concrète* is the latter's concern with sounds as self-contained entities complete in themselves without reference to their source.

11. David Dunn, "Chaos and the Emergent Mind of the Pond," on *Angels and Insects* (Albuquerque, N.M.: ¿What Next?, 1999); the quotation here and those in the following paragraphs are from the CD liner notes.

12. Doug Struck, "Climate Change Drives Disease to New Territory," *Washington Post*, May 5, 2006; Paul R. Epstein, "Climate Change and Human Health," *New England Journal of Medicine* 353, no. 14 (2005): 1433–36; Paul R. Epstein and Evan Mills, eds., *Climate Change Futures: Health, Ecological, and Economic Dimensions* (Boston: Harvard Medical School/United Nations Development Program, 2006). For a careful study suggesting that causative models centered on climate change sideline the remediable social factors critical to epidemiology (for example, health care, poverty, drug resistance, urban development), see Simon I. Hay, Jonathan Cox, David J. Rogers, Sarah E. Randolph, David I. Stern, G. Dennis Shanks, Monica F. Myers, and Robert W. Snow, "Climate Change and the Resurgence of Malaria in the East African Highlands," *Nature* 415 (2002): 905–9.

13. Data from Dunn and Crutchfield, "Insects, Trees, and Climate," 3, citing Dan Jolin, "Destructive Insects on Rise in Alaska," Associated Press, September 1, 2006; Doug Struck, " 'Rapid Warming' Spreads Havoc in Canada's Forest: Tiny Beetles Destroying Pines," *Washington Post*, March 1, 2006; Jerry Carlson and Karin Verschoor, "Insect Invasion!," *New York State Conservationist*, April 26–27, 2006; Jesse A. Logan and James A. Powell, "Ghost Forests, Global Warming, and the Mountain Pine Beetle (Coleoptera: Scolytidae)," *American Entomologist* 47, no. 3 (2001): 160–73. See also Jim Robbins, "Bark Beetles Kill Millions of Acres of Trees in West," *New York Times*, November 17, 2008, in which the additional point is made about lodge pole pine stands that "because fires have been suppressed for so long, all forests are roughly the same age, and the trees are big enough to be susceptible to beetles." For an interesting account of mountain pine beetle activity in western forests, see Robbins, "Some See Beetle Attacks on Western Forests as a Natural Event," *New York Times*, July 6, 2009.

14. Dunn and Crutchfield, "Insects, Trees, and Climate," 4.

15. Thomas Eisner, *For Love of Insects* (Cambridge, Mass.: Harvard University Press, 2003).

16. For overviews, see David L. Wood, "The Role of Pheromones, Kairomones, and Allomones in the Host Selection and Colonization Behavior of Bark Beetles," *Annual Review of Entomology* 27 (1982): 411–46; and John A. Byers, "Host-Tree Chemistry Affecting Colonization of Bark Beetles," in *Chemical Ecology of Insects 2*, ed. Ring T. Cardé and William J. Bell (New York: Chapman and Hall, 1995), 154–213.

17. Dunn and Crutchfield, "Insects, Trees, and Climate," 8.

18. Jayne Yack and Ron Hoy, "Hearing," in *Encyclopedia of Insects*, ed. Vincent H. Resh and Ring T. Cardé (New York: Academic Press, 2003), 498–505.

19. Dunn and Crutchfield, "Insects, Trees, and Climate," 10.

20. Reginald B. Cocroft and Rafael L. Rodríguez, "The Behavioral Ecology of Insect Vibrational Communication," *BioScience* 55, no. 4 (2005): 323, 331.

21. Dunn and Crutchfield, "Insects, Trees, and Climate," 10.

22. Ibid., 7.

Ex Libris, Exempla

1. Claudine Frank, introduction to *The Edge of Surrealism: A Roger Caillois Reader*, ed. Claudine Frank (Durham, N.C.: Duke University Press, 2003), 28–31.

2. Roger Caillois, "Letter to André Breton," in *Edge of Surrealism*, 84.

3. Ibid., 85.

4. Ibid. (emphasis in the original).

5. Denis Hollier, "On Equivocation (between Literature and Politics)," trans. Rosalind Krauss, *October* 55 (1990): 20.

6. Caillois, "Letter to André Breton," 85.

7. Maria Sibylla Merian, *Dissertation sur la génération et la transformation des insectes de Surinam* (Hague, Netherlands: Pieter Gosse, 1726), 49, quoted in Roger Caillois, *The Mask of Medusa*, trans. George Ordish (New York: Clarkson N. Potter, 1964), 113.

8. On Bates, see my *In Amazonia: A Natural History* (Princeton, N.J.: Princeton University Press, 2002).

9. Caillois, *Mask of Medusa*, 118–20.

10. Ibid., 104.

11. Ibid., 117.

12. Ibid., 121.

13. Roger Caillois, "Mimicry and Legendary Psychasthenia," trans. John Shepley, *October* 31 (1984): 19; Roger Caillois, *The Writing of Stones*, trans. Barbara Bray (Charlottesville: University Press of Virginia, 1985), 2, 3, 104.

14. Gustave Flaubert, *The Temptation of Saint Anthony* (1874), quoted in Caillois, "Mimicry and Legendary Psychasthenia," 31.

15. Caillois, "Mimicry and Legendary Psychasthenia," 27.

16. Hans Zinsser, *Rats, Lice and History: Being a Study in Biography, Which, after Twelve Preliminary Chapters Indispensable for the Preparation of the Lay Reader, Deals with the Life History of Typhus Fever* (Boston: Atlantic Monthly Press/Little, Brown, 1935), 183.

17. See William Gates, ed. and trans., *An Aztec Herbal: The Classic Codex of 1552* (Mineola, N.Y.: Dover Publications, 2000).

18. Pedro de Cieza de León, *The Second Part of the Chronicle of Peru*, trans. Clements R. Markham (London: Hakluyt Society, 1883), 51, 219.
19. Virginia Sáenz, *Symbolic and Material Boundaries: An Archaeological Genealogy of the Urus of Lake Poopó, Bolivia* (Uppsala, Sweden: Uppsala University, 2006), 50–51; Reiner T. Zuidema, *The Ceque System of Cuzco: The Social Organization of the Capital of the Inca*, trans. Eva M. Hooykas (Leiden, Netherlands: E. J. Brill, 1964), 100.
20. Günter Morge, "Entomology in the Western World in Antiquity and in Medieval Times," in *History of Entomology*, ed. Ray F. Smith, Thomas E. Mittler, and Carroll N. Smith (Palo Alto, Calif.: Annual Reviews, 1973), 77.
21. George Poinar, Jr., and Roberta Poinar, *The Amber Forest: A Reconstruction of a Vanished World* (Princeton, N.J.: Princeton University Press, 2001), 129.
22. Jo-shui Chen, *Liu Tsung-yüan and Intellectual Change in T'ang China, 773–819* (Cambridge: Cambridge University Press, 1992), 32. Also, Anthony DeBlasi, *Reform in the Balance: The Defense of Literary Culture in Mid-Tang China* (Albany, N.Y.: SUNY Press, 2002), and Richard E. Strassberg, *Inscribed Landscapes: Travel Writing from Imperial China* (Berkeley: University of California, 1994).
23. Richard E. Strassberg, *Inscribed Landscapes*, 141; Liu Zongyuan, "My First Excursion to West Mountain," in Strassberg, *Inscribed Landscapes*, 141.
24. Liu Zongyuan quoted in Chou Io, *A History of Chinese Entomology*, trans. Wang Siming (Xi'an, China: Tianze Press, 1990), 174 (translation amended).
25. Liu Zongyuan, *Liu Tsung-yüan chi* [*Collected Works of Liu Zongyuan*] (Beijing: Zhong Hua Books, 1979), quoted in Chen, *Liu Tsung-yüan*, 112.
26. Karl von Frisch, *Ten Little Housemates*, trans. Margaret D. Senft (New York: Pergamon Press, 1960), 141.
27. Ibid., 84.
28. Ibid., 107–8.
29. Roger Caillois, "The Praying Mantis: From Biology to Psychoanalysis," in *Edge of Surrealism*, 79.
30. Von Frisch, *Ten Little Housemates*, 107–8.

Yearnings

1. Kawasaki's website can be found at http://ww3.ocn.ne.jp/~fulukon/.
2. See Miyazaki's manga in Yoro Takeshi and Miyazaki Hayao, *Mushime to anime* (Tokyo: Tokuma Shoten, 2002). Reports from 2003 suggest that the city government of Nagoya was hoping to build a development based on Miyazaki and Arakawa's designs.
3. Matsuo Basho quoted in *Haiku*, vol. 3, *Summer–Autumn*, ed. and trans. R. H. Blyth (Tokyo: Hokuseido Press, 1952), 229.
4. Lafcadio Hearn, *Shadowings* (Tokyo: Tuttle, 1971), 101.
5. See K. Takeuchi, R. D. Brown, I. Washitani, A. Tsunekawa, and M. Yokohari, *Satoyama: The Traditional Rural Landscape of Japan* (Tokyo: Springer-Verlag, 2003).
6. See, for example, Yasuhiko Kasahara's Kay's Beetle Breeding Hobby, http://www.geocities.com/kaytheguru. It is worth noting that Japan has long been the world leader in insect breeding. To the best of my knowledge, the country's butterfly

houses are still the only ones in which the animals are raised on-site rather than bought in as pupae.

7. See Harumi Befu, *Hegemony of Homogeneity: An Anthropological Analysis of Nihonjinron* (Melbourne, Australia: Trans Pacific Press, 2001). On Japanese ideas of nature, see Arne Kalland and Pamela J. Asquith, "Japanese Perceptions of Nature: Ideals and Illusions" and other chapters in *Japanese Images of Nature: Cultural Perceptions,* ed. Pamela J. Asquith and Arne Kalland (Richmond, U.K.: Curzon Press, 1997); Julia Adeney Thomas, *Reconfiguring Modernity: Concepts of Nature in Japanese Political Ideology* (Berkeley: University of California Press, 2001); and Tessa Morris-Suzuki, *Re-Inventing Japan: Time, Space, Nation* (Armonk, N.Y.: M. E. Sharpe, 1998). All of these authors work hard to historicize what is sometimes regarded—both inside and outside Japan—as a timeless and unique Japanese relationship with nature, showing how ideas of nature have taken particular forms at particular moments and trying to make sense of the coexistence of a widely held ideology of oneness with nature and long-standing commercial practices that have produced large-scale environmental destruction.

8. Tsunoda Tadanobu, *The Japanese Brain: Uniqueness and Universality,* trans. Yoshinori Oiwa (Tokyo: Taishukan, 1985). For a scathing response that locates Tsunoda's work in the context of nationalist *nihonjinron,* see Peter Dale, "The Voice of the Cicadas: Linguistic Uniqueness, Tsunoda Tadanobu's Theory of the Japanese Brain and Some Classical Perspectives," *Electronic Antiquity: Communicating the Classics* 1, no. 6 (1993).

9. Shoko Kameoka and Hisako Kiyono, *A Survey of the Rhinoceros Beetle and Stag Beetle Market in Japan* (Tokyo: TRAFFIC East Asia—Japan, 2003), 47.

10. Japan External Trade Organization (JETRO), *Marketing Guidebook for Major Imported Products 2004,* vol. 3, *Sports and Hobbies* (Tokyo: JETRO, 2004), 235.

11. Kouichi Goka, Hiroshi Kojima, and Kimiko Okabe, "Biological Invasion Caused by Commercialization of Stag Beetles in Japan," *Global Environmental Research* 8, no. 1 (2004): 67.

12. A survey of insect stores in Tokyo carried out by TRAFFIC East Asia, the regional network monitoring the wildlife trade, found two imported *Dorcus antaeus* stag beetles—a species classed as "nondetrimental" but whose collection is banned in its countries of origin—each selling for U.S. $3,344. See Kameoka and Kiyono, *Survey.*

13. Goka, Kojima, and Okabe, "Biological Invasion."

14. Stag beetles can live up to five years, much longer than rhinoceros beetles, hence their relatively higher price. See T. R. New, " 'Inordinate Fondness': A Threat to Beetles in South East Asia?," *Journal of Insect Conservation* 9 (2005): 147.

15. Kameoka and Kiyono, *Survey,* 41.

16. JETRO, *Marketing Guidebook,* 3:242.

17. Kameoka and Kiyono, *Survey.*

18. See Goka, Kojima, and Okabe, "Biological Invasion," for a detailed discussion of these concerns; see also Kameoka and Kiyono, *Survey;* and New, " 'Inordinate Fondness.' "

19. Goka, Kojima, and Okabe, "Biological Invasion."

20. Yajima Minoru, *Mushi ni aete yokatta* [*I Am Happy That I Met Insects*] (Tokyo:

Froebel-kan, 2004), 42. I am grateful to Yumiko Iwasaki for all translations from this book and those in note 20 below.

21. Konishi Masayasu, *Mushi no bunkashi* [*A Cultural History of Insects*] (Tokyo: Asahi Sensho, 1992), 29–30. For synoptic histories of Japanese insect culture, see also Konishi's *Mushi no hakubutsushi* [*A Natural History of Insects*] (Tokyo: Asahi Sesho, 1993), and Kasai Masaaki, *Mushi to Nihon bunka* [*Insects and Japanese Culture*] (Tokyo: Daikosha, 1997), and for a review of these and other accounts, see Norma Field's "Jean Henri Fabre and Insect Life in Modern Japan" (unpublished manuscript, n.d.), courtesy of the author.

22. Like all other narrators of this history (including everyone whom CJ and I spoke to about this), Konishi also emphasizes the collecting work in Japan by three foreign naturalists: Engelbert Kaempfer, Carl Peter Thunberg, and Philipp Franz von Siebold. All three returned to Europe to publish accounts of Japanese fauna, including insects (Kaempfer's work was published posthumously in 1727; Thunberg's was published in 1781; and Siebold's in 1832), contributions that stand as the initial contact of Japanese nature with formal Western science.

23. The literature on the emergence of European science is, not surprisingly, huge. For a nuanced introductory view of the European scientific revolution, see Steven Shapin, *The Scientific Revolution* (Chicago: University of Chicago Press, 1996). In *The Formation of Science in Japan: Building a Research Tradition* (New Haven, Conn.: Yale University Press, 1989), James R. Bartholomew argues that institutional and social continuities from the Tokugawa period provided the basis for the rapid development of Japanese science in the Meiji period. For an interesting account of the ways in which scientific knowledge and institutions can travel, see Gyan Prakash, *Another Reason: Science and the Imagination of Modern India* (Princeton, N.J.: Princeton University Press, 1999). For a programmatic revision of conventional scientific histories of the leap from pre-modern to modern, see Bruno Latour, *We Have Never Been Modern*, trans. Catherine Porter (Cambridge, Mass.: Harvard University Press, 1993).

24. Shiga Usuke, *Nihonichi no konchu-ya* [*The Best Insect Shop in Japan*] (Tokyo: Bunchonbunko, 2004). Thanks to Hisae Kawamori for translations from this book.

25. See government of Japan, Ministry of the Environment, "List of Regulated Living Organisms under the Invasive Alien Species Act," law 78, June 2, 2004, http://www.env.go.jp/nature/intro/1outline/files/siteisyu_list_e.pdf.

Zen and the Art of Zzz's

1. My thanks to Barrett Klein for introducing me to the literature on this topic.

SELECTED BIBLIOGRAPHY

Abbas, Ackbar. "Play it Again Shanghai: Urban Preservation in the Global Era." In *Shanghai Reflections: Architecture, Urbanism and the Search for an Alternative Modernity*, edited by Mario Gandelsonas, 37–55. New York: Princeton Architectural Press, 2002.

Abramson, Charles I., ed. *Selected Papers and Biography of Charles Henry Turner (1867–1923). Pioneer in the Comparative Animal Behavior Movement*. New York: Edwin Mellen Press, 2002.

Achebe, Chinua. *Things Fall Apart*. London: Heinneman, 1976.

Aldrovandi, Ulisse. *De animalibus insectis libri septem*. 1602.

Almog, Shmuel. "Alfred Nossig: A Reappraisal." *Studies in Zionism* 7, (1983): 1–29.

Alpha Gado, Boureima. *Une histoire des famines au Sahel: étude des grandes crises alimentaires, XIXe–XXe siécles [A History of Famine in Sahel: A Study of the Great Food Crises, Nineteenth to Twentieth Centuries]*. Paris: L'Harmattan, 1993.

Aly, Götz, Peter Chroust, and Christian Pross. *Cleansing the Fatherland: Nazi Medicine and Racial Hygiene*. Translated by Belinda Cooper. Baltimore: Johns Hopkins University Press, 1994.

Appelfeld, Aharon. *The Iron Tracks*. Translated by Jeffrey M. Green. New York: Schocken Books, 1999.

Aristotle. *Generation of Animals*. Translated by A. L. Peck. Cambridge, Mass.: Loeb Classical Library/Harvard University Press, 1979.

———. *History of Animals*. Translated by A. L. Peck. 3 vols. Cambridge, Mass.: Loeb Classical Library/Harvard University Press, 1984.

———. *Parts of Animals. Movement of Animals. Progression of Animals*. Translated by A. L. Peck and E. S. Forster. Cambridge, Mass.: Loeb Classical Library/Harvard University Press, 1968.

Aschheim, Steven E. *Brothers and Strangers: The East European Jew in German and German-Jewish Consciousness, 1800–1923*. Madison: University of Wisconsin Press, 1982.

Atran, Scott. *Cognitive Foundations of Natural History: Towards an Anthropology of Science*. Cambridge: Cambridge University Press, 1993.

Backus, Robert, trans. *The Riverside Counselor's Stories: Vernacular Fiction of Late Heian Japan*. Palo Alto, Calif.: Stanford University Press, 1985.

Bacon, Francis. *Sylva sylvarum: or a Naturall History in Ten Centuries*. London, 1627.

Bachelard, Gaston. *The Poetics of Space*. Translated by Maria Jolas. New York: Beacon Press, 1969.

Bagemihl, Bruce. *Biological Exuberance: Animal Homosexuality and Natural Diversity.* New York: St. Martin's Press, 1999.

Bartholomew, James R. *The Formation of Science in Japan: Building a Research Tradition.* New Haven, Conn.: Yale University Press, 1993.

Bataille, Georges. *The Tears of Eros.* Translated by Peter Connor. San Francisco: City Lights, 1989.

Bauman, Zygmunt. "Allosemitism: Premodern, Modern, Postmodern." In Modernity, Culture, and "the Jew," edited by Bryan Cheyette and Laura Marcus. Palo Alto, Calif.: Stanford Universtiy Press, 1998.

Bayart, Jean-François. *The State in Africa: The Politics of the Belly.* Translated by Mary Harper, Christopher Harrison, and Elizabeth Harrison. London: Longman, 1993.

Beebe, William. "Insect Migration at Rancho Grande in North-Central Venezuela: General Account." *Zoologica* 34, no. 12 (1949): 107–10.

Bein, Alex. "The Jewish Parasite: Notes on the Semantics of the Jewish Problem with Special Reference to Germany." *Leo Baeck Institute Yearbook* 9 (1964): 3–40.

Bekoff, Marc, Colin Allen, and Gordon M. Burghardt, eds. *The Cognitive Animal: Empirical and Theoretical Perspectives on Animal Cognition.* Cambridge, Mass.: MIT Press, 2002.

Benjamin, Walter. *Illuminations: Essays and Reflections.* Translated by Harry Zohn. New York: Schocken Books, 1968.

———. *Reflections: Essays, Aphorisms, Autobiographical Writings.* Edited by Peter Demetz. Translated by Edmund Jephcott. New York: Schocken Books, 1986.

Bergson, Henri. *Creative Evolution.* Translated by Arthur Mitchell. New York: Dover, [1911] 1989.

Bolaño, Roberto. *2666.* Translated by Natasha Wimmer. New York: Farrar, Straus and Giroux, 2008.

Bramwell, Anna. *Ecology in the Twentieth Century: A History.* New Haven, Conn.: Yale University Press, 1989.

Burkhardt, Richard W., Jr. *Patterns of Behavior: Konrad Lorenz, Niko Tinbergen, and the Founding of Ethology.* Chicago: University of Chicago Press, 2005.

Busby, Chris. *Wings of Death: Nuclear Pollution and Human Health.* Aberystwyth, U.K.: Green Audit, 1995.

Caillois, Roger. *The Mask of Medusa.* Translated by George Ordish. New York: Clarkson N. Potter, 1964.

———. "Mimicry and Legendary Psychasthenia." Translated by John Shepley. *October* 31 (1984): 16–32.

———. *The Writing of Stones.* Translated by Barbara Bray. Charlottesville: University Press of Virginia, 1985.

Calarco, Matthew. *Zoographies: The Question of the Animal from Heidegger to Derrida.* New York: Columbia University Press, 2008.

Canetti, Elias. *Crowds and Power.* Translated by Carol Stewart. New York: Farrar, Straus and Giroux, 1984.

Chen, Jo-shui. *Liu Tsung-yuan and Intellectual Change in T'ang China, 773–819.* Cambridge: Cambridge University Press, 1992.

Chou, Io. *A History of Chinese Entomology.* Translated by Wang Siming. Xi'an, China: Tianze Press, 1990.

Coad, B. R. "Insects Captured by Airplane Are Found at Surprising Heights." *Yearbook of Agriculture, 1931*. Washington, D.C.: USDA, 1931.

Cocroft, Reginald B., and Rafael L. Rodríguez. "The Behavioral Ecology of Insect Vibrational Communication." *Bioscience* 55, no. 4 (2005): 323–34.

Cohen, Richard I. *Jewish Icons: Art and Society in Modern Europe*. Berkeley: University of California Press, 1998.

Collodi, Carlo. *Pinocchio*. Translated by Mary Alice Murray. London: Penguin, 2002.

Cooper, Barbara M. *Marriage in Maradi: Gender and Culture in a Hausa Society in Niger, 1900–1989*. Abingdon, U.K.: James Currey, 1997.

———. "Anatomy of a Riot: The Social Imaginary, Single Women, and Religious Violence in Niger." *Canadian Journal of African Studies* 37, nos. 2–3 (2003): 467–512.

Crary, Jonathan. *Techniques of the Observer: On Vision and Modernity in the Nineteenth Century*. Cambridge, Mass.: MIT Press, 1992.

Crist, Eileen. "The Ethological Constitution of Animals as Natural Objects: The Technical Writings of Konrad Lorenz and Nikolaas Tinbergen." *Biology and Philosophy* 13, no. 1 (1998): 61–102.

———. "Naturalists' Portrayals of Animal Life: Engaging the Verstehen Approach." *Social Studies of Science* 26, no. 4 (1996): 799–838.

Dale, Peter. "The Voice of the Cicadas: Linguistic Uniqueness, Tsunoda Tananobu's Theory of the Japanese Brain and Some Classical Perspectives." *Electronic Antiquity: Communicating the Classics* 1, no. 6 (1993).

Darwin, Charles. *The Descent of Man, and Selection in Relation to Sex*. New York: Penguin, [1871] 2004.

———. *The Expression of the Emotions in Man and Animals*. New York: Oxford University Press, [1872] 1998.

Daston, Lorraine. "Attention and the Values of Nature in the Enlightnment." In *The Moral Authority of Nature*, edited by Lorraine Daston and Fernando Vidal, 100–26. Chicago: University of Chicago Press, 2004.

Daston, Lorraine, and Katherine Park. *Wonders and the Order of Nature, 1150–1750*. New York: Zone Books, 1998.

Davis, Natalie Zemon. *Women on the Margins: Three Seventeenth-Century Lives*. Cambridge, Mass.: Belknap/Harvard, 1995.

Degler, Carl N. *In Search of Human Nature: The Decline and Revival of Darwinism in American Social Thought*. Oxford, U.K.: Oxford University Press, 1991.

Deichmann, Ute. *Biologists under Hitler*. Translated by Thomas Dunlap. Cambridge, Mass.: Harvard University Press, 1996.

Deleuze, Gilles, and Félix Guattari. *A Thousand Plateaus: Capitalism and Schizophrenia*. Translated by Brian Massumi. Minneapolis: University of Minnesota Press, 1987.

Deleuze, Gilles, and Leopold von Sacher-Masoch. *Masochism*. New York: Zone Books, 1991.

Derrida, Jacques. *The Animal That Therefore I Am*. Translated by David Wills. New York: Fordham University Press, 2008.

Dingle, Hugh. *Migration: The Biology of Life on the Move*. New York: Oxford University Press, 1996.

Dudley, Robert. *The Biomechanics of Insect Flight: Form, Function, Evolution*. Princeton, N.J.: Princeton University Press, 2000.

Dunn, David. *Angels and Insects*. Santa Fe, N.M.: ¿What Next?, 1999.

——. *The Sound of Light in Trees*. Santa Fe, N.M.: EarthEar/Acoustic Ecology Institute, 2006.

Dunn, David, and James P. Crutchfield. "Insects, Trees, and Climate: The Bioacoustic Ecology of Deforestation and Entomogenic Climate Change." Santa Fe Institute Working Paper 06–12–055, 2006.

Efron, John M. *Defenders of the Race: Jewish Doctors and Race Science in Fin-de-Siècle Europe*. New Haven, Conn.: Yale University Press, 1994.

Eisner, Thomas. *For Love of Insects*. Cambridge, Mass.: Harvard University Press, 2003.

Evans, E. P. *The Criminal Prosecution and Capital Punishment of Animals: The Lost History of Europe's Animal Trials*. Boston, Mass.: Faber, [1906] 1987.

Evans, R.J.W. *Rudolf II and His World: A Study in Intellectual History, 1576–1612*. London: Thames and Hudson, 1973.

Exner, Sigmund. *The Physiology of the Compound Eyes of Insects and Crustaceans*. Translated by R. C. Hartree. Berlin: Springer Verlag, [1891] 1989.

Fabre, Jean-Henri. *The Hunting Wasps*. Translated by Alexander Teixeira de Mattos. New York: Dodd, Mead and Company, 1915.

——. *The Life of the Fly*. Translated by Alexander Teixeira de Mattos. New York: Dodd, Mead and Company, 1913.

——. *The Mason-Wasps*. Translated by Alexander Teixeira de Mattos. New York: Dodd, Mead and Company, 1919.

——. *Social Life in the Insect World*. Translated by Bernard Miall. New York: Century, 1912.

Favret, Colin. "Jean-Henri Fabre: His Life Experiences and Predisposition Against Darwinism." *American Entomologist* 45, no. 1 (1999): 38–48.

Feld, Steven, and Donald Brenneis. "Doing Anthropology in Sound." *American Ethnologist* 31, no. 4 (2004): 461–74.

Feyerabend, Paul. *Against Method: Outline of an Anarchistic Theory of Knowledge*. London: New Left Books, 1975.

Field, Norma. "Jean-Henri Fabre and Insect Life in Japan." Unpublished manuscript, n.d.

Findlen, Paula. *Possessing Nature: Museums, Collecting, and Scientific Culture in Early Modern Italy*. Berkeley: University of California Press, 1994.

Foster, Hal, ed. *Vision and Visuality*. Seattle: Bay Press/Dia Art Foundation, 1988.

Frank, Claudine, ed. *The Edge of Surrealism: A Roger Caillois Reader*. Durham, N.C.: Duke University Press, 2003.

Frazer, James George. *The Golden Bough: A Study in Magic and Religion*, 12 vols. London: MacMillan, 1906–15.

Freccero, Carla. "Fetishism: Fetishism in Literature and Cultural Studies." In *New Dictionary of the History of Ideas*. Vol. 2. New York: Scribner's, 2005.

Frisch, Karl von. *Bees: Their Vision, Chemical Senses, and Language*. Ithaca: Cornell University Press, 1950.

——. *A Biologist Remembers*. Translated by Lisbeth Gombrich. Oxford, U.K.: Pergamon Press, 1967.

——. *The Dance Language and Orientation of Bees*. Translated by Leigh E. Chadwick. Cambridge, Mass.: Harvard University Press, [1965] 1993.

———. *The Dancing Bees: An Account of the Life and Senses of the Honey Bee.* Translated by Dora Isle and Norman Walker. New York: Harcourt, Brace and World, 1966.

———. *Ten Little Housemates.* Translated by Margaret D. Senft. New York: Pergamon Press, 1960.

Fudge, Erica. *Animal.* New York: Reaktion Books, 2002.

Gates, Katharine. *Deviant Desires: Incredibly Strange Sex.* New York: Juno Books, 2000.

Glick, P. A. *The Distribution of Insects, Spiders, and Mites in the Air.* U.S. Department of Agriculture Technical Bulletin 673. Washington, D.C.: USDA, 1939.

Goethe, Johann Wolfgang von. *Italian Journey, 1786–1788.* Translated by W. H. Auden and Elizabeth Mayer. London: Penguin Books, 1962.

———. *Theory of Colors.* Translated by Charles Locke Eastlake. Cambridge, Mass.: MIT Press, 1970.

Gossman, Lionel. "Michelet and Natural History: The Alibi of Nature." *Proceedings of the American Philosophical Society* 145, no. 3 (2001): 283–333.

Gould, James L. *Ethology: The Mechanisms and Evolution of Behavior.* New York: W. W. Norton, 1983.

Gould, James L., and Carol Grant Gould. *The Honey Bee.* New York: Scientific American, 1988.

Gould, Stephen Jay. *Hen's Teeth and Horse's Toes: Further Reflections in Natural History.* New York: W. W. Norton, 1994.

Gould, Stephen Jay, and Richard Lewontin. "The Spandrels of San Marco and the Panglossian Paradigm: A Critique of the Adaptationist Program." *Proceedings of the Royal Society B: Biological Sciences* 205 (1979): 581–98.

Graeub, Ralph. *The Petkau Effect: The Devastating Effect of Nuclear Radiation on Human Health and the Environment.* New York: Four Walls Eight Windows, 1994.

Grant, Edward. "Aristotelianism and the Longevity of the Medieval World View." *History of Science* 16 (1978): 95–106.

Greenspan, Ralph J., and Herman A. Dierick. " 'Am Not I a Fly Like Thee?' From Genes in Fruit Flies to Behavior in Humans." *Human Molecular Genetics* 13, no. 2 (2004): R267–R273.

Grégoire, Emmanuel. *The Alhazai of Maradi: Traditional Hausa Merchants in a Changing Sahelian City.* Translated by Benjamin H. Hardy. Boulder, Colo.: Lynne Rienner, 1992.

Griffin, Donald R. *Animal Minds: Beyond Cognition to Consciousness.* Rev. edition. Chicago: University of Chicago Press, 2001.

Guerrini, Anita. *Experimenting with Humans and Animals: From Galen to Animal Rights.* Baltimore: Johns Hopkins University Press, 2003.

Hacking, Ian. "On Sympathy: With Other Creatures." *Tijdschrift voor Filosofie* 63, no. 4 (2001): 685–717.

Haraway, Donna J. *Primate Visions: Gender, Race and Nature in the World of Modern Science.* New York: Routledge, 1989.

———. *When Species Meet.* Minneapolis: University of Minnesota Press, 2007.

Hart, Mitchell B. "Moses the Microbiologist: Judaism and Social Hygiene in the Work of Alfred Nossig." *Jewish Social Studies* 2, no. 1 (1995): 72–97.

———. "Racial Science, Social Science, and the Politics of Jewish Assimilation." *Isis* 90 (1999): 268–97.

————. *Social Science and the Politics of Modern Jewish Identity.* Palo Alto, Calif.: Stanford University Press, 2000.

Hearn, Lafcadio. *Shadowings.* Tokyo: Tuttle, 1971.

Hearne, Vicki. *Adam's Task: Calling Animals by Name.* New York: Alfred A. Knopf, 1986.

————. *Animal Happiness.* New York: HarperCollins, 1994.

Heidegger, Martin. *The Fundamental Concepts of Metaphysics: World, Finitude, Solitude.* Translated by William McNeill and Nicholas Walker. Bloomington: Indiana University Press, 1995.

Helmreich, Stefan. *Alien Ocean: Anthropological Voyages in Microbial Seas.* Berkeley: University of California Press, 2009.

Hendrix, Lee. "Joris Hoefnagel and *The Four Elements:* A Study in Sixteenth-Century Nature Painting." Ph.D. diss., Princeton University, 1984.

————. "Of Hirsutes and Insects: Joris Hoefnagel and the Art of the Wondrous." *Word and Image* 11, no. 4 (1995): 373–90.

Hendrix, Lee, and Thea Vignau-Wilberg. *Mira calligraphiae monumenta: A Sixteenth-Century Calligraphic Manuscript Inscribed by Georg Bocskay and Illuminated by Joris Hoefnagel.* Malibu, Calif: J. Paul Getty Museum, 1992.

Herrnstein, R. J. "Nature as Nurture: Behaviorism and the Instinct Doctrine." *Behavior and Philosophy* 26 (1998): 73–107; reprinted from *Behavior* 1, no. 1 (1972): 23–52.

Hesse-Honegger, Cornelia. *After Chernobyl.* Bern: Bundesamt für Kultur/Verlag Lars Müller, 1992.

————. "Der Verdacht." [The Suspicion]. *Tages-Anzeiger Magazin* (April 1989): 28–35.

————. *The Future's Mirror.* Translated by Christine Luisi. Newcastle upon Tyne, U.K.: Locus+, 2000.

————. *Heteroptera: The Beautiful and the Other, or Images of a Mutating World.* Translated by Christine Luisi. New York: Scalo, 2001.

————. *Warum bin ich in Österfärnebo? Bin auch in Leibstadt, Beznau, Gösgen, Creys-Malville, Sellafield gewesen . . . [Why am I in Österfärnebo? I Have Also Been to Leibstadt, Beznau, Gösgen, Creys-Malville, Sellafield . . .].* Basel, Switzerland: Editions Heuwinkel, 1989.

————. "Wenn Fliegen und Wanzen anders aussehen als sie solten." [*When Flies and Bugs Don't Look the Way They Should*]. *Tages-Anzeiger Magazin* (January 1988): 20–25.

Hoefnagel, Joris. *Animalia rationalia et insecta (Ignis).* 1582.

Hooke, Robert. *Micrographia; or Some Physiological Descriptions of Minute Bodies Made by Magnifying Glasses with Observations and Inquiries Thereupon.* New York: Dover, [1665] 2003.

Hsiung Ping-chen. "From Singing Bird to Fighting Bug: The Cricket in Chinese Zoological Lore." Unpublished manuscript, Taipei, Taiwan, n.d.

Imanishi Kinji. *The World of Living Things.* Translated by Pamela J. Asquith, Heita Kawakatsu, Shusuke Yagi, and Hiroyuki Takasaki. London: RoutledgeCurzon, 2002.

Jacoby, Karl. "Slaves by Nature? Domestic Animals and Human Slaves." *Slavery and Abolition* 15 (1994): 89–99.

Japan External Trade Organization (JETRO). *Marketing Guidebook for Major Imported Products 2004.* Vol. 3, *Sports and Hobbies.* Tokyo: JETRO, 2004.

Jay, Martin. *Downcast Eyes: The Denigration of Vision in Twentieth-Century French Thought.* Berkeley: University of California Press, 1994.

Jin Xingbao. "Chinese Cricket Culture." *Cultural Entomology Digest* 3 (November 1994). Available at http://www.insects.org/ced3/chinese_crcul.html.

Jin Xingbao and Liu Xianwei. *Qan jian min cun de xuan yan han guang shan. [Common Singing Insects: Selection, Care, and Appreciation]*. Shanghai: Shanghai Science and Technology Press, 1996.

Joffe, Steen R. *Desert Locust Management: A Time for Change.* World Bank Discussion Paper, no. 284, April 1995. Washington, D.C.: World Bank, 1995.

Johnson, C. G. *Migration and Dispersal of Insects by Flight.* London: Methuen, 1969.

Jullien, François. *The Propensity of Things: Toward a History of Efficacy in China.* Translated by Janet Lloyd. New York: Zone Books, 1995.

Kafka, Franz. *The Transformation and Other Stories.* Translated by Malcolm Pasley. London: Penguin, 1992.

Kalikow, Theodora J. "Konrad Lorenz's Ethological Theory: Explanation and Ideology, 1938–1943." *Journal of the History of Biology* 16, no. 1 (1983): 39–73.

Kalland, Arne, and Pamela J. Asquith, eds. *Japanese Images of Nature: Cultural Perceptions.* Richmond, U.K.: Curzon, 1997.

Kapelovitz, Dan. "Crunch Time for Crush Freaks: New Laws Seek to Stamp Out Stomp Flicks." *Hustler,* May 2000.

Kaufmann, Thomas DaCosta. *The Mastery of Nature: Aspects of Art, Science, and Humanism in the Renaissance.* Princeton, N.J.: Princeton University Press, 1993.

———. *The School of Prague: Painting at the Court of Rudolf II.* Chicago: University of Chicago Press, 1988.

Kessel, Edward L. "The Mating Activities of Balloon Flies." *Systematic Zoology* 4, no. 3 (1955): 97–104.

Kohler, Robert E. *Lords of the Fly: Drosophila Genetics and the Experimental Life.* Chicago: University of Chicago Press, 1994.

Konishi Masayasu. *Mushi no bunkashi [A Cultural History of Insects]*. Tokyo: Asahi Sensho, 1992.

Kouichi Goka, Hiroshi Kojima, and Kimiko Okabe. "Biological Invasion Caused By Commercialization of Stag Beetles in Japan." *Global Environmental Research* 8, no. 1 (2004): 67–74.

Kral, Karl, and Frederick R. Prete. "In the Mind of a Hunter: The Visual World of a Praying Mantis." In *Complex Worlds from Simpler Nervous Systems,* edited by Frederick R. Prete. Cambridge, Mass.: MIT Press, 2004.

Krall, Hanna. *Shielding the Flame: An Intimate Conversation with Dr. Marek Edelman, the Last Surviving Leader of the Warsaw Ghetto Uprising.* Translated by Joanna Stasinska and Lawrence Weschler. New York: Henry Holt, 1986.

Krizek, George O. "Unusual Interaction between a Butterfly and a Beetle: 'Sexual Paraphilia' in Insects?" *Tropical Lepidoptera* 3, no. 2 (1992): 118.

Land, Michael F. "Eyes and Vision." In *Encyclopedia of Insects,* edited by Vincent H. Resh and Ring T. Cardé, 393–406. New York: Academic Press, 2003.

Land, Michael F., and Dan-Eric Nilsson. *Animal Eyes.* Oxford, U.K.: Oxford University Press, 2002.

Lapini, Agostino. *Diario fiorentino dal 252 al 1596 [Florentine Diary 252–1596]*. Edited by Gius. Odoardo Corazzini. Florence: G. C. Sansoni, 1900.

Lasden, Martin. "Forbidden Footage." *California Lawyer* (September 2000). Available at californialawyermagazine.com/index.cfm?sid=&tkn=&eid=306417&evid=1.

Launois-Luong, M. H., and M. Lecoq. *Vade-mecum des criquets du Sahel* [*Vade Mecum of Locusts in the Sahel*]. Paris: CIRAD/PRIFAS, 1989.

Lauter, Marlene, ed. *Concrete Art in Europe after 1945*. Ostfildern-Ruit, Germany: Hatje Cantz, 2002.

LeBas, Natasha R., and Leon R. Hockham. "An Invasion of Cheats: The Evolution of Worthless Nuptial Gifts." *Current Biology* 15, no. 1 (2005): 64–67.

Legros, Georges Victor. *Fabre: Poet of Science*. Translated by Bernard Miall. Whitefish, Mont.: Kessinger Publishing, [1913] 2004.

Leopardi, Giacomo. *Zibaldone dei pensieri*. Vol. 1. Edited by Rolando Damiani. Milan: Arnoldo Mondadori Editore, 1997.

Levy-Barzilai, Vered. "The Rebels among Us." *Haaretz Magazine*, October 13, 2006, 18–22.

Li Shijun. *Min jien cuan shi: shang pin xishuai* [*An Anthology of Lore of One Hundred and Eight Excellent Crickets*]. Hong Kong: Wenhui, 2008.

———. *Zhonggou dou xi jian shang* [*An Appreciation of Chinese Cricket Fighting*]. Shanghai: Shanghai Science and Technology Press, 2001.

———. *Zhonghua xishuai wushi bu xuan* [*Fifty Taboos of Cricket Collecting*]. Shanghai: Shanghai Science and Technology Press, 2002.

Libertaire Group, ed. *A Short History of the Anarchist Movement in Japan*. Tokyo: Idea Publishing House.

Lindauer, Martin. *Communication among Social Bees*. Cambridge, Mass.: Harvard University Press, 1961.

Lingis, Alphonso. *Abuses*. New York: Routledge, 1994.

———. *Dangerous Emotions*. New York: Routledge, 2000.

———. *Excesses: Eros and Culture*. Albany, N.Y.: State University of New York Press, 1983.

Liu Xinyuan. "Amusing the Emperor: The Discovery of Xuande Period Cricket Jars from the Ming Imperial Kilns." *Orientations* 26, no. 8 (1995): 62–77.

Lloyd, G.E.R. *Science, Folklore and Ideology: Studies in the Life Sciences in Ancient Greece*. Cambridge: Cambridge University Press, 1983.

Luckert, Stephen. *The Art and Politics of Arthur Szyk*. Washington, D.C.: U.S. Holocaust Memorial Museum, 2002.

Mamdani, Mahmood. *When Victims Become Killers: Colonialism, Nativism, and the Genocide in Rwanda*. Princeton, N.J.: Princeton University Press, 2002.

Mazokhin-Porshnyakov, Georgii A. *Insect Vision*. Translated by Roberto Masironi and Liliana Masironi. New York: Plenum Press, 1969.

McCartney, Andra. "Alien Intimacies: Hearing Science Fiction Narratives in Hildegard Westerkamp's *Cricket Voice* (or 'I Don't Like the Country, the Crickets Make Me Nervous')." *Organized Sound* 7 (2002): 45–49.

Mendelsohn, Ezra. "From Assimilation to Zionism in Lvov: The Case of Alfred Nossig." *Slavonic and East European Review* 49, no. 17 (1971): 521–34.

Merian, Maria Sibylla. *Metamorphosis insectorum Surinamensium*. Amsterdam: Gerard Valck, 1705.

Michelet, Jules. *The Insect*. Translated by W. H. Davenport Adams. London: T. Nelson and Sons, 1883.

Mol, Annemarie. *The Body Multiple: Ontology in Medical Practice*. Durham, N.C.: Duke University Press, 2003.

Montaigne, Michel de. *The Complete Works*. Translated by Donald M. Frame. New York: Everyman's Library, 2003.

Mousseau, Frederic, with Anuradha Mittal. *Sahel: A Prisoner of Starvation? A Case Study of the 2005 Food Crisis in Niger*. Oakland, Calif.: The Oakland Institute, 2006.

Munz, Tania. "The Bee Battles: Karl von Frisch, Adrian Wenner and the Honey Bee Dance Language Controversy." *Journal of the History of Biology* 38, no. 3 (2005): 535–70.

Nilsson, Dan-Eric, and Susanne Pelger. "A Pessimistic Estimate of the Time Required for an Eye to Evolve." *Proceedings of the Royal Society B: Biological Science* 256 (1994): 53–58.

Nossig, Alfred, ed. *Jüdische Statistik* [*Jewish Statistics*]. Berlin: Der Jüdische Verlag, 1903.

———. *Die Sozialhygiene der Juden und des altorientalischen Völkerkreises* [*Social Hygiene of the Jews and Ancient Oriental Peoples*]. Stuttgart: Deutsche Verlags-Anstalt, 1894.

———. *Zionismus und Judenheit: Krisis und Lösung* [*Zionism and Jewry: Crisis and Solution*]. Berlin: Interterritorialer Verlag "Renaissance," 1922.

Nuti, Lucia. "The Mapped Views by George Hoefnagel: The Merchant's Eye, the Humanist's Eye." *Word and Image* 4 (1988): 545–70.

Nye, Robert A. "The Rise and Fall of the Eugenics Empire: Recent Perspectives on the Impact of Biomedical Thought in Modern Society." *Historical Journal* 36 (1993): 687–700.

Okumoto Daizaburo. *Hakubutsugakuno kyojin Anri Faburu* [*Henri Fabre: A Giant of Natural History*]. Tokyo: Syueisya, 1999.

Osten-Sacken, Carl Robert. "A Singular Habit of *Hilara*." *Entomologist's Monthly Magazine* 14 (1877): 126–27.

Ovid. *Tales from Ovid*. Translated by Ted Hughes. London: Faber and Faber, 1997.

Pavese, Cesare. *This Business of Living: Diaries 1935–1950*. Translated by Alma E. Murch. New York: Quartet, 1980.

Perec, Georges. *Species of Spaces and Other Pieces*. Translated by John Sturrock. London: Penguin, 1998.

Philipp, Feliciano. *Protection of Animals in Italy*. Rome: National Fascist Organization for the Protection of Animals, 1938.

Pliny. *Natural History*, book XI. Translated by H. Rackham. Cambridge, Mass.: Loeb Classical Library/Harvard University Press, 1983.

Ploetz, Alfred. *Die Tüchtigkeit unserer Rasse und der Schutz der Schwachen: Ein Versuch über die Rassenhygiene und ihr Verhältnis zu den humanen Idealen, besonders zum Sozialismus* [*The Efficiency of Our Race and the Protection of the Weak: An Essay Concerning Racial Hygiene and Its Relationship to Humanitarian Ideals, in Particular to Socialism*]. Berlin: S. Fischer, 1895.

Plutarch. *Moralia*. Vol. XII. Translated by Harold Cherniss and William C. Helmbold. Cambridge, Mass.: Harvard University Press, 1957.

Proctor, Robert N. *Racial Hygiene: Medicine under the Nazis*. Cambridge, Mass.: Harvard University Press, 1988.

Pu Songling. "The Cricket." in *Strange Tales from Make-Do Studio*. Translated by Denis C. Mair and Victor H. Mair. Beijing: Foreign Languages Press, 2001.

Raffles, Hugh. *In Amazonia: A Natural History*. Princeton, N.J.: Princeton University Press, 2002.

Ratey, John J. *A User's Guide to the Brain: Perception, Attention, and the Four Theaters of the Brain.* New York: Vintage, 2002.

Reischauer, Edwin O., and Joseph K. Yamagiwa. *Translations from Early Japanese Literature.* Cambridge, Mass.: Harvard University Press, 1951.

Resh, Vincent H., and Ring T. Cardé, eds. *Encyclopedia of Insects.* New York: Academic Press, 2003.

Roitman, Janet. *Fiscal Disobedience: An Anthropology of Economic Regulation in Central Africa.* Princeton, N.J.: Princeton University Press, 2004.

Roughgarden, Joan. *Evolution's Rainbow: Diversity, Gender, and Sexuality in Nature and People.* Berkeley: University of California Press, 2004.

Rowley, John, and Olivia Bennett. *Grasshoppers and Locusts: The Plague of the Sahel.* London: The Panos Institute, 1993.

Ryan, Lisa Gail, ed. *Insect Musicians and Cricket Champions: A Cultural History of Singing Insects in China and Japan.* San Francisco: China Books and Periodicals, 1996.

Sacks, Oliver. *An Anthropologist on Mars: Seven Paradoxical Tales.* New York: Vintage, 1995.

Sax, Boria. *Animals in the Third Reich: Pets, Scapegoats, and the Holocaust.* New York: Continuum, 2003.

———. "What is a 'Jewish Dog'? Konrad Lorenz and the Cult of Wildness." *Society and Animals: Journal of Human-Animal Studies* 5, no. 1 (1997).

Scarborough, John. "On the History of Early Entomology, Chiefly Greek and Roman with a Preliminary Bibliography." *Melsheimer Entomological Series* 26 (1979): 17–27.

Schafer, R. Murray. *The Soundscape: Our Sonic Environment and the Tuning of the World.* Rochester, Vt.: Destiny Books, 1994.

Schiebinger, Londa. *Plants and Empire: Colonial Bioprospecting in the Atlantic World.* Cambridge, Mass.: Harvard University Press, 2004.

Searle, John R. *Mind: A Brief Introduction.* Oxford, U.K.: Oxford University Press, 2004.

Sebald, W. G. *Austerlitz.* Translated by Anthea Bell. New York: Random House, 2001.

———. *On the Natural History of Destruction.* Translated by Anthea Bell. New York: Random House, 2003.

Seeley, Thomas D. *The Wisdom of the Hive: The Social Physiology of Honey Bee Colonies.* Cambridge, Mass.: Harvard University Press, 1995.

Seeley, Thomas D., S. Kühnholz, and R. H. Seeley. "An Early Chapter in Behavioral Physiology and Sociobiology: The Science of Martin Lindauer." *Journal of Comparative Physiology A: Neuroethology, Sensory, Neural, and Behavioral Phisiology* 188 (2002): 439–53.

Serres, Michel. *The Parasite.* Translated by Lawrence R. Schehr. Minneapolis: University of Minnesota Press, 2007.

Seyfarth, Ernst-August, and Henryk Perzchala. "Sonderaktion Krakau 1939: Die Verfolgung von polnischen Biowissenschaftlern und Hilfe durch Karl von Frisch" [Sonderaktion Krakau, 1939: The Persecution of Polish Biologists and the Assistance Provided by Karl von Frisch]. *Biologie in unserer Zeit* 22, no. 4 (1992): 218–25.

Shapin, Steven. *The Scientific Revolution.* Chicago: University of Chicago Press, 1998.

Shiga Usuke. *Nihonichi no konchu-ya* [*The Best Insect Shop in Japan*]. Tokyo: Bunchon-bunko, 2004.

Shoko Kameoka and Hisako Kiyono. *A Survey of the Rhinoceros Beetle and Stag Beetle Market in Japan.* Tokyo: TRAFFIC East Asia—Japan, 2003.

Smith, Ray F., Thomas E. Mittler, and Carroll N. Smith, eds. *History of Entomology.* Palo Alto, Calif.: Annual Reviews, Inc., 1973.

Sommer, Volker, and Paul L. Vasey, eds. *Homosexual Behavior in Animals: An Evolutionary Perspective.* Cambridge: Cambridge University Press, 2006.

Spicer, Dorothy Gladys. *Festivals of Western Europe.* New York: H. W. Wilson, 1958.

Stein, Rolf A. *The World in Miniature: Container Gardens and Dwellings in Far Eastern Religious Thought.* Translated by Phyllis Brooks. Palo Alto, Calif.: Stanford University Press, 1990.

Strassberg, Richard E. *Inscribed Landscapes: Travel Writing from Imperial China.* Berkeley: University of California Press, 1994.

Szymborska, Wisława. *Miracle Fair: Selected Poems of Wisława Szymborska.* Translated by Joanna Trzeciak. New York: W. W. Norton, 2001.

Taussig, Michael. *Mimesis and Alterity: A Particular History of the Senses.* New York: Routledge, 1993.

———. *My Cocaine Museum.* Chicago: University of Chicago Press, 2004.

The Warsaw Diary of Adam Czerniakow: Prelude to Doom. Edited by Raul Hilberg, Stanislaw Staron, and Josef Kermisz. Translated by Stanislaw Staron and the staff of Yad Vashem. New York: Stein and Day, 1979.

Thomas, Julia Adeney. *Reconfiguring Modernity: Concepts of Nature in Japanese Political Ideology.* Berkeley: University of California Press, 2001.

Thomas, Keith. *Man and the Natural World: A History of the Modern Sensibility.* New York: Pantheon, 1983.

Toor, Frances. *Festivals and Folkways of Italy.* New York: Crown, 1953.

Topsell, Edward. *The History of Four-Footed Beasts and Serpents.* Vol. 3, *The Theatre of Insects or Lesser Living Creatures* by Thomas Moffet. New York: De Capo, [1658] 1967.

Tort, Patrick. *Fabre: Le Miroir aux Insectes.* Paris: Vuibert/Adapt, 2002.

Tregenza, T., N. Wedell, and T. Chapman. "Introduction. Sexual Conflict: A New Paradigm?" *Philosophical Transactions of the Royal Society B: Biological Sciences* 361 (2006): 229–34.

Tsunoda Tadanobu. *The Japanese Brain: Uniqueness and Universality.* Translated by Yoshinori Oiwa. Tokyo: Taishukan, 1985.

Tuan, Yi-Fu. "Discrepancies Between Environmental Attitude and Behaviour: Examples from Europe and China." *Canadian Geographer* 12, no. 3 (1968): 176–91.

Uexküll, Jakob von. "A Stroll through the World of Animals and Men: A Picture Book of Invisible Worlds." In *Instinctive Behavior: The Development of a Modern Concept,* edited and translated by Claire H. Schiller, 5–80. New York: International Universities Press, 1957.

Uvarov, Boris Petrovich. *Grasshoppers and Locusts: A Handbook of General Acridology.* Vol. 1. Cambridge: Cambridge University Press, 1966.

Vignau-Wilberg, Thea. *Archetypa studiaque patris Georgii Hoefnagelii (1592): Nature, Poetry and Science in Art around 1600.* Munich, Germany: Staatliche Graphische Sammlung, 1994.

Vilencia, Jeff. *The American Journal of the Crush-Freaks.* 2 vols. Bellflower, Calif.: Squish Publications, 1993–96.

Wade, Nicholas. "Flyweights, Yes, but Fighters Nonetheless: Fruit Flies Bred for Aggressiveness." *New York Times*, October 10, 2006.

Wagner, David L. *Caterpillars of Eastern North America: A Guide to Identification and Natural History*. Princeton, N.J.: Princeton University Press, 2005.

Weindling, Paul Julian. *Epidemics and Genocide in Eastern Europe, 1890–1945*. New York: Oxford University Press, 2000.

Weiss, Sheila Faith. "The Race Hygiene Movement in Germany." *Osiris* 3 (1987): 193–226.

Wolfe, Cary, ed. *Zoontologies: The Question of the Animal*. Minneapolis: University of Minnesota Press, 2003.

Wu Zhao Lian. *Xishuai mipu* [*Secret Cricket Books*]. Tianjin, China: Gu Ji Shu Dan Ancient Books, 1992.

Yajima Minoru. *Mushi ni aete yokatta* [*I Am Happy That I Met Insects*]. Tokyo: Froebelkan, 2004.

Yoro Takeshi and Miyazaki Hayao. *Mushime to anime*. Tokyo: Tokuma Shoten, 2002.

Yoro Takeshi, Okumoto Daizaburo, and Ikeda Kiyohiko. *San-nin yoreba mushi-no-chi'e* [*Put Three Heads Together to Match the Wisdom of a Mushi*]. Tokyo: Yosensya, 1996.

Zinsser, Hans. *Rats, Lice and History: Being a Study in Biography, which, after Twelve Preliminary Chapters Indispensable for the Preparation of the Lay Reader, Deals with the Life History of Typhus Fever*. Boston, Mass.: Atlantic Monthly Press/Little, Brown, and Company, 1935.

Zylberberg, Michael. "The Trial of Alfred Nossig: Traitor or Victim." *Wiener Library Bulletin* 23 (1969): 41–45.

ACKNOWLEDGMENTS

During the years it took to research and write this book I was almost always outside my areas of expertise and more than usually dependent on the generosity of others. A huge number of people helped me, some with individual chapters, others with advice and encouragement throughout the entire time. In most cases, I can only list them by name and add simply that one of the great pleasures of the past few years has been the opportunity to learn so much from so many of them.

As always, my first and deepest thanks are to my dearest friend and co-conspirator Sharon Simpson. Every idea and feeling in this book has traveled back and forth between us endless times. It is not just that this book would be different without her, it simply wouldn't exist.

My gratitude and appreciation goes also to everyone who trusted me enough to let me write about their lives. In particular, I'm grateful to Cornelia Hesse-Honegger, David Dunn, Fang Dali, Jeff Vilencia, Kawasaki Mitsuya, Li Shijun, Sugiura Tetsuya, Yajima Minoru, and Yoro Takeshi.

Equally significant has been the contribution of the three talented and dedicated research collaborators, now friends, who in fundamental ways co-wrote the major fieldwork chapters with me: Hu YanJun in China, Shige (CJ) Suzuki in Japan, and Abdoulkarim Saidou in Niger.

That fieldwork could not have happened without some extraordinary kindness from other friends old and new. For this, I'm especially grateful to Mei Zhan, Huang Jingying, Tyler Rooker, Ding Xiaoqian, Mahamane Tidjani Alou, Nassirou Bako Arifari, Shiho Satsuka, Gavin Whitelaw, and Thomas Bierschenk.

Back in the United States, I benefited greatly from the skilled bibliographic, translation, and interpretive work of Steve Connell, Ling Chen, Hisae Kawamori, Gabrielle Popoff, and Yumiko Iwasaki.

I'm indebted to Denise Shannon, my literary agent, for her good humor, patience, and wisdom, and to Dan Frank, my editor at Pantheon, for not only encouraging me to go my own way but gently insisting I do so. My thanks also to Michiko Clark, Altie Karper, Jill Verrillo, and Abigail Winograd at Pantheon.

I'm grateful to The New School for providing me with an exhilarating work environment and for the paycheck and research funds that allowed all this to happen, and to Jim Scott and Kay Mansfield at the Yale Program in Agrarian Studies for the year's fellowship (in all senses of the term) that gave me the chance to develop the initial shape of this project.

Without the following people—and I'm certain also others whom I've inadvertently omitted—this book would have been far less: Adriana Aquino, Al Lingis, Alan Christy, Alex Bick, Alexei Yurchak, Alondra Nelson, Amber Benezra, Anand Pandian, Ann Stoler, Anna Tsing, Anne-Marie Slézec, Annemarie Mol, Antoinette Tidjani Alou, Arjun Appadurai, Arun Agrawal, Ayako Furuta, Barrett Klein, Ben Orlove, Beth Povinelli, Bill Maurer, Boureima Alpha Gado, Brantley Bardin, Bruce Braun, Carla Freccero, Carol Breckenridge, Charles Whitcroft, Charlie Piot, Christine Padoch, Claudio Lomnitz, Dan Linger, David Porter, Dejan Lukic, Dieter Hall, Dilip Menon, Ding Xuewen, Don Kulick, Don Moore, Donna Haraway, Ed Kamens, Emily Martin, Eric Hamilton, Eric Worby, Ernst-August Seyfarth, Faisal Devji, Fatema Ahmed, Federico Finchelstein, Fred Appel, Fu Shui Miao, Fu Zhou Liang, Gabriel Vignoli, Gail Hershatter, Gary Shapiro, Graham Burnett, Grzegorz Sokol, Heather Watson, Hoon Song, Hsiung Ping-chen, Hylton White, Iijima Kazuhiko, Ilana Gershon, I-Yi Hsieh, Jacek Nowakowski, Jake Kosek, Janelle Lamoreaux, Janet Roitman, Janet Sturgeon, Jean-Yves Durand, Jim Clifford, Jin Xingbao, Jody Greene, Joe Masco, John Marlovits, Jonathan Bach, June Howard, Karen Davidson, Katharine Gates, Kimio Honda, Larry Hirschfeld, Lawrence Cohen, Leander Schneider, Lee Hendrix, Li Jun, Lisa Rofel, Louise Fortmann, Martin Lasden, Matt Wolf-Meyer, Maya Gautschi, Mick Taussig, Miguel Pinedo-Vásquez, Miriam Ticktin, Monica Phillipo, Nancy Jacobs, Nancy Peluso, Nataki Hewlett, Natasha Copeland, Neferti Tadiar, Niki Labruto, Noriko Aso, Norma Field, Oana Mateescu, Ohira Hiroshi, Okumoto Daizaburo, Orit Halpern, Paolo Palladino, Paul Gilroy, Peter Lindner, Ralph Litzinger, Rebecca Hardin, Rebecca Solnit, Rebecca Stein, Reiko Matsumiya, Rhea Rahman, Riccardo Innocenti, Roberto Koshikawa, Rotem Geva, Saba Mahmood, Sally Heckel, Shao Honghua, Sina Najafi, Stefan Helmreich, Stuart McLean, Susan Harding, Susan O'Donovan, Susanna Hecht, Tao Zhi Qing, Tim Choy, Tjitske Holtrop, Tom Baione, Toni Schlesinger, Vicky Hattam, Vron Ware, Vyjayanthi Rao, Wang Yuegen, Wendy Yu, Wulan, Yangtian Feng, Yen-ling Tsai, Yi Yinjiong, and Yukiko Koga.

Finally, there are a good number of people in this book whom, for various reasons, I refer to by pseudonym. Some are people in Shanghai who talked to me in unsafe circumstances. Others are people whose names I never learned but who shared their knowledge with me in markets, stores, museums, on street corners, and in all those places where insects find their way into our lives. To them, and to the residents of Dandasay, Dan mata Sohoua, and Rijio Oubandawakim in Niger and, once again, to my friends in Igarapé Guariba in Brazil, I extend my heartfelt thanks.

INDEX

Aargau, Switzerland, nuclear power plant in, 27, 33, 36
abolitionist movement, 250
abstract art, 31. *See also* concrete art
Academy Studios, 301–2
Acéphale (Headless) group, 331
Achebe, Chinua, 211–12, 215, 220, 235
acoustic ecology, 421n.6, 422n.10. *See also* soundscapes
Acrididae family, 216. *See also* locusts
adaptation, functionless by-products of, 262, 416n.13
adulthood, conceptualizing, 163–4, 165–9
Aesop, 245
Africa: colonial, concentration camps in, 157, 403–4n.42; disease control in, 157. *See also* Niger; Sahel
aggression, fruit flies bred for, 116–17, 120–1, 122
AGRHYMET (Sahelian agricultural research organization), 216, 220
agriculture, insect invasions and, 6, 209, 210, 352, 372. *See also* locusts
Agriculture Department, U.S., 5–6
Ahasuerus, the Wandering Jew, 142, 143, 146, 147
airborne dispersal of insects, 5–12; and first attempts to collect insects by airplane, 5–7, 10; miniaturization of insects and, 9
Albers, Josef, 29
Aldrovandi, Ulisse, 81, 124–5, 133, 167

Alexander II, Russian Czar, 147
alhazai, 224–5, 229
Allgemeine Jüdische Kolonisations Organisation (AJKO), 152
allomones, 326–7
Almog, Shmuel, 147
Alpha Gado, Boureima, 209–10, 215
Amazonia, 85–6; arrival of butterflies in, 13–14; *Plasmodium* protozoa in, 71–3
American Journal of the Crush-Freaks, The (Vilencia), 269–71, 273, 278, 279, 281, 288
American Sign Language, 197
Ammophila wasps, 53, 58, 59–60, 61–2, 70, 162
Ando Tadao, 370
animal sacrifice, 284
animal welfare, 414–15n.17; crush films and, 267, 273–6, 281–4, 288–9, 290; fascists' espousal of, 249–51; First Amendment and, 284, 289; in Italy, 245–6, 249–51, 256
Anning, Mary, 18–19
Answer, The, 142–3
ant lion larvae, 337
Anthropogenie oder Entwickelungsgeschichte des Menschen (The Evolution of Man) (Haeckel), 192
anti-nuclear movement, 26, 32, 34, 37; radiation effects studied by, 23–5
antisemitism, 141–61, 174; delousing metaphor and, 141–2, 155;

antisemitism *(continued)*
    in early-modern France, 145; fears
        of contamination and disease and,
        157–60; Holocaust and, 146, 155–7,
        158, 399n.4, 403n.36; parasite
        concept and, 145–6, 156–7;
        pogroms of 1881 and, 143, 147,
        158. *See also* Jews
ants, 7, 42, 52, 186, 313, 324; carpenter,
    321; leaf-cutter, 328–9
aphids, 6, 9, 324
Appelfeld, Aharon, 141
apposition eye, 312, 313
aquatic insects, Dunn's soundscape of,
    323–4
Arakawa Shusaku, 346–7
Aristotle, 121, 123, 127, 128, 129–31, 167,
    397n.20
Article 70 of the Public Safety Act (Italy),
    250–1
Ascension Sunday, Florence's *festa del
    grillo* on, 241, 243, 246–9, 251–6
Augustine, Saint, 45
Auschwitz, 155, 158, 403n.36
Austin, J. L., 68
Aztecs, 335–6

Bachus, Spencer, 284
Bacon, Francis, 126–7, 129
balloon flies, 291–2
bark beetles (Scolytidae), 319, 321, 325,
    326, 327–8, 329–30
Basho, 352
Bataille, Georges, 281, 331
Bates, Henry Walter, 333
Bauhaus, 31
"Beasts Are Rational" (Plutarch),
    258–9
bed bugs, 339
Beebe, William, 8–9, 10
bees: European bumblebees (*Bombus
    terrestris*), 361, 379. *See also*
    honeybees
beetles, 9, 42, 52; bark (Scolytidae), 319,
    321, 325, 326, 327–8, 329–30;
    bombardier, 326; collected in Japan,

343–4, 350–2, 354–67, 373, 378–80,
    425n.12; global warming and,
    325–6, 327–8, 329–30; Japanese
    (*Popillia japonica*), postcoital
    embrace of, 261; piñon engraver
    (*Ips confusus*), 319, 321, 327–8,
    329–30; tortoiseshell, 329. *See also*
    rove beetles
behaviorists, 172, 178, 192; instinct and,
    60, 61
Bein, Alex, 145–6
Be-kuwa!, 363, 379
Bembix wasps, 52, 70
Benjamin, Walter, 135, 137–8
Bergdolt, Ernst, 190–1, 192
Bergson, Henri, 61–2, 391n.39
Bergsonites, 142–3
Berlese, Antonio, 259
Beutler, Ruth, 176, 177, 178, 185
Bill, Max, 30, 31, 32
bioluminescence, 333, 351
birds, quantity of insects eaten by, 251
Black Death, 157
black-eyed susans (*Rudbeckia hirta*),
    304, 315
blowflies, 304
Bocskay, Georg, 137
Bolaño, Roberto, 163
bollworm moths, 6, 11
Book of Crickets (Jia), 79, 80–2, 85, 86
Bottigelli, Mauro, 251
boundary layer, 10
Bradbury, Michael, 281, 283
brain: aggression levels and, 117; human
    exceptionalism and, 308, 309,
    419n.10; image transmitted from
    compound eye to, 312; Japanese
    exceptionalism and, 358–9;
    neuroscience and, 307–8, 309;
    perceptual algorithms and, 305–9;
    social, 308–9
breeders, amateur, 357, 358, 378, 380
Breton, André, 331, 332–3
Brod, Max, 170
Brücke, Ernst, 311
Bry, Théodore de, 166

Bugliani, Vincenzo, 252
bumblebees, European (*Bombus terrestris*), 361, 379
Büro für Statistik der Juden, 150
Busby, Chris, 23–5
butterflies, 42, 44, 52, 131, 167, 169, 170, 328; in Amazonia, 13–14; color vision of, 303, 304; in Japan, 351, 352, 353, 369, 370, 373, 378, 424–5n.6; larva of (*see* caterpillars); migration of, 6, 8, 9, 11; mimicry of, 333, 334; orogenital contact of rove beetle and, 257–8, 262–3

cabinets of curiosities, 125, 128
caddis fly larvae, 340
Caillois, Roger, 331–5, 341
California, animal-cruelty laws in, 273–6
Caligo butterflies, 334
Calvino, Italo, 254
Canetti, Elias, 121
Cap de la Hague nuclear power plant, France, 33, 34, 39–40
Capriola, Thomas, 281
carpenter ants, 321
caste societies, 186
caterpillars, 69; of clothes moths, 340; Merian's paintings of, 166–9; metamorphosis of, 63, 163, 165–9; predation and, 59–60, 62–3, 68–9, 162–3, 170
cavitation, 319–20, 321, 328
cells, vulnerability of, to radiation, 24–5
Cerceris wasps, 52–3
Cézanne, Paul, 28
Chaffin, Diane, 275–6
Chalybion wasps, 53
"Chaos and the Emergent Mind of the Pond" (Dunn), 323–4
Cheke, Robert, 218
chemical ecology, 326–7, 329
Chen, Jo-shui, 338
Chernobyl disaster, 40; Hesse-Honegger's research into effects of, 17–18, 20–2, 25–7, 34, 36; official assessments of danger of, 22–3, 25

China: cicadas in, 77–8; cricket fighting in, 74–115, 120–1, 122 (*see also* cricket fighting); Liu Zongyuan in exile in, 337–9; materia medica of, 85, 371, 377
cholera, 157, 158
Churchill, Winston, 404n.50
cicadas, 353, 377; in China, 77–8; mutated, found by Hesse-Honegger, 26–7; singing of, 50, 244, 265, 352
Cieza de Léon, Pedro de, 336
CITES (Convention on International Trade in Endangered Species), 363
classification. *See* taxonomy
Clever Hans, 172
climate change. *See* global warming
Clinton, Bill, 288
clothes moths, 340
cockroaches, 339, 341, 355, 377; Tutsi identified with, 146. *See also* water bugs
Cocroft, Reginald, 328
COGEMA, 33, 34, 39–40, 229
cognitive processes, 419n.9; perceptual algorithms and, 305–9
collecting insects: breeding by hobbyists and, 357, 358, 378, 380; class distinctions and, 375, 377–8; for cricket fighting, 76, 87, 89; cultural attachment to insects in Japan and, 350–3, 355; explanations for surging interest in, 362; by girls and young women, 362–3; importation of foreign specimens and, 355, 357, 360–1, 363–4, 365–7, 379–80; insect boys (*konchu-shonen*) and, 343–50, 356, 367, 374, 375; in Japan, 322, 343–82; Japanese exceptionalism and, 358–9; paintings of specimens and, 371–2; positive outcomes ascribed to, 18, 322, 343, 345, 375–6, 380–1, 382; in postwar Tokyo, 370–1, 377–8; in prewar Tokyo, 374–7; sanctioned killing and, 380–2; scholarly, 356, 371–3, 377; Shiga insect store

collecting insects *(continued)*
 and, 351, 374–9, 381–2; summer
 assignments for Japanese students
 and, 63–4, 348–9, 378–9, 380
Collodi, Carlo, 243, 245–6, 255
color, in painting, 28–9
color vision, 174, 302–4, 419n.5; cultural-
 historical meaning and, 308
Columbia University, Fly Room at,
 117–20
communication: human-nonhuman,
 196–7, 198, 411n.61. *See also*
 language
Communication among Social Bees
 (Lindauer), 187–8
compound eyes, 302, 309, 310–14; two
 types of, 312–13
concentration camps: in colonial Africa,
 157, 403–4n.42. *See also* Holocaust
concrete art, 16, 30–2, 36–7
Connors, Tom, 275, 283
conservation legislation, in Japan, 360–1,
 363, 379–80
constructivism, 30
Cooper, Barbara, 224
cooperation: honeybee social order and,
 186–90; as motor of evolution,
 66–7, 392n.48
Cortés, Hernán, 335
Cosimo I, Grand Duke of Tuscany,
 247–8
Court TV, 283, 285
creationists, 58, 61, 63, 420n.24
Creede, Susan "Minnie," 274–5, 284–5,
 287, 288
"Cricket, The" (Pu), 80
cricket fighting, 74–115, 120–1, 122; anti-
 gambling campaigns and, 105–12;
 care and training of crickets for,
 84–6; collecting crickets for, 76, 87,
 89; description of matches, 97–101;
 doping and chemical manipulations
 in, 102; Five Virtues and, 78–9, 113;
 gambling on, 77–81, 88, 91, 93–105,
 108–10, 113; Jia Sidao and, 79–82,
 85, 86, 111, 113; as link to traditional

Chinese culture, 78–80, 110–11;
 losers released after, 101; market in
 crickets and, 88–93, 107, 111;
 matching of opponents by weight
 in, 104; morphological
 characteristics and, 82–4, 112,
 393n.8; museum dedicated to, 76–7,
 95; paraphernalia for, 94; at public
 house, 101–2, 103–4, 105; Qibao
 Golden Autumn Cricket Festival
 and, 77, 95; revival of, 78, 108, 109;
 season for (happy times), 86–7;
 social selves of crickets and, 100–1;
 Three Reversals and, 113–14; as
 vehicle for cultivation and elevation
 of self, 109; wild crickets deemed
 superior for, 85–6
cricket friends, 113
crickets, 116, 241–56, 328; animal-
 welfare advocates and, 245–6,
 251–3, 256; attempts to save crops
 from, 246–7; in crush videos, 276,
 277; female, 91, 114; and *festa del
 grillo* in Parco delle Cascine,
 Florence, 241, 243, 246–9, 251–6; in
 Japan, 241, 352, 359, 371, 377, 378;
 longstanding Italian traditions and,
 244; singing of, 80, 87, 113, 241,
 244, 247, 252, 359; talking, in
 Collodi's tale of Pinocchio, 243,
 245–6, 347
criquet migrateur, 216, 219
criquet pèlerin, 209, 216–17, 218, 233,
 234, 239
criquet sénégalais, 216, 218, 219, 239
criquets, 216, 219. *See also* locusts
Cromwell, Oliver, 73
crush fetishism, 267–90; California's
 animal-cruelty laws and, 273–6;
 demographic analysis of, 269;
 explanation for, 280–1, 285–7; First
 Amendment and, 284, 289; guy-
 bug identification and, 278–80;
 House Resolution 1887 and, 281–4,
 288–9, 290; Toogood's arrest and,
 267, 273; Vilencia's *American*

Journal of the Crush-Freaks and, 269–71, 273, 278, 279, 281, 288; Vilencia's films and, 267–8, 271–3, 276–8; YouTube videos and, 289–90

Crush Goddess, 281

Crushcentral, 274, 284–5

Crutchfield, James, 326, 327–8, 329–30

cubists, 28, 29

Cultural Revolution, 76, 108, 110

Cuvier, Georges, 62

Czerniakow, Adam, 149, 160–1

Dachau, 157

dance flies. *See* empidids

Dance Language and Orientation of Bees, The (von Frisch), 196

Dancing Bees, The (von Frisch), 186, 410n.45

Dante, 244

Darwin, Charles, 50, 52, 58, 64, 313, 333, 420–1n.24; Imanishi's critique of, 66–7

Daston, Lorraine, 128

DDT, 71, 341

De animalibus insectis libri septem (Aldrovandi), 81, 124–5

De Stijl, 30

death, 41–5; animal sacrifice and, 284; decomposition and, 45, 47; displays of insect bodies and, 42–4; of experimental animals, 119, 120–2; human sacrifice and, 331; sanctioned killing of insects and, 380–2. *See also* genocide

"Decoding the Language of the Bee" (von Frisch), 195

decomposition, 45, 47

deforestation: global warming and, 325–6, 330; piñon pine die-off and, 319–20, 323, 327–8, 329–30

Deleuze, Gilles, 286, 391n.39

Deng Xiaoping, 95, 108

dengue fever, 325

Descent of Man, The (Darwin), 58

"diagonal science," 332

Diario fiorentino (Lapini), 246–7

Dierick, Herman A., 116–17

Direction de la protection des végétaux, Maradi, Niger, 220, 221, 222, 239

disease: associated with Jews, 157–60, 404n.45. *See also* insect-borne diseases

dissections, performed by Fabre, 54, 56–7

dog-fighting videos, 289

Doris Day Animal League, 281

dragonflies, 9, 10, 352, 377; in bomb crater in Tokyo, 367, 369, 373; Hoefnagel's depiction of, 139–40; Hooke's engraving of, 310; vision of, 303, 313–14

dreaming, 385–6

droughts: deforestation and, 325–6; Nigerien famine of 1968 to 1974 and, 223–4, 228; piñon pine die-off and, 319–20, 323, 325; in Sahel, 210

Dunn, David, 319, 321–5, 326, 327–8, 329–30

Dürer, Albrecht, 135–6

ecstasy, fighting crickets doped with, 102

Edelman, Marek, 153–4, 156, 402n.33

Efron, John, 150

eggs, maggots' development from, 167, 398n.24

Einsatzgruppen (SS paramilitaries), 148

Eisner, Thomas, 326

Elizondo, Erika, 271–2, 299, 300

empidids (dance flies), 291–7; male cheating and, 294–6; nuptial gifts of, 292–6, 297; Osten-Sacken's observation of, 291–2, 293, 295, 296–7

Empis bullifera, 293–4, 297

Encyclopedia of Insects (Resh and Cardé), 386

Enlightenment, European, 127, 372–3

entoma, 130–1, 397n.20

environment: evolution affected by, 151; instincts influenced by, 61, 62–3

epistemological limitations of science, 37–8

ethology, 61, 171, 172, 192, 199, 406nn.1, 3. *See also* Frisch, Karl von

eugenics, 145, 151, 155, 157, 160, 191–2, 401n.25, 402–3n.35, 407n.11

Eumenes wasps, 53, 57

European spruce bark beetles, 330

eusocial insects, 171–200, 324, 327

evil, God and problem of, 68–9

evolution, 9, 46–70, 177, 296; cooperation as motor of, 66–7, 392n.48; of eye, 420–1n.24; Fabre's rebuttal of, 50, 52, 56, 58–9, 68; functionless by-products of adaptation and, 262, 416n.13; of honeybees, 190; instinct as Achilles' heel of, 52, 58–9; miniaturization of insects and, 9; Nazi race policy and, 191–2; nonreproductive sexual interactions and, 260–2; role of environment in, 151. *See also* natural selection

Exner, Sigmund, 176, 311–13

experimentation: destruction of animal subjects in, 119, 120–2; genetic, fruit flies in, 116–22 (*see also* fruit flies)

Expressions Videos, 267

extermination methods, 341; in Holocaust, 155, 403n.36

eyes: of fruit flies, Hesse-Honegger's paintings of, 16–17. *See also* vision

Fables (La Fontaine), 50–1

Fabre, Frédéric, 55, 57

Fabre, Jean-Henri, 46–70, 165, 244, 351, 370, 377, 380; dissections performed by, 54, 56–7; engagement of, with nature, 51–2, 56–7, 68, 368; hardships, frustrations, and disappointments in life of, 54–6; house of, in Sérignan du Comtat (l'Harmas), 46–50, 52; instinct as viewed by, 52, 57–63, 68, 315;

Japanese esteem for, 63–8; transformism (evolution) disputed by, 50, 52, 56, 58, 68; wasps studied by, 52–4, 57, 58–63, 70

Fabre Museum, Tokyo, 64

Fang, Master (museum director), 76–7, 78, 82, 84–6, 94–5, 110

fascists: animal welfare espoused by, 249–51. *See also* Nazis

Feld, Steven, 321

festa del grillo, 241, 243, 246–9, 251–6; animal-welfare advocates and, 251–3, 256; current cricketless incarnation of, 253–6; origin of, 246–7

Festival international de la mode africaine, 225

Festivals and Folkways of Italy (Toor), 247

Festivals of Western Europe (Spicer), 241, 242, 247, 253

"Fetishes/Paraphilia/Perversions" (Vilencia), 287–8

fetishism, 280; causation of, 280, 285–6, 287–8. *See also* crush fetishism

Feyerabend, Paul, 37

Field, Norma, 51

Fifty Taboos of Cricket Collecting (Li), 109

fireflies: in Japan, 351, 352, 377; *Lampyris*, compound eye of, 311–12, 313; *Photuris*, defenses of, 326

First Amendment, 284, 289

Flaubert, Gustave, 334–5, 353

fleas, 130, 339

flies, 6, 42, 45, 46, 131, 328; at beach, 385, 386; dance (*see* empidids); fruit (*see* fruit flies); lantern (*Laternaria phosphorea*), 331, 333, 334; larvae of (*see* maggots); space-time occupied by, 314

Florence: *festa del grillo* in, 241, 243, 246–9, 251–6; *scoppio del carro* in, 251; tourists and cultural consumption in, 241–3

flowers, as seen by insects vs. humans, 304

food, insects as, 353–4, 368, 377; locusts, 211, 212–15, 220, 226–7, 229–33

Four Elements, The (Hoefnagel), 123–40. See also Hoefnagel, Joris

France: African colonies and, 208, 223, 224; antisemitism in, 145; revolutionary upheavals in, 165

Francis of Assisi, Saint, 249

Frazer, Sir James, 134–5, 136, 398n.33

Freud, Sigmund, 280, 311

Frisch, Karl von, 61, 171–200, 299, 369–70, 410n.44, 418n.1; anthropomorphic approach of, 183–4; bees loved and tended by, 172–3; dance theory of, 174–8, 177–80, 408nn.20, 22; experiment design and, 180–3; as founder of ethology, 192; honeybees' cognitive capabilities and, 195–200, 410n.45; honeybees studied by, 171–200, 302, 303 (see also honeybees); laboratory subjects mutilated by, 173, 341; Lindauer as protégé of, 185–6, 187; natural history museum founded by, 176, 311; Nazi regime and, 174, 175–6, 185, 190–2; race hygiene and, 407n.11; *Ten Little Housemates* by, 339–41

fruit flies (*Drosophila melanogaster*), 7, 9, 117–22; bred for aggression, 116–17, 120–1, 122; Chernobyl disaster and, 22; destroyed in laboratory, 119, 120–1, 122; Hesse-Honegger's paintings of, 16–17; mutations in, 16–17, 18, 117–18, 120; naturally well suited to experimental life, 117–18; redesigned for laboratory, 118–19, 120

Fujimori Terunobu, 346

Galileo, 19–20, 35–6, 248

Gallegly, Elton, 281–2, 283–4, 285, 288, 290

gambling: on cricket fighting, 77–81, 88, 91, 93–105, 108–10, 113; PRC's campaigns against, 110; in traditional Chinese culture, 111

Gardner, Beatrix, 197, 198

Gardner, R. Allen, 196–7, 198

Garibaldi, Giuseppe, 245–6, 249

Gekkan-mushi (*Insect Monthly*), 356

genetics: aggression levels and, 116–17; eugenics and, 145, 151, 160, 401n.25, 402–3n.35; fruit flies as experimental subjects in, 116–22; interbreeding of native and foreign species and, 364

genocide: in colonial Africa, 403–4n.42; Rwandan, 146, 400n.12. See also Holocaust

German Social Democratic Party, 26

Germany: insect deformities near nuclear power plants in, 15, 27–9, 34. See also Nazis

Gesner, Conrad, 18–19, 35–6, 395–6n.2

Gilman, Charlotte Perkins, 186

Giornale per i bambini, 243

Glick, P. A., 5–7, 10, 11

global warming, 318–30; bark beetles' contribution to, 329–30; droughts in Sahel and, 210; habitat ranges and, 325; piñon pine die-off and, 319–20, 323, 325, 327–8, 329–30; recordings of insect sound-world and, 327–8, 329–30; widespread deforestation and, 325–6, 330

God, 45; problem of evil and, 68–9; pursuit of divinity in nature and, 60–1, 66, 68, 69

Goebbels, Joseph, 142, 175

Goethe, Johann Wolfgang von, 29, 243, 419n.5

Goka, Kouichi, 361, 364, 379

González, Pedro, 132–4, 136, 398n.30

Göring, Hermann, 142

Gould, Carol, 195

Gould, James, 195

Gould, Stephen Jay, 68–9, 262, 296, 416n.13

grape borer weevils, 261

grasshoppers, 131, 216, 217–18, 220, 326, 328; *criquet senegalensis*, 216, 218, 219, 239; *Kraussaria angulifera*, 220. *See also* locusts

Great Britain, African colonies and, 211, 212, 224

Greenspan, Ralph J., 116–17

Griffin, Donald, 178, 195, 199

grillo parlante, in Collodi's tale of Pinocchio, 243, 245–6, 255

Guattari, Félix, 391n.39

Gunma Insect World, 370

habitat ranges, global warming and, 325

Hacking, Ian, 414–15n.17

Haeckel, Ernst, 192

Haldane, J.B.S., 120

Hamburg, Allied bombing raids on, 45

Hanford, Wash., nuclear power plant in, 39, 40

Haraway, Donna, 146

l'Harmas, Sérignan du Comtat, France, 46–50, 52

Hartley, Mike, 267

healing, insects in, 371, 377

hearing: among insects, 328–9. *See also* soundscapes

Hearne, Vicki, 197, 411n.61

Heidegger, Martin, 249–50

Helsinki International Film Festival, 273

Hendrix, Lee, 133

Herero, concentration camps and, 403–4n.42

Herrnstein, Richard, 60, 61, 63

Herzl, Theodor, 148, 149, 152

Hesse-Honegger, Cornelia, 15–40, 120, 248, 369–70, 381; aesthetics of, 16–17, 19–20, 27–32, 35–7, 38–9; Chernobyl's effects studied by, 17–18, 20–2, 25–7, 34, 36; insect deformities near nuclear power plants studied by, 15, 27–40; journals of field trips made by, 39–40; methodological issues addressed by, 34–5; scientific community's hostility toward, 25–7, 34–5

hierarchies: Aristotelian, 121, 123, 130; of fascists, 191–2, 249–50; human exceptionalism and, 177, 308, 309, 419n.10; insect vision and, 305–7; of social insects, 186, 191

high-altitude entomology, 5–9, 10. *See also* airborne dispersal of insects

Hilara sartor, 294, 297

Himmler, Heinrich, 141–2, 146, 148, 155, 156, 402n.34

Hirayama Insect Specimen Store, Tokyo, 374–5, 376

Hirohito, Emperor, 378

Hiroshima bombing, 23

hirsutism, of Hoefnagel's *animalia rationalia*, 132–4

Hirszenberg, Shmuel, 143, 147

history: perceptual understanding and, 308; too much, problem of, 295–6

Hitler, Adolf, 142

Hoefnagel, Jacob, 167

Hoefnagel, Joris, 123–40, 167, 369–70; Aristotelian taxonomy and, 129–31; *The Four Elements* by, 123–40; González as *animalia rationalia* of, 132–4, 136; mimetic method of, 134–7, 138–9; *Mira calligraphiae monumenta* by, 137–8; real wings attached to insect painting by, 139–40

Holocaust, 146, 155–7, 158, 399n.4, 403n.36

Holocaust Memorial Museum, Washington, D.C., 142

homosexuality. *See* queerness

Honegger, Gottfried, 30

honeybees, 128, 131, 171–200, 201, 204, 304, 364; absence of observable tension among, 190, 409n.38; attracting, for experiments, 171; cognitive capabilities of, 195–200, 307, 410n.45; color vision of, 174, 302, 303; compound eyes of, 302, 309; dances of, 174–5, 177–80, 182, 183, 187, 193–5, 197, 199, 408nn.20, 22, 24, 25; evolution of, 190;

experiment design and, 180–3; von
    Frisch's affinities with, 172–3, 183–4;
    von Frisch's love and care for, 172–3;
    individuality of hive members and,
    183–4, 190; Lindauer's research on,
    185–6, 187–9, 191, 192–5, 196, 198,
    200, 408n.24; location of food
    sources communicated by, 174–5,
    177–80, 408nn.20, 22, 24, 25;
    mechanical, 196, 411n.60; mutilated
    by von Frisch, 173, 341; National
    Socialist war effort and, 175–6; nest
    selection of, 187, 192–5, 199;
    physical contact of, 188–9, 262;
    sense of smell of, 179, 180; social
    order of, 186–90, 191–2, 324, 327;
    trained to respond to scent, 176;
    worker labor allocation of, 187–9
honji (original form or state), 169
honzo (Chinese materia medica),
    371, 377
Hooke, Robert, 310
hormic psychology, 61, 62
Horyuji Temple, Nara, 353
houara, 216, 219. See also locusts
House Judiciary Committee's
    Subcommittee on Crime, 284–5,
    287, 288
House Resolution 1887, 281–4,
    288–9, 290
houseflies, 130, 339, 341, 377; Umwelten
    of, 315
Hsiung Ping-chen, 79
Huayna Capac, 336
Hughes, Ted, 162
Hugo, Victor, 55
human exceptionalism, 177, 308, 309,
    419n.10; language and, 197–8, 199,
    412n.69
Humane Society, 273
Hurricane Katrina, 320
hygiene, 161; disease control and,
    157–60; race (see eugenics)

Ignis (Hoefnagel), 123–40. See also
    Hoefnagel, Joris

Iijima Kazuhiko, 355–8, 361
Imanishi Kinji, 66–8
immigration controls, 159, 404n.50
importation of foreign insects, 355, 357,
    363–4, 365–7; genetic introgression
    and, 364; legislation on, 360–1, 363,
    379–80
In Step, 269
Incas, 336–7
insect boys, in Japan (konchu-shonen),
    343–50, 356, 367, 374, 375
insect-borne diseases: global warming
    and, 325; Plasmodium protozoa and,
    71–3
insecte, L' (Michelet), 163–6, 405n.8
insectification: equation of Jews with lice
    and, 141–2, 144, 146, 148, 153–4, 155;
    Rwandan genocide and, 146,
    400n.12
Insectorum sive minimorum animalium
    theatrum (Moffett), 81, 124–5, 127–8
instinct, 192, 324; Darwin's views on, 58;
    Fabre's views on, 52, 57–63, 68, 315;
    intuitional, reflexive, and hormic
    positions on, 60–3; Lorenz's views
    on, 61, 191–2, 410n.42; responsive
    to external stimuli, 61, 62–3
Institute of Physiology, Vienna, 311
Institute of Zoology, University of
    Munich, 174–5, 177, 185, 190, 339
Institute of Zoology, University of
    Zürich, 16–17, 25, 36
International Commission on
    Radiological Protection (ICRP),
    22–3, 25
Invasive Alien Species Act (Japan),
    379–80
Iron Tracks, The (Appelfeld), 141
Islamists, in Niger, 224–5
Italian language, derivation of, 244
Italy, 241–56; animal protection in, 246,
    249–51, 256; and Collodi's tale of
    Pinocchio, 243, 245–6, 255;
    Florence's festa del grillo in, 241, 243,
    246–9, 251–6; tourists and cultural
    consumption in, 241–3

Itami City Insectarium, Hyogo
Prefecture, 355, 365
Itaya, Kikuo, 299

Jackson, Michael, 245
James, William, 60–1
Janzen, Daniel, 163
Japan, 322, 343–82; conservation
legislation in, 360–1, 363, 379–80;
crickets in, 241, 352, 359, 371, 377,
378; cultural attachment to insects
in, 350–3, 355; environmental
disasters in, 378; exceptional
sensitivity to nature ascribed to, 68,
358–9, 425n.7; Fabre's reputation in,
63–8; foreign insects imported into,
355, 357, 360–1, 363–4, 365–7,
379–80; history of insect studies in,
371–3, 426n.23; horrors of World
War II in, 23, 367–71, 373; insect
boys (konchu-shonen) in, 343–50,
356, 367, 374, 375; insect collecting
in, 63–4, 322, 343–82, 425n.12 (see
also collecting insects); insect
habitats in, 356–7, 363–4, 370, 379,
380; soundscape of Osaka
Prefecture's Minoo Park in, 264–5;
stages of ideal man's ideal life in,
359–60
Japan External Trade Organization, 362
Japanese beetles (Popillia japonica),
postcoital embrace of, 261
Jecmen, Greg, 123, 138, 139
jewel beetles, 377
Jewish Agency, 152
Jews, 141–61; disease associated with,
157–60, 404n.45; equated with lice,
141–2, 144, 146, 148, 153–4, 155,
420n.34; explanation of differences
between non-Jewish Germans and,
150–1; German vs. "eastern,"
401n.27; Nazi civil service law and,
174, 175; Nossig's statistical analysis
of, 149–50, 152; parasite concept
and, 145–6, 156–7; Szyk's drawings
and, 142–3, 147; Zionism and, 142,

147–8, 149, 151–3, 154, 399n.3. See
also antisemitism
Jia Sidao, 79–82, 85, 86, 111, 113
Jiminy Cricket, 243, 245, 246, 347
Jin Xingbao, 82–3
Johnson, Cecil, 11
J. Paul Getty Museum and Research
Institute, Los Angeles, 137
Judenfrage (Jewish Question), 148, 150
Judenstaat, Der (Herzl), 148
Jüdische Statistik, 150
Justice Department, U.S., 288–9

kabutomushi. See rhineroceros beetles
Kafka, Franz, 162–70
kaiju (strange-beast) movies, 378
kairomones, 327
kampo medicine, 377
Kashihara City Insectarium, 353–4
Kaufmann, Thomas DaCosta, 125
Kawabata Yasunari, 352
Kawasaki Mitsuya "Kuwachan," 343–4,
345–6, 347, 349, 356, 357, 360,
363, 380
Keats, John, 218
Kessel, Berta, 293–4, 297
Kessel, Edward, 292–5, 297
killing. See death
Koch, Robert, 157, 404n.42
Kohler, Robert, 117, 118
Koizumi Yakumo (Lafcadio Hearn),
352–3
Kojima Hiroshi, 361
Konchukai (Insect World), 376–7
Konishi Masayasu, 370–3
Konkrete Gestaltung (Concrete Formation)
(Bill), 31
Krafft-Ebing, Richard von, 288
Kral, Karl, 306–7, 308
Kraussaria angulifera, 220
Krizek, George O., 257–8, 261, 262–3
Kropotkin, Peter, 66, 392n.48
Kumagusu Minakata, 66
Kurimoto Tanshu, 371–2
kuwagata. See stag beetles
Kuwagata Tsumami, 351

La Fontaine, Jean de, 50–1
lac, 353
Lacan, Jacques, 198, 199
"Lady Who Loved Worms, The,"
    166–7, 169, 318, 352, 367
Lamarck, Jean-Baptiste, 50, 151,
    401n.23
Land, Michael, 313
Landauer, Martin, 369–70
language: animal cognition and,
    195–200, 410n.45, 411–12n.69; of
    honeybees, 171–200 (see also
    honeybees); human, talking
    insects and, 244; human
    exceptionalism and, 197–8, 199,
    412n.69
lantern flies (Laternaria phosphorea), 331,
    333, 334
Lapini, Agostino, 246–7
larva, meaning of word, 164
larvae: fly (see maggots); Lepidoptera (see
    caterpillars); owl-fly, 337, 338
Lasden, Martin, 274–5
Laspeyresia saltitans moths, 332
Launois-Luong, My-Hanh, 216
Lavater, Warja, 30
leafhoppers (unka), 372
LeBas, Natasha, 297
Lecoq, Michel, 216
Leeuwenhoek, Anton van, 310–11, 312
Lega anti-vivesezione, 251
Legros, Georges Victor, 56, 61
Leopardi, Giacomo, 244
Leopold II, Holy Roman Emperor (Pietro
    Leopoldo, Grand Duke of
    Tuscany), 248
Levi, Primo, 44
Lewontin, Richard, 416n.13
Li Jun, 106–7, 112
li qiu (start of autumn), 87–9
Li Shijun, 105–12, 369–70
lice, 130, 339, 341; Jews equated with,
    141–2, 144, 146, 148, 153–4, 155,
    402n.34; as tribute in pre-
    Columbian empires, 335–7; as
    typhus vector, 159

Lindauer, Martin, 185–6, 187–9, 191,
    192–5, 196, 198, 200, 408n.24
Linnaeus, 82, 130, 164, 397n.20
Liu Zongyuan, 337–9
Lloyd, G.E.R., 130
locusts, 354, 368; Achebe's paradox and,
    211–12, 215, 220; catching, as child's
    game, 240; crop protection
    techniques and, 221–2, 234–6, 239;
    destructiveness of, 209–10, 215–20,
    233, 234–8; distinct from other
    grasshoppers, 217–18; as food, 211,
    212–15, 220, 226–7, 229–33;
    migration of, 8, 11, 217; in Niger,
    209–40; Nigerien terms for, 216,
    219–20; phase transformation of,
    216–17; various species of, 216
Loeb, Jacques, 60, 178
Lohse, Richard Paul, 30
Lorenz, Konrad, 61, 171, 191–2,
    410nn.42, 44
low-frequency emissions, 321, 328
Lu Xun, 98
Lukumí Babalu Aye, church of, 284
Lyme disease, 325

macaques, female-female sex play of,
    261–2
maggots, 41, 45, 46, 167, 398n.24
magic, mimetic, 134–5, 398nn.33, 34
Mahamane, Abdou, 207, 208
malaria, 73, 157, 325
male cheating, of empidids, 294–6
Malevich, Kazimir, 30, 31
Mallock, Henry, 309
Mamdani, Mahmood, 146
mantid shrimp, 303
mantises, 328, 331, 333, 334, 341; vision
    of, 305, 306–7
Man'yo-shu, 352
Mao Zedong, 330
Maruyama Okyo, 371
Marx, Karl, 409n.38
Matsumoto Leiji, 351
Maya, 337
mayflies, 352

Mazokhin-Porshnyakov, Georgii, 305
McDougall, William, 61
McNamara, Robert, 367
Médecins Sans Frontières, 237
Medicis, 247–8
Meiji Japan, 372–3, 375, 392n.48,
    426n.23
Mémoires pour servir à l'histoire des insectes
    (Réaumur), 57
Mendez-Lopez, Maria "Lupe," 274–5
Merian, Maria Sibylla, 18–19, 35–6,
    166–8, 169, 333
metamorphosis, 63, 163, 165–70;
    Merian's paintings and, 166–8;
    Michelet's understanding of, 163–4,
    165–6, 168–9; phase transformation
    of locusts and, 216–17
Metamorphosis insectorum Surinamensium
    (Merian), 167, 168
Mexican jumping beans, 331, 332–3
Michelet, Jules, 163–6, 168–70, 405n.8
Micrographia (Hooke), 310
micro/macrocosmic reasoning, 124,
    125, 127
microscope, 15, 167
migration, 5–11; and arrival of butterflies
    in Amazonia, 13–14; high-altitude
    research on, 5–9, 10; of locusts, 8,
    11, 217
Mik, Josef, 292
Mill, John Stuart, 55
mimesis: in Hoefnagel's *Ignis*, 134–7,
    138–9; insect masters of, 331, 333–5
Ming dynasty (China), 80, 110
miniaturization of insects, 9
Ministry of Agriculture, Forestry, and
    Fisheries (Japan), 361
Ministry of Education (Germany), 190
Ministry of Education (Japan), 378–9
Ministry of Food (Germany), 175–6
Ministry of the Environment (Japan), 361
Minoo Park, Osaka Prefecture, Japan,
    264–5, 348–9
Mira calligraphiae monumenta (*Model
    Book of Calligraphy*) (Hoefnagel),
    137–8

Mistral, Frédéric, 55
mites, 10, 364
Miyazaki, Hayao, 318, 346–7, 352,
    360, 363
Moctezuma II, 335, 336
Moffett, Thomas, 81, 124–5, 127–8,
    140, 167
Mol, Annmarie, 121–2, 316
monarch butterflies, 8
Mondrian, Piet, 30
Monstrorum historia (Aldrovandi), 133
Montaigne, Michel de, 133
Monte Cantagrilli (Singing Cricket
    Mountain), Tuscany, 248
Montreal Insectarium, 42–4
moon, Galileo's ink washes of,
    19–20, 35
Moquin-Tandon, Alfred, 56
Moralia (Plutarch), 258–9
Morgan, Thomas Hunt, 117–20
Morishima Churyo, 371
morphology, 51; in caste societies, 186;
    classification systems and, 130,
    397n.20; fighting crickets and,
    82–4, 112, 393n.8
mosquitoes, 131, 325, 339, 341;
    Plasmodium protozoa and, 72–3
Mothra, 378
moths, 130, 170, 328, 332; bollworm, 6,
    11; clothes, 340; larva of (*see*
    caterpillars); Silver Y, 8; *Utetheisa
    ornatrix*, 326
motion detection, 314
mountain pine beetles, 325
Mouvement des Nigériens pour la justice
    (MNJ), 207
Murasaki Shikibu, 352
Muséum national d'Histoire naturelle,
    Paris, 47, 48
Mushi Productions, 347
MushiKing, 351, 354, 356, 363, 364–7
mushiokuri festivals, 352
Mushi-sha, Tokyo, 355–8, 363, 380
mushi-uri (itinerant sellers of singing
    insects), 370–1
musique concrète, 322–3, 422n.10

Mussolini, Benito, 249, 250–1
mutations: Chernobyl disaster and, 17–18, 20–7; in fruit flies, 16–17, 18, 117–18, 120; Hesse-Honegger's paintings of, 15–19, 27–38
"My First Excursion to West Mountain" (Liu), 338

Nagasaki bombing, 23
National Fascist Organization for the Protection of Animals, 249
National Gallery of Art, Washington, D.C., 123, 133, 138
National Science Foundation, 116
Natural History Museum, London, 344–5
natural selection, 66–7, 333, 407n.11; eye and, 420–1n.24; instincts and, 58; queer sex and, 260–2. See also evolution
naturalism, in art, 17
nature: divinity in, 60, 66, 68, 69; natural sciences distinct from, 67; as vehicle of moral instruction, 51, 69. See also sympathy with nature
Nausicaä of the Valley of the Wind (Miyazaki), 318, 352, 363
Nazis: animal welfare and, 249; antisemitism of, 141–61, 174, 175 (see also antisemitism); von Frisch's relations with, 174, 175–6, 185, 190–2, 410nn.42, 44; Lorenz's involvement with, 191–2, 410nn.42, 44; Szyk's drawings of, 142–3
Nepal, 205–6
nests: of eusocial insects, 324, 327; honeybees' selection of sites for, 187, 192–5, 199. See also wasp nests
Neuroptera, 328
neuroscience, 307–8, 309, 311
Neurosciences Institute, San Diego, 116–17, 120–1, 122
New Mexico, piñon pine die-off in, 319–20, 323, 327–8, 329–30
New York Times, 116

Niger, 207–40; criquet sénégalais grasshopper in, 218, 239; destructiveness of locusts in, 209–10, 215–20, 233, 234–8; drought and famine of 1968 to 1974 in, 223–4, 228; Islamic activists in, 224–5; locust species in, 216; locusts as food in, 211, 212–15, 220, 226–7, 229–33; natural disasters in, 209–10; NGOs in, 237–8; pesticide use in, 221–2, 226, 234–5; political instability and violence in, 207–9, 239; standard of living indices for, 213–14; uranium in, 208, 228–9, 413n.22; various names for locusts in, 216, 219–20
Nigeria, 215, 223, 224, 225, 226, 229, 230
nightmares, 120, 201–4
nihonjinron (Japanese exceptionalism), 68, 358–9, 425n.7
Nilsson, Dan-Eric, 313, 420–1n.24
Nobel Prize, 61, 157, 171, 195, 302, 390n.21, 410n.42
North Carolina State Museum of Natural Sciences, Arthropod Zoo at, 301–2
Nosema apis, 175–6
Nossig, Alfred, 143, 146–53, 154, 155, 156, 160–1, 402–3n.35; as sculptor, 143, 147, 153; statistics enterprise of, 149–50, 152; trial and execution of, 146–7, 148, 153; Zionism and, 147–8, 149, 151–3
nuclear power plants: Hesse-Honegger's encounters with workers at, 39–40; Hesse-Honegger's study of insect deformities near, 15, 27–40; international nuclear regulatory agencies and, 22–3; research on low-level radiation and, 23–5. See also Chernobyl disaster
nuptial gifts, of empidids, 292–6, 297; male cheating and, 294–6

Odynerus wasps, 57
Ojeda, Alonso de, 335

Okabe Kimiko, 361
Okumoto Daizaburo, 64, 66, 68, 353,
    358–60, 377, 380, 381
O'Leary, Bill, 267
ommatidia, 312–14
"On Cannibals" (Montaigne), 133
"On the Mimetic Faculty"
    (Benjamin), 135
Organization of Reich Beekeepers,
    176
orogenital contact, of butterfly and rove
    beetle, 257–8, 262–3
Osten-Sacken, Baron Carl Robert, 291–2,
    293, 295, 296–7
Österfärnebo, Sweden, Chernobyl
    disaster's effects in, 17, 20–2
Osugi Sakae, 64–6, 368, 392n.48
Ottoman Empire, 152
owl-fly larvae, 337, 338
Oxfam, 238

paintings of insects: by Hesse-Honegger,
    15–22, 25–40; by Hoefnagel,
    123–40; by Merian, 166–8, 169; as
    research rather than mere
    documentation, 18–19; in Tokugawa
    Japan, 371–2
Paleozoic, 9
Palestine, Jewish homeland in, 148,
    151–2, 402n.31
parasites, 25; Jews associated with,
    145–6, 156–7; Nosema apis, 175–6;
    Plasmodium protozoa, 71–3; problem
    of evil and, 68–9
Parco delle Cascine, Florence: creation
    of, 247–8; festa del grillo in, 241, 243,
    246–9, 251–6
Park, Katharine, 128
Parry, William, 6
Pasteur, Louis, 395n.4, 398n.24
Pavese, Cesare, 201
People v. Thomason, 275, 281
perceptual algorithms, 305–9
Perec, Georges, 295
Perelli, Tommaso, 248
perspective, 308–9

pesticides, 25, 71, 218, 221–2, 226,
    234–5
Petkau, Abram, 23, 36
Pfungst, Oskar, 172
pheromones, 326, 327, 330
Philipp, Feliciano, 249, 251
photoreceptive cells, 303, 304
Photuris fireflies, defenses of, 326
Physiology of the Compound Eyes of Insects
    and Crustaceans, The (Exner), 311
Pietro Leopoldo, Grand Duke of Tuscany
    (Leopold II, Holy Roman
    Emperor), 248
Pillow Book (Sei), 352
Pinocchio, Collodi's tale of, 243,
    245–6, 255
piñon engraver beetles (Ips confusus), 319,
    321, 327–8, 329–30
piñon pines (Pinus edulis), 319–23; die-off
    of, 319–20, 323, 327–8, 329–30;
    Dunn's soundscapes and, 319,
    321–3, 326, 327–8, 329–30
Plant Protection Act of 1950 (Japan),
    360–1, 363, 379
plants, deformed after Chernobyl
    disaster, 20
Plasmodium protozoa, 71–3
Plato, 125
Pliny, 127, 130
Ploetz, Alfred, 154–5, 192, 403n.35
Plutarch, 258–9
pogroms of 1881, 143, 147, 158
Poland, 158, 159
Pompeii, 244
praying mantises. See mantises
pre-Columbian empires, lice as tribute
    in, 335–7
predation, 10, 218; caterpillars' defenses
    against, 162–3; Fabre's wasp studies
    and, 57, 58, 59–60, 61–3, 70;
    insects' sound-world and, 328, 329;
    owl-fly larvae and, 337, 338; problem
    of evil and, 68–9
Prete, Frederick, 305–7, 308
Psychopathia sexualis (Krafft-Ebing),
    288

psychophysiological research, 306
Pu Songling, 80
pupation, 163–4, 169

Qibao, China, fighting crickets in, 76–7, 95
Qing dynasty (China), 76, 80, 110
queerness, 257–63; among animals, discounting of, 258–60; of female Japanese macaques, 261–2; Krizek's photo of orogenital contact of butterfly and rove beetle and, 257–8, 261, 262–3; pleasure of same-sex encounters and, 261–3; scientists' explanations for, 260–1

race branding: insectification and, 146, 400n.12. *See also* antisemitism
race hygiene. *See* eugenics
radiation: artificial, random behavior of, 24–5; calculating dangers of, 22–5; Hesse-Honegger's investigation into effects of, 15–22, 25–40; ingestion vs. external exposure to, 24; international nuclear regulatory agencies and, 22–3, 25; low-level emissions and, 23–5. *See also* Chernobyl disaster; nuclear power plants
Ramunno, Stefano, 252
randomness: of artificial radiation, 24–5; concrete art and, 31, 36; in Hesse-Honegger's insect paintings, 16–17, 31–2, 36–7
Réaumur, René-Antoine Ferchault de, 57, 127
Record of Fu Ban, A (Liu), 338
Redi, Francesco, 167, 398n.24
Reich, Das, 175
Renaissance, 123–40; Aristotelian thought in, 123, 127, 128, 129–31; compendiums devoted to insects in, 123–37 (*see also* Hoefnagel, Joris); micro/macrocosmic reasoning in, 124, 125, 127; observational practice developed in, 125; religious

intolerance in, 126, 133; wonder in, 19–20, 124, 125, 127–8, 136
Repubblica, La, 252
Revisionists, 142–3, 399n.3
rhabdom, 312, 313
Rhamphomyia sulcata, 297
rhinoceros beetles, 425n.14; in Japan (*kabutomushi*), 349, 350, 354–67, 378, 379–80
rice paddies, insect invasions and, 352, 372
robber flies, 313
Rodríguez, Rafael, 328
Rolland, Romain, 55
Rooney, Mickey, 283
Rostand, Edmond, 55
Roughgarden, Joan, 296
rove beetles: male, "feminine" behavior of, 260; orogenital contact of butterfly and, 257–8, 262–3
Royal Society of London, 311
Rudolf II, Holy Roman Emperor, 125, 137
Russell, Bertrand, 62
Russia, 158; pogroms in, 143, 147, 158
Russian Civil War, 159, 404n.50
Rwandan genocide, 146, 400n.12

Saadou, Mahamane, 208–9, 210, 234
Sacher-Masoch, Leopold von, 286, 287
sacrifice: animal, 284; human, 331; of laboratory subjects, 119, 120–2
Sahel: *criquet sénégalais* grasshopper in, 216, 218, 219, 239; famines in, 209–10, 223–4, 228, 237; locust species in, 216; phase transformation of locusts in, 216–17. *See also* Niger
Saichu shinam (Tanaka), 373
San Martino a Strada, Tuscany, 246–7
Santería, 284
satoyama, 356, 357, 370
Satoyama Society, 379–80
sawfly larvae, 326
scale insects, 353

scarab beetles, 353
scavengers, 340
Scolytidae. *See* bark beetles
Scott, Robert, 284, 289
Sebald, W. G., 200
Seeley, Thomas, 187
Sega, 351, 362, 364–7
Sei Shonagon, 352
Seidou, Mahaman, 220
self-referentiality, 198–9, 200,
    410n.45
Sellafield, England, nuclear power plant
    in, 33, 36
Senchufu (Kurimoto), 371–2
sex, 131; among crickets, 84, 91, 114;
    empidids' nuptial gifts and,
    292–6, 297; of queen bees, 186.
    See also crush fetishism;
    queerness
Shanghai: Communist Party's relations
    with, 108; cricket fighting in, 74–115,
    120–1, 122 (*see also* cricket fighting);
    divisions between urban and
    provincial in, 90–1, 92–3; urban
    growth and transformation in,
    75–6
Shanghai Evening Post, 106–7
Shiga Konchu Fukyu-sha, Tokyo, 351,
    375–9, 381–2
Shiga Usuke, 373, 374–9, 381–2
Shijing (*The Book of Songs*), 113
Shosoin, Todaiji Temple, Nara, 353
sign language, 196–7
silkworms (*Bombyx mori*), 166,
    259, 354
Silver Y moths, 8
silverfish (*Lepisma saccharina*),
    339, 341
Simmons, L. W., 114
Singer, Isaac Bashevis, 250
slaves, 93, 223, 250
sleep, 385–6
Slézec, Anne-Marie, 47–9, 50
Smush, 267–8, 271–3, 276, 288
social Darwinism, 160, 392n.48
sociosexual behaviors, 260–1

SOMAIR (uranium enterprise), 229
Sommer, Volker, 259
"somnambulist" consciousness, 62
Sound of Light in Trees, The (Dunn), 319,
    321–3, 326
soundscapes, 319, 321–5, 421n.6,
    422n.10; aquatic insects and, 323–4;
    research on insect behavior and,
    326, 327–30; sonic way of knowing
    and, 321–3
Southern Song dynasty (China),
    79–80
Souvenirs entomologiques (Fabre), 50, 52,
    64, 66, 368
Soviet Union, 176
space-time worlds, uniqueness of,
    314–17
Spencer, Herbert, 60, 61
Sphex wasps, 52, 53, 70. *See also*
    Ammophila wasps
Spicer, Dorothy Gladys, 241, 242,
    247, 253
spiders, 66, 329, 339; aerial travel
    of, 7, 10
spontaneous generation, 130–1, 167,
    398n.24
spring, cricket as harbinger of, 241,
    247, 248
spruce bark beetles, 325
Squish, 267–8, 271, 272–3, 276
Squish Playhouse, 276–8
Squish Productions, 268–9
Srinivasan, Mandyam, 307
SS, 148, 161, 185
stag beetles, 425n.14; depictions of, 131,
    136; in Japan (*kuwagata*), 343–4,
    350, 354–67, 377, 378, 379–80,
    425n.14
Steiner, Rudolph, 29
Steponit, 273
Strom ohne Atom (Electricity without
    Nuclear Power), 34
subjectivity: concrete art's rejection of, 31;
    Umwelten and, 314–16, 410n.46,
    411n.61
Suchin, Peter, 35

Suffolk County, N.Y., D.A.'s
    office, 281
Sugiura Tetsuya, 353–5, 356, 377
sun, as reference in honeybees' dances,
    179–80
superposition eye, 312–13, 420–1n.24
Supreme Court, U.S., 284, 289
Surrealism, 31, 135, 136, 331–2
survival, quantifying, 163
suzumushi (bell crickets), 371, 378
swallowtail butterflies, 369, 370
Swammerdam, Jan, 127
Sweden, Chernobyl disaster's effects in,
    17, 20–2, 27
Switzerland: Chernobyl disaster's effects
    in, 20, 22, 26, 36; insect deformities
    near nuclear power plants in, 27, 33,
    36, 37
Sylva sylvarum (Bacon), 126–7
sympathy with nature, 414–15n.17;
    cricket fighting and, 100, 114–15;
    crush fetishism and, 278–80;
    Fabre's narrative approach and,
    51–2, 368; fascists' concern for
    animal welfare and, 249–50; von
    Frisch's anthropomorphism and,
    183–4; von Frisch's way of telling
    and, 172; Hesse-Honegger's intense
    focus and, 15, 18, 38–9; Hoefnagel's
    images and, 128–9, 134–7; insect
    collecting and, 18, 322, 345, 375–6,
    380–1, 382; sonic way of knowing
    and, 321–3
Szyk, Arthur, 142–3, 147, 399n.3
Szymborska, Wisława, 42

Tages-Anzeiger Magazin, 20, 25,
    27, 36
Tale of Genji (Murasaki), 352
Tales from Ovid (Hughes), 162
talking insects: cicadas, 50, 244, 265, 352;
    connections between human speech
    and, 244; crickets, 80, 87, 113, 241,
    244, 247, 252, 359
Tama Zoo, Tokyo, 378
Tamagotchi, 255–6

Tanaka Yoshio, 373
Tandja, Mamadou, 207, 237
Tang dynasty (China), 80
Taussig, Michael, 135
taxonomy, 51, 66; Aristotelian, 129–31,
    167, 397n.20; fighting crickets and,
    82–4, 112, 393n.8; Linnaean, 130,
    397n.20
Taylor, Harriet, 55
Tears of Eros (Bataille), 281
Temptation of Saint Anthony, The
    (Flaubert), 334–5, 353
Ten Little Housemates (von Frisch),
    339–41
termites, 186, 324
Tezuka Osamu, 347–8, 351, 360, 378
Thailand, insect cuisine of, 353–4
Theophrastus, 129
Things Fall Apart (Achebe), 211–12, 215,
    220, 235
Thomason, Gary, 274–5, 281
thornbug leafhoppers, 329
Three Mile Beach, Wilder Ranch State
    Park, Calif., 383–6
Three Mile Island nuclear power plant,
    Pa., 20, 33
thrips, 9, 324
Ticino, Switzerland, Chernobyl disaster's
    effects in, 20, 22, 26
ticks, 325, 339
Tinbergen, Nikolaas, 61, 171, 410n.44
Tokai Media, 379–80
Tokugawa Japan, 371–2, 375,
    426n.23
Tokyo, firebombing of, 367–8,
    370–1, 373
Tokyo University, 373
Toogood, Keith, 267, 273
Toor, Frances, 247
Torquemada, Juan de, 335
Trueheart, Charles, 273
Tsunoda Tadanobu, 359
Turner, Charles Henry, 302, 303,
    418–19n.1
turnip moths (*Agrotis segetum*), 162
Tutt, James William, 8

typhus, 158, 159, 160, 404n.51; Jews associated with, 153–4, 157

Uexküll, Jakob von, 314–16, 410n.46, 411n.61
Ultraman, 378
ultrasonic emissions, 321, 328
ultraviolet filtering, 304
Umwelten, 314–16, 410n.46, 411n.61
United Nations, 213, 214; Food and Agriculture Organization (FAO), 239; Scientific Committee on the Effects of Atomic Radiation, 22–3
Université Abdou Moumouni, Niamey, Niger, 208–10
University of Florida Book of Insect Records, 217
unka leafhoppers, 372
uranium, 208, 228–9, 413n.22
Utetheisa ornatrix moths, 326

Vade-Mecum des criquets du Sahel (Launois-Luong and Lecoq), 216, 220
Vasey, Paul, 259, 261–2
Ventura County, Calif., D.A.'s office, 273–6, 281, 283
Venus in Furs (Sacher-Masoch), 287
Verein für jüdische Statistik (Association for Jewish Statistics), 149–50
Versailles Treaty, 159, 160
vibrational signals, 188, 328–9
vibrocrypticity, 329
Viel, Jean-François, 34
Vilencia, Jeff, 267–73, 275, 276–81, 282–3, 285–8, 289; *The American Journal of the Crush-Freaks* by, 269–71, 273, 278, 279, 281, 288; crush films made by, 267–8, 271–3, 276–8
Virchow, Rudolf, 150, 401n.21
vision, 301–17; color, 174, 302–4, 308, 419n.5; compound eye and, 302, 309, 310–14; cultural-historical

meaning and, 308–9; distinct space-time worlds and, 314–17; evolution of eye and, 420–1n.24; insect, re-creating for humans, 301–2, 304, 305, 309–10; inversion of image and, 312, 313; motion detection and, 314; perceptual algorithms and, 305–9

Wade, Nicholas, 116
Walt Disney Productions, 243, 245, 246, 347
Wandering Jew, 142, 143, 146, 147
Warsaw Ghetto, 146–7, 148, 149, 152, 153–4, 160–1, 400n.14
Washington Post, 273
Washoe, 197, 198
Wasmann Journal of Biology, 294
wasp nests, 52–4, 61, 162; eggs suspended from roof of, 57; missiles constructed from, 337; preparation of, 52–3; variations in wasp behavior and, 62–3
wasps, 6, 7, 9, 162, 304, 324, 337, 391n.39; Fabre's studies of, 52–4, 57, 58–63, 70; parasitic, problem of evil and, 68–9
water bugs (cockroaches), 299–300; bisexual "promiscuity" of, 260–1
Watson, John B., 60, 178
Weindling, Paul, 159
West Nile virus, 325
Wilder Ranch State Park, Santa Cruz, Calif., 383–6
Wittgenstein, Ludwig, 197, 411n.61
wonder: in Fabre's intuitive approach to instinct, 60–1, 62, 63; in late Renaissance, 19–20, 124, 125, 127–8, 136
wood louse, 131
World Bank, 234
World Health Organization, 73
World War I, 152–3, 158, 159
World War II, 175–6, 177, 367–71, 373; Hamburg bombings in, 45;

Hiroshima and Nagasaki bombings, 23; Tokyo firebombing in, 367–8, 370–1, 373
World Wildlife Fund, 32
Writing of Stones, The (Callois), 334

Yagura, Robert, 302
Yajima Minoru, 367–70, 373, 374, 375, 378, 382
yakuza, 360, 363

Yoro Takeshi, 322, 344–7, 356, 377, 380–1
YouTube, crush videos on, 289–90

Zakari, Ousmane Moussa, 239
Zionism, 142, 147–8, 149, 151–3, 154, 399n.3, 401n.27
Zionist Organization, 149, 151, 152–3
ZOB (Jewish Fighting Organization), 146, 147, 153, 400n.14
zoophilia, 258

Illustration Credits

5   Image courtesy of USDA

8   Image courtesy of USDA

14   Photo by author

15   Photo by author

16   Image courtesy of Cornelia Hesse-Honneger

19   Image courtesy of New York University Libraries

21   Image courtesy of Cornelia Hesse-Honneger

24   From Jay M. Gould and Benjamin A. Goldman with Kate Millpointer, *Deadly Deceit: Low-Level Radiation High-Level Cover-up*, New York: Four Walls Eight Windows, 1990. Reprinted by permission of Basic Books, a member of Perseus Books Group

28   Images courtesy of Cornelia Hesse-Honneger

33   Map courtesy of Cornelia Hesse-Honnegger

40   Image courtesy of Cornelia Hesse-Honneger

43   Photo by author

45   The Metropolitan Museum of Art, Purchase, Jennifer and Joseph Duke Gift, 1999 (1999.411) Copy Photo © The Metropolitan Museum of Art

46   Photo by author

48   Image courtesy of the Muséum national d'Histoire naturelle, Paris

49   Photo by author

53   Photo by P.-H. Fabre

56   Image courtesy of the Muséum national d'Histoire naturelle, Paris

59   Photo by C. Truc

65   Republished with kind permission of All-Nippon Airlines

66   Photo by author

75   Image courtesy of Hu YanJun

77   Photograph by author

81   Images courtesy of Dai Honghai

90   Photo by author

93   Photo by author

98   By kind permission of Li Shijun

99   Photo by author

107   Photo reproduced with kind permission of *The Shanghai Evening Post*

114   Photo by author

116   Images courtesy of Herman A. Dierick

118   Photo by author

119   Image from Calvin B. Bridges and T. H. Morgan, "The Third Chromosome Group of Mutant Character of *Drosophila melanogaster*" (Carnegie Institute, 1923), reprinted courtesy of The Carnegie Institute

124 *Animalia Rationalia et Insecta (Ignis): Plate LVII,* Gift of Mrs. Lessing J. Rosenwald. Image courtesy of the Board of Trustees, National Gallery of Art, Washington

132 *Animalia Rationalia et Insecta (Ignis): Plate I,* Gift of Mrs. Lessing J. Rosenwald. Image courtesy of the Board of Trustees, National Gallery of Art, Washington

134 *Animalia Rationalia et Insecta (Ignis): Plate XLIII,* Gift of Mrs. Lessing J. Rosenwald. Image courtesy of the Board of Trustees, National Gallery of Art, Washington

136 *Animalia Rationalia et Insecta (Ignis): Plate V,* Gift of Mrs. Lessing J. Rosenwald. Image courtesy of the Board of Trustees, National Gallery of Art, Washington

139 *Animalia Rationalia et Insecta (Ignis): Plate LIV,* Gift of Mrs. Lessing J. Rosenwald. Image courtesy of the Board of Trustees, National Gallery of Art, Washington

143 Arthur Szyk, *Oh Ye Dry Bones, Hear the Word of the Lord,* cover of *The Answer* (1944). Reproduced with the cooperation of The Arthur Szyk Society, Burlingame, Calif. www.szyk.org

144 Shmuel Hirszenberg, *The Wandering Jew* (1899). Collection of the Israel Museum, Jerusalem. Photo © The Israel Museum/David Harris

144 Alfred Nossig, *The Wandering Jew* (1901). From the Archives of the YIVO Institute for Jewish Research, New York

144 Garry Hunter/Wellcome Images

149 Opening event of the "Ausstellung jüdischer Künstler" (Exhibition of Jewish Artists), Berlin, 1907. From the Archives of the YIVO Institute for Jewish Research, New York

154 Generalgouvernment poster "Jews-Lice-Typhus" (1940). Reproduced from the collection of the Biblioteka Jagiellonska, Krakow, sygn. BJ 749040 III 59 Rara

156 Model of the Auschwitz-Birkenau extermination facilities by Mieczyslaw Stobierski. Courtesy of the U.S. Holocaust Memorial Museum

168 Maria Sibylla Merian, *Metamorphosis insectorum surinamensium,* 1705, plate 14, Courtesy of American Museum of Natural History Library

173 Wilhelm von Osten and his horse "The Clever Hans." 1904. Bildarchiv Preussischer Kulturbesitz/Art Resource, N.Y.

174 (*left*)After Hildtraut Steinhoff, *Z. vergl. Physiol.* 31, 38–57, 1948; (*right*) Photo by Dr. Schick

176 Photo from *A Biologist Remembers* by Karl von Frisch, translated by Lisbeth Gombrich, p.41, Oxford: Pergamon Press, 1967

177 Photo from *A Biologist Remembers* by Karl von Frisch, translated by Lisbeth Gombrich, p.28, Oxford: Pergamon Press, 1967

179 After Karl von Frisch, "Sprechende Tänze im Bienenvolk," Festrede in der Bayer. Akad. Wiss., 1954

181 Reprinted by permission of the publisher from *The Dance Language and Orientation of Bees* by Karl von Frisch, translated by Leigh E. Chadwick, p. 137, Cambridge, Mass.: The Belknap Press of Harvard University Press, Copyright © 1967, 1993 by the President and Fellows of Harvard College

182 (*top*)Reprinted from *Bees, Their Vision, Chemical Senses, and Language* by Karl von Frisch, p. 88, by permission of the publisher, Cornell University Press; (*bottom*) After M. Renner, *Z. vergl. Physiol.* 42, 449–83, 1959

183 (*top*) Reprinted from *Bees, Their Vision, Chemical Senses, and Language* by Karl von Frisch, p. 55, by permission of the publisher, Cornell University Press; (*bottom*) Photo by M. Renner

184 Reprinted by permission of the publisher from *The Dance Language and Orientation of Bees* by Karl von Frisch, translated by Leigh E. Chadwick, p. 166, Cambridge, Mass.: The Belknap Press of Harvard University Press, Copyright © 1967, 1993 by the President and Fellows of Harvard College

186 Reprinted from *Bees, Their Vision, Chemical Senses, and Language* by Karl von Frisch, p.1, by permission of the publisher, Cornell University Press

187 Reprinted by permission of the publisher from *Communication Among Social Bees,* Revised Edition by Martin Lindauer, p. 14, Cambridge, Mass.: Harvard University Press, Copyright © 1961 by the President and Fellows of Harvard College. Copyright © renewed 1989 by Martin Lindauer

189 Reprinted by permission of the publisher from *Communication Among Social Bees,* Revised Edition by Martin Lindauer, p. 18, Cambridge, Mass.: Harvard University Press, Copyright © 1961 by the President and Fellows of Harvard College. Copyright © renewed 1989 by Martin Lindauer

197 Photo by Harald Doering

203 Illustration by Bill Russell www.billustration.com

210 Map of breeding areas and major movements of locusts during plagues reproduced by permission of the publisher from G. B. Popov, *Atlas of Desert Locust Breeding Habits,* Rome: Food and Agriculture Organization, 1997

214 Photo by author

221 Photo by author

228 Photo by author

230 Photo by author

232 Photo by author

234 Map of breeding areas and major movements of locusts during recessions reproduced by permission of the publisher from G. B. Popov, *Atlas of Desert Locust Breeding Habits,* Rome: Food and Agriculture Organization, 1997

237 Photo by author

242 Image courtesy of Gillian Raffles

244 Photo by author

248 Image reproduced with kind permission of Franca Principe, IMSS–Florence

253 Photo by author

255 Image courtesy of Banca Dati dell'Archivio Storico Foto Locchi Firenze (Archivio Foto Locchi Databank, Florence)

256 Photo by author

257 Image courtesy of George O. Krizek

259 Photo of West Indian manatees copyright © Phillip Colla/www.oceanlight.com

264 Photo by author

266 Photo by author

268 Image courtesy of Jeff Vilencia

270 Image courtesy of Jeff Vilencia

272 Images courtesy of Jeff Vilencia

278 Image courtesy of Jeff Vilencia

279 Image courtesy of Jeff Vilencia

282 AP Photo/Los Angeles Daily News, Michael Owen Baker

286 Image courtesy of Jeff Vilencia

294 Photo by Onno Zweers, Creative Commons Attribution and ShareAlike license (CC-BY-SA)

295 Reprinted with kind permission of Natasha LeBas

301 Courtesy of the North Carolina Museum of Natural Sciences and Academy Studios, Novato, California

303 Reprinted from *Bees, Their Vision, Chemical Senses, and Language* by Karl von Frisch, p. 7, by permission of the publisher, Cornell University Press

304 (*both*) Images courtesy of Thomas Eisner, Cornell University

311 "Grey drone-fly" reproduced from Robert Hooke, Micrographia. Science Museum / Science & Society Picture Library

312 (*top*) Image reproduced from Sigmund Exner, *The Physiology of the Compound Eyes of Insects and Crustaceans*, R. C. Hartree, ed. Berlin: Springer Verlag, 1989; (*bottom*) Image reprinted from Edward Gaten, "Optics and Phylogeny: Is There an Insight? The Evolution of Superposition Eyes in the Decapoda (Crustacea)," *Contributions to Zoology*, 67 (4) 223–36 (1998), with kind permission of Edward Gaten and *Contributions to Zoology*

313 (*top*) Image reprinted from Edward Gaten "Optics and Phylogeny: Is There an Insight? The Evolution of Superposition Eyes in the Decapoda (Crustacea)," *Contributions to Zoology*, 67 (4) 223–36 (1998), with kind permission of Edward Gaten and *Contributions to Zoology*; (*bottom*) Image reprinted by permission of the publisher from Michael F. Land and Dan-Eric Nilsson, *Animal Eyes*, Oxford: Oxford University Press, 2002

315 Reprinted from *Instinctive Behavior* by Claire Schiller by permission of International Universities Press, Inc. Copyright 1957 by IUP

321 Photo courtesy of Paul Ingles http://www.paulingles.com/

324 Image courtesy of David Dunn

326 Photo courtesy of A. Steven Munson, USDA Forest Service, Bugwood.org

330 By kind permission of William M. Ciesla, Forest Health Management International, United States

332 Photo by author

340 Reprinted from Karl von Frisch, *Ten Little Housemates*, Oxford: Pergamon Press, 1960

344 Photo by author

345 Image courtesy of Yoro Takeshi

346 Image courtesy of Yoro Takeshi

348 Image courtesy of the Tezuka Osamu Museum, Takarazuka, Japan

349 Photo by author

350 Photo by author

354 Photo by author

356 Photo by author

358 Photo by author

359 Photo by author

362 Photo by author

365 Photo by author

366 Images made available courtesy of Sega Corporation. © SEGA. All rights reserved

369 Image courtesy of Yajima Minoru

372 Images from *Senchufu* by Tanshu Kurimoto reproduced courtesy of the National Diet Library, Japan

376 Image reproduced with kind permission of Shiga Usuke

381 Poster courtesy of Mushi-sha, Tokyo

382 Image reproduced with kind permission of Shiga Usuke

384 Photo by author

408 (*endnotes*) Reprinted by permission of the publisher from *The Dance Language and Orientation of Bees* by Karl von Frisch, translated by Leigh E. Chadwick, p. 132, Cambridge, Mass.: The Belknap Press of Harvard University Press, Copyright © 1967, 1993 by the President and Fellows of Harvard College

About the Author

Hugh Raffles lives in New York City and teaches anthropology at the New School. He is the author of *In Amazonia: A Natural History,* which received the Victor Turner Prize in Ethnographic Writing. His essays have been published in *The Best American Essays* and *Granta.* He is the recipient of a Whiting Writers' Award.

A Note on the Type

This book was set in Scala, a typeface designed by the Dutch designer Martin Majoor (b. 1960) in 1988 and released by the FontFont foundry in 1990. While designed as a fully modern family of fonts containing both a serif and a sans serif alphabet, Scala retains many refinements normally associated with traditional fonts.

Composed by North Market Street Graphics,
Lancaster, Pennsylvania

Printed and bound by Berryville Graphics,
Berryville, Virginia

Designed by M. Kristen Bearse